1175 ND

Patterns of Discovery
in the Social Sciences

OBSERVATIONS

A series edited by Howard S. Becker
Northwestern University

Patterns of Discovery in the Social Sciences

Paul Diesing
State University of New York at Buffalo

Aldine · Atherton
Chicago · New York

THE AUTHOR

Paul Diesing is Professor of Philosophy and Political Science, State University of New York at Buffalo. He received his Ph.D. in philosophy from the University of Chicago in 1952 and has taught at that university, the University of Illinois, and the University of Colorado. Professor Diesing is also a Faculty Associate at the Buffalo Center for International Conflict Studies, where he is participating in the Center's program of research in bargaining theory and international crises. He is the author of *Reason in Society: Five Types of Decisions and Their Social Conditions*.

Copyright © 1971 by Paul Diesing

First published 1971 by
Aldine · Atherton, Inc.
529 South Wabash Avenue
Chicago, Illinois 60605

ISBN 0-202-30101-X
Library of Congress Catalog Number 72-106978

Printed in the United States of America

In memory of

ROBERT REDFIELD

Acknowledgments

My primary indebtedness is to the many social scientists who let me hang around and listen to them, showed me their experimental apparatus, invited me to their private discussion groups and endured my sometimes disruptive questions, listened and commented on my presentations in various seminars, colloquia, and discussion groups, tried to answer my questions, and read and commented on some portion of this work, Dean Pruitt and Morris Zelditch especially. I am also grateful to Richard McKeon for teaching me that there are several different modes of knowing.

I also wish to thank Sue Pidgeon and Lucille Peterson for their diligent typing and retyping of various drafts of the manuscript.

The following work was written over a period of time and unfortunately could not take account of the most recent developments in the areas investigated. The chapters on mathematical modeling were substantially completed in 1966, those on computer simulation in May 1967, and the rest in June 1969.

The publisher, Alexander J. Morin, is mainly responsible for the inclusion of the last chapter. I had earlier deleted it as superficial and sketchy, but he insisted I put it back in, perhaps because he wanted a happy ending.

Contents

III. Methods in the Philosophy of Science

Patterns of Discovery
in the Social Sciences

1

Introduction

Books on social science methodology mostly fall into one of two classes. First, there are "methods" books, works which introduce the student to research techniques in some specialized area of the social sciences. Each field has its own methods: there are methods in social research, methods in cultural anthropology, research methods in human relations, and so on. These are "how-to-do-it" books. The student is taught how to write questionnaries, conduct interviews, calculate chi-squares, administer tests, write computer programs, and do whatever else is required in his special field of interest. Such books must be revised frequently, because new techniques are constantly appearing and old ones being modified. Then there are "method" or "scientific method" books. These are more abstract discussions of science in general, referring to specific fields only to illustrate what is true of all science at all times.

My approach is midway between these two. The methods I investigate are not the hundreds of particular scaling, testing, interviewing, and statistical techniques, nor the timeless logic of science in general, but rather the four or five different methods or modes of procedure, incorporating particular techniques as parts, that social scientists use today. By "method" or "mode of procedure" I mean the whole series of steps that a scientist or research team follows in the process of making a contribution to a field of knowledge. Not everything a scientist does is part of his method—teaching seminars in the subject, applying for research grants, politicking to get his theories accepted—but only those things that are an essential part of the achievement of knowledge. I call these methods "patterns of discovery," using the terminology of the late Norwood Hanson (1958), because I am dealing with the whole process of inquiry, the whole process of "discovering" or creating or developing knowledge, and not just the verification aspect.

To discuss "methods" rather than method does not imply that there is

1

no one basic method of science. However, a premature interest in this one method forces one's attention to move to so abstract a level that much of what scientists do must be ignored as technical detail. Consequently, one's account tends to become thin and abstract, and attention shifts to philosophical puzzles of little interest to scientists; or, in the attempt to achieve richness of detail, one tends mistakenly to identify a particular method, say, the method of nuclear physicists or experimental psychologists, with the general method of science. General scientific method is best discussed only after one has begun to appreciate the variety that exists in methods now in use.

Types of Methods

If one's attention is directed to differences among methods, the most obvious difference is that between the clinical and the experimental method. This difference has often been noticed and has been accounted for in a great variety of ways. If one wishes to reduce differences to a minimum, one can say that there are only these two basic methods, the clinical and the experimental. However, with a bit of attention, one notices that survey methods are distinguishable from experimentation and that there are also variants of the clinical method, notably participant observation. One also finds that formal methods have characteristics that distinguish them from both clinical and experimental approaches, and that there are in turn several formal methods.

One could go on and make further distinctions, but let us provisionally stop here and say there are at present four main types of methods in use: experimentation, statistical survey research, participant-observer and clinical methods, and formal methods. For the time being, computer simulation can still be treated as a formal method, though perhaps in a few more years it may be more appropriately regarded as a fifth and distinct method.

Participant-observer and clinical methods can also be distinguished, but it is more convenient to group them together, to keep the list down to four. Such a list is not intended as a definitive classification of existing methods, but only as a set of initial distinctions useful for exploring the field. As one continues his investigations, it may become necessary to make further distinctions of varying degrees of sharpness and to notice continuities or overlapping between methods initially distinguished from each other.

Let us glance at each of these methods briefly to note their main characteristics.

The experimental method has been most fully developed among the social sciences in psychology and in social psychology. It has variables as its subject matter, that is, any natural occurrences that exhibit measurable variations in incidence, or rate of occurrence, or rate of change of occurrence. Its principal objectives are to discover variables that behave in a lawlike fashion and to discover the laws governing their variation. Presumably everything in nature changes somehow, but the experimentalist tries to find regular changes that can be described in relatively simple and precise terms. Originally variables were studied in pairs, but later Fisher's statistical work (1935) enabled experimenters to deal with three or more variables simultaneously. When a pair of variables is being studied, one is ordinarily treated as an independent variable ("cause") and the other as a dependent variable ("effect"). The correlations that may be found between the two serve as a first approximation or ingredient of some prospective law. More complex correlations and partial correlations among three or more variables point to more complex laws.

The experimental procedure, in outline, is to locate a potentially lawlike variable by examining previous experimental results and trying to find masking effects that disguised or covered over some hidden correlation. Theory is useful for suggesting possible masking effects and possible hidden correlations. It is also possible to examine a case study or even one's own experience with the help of theory, to locate a possible lawlike variable, but this approach is more difficult and less likely to succeed because of the chaotic appearance of ordinary experience. The searching of ordinary experience is likely to be a haphazard, hit-or-miss affair, while the searching of experimental results can be more systematic because of the regularity of the data.

Next, one imagines an experimental situation in which the masking effects are removed or controlled so that the hidden correlation can be plainly observed. Control can be achieved in a variety of ways, including holding the masking factors constant, eliminating them entirely, limiting their range of variation, counteracting them, and subtracting their presumed effects statistically from the results. Once the controls are set up, the next steps are to introduce the independent variable and then measure the change in the dependent variable. The results are then compared with previous experimental results to see whether one has moved closer to the presumed hidden correlation. If one has moved closer, one continues the search in the same direction; if not, one starts looking in a different direction. Tests of significance are used to determine whether it is worthwhile to continue the search in the same direction or advisable to try something different. Significance criteria are set at a level such that not too many promising leads are discarded prematurely and not too many blind alleys are preserved; however, such tests are advisory only.

It is also possible to begin one's work by examining plausible speculations on a subject, then operationalizing some of the key concepts and devising ground-breaking experiments. Such initial experiments cannot be expected to produce immediate success; they serve only to start the long search for hidden variables and correlations.

As the investigator gradually refines his variables and strengthens his correlations, he also tries to determine the limits of their validity. Do they hold only for college sophomores? For men only, or for women, too? For Japanese? Navahos? Frequently some speculation or theory can be used to suggest a class of subjects for whom the correlation might not hold, or for whom it holds very strongly. Such investigations not only uncover limits but also put one on the track of more general laws of which the original correlation was an instance.

Checking can occur throughout the search process. It is possible at any stage to repeat the experiment in a different place with a different experimenter and different instances of the variable to see whether the same results occur. However, most published instances of what are called "replication" are actually part of the search process, since small changes are made in the experimental setup in hopes of getting a slightly better correlation or of uncovering new limits on the original correlation. True replications, changing only experimenter, place, and specific subjects, are usually left to students, and their frequent failures to get the same results are explained as being due to inexperience.

Once the initial objective, a general law, is achieved and checked, attention shifts to the discovery of new laws. These may be supplementary, in that they limit the range of validity or applicability of the original law, or they may state the effects of the original dependent variable on other variables. The eventual result envisioned is a kind of network of linked variables, extending endlessly in all directions.

In the experimental method, definitions are always at least partly operational. Definitions of independent variables include a statement of the operations by which they are introduced and controlled, and definitions of dependent variables include a statement of the operations and measurements by which their presence can be determined. The reason is that the experimental discovery of laws depends on actual operations with the variables involved, which is possible only if the variables are reduced to operational terms. Similarly, replication is possible only if the original operations have been specified. It is not necessary to have a completely operational definition; in many cases it is thought that a single concept, for instance "group cohesion," can have several different operational definitions, all sharing a vague common core of meaning. However, each new operational definition produces some shift of meaning, perhaps a large shift. Consequently, widespread use of the experimental method tends to produce a proliferation of variables and laws, many vaguely overlapping, rather than the single clear network of laws originally anticipated. When attempts are made to collect and systematize large numbers of empirical laws, as in March and Simon's *Organizations* (1958), the results are suggestive rather than precise because of the shifting meanings of the central variables.

This difficulty in producing truly general laws is one of the chief problems in the experimental method in the social sciences, along with such problems of controlling variables as experimenter bias. Experimentation is effective in producing five-page reports in psychology journals, but these reports are consolidated only very gradually into a system of general laws. Conse-

quently, scientists interested in developing general theory in a hurry sometimes shift to other methods, particularly the formal method, which are
better adapted to the problems of general theory.

The survey method was devised to overcome another problem of the
experimental method: the difficulty of dealing experimentally with large and
complex subject matter. Experimentation always involves a considerable
abstraction from natural complexity, and scientists who wanted to study complex sets of variables in their natural setting devised the survey method for
this purpose. However, survey research has developed well beyond this original purpose and become a method in its own right, one that has been
combined with and enriched other methods and has also produced its own
kind of theory.

The experimental difficulty of dealing with large and complex subjects is
met in the survey method by sampling and by substituting statistical controls for experimental ones. Similarly, correction and validation involve
primarily the statistical manipulation of data. With the continuing development of statistical techniques it has become possible to devise quite complex
research designs, involving many variables in a variety of relationships
and yielding complex correlations. Thus the austere limits of the classical
experimental method are transcended, and the complexity of actual societies
can be more adequately handled.

Another advantage of the survey method is that it combines readily with all
other methods. Experimentation has been enriched by statistical controls,
for instance by using sampling techniques to select experimental subjects.
Participant observers have used sample surveys to extend the range of their
observations, while survey researchers have used a variety of clinical and
quasi-clinical techniques, such as focused and unfocused interviews, various degrees of participant observation, and projective devices, to enrich their
data. The variety of combinations in use is so great that survey research
and participant observation can now be seen as two ends of a continuum
rather than as two distinct kinds of methods. Formal methods have also
used survey research data to provide interpretations and probable values
of formal variables and to suggest new variables and relationships.

The participant-observer method was first developed by anthropologists, though it is also frequently used by sociologists, social psychologists, political scientists, and organization theorists. Its primary subject
matter is a single, self-maintaining social system. The system may be a
small community with its own culture, or a larger society with its culture,
or a small and relatively isolated neighborhood, or a gang, clique, voluntary organization, or family, or a formal organization or institution,
or a person (clinical method), or a historical period. In each case the
emphasis is on the individuality or uniqueness of the system, its wholeness
or boundedness, and the ways it maintains its individuality. The primary
objective is to describe the individual in its individuality, as a system of
rules, goals, values, techniques, defense or boundary-maintaining mech-

anisms, exchange or boundary-crossing mechanisms, socialization procedures, and decision procedures. In one important variant, the primary
interest is in recurring processes within or around such individual systems.

The procedure is, first, to become socialized into the system, to learn a
set of roles and normative elements, to form relationships, and thus to
participate in the normal routines and occasional crises of the system. If
the system is small, the researcher can gradually turn himself into an analogue of the system, so that he reacts as it reacts, feels as it feels, thinks
and evaluates as it does. The next step is to make this implicit knowledge
(Polanyi's "personal knowledge," *verstehen* in a sense) explicit. The
researcher constructs hypotheses about parts of the system out of the recurrent themes that come to his attention and tests these hypotheses against a
variety of data—what he sees, what others tell him, how he reacts, and
how others react to his probing actions. Many detailed hypotheses are gradually combined into a model of the whole system, whose parts are tested
by how well they fit together and how well they agree with the data.

The system model is continually checked against new data and revised.
Since the researcher is part of the system he studies, new data are continually coming in and the model is never quite completed. Other researchers
contribute further checks by providing their own models of the system, which
are compared with one another for coherence as well as with the various
sets of data.

All through this process the researcher is continually comparing his case
with others familiar to him, looking for similarities and differences, and
using one case to suggest things to look for in another. One eventual result
of such a process of comparison is a typology, a classification of cases according to similarities and differences. Further study of a type should lead
to hypotheses about which of its characteristics are particularly important
in determining the rest and what are the dynamics of the type. Comparison
of widely differing types enables one to search for still more general characteristics of many kinds of human systems—universal or nearly universal values, institutions, system problems, mechanisms, and the like. General theorizing of this sort tries to transcend the relativity inherent in the participant-
observer method by looking for general characteristics of human systems,
though it still recognizes that these characteristics vary considerably in detail.

At least three other methods similar to participant observation can be
distinguished. First, the clinical method used in clinical psychology and
psychiatry is basically the same in that it deals with a whole, unique, self-
maintaining system—in this case a person—and aims at construction of a
system model; it involves the intimate participation of the therapist in the
functioning of his subject matter, so as to develop an intuitive understanding of it; it involves the development of specific hypotheses out of recurring
themes and the testing of them against several kinds of data, including
the clinician's own reactions and the responses to his probing actions; and

it involves the continuous reconstruction of the system model in terms of internal coherence and of agreement with the continuing supply of data. It falls short of participant observation at its best in that the clinician cannot, in principle, get as complete an inside understanding of his subject as can a group of field workers. If the personality is, in part, a system of roles and role expectations, the clinician participates in it by taking one or two roles that are offered him. He can then participate in and observe the activity of his subject in those roles. But the subject's activity in other roles, as husband, father, employee, and the like, is not accessible to direct observation and must be reconstructed intuitively from the subject's reports. This makes for an incompleteness of observation that is not necessarily the case for field studies. A partial solution to the clinician's problem is to study a whole family, but this approach is likely to sacrifice some of the depth of knowledge that can be achieved by concentrating on a single subject or part of one.

Another similar method is used by some historians when they attempt to reconstruct a whole historical period out of available data and try to understand it, intuitively or "from the inside," as a kind of integrated system with its own unique character or spirit. This method falls far short of the clinical method in that the historian cannot participate in his subject matter at all but must experience it vicariously and imaginatively. Nor is a historical period actually a self-maintaining system with actual boundaries; even if it were, it would be much too large to reconstruct in all its inner workings.

Still another similar method is occasionally proposed by some institutional economists. In it the self-maintaining system to be studied is the total set of institutions in which a particular economy functions, seen in historical perspective. I have not succeeded in understanding this method adequately since it seems to have remained a proposal rather than an actuality for over a half century. However, it would seem to involve all the difficulties of the historical method and more, owing to the size and complexity of its subject matter. Just as the participant-observer method has been most successful in studies of simple nonliterate societies or small formal organizations, so the most successful institutionalist studies have been of small primitive economies (such as Polanyi, 1957). Attempts to study the U.S. or world economy have necessarily involved great reliance on statistics and thus have moved toward the survey research method, which is much better suited to a large subject matter. My impression is that there is no one institutionalist method predominant at the present time; some people who call themselves institutionalists use statistical surveys, some use elaborate econometric models, some use participant observation supplemented by numerous statistics, and some use historical reconstruction. Conversely, if a unified institutionalist method is ever fully developed, it will probably be some amalgam of clinical-historical, survey research, and even formal methods.

Formal methods have long been in use in economics, and in recent years have become important in a number of fields, including psychology, sociology, international politics, and some newer interdisciplinary fields. These methods are in particularly rapid development right now, so it is difficult to give an adequate description that will not soon be outdated. Nor is it easy to summarize all the varied and sometimes contradictory methodological devices that are being tried out.

The subject matter of a formal method is a formal system of logical relationships abstracted from all the varied empirical content it might have in the real world. For example, the classical economic theory of the firm dealt with the structure involved in any process of production using any materials at any set of relative prices with any technology. It is supposed that this formal structure is present in the real world in some way or to some extent, and that there it determines the course of events. The initial objective of the formal method is to construct a model of a system or process that can be exemplified empirically.

The first step in the procedure is to set up a first approximation or baseline model by laying down a minimum set of postulates and definitions. These may be derived from some empirical theory by abstracting from its empirical content and thus laying bare its implicit logical structure, as Simon did with Homans' theory (Simon, 1957, ch. 6). More frequently, they are derived by dividing an empirical process into its obvious parts and stating the necessary relations (or in some cases, all possible relations) between those parts.

A minimum set of postulates is one that is sufficient to generate roughly the kind of dynamics the scientist wishes to study. The next step is to deduce, either logically or mathematically or by computer simulation, the inherent dynamics of the system, that is, the set of changes that is determined by the system's internal structure, apart from external influences and apart from any empirical content such as particular values of the system's variables or parameters. (A variable here is some quantitative characteristic of the system that can change, and a parameter is some characteristic of the environment that is given for the system.) Some systems, such as neoclassical price theory, are equilibrium systems; that is, their inherent dynamics lead toward a steady state. In this case the factors that produce and maintain equilibrium can be determined, together with the way the equilibrium value depends on the value of each factor. Other systems fluctuate around an equilibrium point or line, as, for instance, business cycle models. In this case the shape and range of the fluctuations and the location of the equilibrium point can be deduced, together with the dependence of each on the system variables. Other systems, such as those of stochastic learning theory, approach a limit whose value is determinately related to structure and to initial values. Still others, such as population models, go off to infinity if left to themselves, at a determinate rate; and some simply fluctuate indeterminately. Many systems are compound; that is, they have multiple possible outcomes, depending on the initial values of certain variables. For example, in Simon's Berlitz model there is an indifference line; any state of the system lying above the line moves to infinity (the person learns the language), any state below it moves to zero (he stops studying). In some economic growth models any ratio of capital formation to population increase above a crucial rate leads to self-sustained growth (infinity), any lesser rate to stagnation (equilibrium), any rate less than a given minimum to bankruptcy (zero). In all these cases the formal theorist can deduce the way in which the system's logical structure determines its dynamics.

The next step is to interpret the model. Interpretation consists of providing a set of rules of correspondence that relate formal terms of the theory to empirical concepts; in this way the theory gets content and is related to the empirical world. Each formal theory may have a variety of empirical theories corresponding to it; the crucial requirement is that all the empirical theories have the same logical structure as the formal theory they interpret. If the initial definitions of the formal theory are derived from some empirical theory, the latter provides a ready-made interpretation, but even here other interpretations should be discoverable. In addition, the formal theorist may provide "heuristic interpretations" as he goes along, to help the empirically minded reader to think through the theory.

Once interpretations are available it is possible to criticize and correct the initial model. This proceeds by what is called the "method of successive approximations." Correction can begin at either of two places, the initial definitions and postulates or the derived system dynamics, and formal theorists have disagreed on which is the more appropriate (cf. MacEsich, 1961). If one corrects through system dynamics, one compares the path or outcome of the system with empirical paths and outcomes and notes the divergence. Then one modifies some postulate or definition, or adds a new variable, in such a way as to shift the system closer to the empirically observed paths. When the two paths are roughly similar (they cannot be identical because random factors always distort the empirical path away from its logical course) the theorist can assert in some fashion (depending on the theory of truth he believes in) that he has now discovered the logical structure in the world that produces the empirically observed paths or outcomes. If one corrects through initial postulates and definitions, one notes the divergence between the variables and relationships postulated in the formal system and those known to exist in empirical reality. Then, one by one, the missing variables are added and their effects on the system dynamics worked out. When the two sets of variables and relationships roughly correspond (again, they cannot be identical) the theorist can assert that the set of relationships present in that part of the world will of itself tend to produce the kind of dynamics expressed in the formal theory.

Formal methods do not normally produce laws relating pairs of variables; they produce models. However, parts of a model or deductions from a model can be selected and restated in the form of a lawlike sentence. Such "formal laws" are not to be confused with empirical generalizations, which describe factual, observable regularities, nor are they like functionalist laws, which state empirical compatibilities and incompatibilities for some type of empirical system. Rather, formal laws are a priori statements of necessary connections between abstract entities. The "iron laws" of economics are examples of such a priori necessities. These laws need not be exemplified in any particular instance because of empirical interferences and accidents, and they cannot be empirically falsified, as I shall argue in chapters 2-4.

This account is not intended as a definitive description and classification of social science methods; it is only a preliminary statement of some obvious differences among methods. It is intended to serve as an initial orientation, a set of guideposts that will enable the reader to plot his approximate position as he wanders deeper into the thicket of actual practice. I am *not* claiming that there are exactly four sharply distinct methods, rather than three, six, or eight; rather, I am picking out four prominent locations in the terrain and contrasting them with one another. Each of the locations can serve not only as a guidepost but also as a point of departure for exploring the whole field of social science methods, and the field will look different whenever one begins from a different point of departure.

Therefore, some of the broad generalizations made above will be qualified or even discarded as we go into more detail. Other generalizations will hold from some standpoints but not from others. One example will illustrate. As we study formal methods more carefully, we find that mathematical modelers also frequently undertake experiments, and when they do, their experiments differ in a number of important ways from the kind of experimentation I have summarized as "experimental method." I shall describe these differences in detail in chapter 4. These differences did not always exist; when mathematical modelers began experimenting about twenty years ago, they used the experimental techniques then current and only gradually made the modifications they found necessary for their purposes. Experimental methods in other hands were developing in a rather different direction or directions, so that by about 1965 one could say that two distinct kinds of experimentation were going on. I shall later call these two "formalist experiments" and "empiricist experiments." The description of experimental method above applies to empiricist experiments, apart from some recent develop ments, but not to formalist experiments.

When we study the distinction between formalist and empiricist experiments, we find that it sometimes wobbles and starts to disappear. When I describe the distinction to a formalist, he understands and agrees, but when I try it on an empiricist, he is puzzled and starts to argue. The distinction seems perverse and pointless or even unintelligible to him. All experiments are basically the same, he will say; the only distinction worth making is between good and bad experiments, and in the latter class belong a number of unfortunate attempts by people who are better at mathematics than they are at science. These attempts, he says, are characterized by crude, unimaginative experimental design, an insensitive and overly rigid experimenter, and utterly routine mechanical treatment of data. When I listen to such an argument, I am at first persuaded that the distinction I thought I saw was an illusion; but then I gradually notice the category of "formalist experiment" appearing in the argument in a distorted fashion. What shall we say, then? Are there two kinds of experiment or one? It seems to me we should say that from a formalist standpoint there are two kinds, while from the standpoint of an empiricist experimenter there is only one. This conclusion, of course, is subject to modification as I talk to more experimenters of various kinds.

The various social science methods—let us assume as a first approximation that there are about four—have developed to their present state gradually over the past fifty years and are still developing, some rapidly and some slowly. It may be that some of them are also instances of basic, timeless modes of human knowledge (Sacksteder, 1963b), but I shall not consider this possibility. As historical developments, they are all imperfect, incomplete, just as scientific theories are always developing and incomplete. On the other hand, they do not have any inherent, a priori shortcomings or limits that may not eventually be overcome. In their present state they represent solutions to past problems of method and contain tensions and difficulties that will induce future development.

The present differences among the methods described are both factual and normative. A clinician and an experimenter, or a formalist and a survey researcher, follow different procedures, evaluate their developing work by different standards, and aim at different goals. An adequate account of these methods should cover all three aspects—procedures, goals and standards; it should show how procedures and goals are related, describe the characteristic problems and typical solutions that arise out of the procedures, and discuss the criteria for solution that the problems require.

The boundaries between the methods cut across the traditional social science fields. Clinical or case study methods occur not only in psychology but also in anthropology, history, sociology, and political science. Statistical surveys are carried out by psychologists and political scientists as well as by sociologists, and formal methods appear in all the social science fields, now even in anthropology. Moreover, communication and co-operation occur primarily within the boundaries of a method, not within a field. Thus, clinical psychologists and anthropologists have co-operated closely for thirty years now, but clinical and experimental psychologists in the main maintain a cold reserve. Economists formerly were relatively isolated, but with the spread of formal methods to other fields have come to co-operate increasingly with other formalists. Formal and institutional economists have little polite to say to each other, but some institutionalists can work with anthropologists and sociologists who deal in problems of social institutions and cultures.

Differences of method are not only barriers to communication and co-operation, but frequently sources of outright hostility and disdain. Experimenters frequently regard clinicians as frauds and quacks, certainly not as scientists, and dismiss psychoanalytic theory as fiction; clinicians sometimes hold equally uncomplimentary attitudes toward the trivialities of experimental theory and the degrading manipulations of experimental method. Both, however, can agree in regarding formalists as prescientific spinners of abstractions; their models are called "toys" (Homans, 1961, pp. 164, 190, 226, 329), useless at best (Martindale, 1959, pp. 88-89), and usually misleading (Pollis and Koslin, 1962); and their mathematical constructions are regarded as deliberate attempts to disguise the triviality and even the falsity of their empirical assumptions.

Not all contenders are equal in this contest of mutual disdain; the experimentalists and survey researchers are dominant, perhaps becuase there are more of them or perhaps because it is easier to argue that all science is essentially experimental. The dominant view goes something like this: Science is the experimental (or experimental-statistical) search for general laws that relate two or more variables. Experimentation is defined with varying degrees of strictness; to the pure experimentalist even statistical work is suspect, while to the survey researcher, laboratory experimentation is too artificial and too limited to be very useful. Clinical work is not science; it is either a kind of history (case history), or a prescientific exploration for appropriate variables with which to experiment, or downright fraud. Formal work is mostly a misguided and premature aping of the "more advanced" sciences. Physicists or chemists (according to this viewpoint) can properly construct mathematical theories because so many empirical general laws have already been discovered in these fields, and their mathematics merely relates or summarizes the laws in a theory, but in social science very few laws (if any) have as yet been thoroughly verified, so there is nothing to summarize. Consequently, if one dissects one of those mathematical monsters that formalists are constructing, one finds its genuine empirical content to be either trivial or false. The only proper use for nonstatistical mathematics at present is in the deduction of hypotheses from other hypotheses for experimental verification.

This view, or something like it, is so pervasive that even some clinicians and formalists adopt it. Periodically one reads declarations by clinicians that psychoanalysis ought to become "scientific," and there are even a few misguided attempts to make it so—misguided because "science" is defined according to the experimental ideal rather than in a way appropriate to clinical experience. An occasional formalist or clinician will confess privately, "I'm not really a scientist at all, you know" (cf. Gladwin and Sarason, 1953, p. 438).

I think this view is false. It thoroughly distorts both clinical and formal methods and may even be misleading in its interpretation of experimental work. More generally, I think the widespread attitude that there is only one scientific method, usually one's own, is unfortunate. It produces a distorted view of what other scientists are doing, and as a result blocks much potentially fruitful co-operation on new methods and new theories. My main purpose in this book is to argue against a single-method ethnocentrism and to argue that each method is valid in its own way and has its own advantages and disadvantages. Insofar as one form of ethnocentrism is dominant, I wish to argue against that form specifically and defend the other methods against it. I wish to argue that social science is not at present, and ought not to be concerned solely with the experimental-statistical verification of hypotheses and the discovery of general laws.

My procedure will be to describe formal and case study methods—both participant-observer and clinical—in detail, exhibiting them as methods of discovery different from, but analogous to, experimental method. I shall show that their strengths and weaknesses do not spring from the closeness of their resemblance to experimentation but are an integral part of their own unique approaches to knowledge. I shall not describe experimentation and survey research in similar detail because these methods have already been thoroughly studied and described by methodologists. However, I shall from time to time summarize various aspects of these methods to contrast them with corresponding aspects of formal and case study methods.

My relative neglect of experimentation and survey research is not intended to disparage these methods, for which I have a high regard, bur rather to correct the unduly low regard that some social scientists have for formal and clinical and field methods. Nor do I think that further detailed study of experimentation and survey research is unnecessary; there have been some interesting recent developments in experimental methodology that make previous accounts partly obsolete. That task, however, I leave to others.

My neglect of the social context of current social science is not based on a belief that society has no impact on science, but only on the need to keep my subject within manageable limits. A careful study of the social context of American social science would undoubtedly lead to reinterpretations of the methodological developments I shall describe, and I hope such studies can build on mine.

The Logic of Discovery

My earlier statement that this book deals with patterns of discovery requires clarification. Philosophers of science have disputed the question whether there is a logic of discovery, and the present work is in part a contribution to that dispute. The dispute turns in part, but only in part, on the meaning assigned to the term "logic."

Some philosophers, defining "logic" as "deduction," have argued that there can be no logic of discovery, since if we could deduce new knowledge from old it would not really be new. They have further argued that there is no order or method in the process of discovery at all, that "the creative side of science *is* wild and undisciplined" (Jarvie, 1964, p. 49).

In this view science is divided into two quite distinct parts, discovery and justification, neither contributing anything to the other. Discovery proceeds according to no rules or regularities of any sort, so all the methodologist can do about it is to tell anecdotes, myths about such things as serpents and benzene rings, to illustrate the proposition that new hypotheses can pop up in the oddest ways. Justification, in contrast, is a regular process involving rules of evidence, rules of inference, and rules of confirmation, so this is the domain of logic and method.

Other philosophers, defining logic more broadly, have argued that there is a logic of discovery. Norwood Hanson (1958, 1963) has argued for this position in physics, while Abraham Kaplan has argued for it in the social sciences (1964, pp. 12-18). Kaplan, following John Dewey's lead, defines logic as the procedures scientists use when they are doing well as scientists (p. 8). The task of the methodologist is to reconstruct, that is describe and clarify, the logic or logics that scientists are using. The question of whether there is a logic of discovery thus becomes empirical; one answers it affirmatively by describing, reconstructing, one or more such logics, and one answers it negatively by disconfirming a proposed reconstruction.

The present work follows Kaplan's lead by attempting to describe or "reconstruct" several logics that social scientists are now using. I have called these logics "patterns of discovery," following Hanson, to indicate the tradition in which I am working. However, this phrase may be vague or misleading for readers not familiar with Hanson's or Kaplan's work, so I shall specify it a bit.

The term *discovery* is misleading inasmuch as it suggests that scientists are limited to finding something that is already there. The suggestion is that social reality is given for the scientist and his only task is to imitate what is there without changing it. But actually scientific knowledge is in large part an invention or development rather than an imitation; concepts, hypotheses, and theories are not found ready-made in reality but must be constructed. Further, scientific knowledge is part of the process of self-awareness by which societies and individuals "reconstruct" themselves, as I shall argue in chapter 18, so that knowledge necessarily changes what is given. The test of truth in the social sciences, as Dewey used to argue, is whether a theory succeeds in changing its social referent, in some fashion that remains to be specified.

Pattern is also a pretty vague term, as vague as *method* and *logic*. It refers here to a regular, systematic, step-by-step series of procedures used by some group of scientists. The procedures are not mechanical or automatic, nor do they constitute an algorithm guaranteed to give results. They are rather to be applied flexibly according to circumstances; their order may vary, and alternatives are available at every step. In this respect they are more like the search procedures incorporated in Newell and Simon's "General Problem Solver" (1963) and in Cyert and March's simulation of managerial decision procedures (1963). To be sure, they are not sufficiently formalized to be put into a computer program, but they resemble the complexity and susceptibility to unexpected results of a computer program more than they do the austere single-mindedness of symbolic logic.

Justification and verification are not treated as a separate set of procedures occurring *after* "discovery," but are included *within* the process of discovery. In some methods verification is scattered throughout the process, and in others it occurs at one definite point; in some methods there are two or more kinds of verification and in others there is only one; but in any case, verification is always a subordinate part of a larger process of discovery. It constitutes the check point or points in the process.

Most important, what is invented or developed is not just hypotheses but the whole conceptual apparatus of science—methods and techniques, scales and indices, variables and factors, concepts, hypotheses, and models. None of these are either given to scientists or arbitrarily created ("conjectured") by them; they are all worked out step by step in the regular procedure that constitutes scientific method.

I myself do not especially like the traditional phrase "logic of discovery," and prefer to describe scientific methods as "heuristics," but this term also may have inappropriate connotations. "Heuristic" means for some people a haphazard trial-and-error process, and I do not intend this connotation. For others it is a term of disparagement applied to scientific work so poor that it has no noticeable results; such work at least has the heuristic value of helping one avoid the same mistakes next time. Then there are the formalist's "heuristic interpretations," which help make his theory intelligible to simple-minded empiricists. These connotations are all exaggerations of a central core of meaning that may be roughly expressed as follows: a heuristic is a loosely systematic procedure for investigation or inquiry that gives good results eventually and on the whole, but does not guarantee them in any particular case and certainly cannot promise "optimum" results. Heuristic is opposed to algorithm and is similar to search (in Herbert Simon's sense), research, inquiry, and the like.

I shall illustrate these points with an example from survey research, a method not treated in detail in this book. One of the principal tasks of the survey research method is the "discovery" of concepts. These concepts should be related by operational definitions to variables that behave in a lawlike manner, and the variables in turn should be reliably measurable by indices, scales, or test scores. All these subsidiary entities are also developed, or in some cases adapted, in the process of developing a concept.

The concept I have chosen for an illustration is "intraception," and the history of its development has been reported by Levinson et al. (1966). Intraception was first discussed and defined by Murray (1938) as follows: "The dominance of feelings, fantasies, speculations, aspirations. An imaginative, subjective human outlook. Romantic action." Vague as this definition and its discussion by Murray may seem, he regarded it as a refinement of still vaguer concepts advanced by James and Jung. He felt that it singled out one component of the tender-mindedness and introversion complexes and made it available for measurement.

Murray proposed several measures of intraception, but his primary interest was in the clarification of the concept. In contrast, the primary methodological focus in the *Authoritarian Personality* studies (Adorno et al., 1950) was on measurement, and in particular on developing the so-called F scale. One of the components of authoritarianism, as measured by the F scale, turned out to be anti-intraception, which, however, was not always inversely correlated with intraception. The F scale could then be used for further study of intraception, anti-intraception, and extraception.

Further refinement of the concept was achieved by Levinson and his associates in their research on mental hospitals, in which they used the F scale among other instruments. They developed the following definition: "Intraception is the disposition, expressed through various modalities, to emphasize and differentiate psychological aspects of oneself and of the external world" (Levinson et al., 1966, p. 126). They also developed an intraception index with four indicators that intercorrelate in the .3 to .6 range. This moderate level of correlation indicates that intraception as revised is still a somewhat vague concept, perhaps multidimensional, and that still better indicators could be developed.

The line of development here seems to move, on the concept side, from vagueness and complexity toward explicitness and simplicity, and from imaginative description toward lawlike correlations. (I have omitted the discovered correlations from my summary.) On the measuring instrument side, the line of development seems to move from broad general scales and indices toward reliable, specific indices with high indicator intercorrelations. The method, at the most general level, moves back and forth between concept and measurement, with the results of each used to refine and improve the other. This back-and-forth movement appears both in the thirty-year history of this line of research and in the detailed work of Levinson and his associates, who describe their work as a continuing dialectic between concept and empirical findings (1966, p. 129).

I select a second contrasting example from experimental work, another method not discussed systematically in these pages. W. K. Estes, in a 1968 colloquium at Buffalo, reported some of his experimental work dealing with the effect of nonreinforced trials on learning. His problem was set by the fact that a number of experimental studies had shown that the learning curve continues to rise during a series of nonreinforced trials, while a number of other studies had reported a level curve for nonreinforced trials. His first step was to search both sets of studies to find, if possible, some characteristics that were uniformly present in one group but not in the other. He found one such characteristic: When the allowable time for response was 2 seconds or less, the learning curve rose during nonreinforcement; when response time was more than 2 seconds, the curve remained level. His next step was to search the experimental literature for findings about response time in the neighborhood of 2 seconds. He found a generalization that response latency (the amount of time it takes to respond) in that type of learning experiment begins at approximately 3 seconds on the average and, with practice, shortens toward approximately 1 second. Este's next step was to put these two findings into a deductive relationship. Together they implied that when allowable response time was 2 seconds or less, for many subjects there was not sufficient time to respond on initial trials; but as latency decreased with practice to below 2 seconds, the response rate would increase independently of whether any additional learning was occurring. This suggested the hypothesis that the rising learning curve during nonreinforcement was an artifact of the brief response time allowed; the rising curve did not measure learning but rather a decrease of response latency. The next step was to devise experiments to test this hypothesis (which, incidentally, was confirmed).

This example differs from the previous one in that it concerns the work of a single experimenter over several months, rather than groups of researchers over thirty years. Also a hypothesis rather than a concept was "discovered," and its development preceded testing. Nevertheless, the development phase was just as regular and systematic as the testing phase and had its own logic and its own check points. Estes did not dream up his hypothesis; he deduced it from propositions discovered by systematic search.

These two reports may not have accurately described what the researchers were actually doing, and their work may have been atypical in various ways and degrees. If I were to study their methods more systematically, I would have to investigate both these questions. I would also have to be more specific about how, in the first example, concept led to improved scale or index and how empirical findings led to improved concept. But the reports serve to illustrate what I mean by calling scientific methods "heuristics" or "search procedures" or "logics of discovery."

Perhaps the reader is now in a position to select his own name for the present account of scientific method.

Method of the Present Work

Anyone who discusses method must eventually face the question of what *his* method is. After some thought I have concluded that my method all along has been that of participant observation. My approach is essentially anthropological; I treat various methods as subcultures within the general culture of science, each subculture belonging to a community within the general society of social scientists. There are as many methods as there are distinguishable communities of scientists, and the boundaries of each method are those of the community that uses it.

A community is located by finding people who interact regularly with one another in their work. They read and use each other's ideas, discuss each other's work, and sometimes collaborate. They have common friends, acquaintances, intellectual ancestors, and opponents, and thus locate themselves at roughly the same point in sociometric space. Their interaction is facilitated by shared beliefs and values—goals, myths, terminology, self-concepts—which make their work mutually intelligible and valuable. Although they do not all use exactly the same procedure in their work, there is a great deal of similarity, and the differences are accepted as variant realizations of the same values.

Conversely, the boundary of a community is marked by noninteraction, and more definitely by interminable polemics and unresolved misunderstandings. Examination of the polemics reveals differences in beliefs, goals, and values that make rational discussion and collaboration difficult or even impossible.

A method consists of the actual procedures used by members of a community, and the variations of procedure illustrate the range of variants of the method. Each method is justified and explained by an ideology or philosophy of science which specifies the goals of science, the available and permissible means, the impermissible errors, the proper subject matter, the heroic exemplars, and the unfortunate failures or pseudoscientific villains. Needless to say, the actual method always deviates from the prescriptions of its associated ideology, and the successful deviations are the source of change in method.

Some deviants are marginal men, in the sense that they have absorbed parts of two different ideologies and have a diffuse or split identity, and these deviants may mediate between two communities of scientists. If they are successful, that is, accepted and imitated, they become the medium for collaboration between the communities. Collaboration may lead to a regular division of labor, to an interpenetration of ideologies, and sometimes eventually to a partial integration of the two communities. In this way two methods may become variants of a single method, though the original methods may also continue in use. Conversely, other deviants may develop variations in a method that eventually becomes a new method used by a new community. Still other deviants may move by stages into some other community and become accepted as members there.

This conception of method is historically oriented and relativistic. Methods change slowly and continually; they develop, combine, and separate. They have no timeless essence—or any essence they may have does not become apparent in this approach—and are not separated by any fixed boundaries. Some boundaries at some times are quite sharp, such as the boundary between the clinical and the experimental method, which nowadays is crossed or straddled by few people. The Murray group at the Harvard Psychological Clinic made such an attempt, but it does not seem to have caught on. Other boundaries are rather indistinct and are freely crossed or well populated, such as the boundary between statistical surveying and mathematical modeling in the 1950's and the boundary between statistical surveying and participant observation at present. In these cases one needs to use a good deal of care (or recklessness) in drawing a boundary, if indeed a boundary is needed. Some border areas may be regarded as belonging indifferently to one or the other adjacent method, and their true status may not become clear until they have developed further. There are at least two such border areas at present, each showing promise (and some achievement) of new methodological developments. One is the combination of experimentation and mathematical modeling that I shall discuss in chapter 4. The other is the combination of some aspects of particpant observation with survey research techniques in the comparative study of particular political systems; much of this work is still unpublished (for example, Frederick Frey's continuing work on Turkish politics). I shall discuss some earlier stages of this development in chapter 12.

The task of the participant observer is to describe methods as they actually exist in a certain time period, which in the present case is the last two to four decades. It is necessary to take account of practices, supporting ideologies, and ranges of deviation, and to relate these to each other.

A variety of techniques is available for this purpose. First, observation of a literate culture includes, but is not limited to, reading its written output. Published scientific work can be treated as artifacts of the culture, analogous to potsherds, and can be used to reconstruct some of its typical modes of behavior. Articles on methodology can be treated like informants' reports in work on nonliterate cultures. Like most such reports, they are likely to be idealized accounts of what happens at best rather than what happens typically (for example, Nagel, 1961, pp. 503-520). Some are outright myths (Lewin, 1936, ch. 1; Radcliffe-Brown, 1957), valuable as indicators of goals, values, and belief systems. Polemical articles are useful indicators of variance in belief systems and of the boundaries of scientific communities.

To find out what actually happens in science, direct observation is necessary in addition to reading. This means observation of work in progress, including the study of experimental apparatus, questionnaires, field notes and diaries, uncompleted models, and particularly the comparison of different stages in the development of an apparatus, questionnaire, or model. It means talking and listening, personally and in colloquia, about a scientist's own work and about the work of others, in order to discover not only actual procedures but also particular modes of thinking, approaches to problems, and critical standards. Direct participation in scientific work, experiencing at first hand the problems and the modes of solution in use, is indispensable if one is to infer the actual performance behind published work and to interpret the meaning of methodological discussions.

Values, beliefs, and attitudes can also be studied as they are being transmitted to new scientists. This socialization process can be observed by taking and visiting courses, attending lectures, and looking at textbooks. One can even learn something by taking part in those barbaric sacred rites called "scientific conventions," though there it is difficult for outsiders to gain proper entry to the mysteries.

I do not mean to imply that I have used all of these techniques to the fullest, though I have done some of each and a great deal of most of them. Like most accounts of method, the above is an idealization, constructed after the fact. My cry is the cry of all fledgling field workers: "If only I had known at the beginning of my field work what I know now, I could have done so much better!" Indeed, my own performance has been so far below the ideal that I fear it resembles more the earliest anthropological work, the reports of naive travelers to far-off lands. Like them, I journeyed to these strange cultures originally in search of the gold of truth, hoping to exchange my shiny philosophical trinkets for it, and stayed to marvel at the intricate customs, the weird rituals, the incomprehensible feuds and wars, the admirable human beings I found there. I hope, however, that I have at times succeeded in approximating what Gluckman calls "the method of apt illustration" (Epstein, 1967, p. xiii), which is a step higher up the ladder than the traveler's report. A still more adequate method, it seems to me now, would be one that makes extensive use of quantitative data and statistical techniques; but if I had adopted such a method this book would never have been finished.

Like all methods, the participant-observer method has its characteristic biases and defects, and it is well to take note of them at the outset. To begin, some biases: First, the observer of a living system expects to find both ideals and practices, norms and facts, in interplay with each other. He looks for mechanisms of social control whereby practice is kept within an acceptable range of ideals, and ideals are reinterpreted to remain relevant to practice. He expects to find ranges of deviation beyond the allowable limit and is interested in the deviants as both indicators of strain and sources of innovation and diffusion.

Second, the process of studying a living system from the inside leads one to identify with it and to accept its own standards and outlook. Among anthropologists this tendency is expressed in the doctrine of cultural relativism, the doctrine that each culture has its own problems and achievements, its own strengths and weaknesses, and that it must be sustained and improved on its own unique terms. However this doctrine may have been misinterpreted by eager philosophical critics and overextended by an occasional enthusiast, as a methodological bias it simply expresses a resolve to understand a culture in its own categories. It has no more metaphysical significance than the experimentalist's postulate of universal determinism, which expresses his resolve to keep looking for causes. Cultural relativism is not incompatible with a search for cultural universals, but it does carry with it a great skepticism about any proposed universals, a belief that there are probably exceptions or that the universal is usually described too narrowly. When an anthropologist does claim to have found a valid universal, it is likely to be something quite abstract, a functional prerequisite that can be satisfied in different ways by different cultures—and even then he would not be surprised to hear of an exception or two. In the present context this characteristic bias becomes a belief that all scientific methods must be understood in their own terms and improved in their own ways, and that any general characteristics of scientific method are likely to be requirements that can be satisfied in a variety of ways.

One difficulty of the participant-observer method is its tendency to draw a sharp boundary around its subject. Any scientific method has this tendency to some extent, since what is studied is treated differently from the surrounding material which is not studied. But the tendency is stronger in participant observation because its practitioners attempt to interpret their subjects as going systems, and systems have boundaries and boundary-maintenance functions. If one's subject is a Pacific island culture or a small jungle tribe, the tendency does not lead to appreciable distortions; indeed, the anthropologist who studies a whole isolated culture can correctly claim that he, of all social scientists, is most justified in drawing a boundary around his subject. But when the subject is a small town, a factory, a street corner gang, a subculture, or in general anything that is also a part of a larger system, the danger of distortion must be faced. In the present context the danger is in a tendency to think that there are four, or five, or some other definite number of methods in use, and to forget that there are also innumerable combinations, variations, and boundary cases. Some of the hybrids are misguided artificial creations that cannot survive, but others may be valuable improvements or precursors of future methods, and still others may turn out to be methods in their own right. There is a similar danger in thinking that the social sciences are themselves sharply defined, simply because we are treating them in that fashion. Actually they are an interdependent part of a larger system, Western society, and probably of other systems as well.

Another difficulty in the participant-observer method is separating the observer's contribution, or bias, from the contribution made by his subject matter. The account in the following chapters must be interpreted as partly an expression of my own biases and partly an account of what is actually there, and it will not be easy to separate the two, particularly if the reader has biases of his own. One solution to the difficulty (though not necessarily the best one) is for the observer to make his biases explicit, and I shall attempt to do this.

In the first place, my original unconscious drift into the participant-observer method expresses a preference for direct observation of particular fact and a self-critical suspicion of all generalization and abstraction. It also expresses a preference for complexity and disorder over clarity and simplicity, or, more accurately, an ambivalence on this point. I regard positively all social science methods and theories, but my admiration for logic and mathematics is a recent acquisition, so recent that I am still a novice rather than a fully initiated adept. I dislike anything that claims superiority, dominance, or orthodoxy, and I prefer to believe that all established truths, including my own, must be mistaken. My particular preference for psychoanalytic theory and my relative dislike for neoclassical economic theory will also soon become apparent. The reader will undoubtedly find additional biases as he goes along.

Preliminary View of the Social Sciences

Before beginning our detailed studies of particular methods, let us take a quick preliminary look at the social sciences as a whole.

The social sciences are a doubly segmented society, divided by two principles of grouping that cut across each other. In this they resemble various Plains Indian societies, such as the Cheyenne, whose members are divided both into clans and into voluntary soldier societies. One principle of grouping, the clan principle, is the professional field: for example, psychology, sociology, or economics. A person enters a field by taking the appropriate course of training (socialization) and by finding a job recognized as belonging to the field—teaching, research, clinical practice, etc. He remains in the field by holding that job or moving to other jobs of higher status. Each field is controlled by its elders, who decide on job offerings, advancement, and co-optation to the ruling group. Each main field has several subdivisions, but control is largely retained by the field elders rather than those in the subfield. Individual departments of a university may combine two or more fields, but control is still by field, as a member may move in and out of departments within his field.

The other principle of grouping is the method. A person adopts a method by engaging in supervised research (socialization) and continues by doing more research, either individually or in teams. Members consult and criticize each other, check each other's results or build on them, exchange techniques, and in general collaborate extensively. Control of a method is a more complex process (which I shall discuss presently), but personal prestige is more important than official position because of extensive personal collaboration. A method provides opportunities for achievement and influence, while a field with its primarily ascriptive values provides financial and emotional security, official advancement, power, and personal identity.

The conflict between these two modes of grouping is a prominent feature of the society. The two are interdependent in that work achievement is demanded for membership and advancement in a field, while financial security is necessary for work. But the strengthening and consolidation of each system tends to weaken the other, because they cut across one another. Increased cohesiveness of a field cuts one off from colleagues in other fields using the same method and thus reduces the wide collaboration that is important for scientific advance. Conversely, wide-ranging collaboration reinforces methodological differences within a field and leads to increased strife and polemics within departments and at field conventions.

The conflict is functional for social science as a whole, because it preserves integration by preventing subsystems from becoming too cohesive. The fact that methods and fields largely cut across one another forces users of different methods together within a field, while it brings members of different fields together within a method. Whenever a field (such as experimental psychology recently or economics fifty years ago) achieves substantial unity of method and high internal cohesion, contact with other fields and with other methods is weakened and theory stagnates. The field moves into a scholastic phase in which attention is focused on smaller and smaller details within an essentially unchanging theoretical framework. A similar stagnation of method would occur if one method were completely isolated from others.

Conflict between the two subsystems, and therefore the unity of the social science system as a whole, can be maintained only insofar as each subsystem maintains its own unity against the disrupting influence of the other. How is this done? The unity of a field, I suspect, is essentially maintained by the job-placement system. The field elders must maintain extensive and close personal contacts to carry out their control task. They must continually exchange information about job applicants and openings, promotions, moves, and departmental politics affecting future openings and applicants. Newer field members develop extensive contacts for the same purpose. My guess is that a content analysis of intimate conversation at conventions and during visits would show a higher frequency of job conversation than of scientific discussion. These contacts unite proponents of different methods as friends and reduce methodological prejudices. If methodological commitment is too strong, contact is limited to those using similar methods, departments become specialized in a particular approach, and the field becomes fragmented. A corollary of this suggestion is that when jobs are plentiful, job control and field unity will be weakened and collaboration across field boundaries will increase.

A second and derivative basis of field unity is the personal identification of individual scientists within a field. A scientist will identify himself as an anthropologist, for instance, rather than as a survey researcher. This means that a field takes on some of the characteristics of a clan; one belongs to it, is accepted by it, and finds security in it. Other field members are brothers and one has an obligation of loyalty to them, even though they may use different methods. Contact with nonfield members may be adventuresome and exciting, but also carries a danger of disloyalty and betrayal and, in extreme cases, even loss of identity. Consequently, collaboration across fields on the basis of a shared method is usually, in the cases I have examined, a cautious affair marked by emotional reserve and frequent reaffirmation of personal differences.

Unity of method is maintained in a more complex way because methods are less institutionalized than fields. Socialization is important in transmitting the culture of a method, but it is often weakened by cross-socialization in a methodologically mixed department. After socialization is completed, deviation is controlled by the methodologists, who function as moralists prescribing canons of methodological purity. In addition, they create myths that dramatize the importance of correct behavior—for example, historical myths that describe the progress of science from error and superstition (false methods) to its present enlightenment (true method). Galileo is the hero of many historical myths, so much so that one turns to a new account of Galileo's work in the confident anticipation of enjoying a new myth. The empiricists tell how their hero dared to look for himself and associate him vaguely with the leaning tower of Pisa and the moons of Jupiter. The formalists point to his crude experimental apparatus—waterclocks and wooden planks—and argue that his infrequent "experimenting" was simply a device to give his formal models an empirical interpretation. Lewin in turn makes him out to be a proto-clinician in disguise (Lewin, 1936, ch. 1). In addition to historical myths, there are utopias showing how the golden future of science will be brought about through methodological correctness. Autobiographical accounts reveal that these myths and methodological prescriptions are taken seriously (Homans, 1962, ch. 1; Skinner, 1959b). (In Skinner's myth he himself is the hero). For those disposed to wander, there are myths about the lost sheep, the pseudo-scientists who use false methods, illustrating the horrible consequences of deviation (Gray, 1962). Here again one finds in conversation that (for example) the experimentalist's fears of sinking gradually into the clinicians' morass or the formalists' mathematical fantasies are real and strong. Against insidious moral danger, constant striving for purity of method is the only protection.

The gentle persuasion of the moralist-methodologist is supplemented by the stronger witchcraft of the journal editor. If one wonders about the remarkable uniformity of method displayed in certain journals and asks the authors of articles why they write that way, they answer, "It's always done that way, that's science, isn't it? You do A, B, C, etc. Besides, we couldn't get it published any other way" (cf. also Riesman and Watson, 1964, p. 311). Then there is the occasional anguished cry of the bewitched victim: "One year of research down the drain to satisfy an editor's pet theory!"

These specific unifying influences give guidance to a more pervasive influence, the diffuse sanctions inherent in widespread collaboration with one's peers. And, finally, the unity of a fellowship of work is strengthened by occasional polemics with misguided proponents of different methods.

The continuous interplay between method and field is, perhaps, occasionally affected by another character, this one an outsider, the philosopher of science. I learned early to avoid these missionary types; their continuous cry, "Repent! You aren't being truly scientific! That was only an explanation sketch, not an explanation!" was unedifying and wearying. Others of a different theological orientation, but equally unedifying, would say "Stop trying to act like scientists! The phrase 'policy science' is logically self-contradictory!" Their numerous theological arguments were also uninteresting; they seemed mainly to disagree over whether social scientists could in principle be saved and go to the heaven of physics or whether they were predestined to damnation. As for this heaven, I cannot tell whether it exists or is another myth, but at any rate I heard marvelously varied accounts of it. Their disputes always seemed to be phrased in terms of how it was in physics, a field which they knew well. Some of them talked in addition of a second heaven above physics, called "fully axiomatized science," a heaven with its own ideal language and method. The doings of social scientists interested them little, except as a basis for a catalog of error; if social scientists did well, they would eventually be in physics anyway, and their present earthly ways would be forgotten.

More recently I have come across a new kind of missionary, exemplified by Kaplan (1964) and perhaps Mischel (1966), who force me to revise my earlier stereotype. This new missionary does not speak of repentance and salvation, but says, rather, "If I am to be helpful to these people, I must first learn to understand them." Instead of making quick forays into the social sciences in pursuit of sinners, he goes to live there and seems actually to enjoy it. With these new missionaries I can be friends, as long as they avoid theology.

Still more recently I have come to appreciate Hempel's work, have seen its value for science, and have used some of his ideas in my own thinking. But it still is the case that my interest is different from that of most philosophers of science. I wish to be neither coach nor umpire, as Kaplan classifies the philosophers. I wish simply to understand and describe the methods of social scientists, to see what they are really up to, and to note both pitfalls and improvements as they appear. I do not wish to dispute about the timeless characteristics of an ideal science, only to describe present developments in all their variety and historical uniqueness. I do not wish to be a philosopher *of* science, where *of* means "different from and superior to." I wish only to participate in the scientific enterprise here and now, contributing those particular things of which I am capable.

I

Formal Methods and Theories

1

Formal Methods
and Theories

2

General Characteristics
of Formal Theories

The method (or methods) I wish to discuss in Part I is given different names by different people—mathematical method, model-building, formal method. Thus we are faced at the outset with a question of terminology. Each of these terms has somewhat different meanings for different people, and each of them also suggests somewhat different boundaries. However, if one remembers that there are no sharp boundaries in the social sciences, that each method shades into and combines with every other, and that all methods are constantly developing and changing anyway, the question of boundaries becomes unimportant. It will be sufficient if we begin with a general characterization of our method, and later mark out its approximate range by means of examples. Each reader can then use any term or terms that he likes to name it.

Some Basic Definitions

The mathematical or formal method is characterized first by the use of formal languages, and second by the development of an axiomatic, deductive structure. A language is a set of concepts and definitions, a set of conventional symbols that stand for the concepts, a set of rules for combining symbols in a statement or sentence, and a set of rules for transforming sentences into equivalent sentences (deduction). The two main groups of formal languages are mathematics and the computer languages, though symbolic logic can also be used (for example, Arrow, 1951; Abelson and Rosenberg, 1958.) There are also intermediate cases in which the basic language is mathematical but a computer is used to perform the necessary calculations. A deductive structure is composed of a set of initial statements, called axioms or postulates, and a set of statements that result or follow from operations on the initial statements. A formal theory is the result of using a formal method; it is written at least partly in a formal language and has an axiomatic, deductive structure.

Both characteristics, language and structure, are equally important. The language of a theory is its matter, in the Aristotelian sense, and its structure is its form. That is, the language of a theory provides it with a certain range of potentialities, and its structure uses or develops those potentialities and thereby becomes a certain definite kind of thing. Both potentiality and its development are necessary for a fully formal theory.

Thus it is not enough to define a formal theory as any theory that uses a formal language; this would be a material definition of a formal theory. There are theories that use mathematical symbols but are not formal theories, for example, Lewin's field theory. Lewin uses symbols and mathematical concepts to describe a situation, but does not make systematic inferences from the initial description. For example, his equation $B = f(P,E)$ is not used to study the mathematical interrelations of personality and environment; the derivatives of the function are not examined, nor are time paths, equilibrium characteristics, asymptotes, ranges of values, etc. Conversely there are theories that are axiomatic-deductive in their structure but use little or no formal language and formal deductive technique, for example, literary economic theories. I shall call these *implicit formal theories* because their structure is incompletely developed owing to the inadequate language used. It is difficult and perhaps impossible to work out a thorough mathematical analysis of a set of propositions that are expressed in verbal terms because the reasoning becomes too complicated. To be sure, literary economists have done considerable analysis of the economics of the firm in perfect competition, but even this quite restricted topic has taken well over a century of effort.

The translation of an implicit formal theory into a formal language enables one to complete its structure and to note points of possible further development. This process is call *formalization*. Formalization is not simply the translation of a theory from one language into another, but is essentially a process of structural development.

The method characterized above may be called either "mathematical" or "model-building" or "formal." Each of these names, however, is open to misinterpretation and must be properly defined. The term *mathematical* may be understood both too broadly and too narrowly—too broadly if it refers to any use of numbers, quantification, or measurement, since these can be an ingredient in any method, and too narrowly if it excludes symbolic logic and computer languages. Properly speaking, a mathematical method is one that uses conventional symbols and techniques for manipulating symbols to achieve an axiomatic, deductive structure. For example, Hurwicz (1963) suggests that there are three essential aspects of the mathematical method: symbolism, axiomatic structure, and a treasury of accumulated techniques and results. He also notes that classical literary economists who use "mathematical reasoning or generalizations, couched in verbal or arithmetical form, but without mathematical symbolism or technique" (1963, p. 5) are doing mathematics but are not using the mathematical method. These points are the same ones I have made above. "Symbolism and technique" approximate what I have called formal language; "axiomatic structure" is the same as axiomatic-deductive structure, and the classical economists who use deductive reasoning without symbolism or technique are implicit formal theorists.

Model can be used broadly to refer to any analogue of anything else, or it may refer to exemplifications, idealized cases, or still other things. For my present purpose it must be defined more narrowly as a system of equations and inequalities, that is, as an axiomatic structure. One can distinguish mathematical models, computer models, and logical models, according to the kind of symbols used in the equations. A model-building method is a way of constructing models and interpreting them, that is, of relating them to the real world. A theory is a model plus one or more interpretations. Occasionally the terms *model* and *theory* are reversed in accounts of the model-building method. A theory is then defined as a system of uninterpreted equations and inequalities, and a model as a theory with one interpretation (for example, Krupp, 1963, p. 199). I have no objection to this terminology, and the reader can use if if he likes, substituting *model* for *theory* and *theory* for *model* in the following pages. But I should warn the reader that I am not following the terminological conventions current in physics or in philosophical accounts of "models" in physics.

Formal means all sorts of things, but its proper meaning here is that opposed to *substantive* (see for example Glaser and Strauss, 1965; more specifically, in Glaser and Strauss' classification I am discussing logico-deductive formal theory [1967, ch. 4]). A formal theory is composed of a model plus an indefinite number of interpretations, and there is a sharp distinction between model and interpretation. A model is not affected by any of its interpretations, but can be understood and studied in abstraction from all of them; one can work with a model—make deductions, search for inconsistencies, study the effects of changes in postulates, add new terms—without referring to anything empirical. A substantive theory, in contrast, is intrinsically about something in the real world, and one cannot make any changes in the theory without referring to the real world to see whether the change is allowable. Any deduction one makes, for example, remains hypothetical until it is empirically verified.

For logicians, the formal/substantive distinction is the same as that between symbolic and Aristotelian logic. One can work on a piece of symbolic logic without asking what the symbols stand for; they can stand for almost anything. Aristotelian logic, in contrast, is designed for work only with essences and properties, not with accidents. Moreover, each syllogism one constructs must be checked against the essence one is studying to see whether the terms have been properly stated. To be sure, Aristotelian logic over the centuries has been formalized and treated as a special kind of symbolic logic, but that was not Aristotle's original intention. The formal/substantive distinction is familiar to sociologists, who probably got it from Simmel or Weber, while the mathematical/literary distinction is used mainly by economists.

One also sometimes finds a distinction made between rational and empirical models. An empirical model is derived from a set of data by some curve-fitting technique and serves to summarize and extrapolate from those data. A rational model attempts to describe some structure that underlies data and produces them, though it can also be used empirically to summarize data. In other words, a rational model is composed of theoretical terms while an empirical model is more nearly observational. Some models, for instance econometric models, are partly rational and partly empirical. Thus in the Klein-Goldberger model, the equation K_t-K_{t-1}=I_t-D_t (increase of capital equals investment minus depreciation) is rational, a tautology in fact, while the equation $(W_2)_t$=$1.82+.578t$ (which describes the average rate of increase in government employee compensation over a certain time period) is empirical. Here we shall be dealing with rational or predominantly rational models.

Since formal theories have, I claim, two sets of characteristics, linguistic and structural, it is necessary to examine each set separately. I shall begin with language.

Formal Languages

Both mathematics and the computer languages can be understood from two quite different though related standpoints. On the one hand, they can be treated as tools for working with quantities; on the other hand, they can be seen as dealing with relations and systems of relations. Mathematics can be understood either as numbers, measurement, and calculation, or as an abstract language of relations. Computers can be treated either as calculators or as simulators. To be sure, both standpoints are legitimate, necessary, and complementary, but in practice one or the other is primary.

From the "quantity" standpoint, arithmetic is the basic branch of mathematics and counting or measuring is the primary operation. Data must be quantified to be subject to mathematical treatment, and the basic advantage of quantification is its exactness. Science is seen as moving from vague verbal predictions to exact quantitative predictions. Non-numerical fields—algebra, topology, graph theory, game theory—are regarded as ways of manipulating potential numbers, their conclusions incomplete until filled in with actual numbers. This is the standpoint represented by the Econometric Society's first motto, "Science is measurement." It is also the standpoint of Schubert's *Quantitative Analysis of Judicial Behavior* and Hull's use of mathematics, the standpoint of statistics, factor analysis, and scaling, and in general, the standpoint of data processing. A typical "quantitative" statement reads: "The use of mathematical models is virtually synonymous with the construction of a quantitative theory of behavior" (Suppes and Atkinson, 1960, p. 282).

From the "relation" standpoint mathematics is an abstract language adapted to describing relations rather than observed qualities. As

Shubik observes, "the language of mathematics is, in general, poor in adjectives" (1964, p. 4) because most adjectives stand for qualities and these are missing in mathematics. G. A. Miller exemplifies the relational standpoint when he says, "Any use of mathematics in science or technology rests on an analogy: something about the way the symbols are related must resemble something about the relations among the observed phenomena. What matters is not the symbols or the objects themselves, but the pattern of interrelations among them. The 'something' that is analogous between the two is generally called their *structure*. The task of an applied mathematician is to construct (or borrow) a system of symbols and rules whose structures is isomorphic with the structure that the empirical scientist discovers in his data and his experience" (1964, p. 222). Alker sums up his account of mathematics: "Mathematics is the logical study of symbolic relationships" (1965, p. 12, but cf. Zinnes, 1968, p. 266). Kemeny and Snell observe "Mathematics is best viewed as the study of abstract relations in the broadest sense of that word. . . . Whatever the nature of the phenomena studied in a given social science, their various components do bear certain relations to each other, and once one succeeds in formulating these abstractly and precisely, one is in a position to apply the full machinery of mathematical analysis" (1962, p. 8).

The various branches of mathematics and logic deal with different kinds of relations, and whenever a new kind of relation is clearly and distinctly conceived, a new branch of mathematics or logic can be invented to deal with it. Algebra and calculus deal with the relations of *greater, less, equal,* and *identical,* together with more complex secondary relations like *proportional to, limit of, partial elasticity.* Utility theory deals with preference relations. Set theory deals with the relation of being included in (ϵ) and the relation of similarity between sets. Graph theory builds on the relations of connnectedness, adjacency, betweenness, and domination, plus more complex secondary relations like reachability; Markov chains are based on the relation of connectedness in time, or transition. Alternativeness, conflict, and cooperation are important relations in game theory. Relations of implication, union (*or*), and intersection (*and*) are fundamental in symbolic logic; and so on. Each of these relations also has its corresponding negative: unequal, indifferent, excluded, unconnected, etc. Also a host of complex relations can be constructed out of the simple ones: a source is a complex kind of domination, a derivative is a relation of greater, less, or equal between a value and an earlier value. Then there are more particularized instances of more abstract relations: being a brother of and being a child of are special kinds of adjacency; being a liaison person or group is a special kind of betweenness; being a friend of is a special kind of connectedness; being a member of is a special kind of inclusion; ideological conversion and changing one's mind are special kinds of transition. Finally there are the three basic modalities of all relations—reflexive, symmetric, and transitive—and their opposites. Computers do not add any new relations to the above but excel in drawing implications from specified relations.

From a relational standpoint, quantification is an operation that is made possible by a very special relation, that of being equal and unconnected. Only equal and unconnected entities can be added, subtracted, etc. This rather unusual relation is more prominent in some societies than in others but is especially prominent in capitalist society, with its ubiquitous buying, selling, and voting transactions. One could call it an alienated relation But for most social science purposes and most types of society, the relations embodied in Markov chains, graph theory, and game theory are more useful and versatile than that assumed in arithmetic. Incidentally, all three of these branches of mathematics were invented in the twentieth century, two of them by and for social scientists. Those quantitatively minded social scientists who think their method is the only valid one commit the error of trying to reduce all social relations to the special relation "equal and unconnected," and this attempt can lead to serious deficiencies in their work.

Conversely, from a quantitative standpoint most of the above relations look like vaguely stated quantities. *Greater* suggests the question "How much greater?" *Adjacent* suggests "How close?" *Preference* suggests "How strong a preference?" *Conflict* suggests "How intense a conflict?" In general the relational use of mathematics may seem primitive and elementary to quantitatively minded scientists, and non-quantitative fields of mathematics like graph theory and topology may seem vague, weak, and uninteresting.

The formal method is based on a relational view of mathematics and computers. The formalist's aim is to build a model or abstract relational structure, and his building materials are the various relations provided by mathematical and computer languages. Formalists also use numbers, but in a secondary and sometimes quite incidental way. The most common use of numbers in a formal method is heuristic; that is, some set of numbers is arbitrarily chosen to illustrate the operation of a model, to set it working so that its operation can be studied. The theorist's interest is not in what happens to the particular numbers but in how the model works with them; this holds true even if the numbers are not arbitrary but represent real data. As Miller observes in speaking of a certain type of model, "the equations are used, not to look at the data, but to look through them at the underlying relations that must hold for any possible set of numerical data" (1964, p. 137). Thus an economist studying supply curves or utility curves (Adams, 1960, pp. 243-252) will be interested not in the absolute numerical value of any point but in the slope of the curve and rates of change in slope, that is, in the derivatives.

A second important use of numbers in a formal method is in the application of a model to a particular case. Here the values of the variables for that case have to be filled in; in particular, the critical values and the limits, where relevant, have to be determined. Which values must be filled in and how exact they must be depends on the model and the use being made of it. In some cases it is only necessary to know that the values lie within, or above or below, certain critical limits; and in some models no numbers may be needed at all.

In most uses of mathematics both quantity and relation will be present, since each requires the other. However, the distinction still is useful in marking the difference between two types of scientific interest. On the one hand the predominant interest is in counting and measuring, data manipulation, prediction; on the other hand the predominant interest is in the construction of relational structures that will order and constrain all possible data. The one is empirical, focusing on specific subject matter; the other is formal, abstracted from empirical content. Failure to make this distinction has led to misunderstandings and needless polemic. Thus the epithet "quantophrenia" may apply to some mathematical social scientists, but not to formalists; and the contention that mathematics, being quantitative, does not apply to economic phenomena, which are qualitative (Byers, 1959, pp. 394-395) is certainly mistaken (cf. also Hurwicz, 1963, pp. 4 ff.). Conversely, the complaint by quantitatively minded scientists (and philosophers) against the formalist's cavalier attitude toward precise numerical data, while perhaps salutary, underestimates the importance of the formalist's characteristic concern with structures of relations.

The Structure of Formal Theories

All formal theories have two parts. First, there is the model or calculus (or theory in some versions of terminology), a set of interrelated propositions stated in a formal language. The propositions of a calculus are nothing more than a network of relations that allow one to move from one term to another in a certain sequence. By itself a calculus is neither true nor false, since it says nothing about the empirical world.

Second, there are one or more sets of rules that relate the calculus to the empirical world. These are called rules of correspondence or rules of interpretation, and each set provides an interpretation of the calculus. That is, it gives a verbal translation of the terms of a calculus and thus tells us what the calculus means empirically. However, unlike ordinary translation, a rule of interpretation never gives a definitive set of possible empirical meanings, since any calculus can have an indefinite number of interpretations. For example, a certain set of equations now known as a "Richardson process model" appears in Alfred Marshall's *Pure Theory of Foreign Trade* (1930) as a model of international trade (Samuelson, 1966, pp. 547-549). Richardson used it to model an armaments race (Rapoport, 1957). Boulding (1962, ch. 2) showed that with certain modifications the same model described some very pervasive characteristics of interpersonal relations, and Pruitt (1967) applied the model to the interaction of certain small groups.

Rules of interpretation do make a truth claim; they claim that the structure of relations in a calculus is the same structure that exists in some part or aspect of the empirical world. That is, they claim that the calculus describes the relational structures (or one of those structures) underlying a certain empirical phenomenon. Stated differently, they claim that if one uses the calculus one can operate successfully with certain empirical phenomena.

Thus the truth or falsity of a formal theory is located entirely in its rules of correspondence (I shall qualify this later when discussing computer models). This is sometimes difficult to realize when reading a formal theory. The propositions of its calculus, which are neither true nor false, are often stated in a categorical way such that they seem to be making a truth claim, while the rules of correspondence are often added carelessly as though they are obvious or trivial details; they may not even be explicitly stated. In the case of implicit formal theories, it not infrequently happens that the author himself is confused as to what sort of truth claim he is making. I shall give examples of this confusion later, when dealing with implicit theories.

No formal theory is ever true without qualification. The rules of interpretation in which its truth is located always relate it to some specific part or aspect of the world, never to the world in general. Indeed, in most cases a formal theory claims only to apply to one aspect of an empirical process or system; it claims to be true *ceteris paribus*. Conversely, no formal theory can ever be totally falsified. Even if a particular interpretation is shown to be invalid, some other interpretation may still be true and since any calculus has an indefinite number of possible interpretations, it is impossible to falsify all its interpretations; there may always be a true one waiting to be discovered. Bush and Mosteller (1955, p. 2) make this point for mathematical learning theories, and Coleman (1964, pp. 516-519) makes it for social process models, calling them "sometimes-true theories." Thus the principle of falsifiability does not apply to formal theories except in a very indirect way. This is one of several striking differences between the kind of truth found in formal theories and that found in the laws sought by empiricists.

The two parts of a formal theory, calculus and interpretation, connect in the terms of the calculus. The calculus is built up out of terms, and each rule of interpretation is attached to some term. Consequently, the terms of a formal theory face in two directions, have two kinds of meaning, and are defined in two different ways. On the one hand they have empirical meanings and operational definitions provided by rules of correspondence, and on the other hand they have formal meanings and relational definitions from their place in the calculus. It may, however, happen that some of the terms of a theory have no empirical meaning but act solely as connectives in the formal network.

Formal meanings and relational definitions are perhaps not so familiar as empirical meanings and operational definitions, so I shall discuss them. A relational definition is simply a statement of how a term is related to other terms. This can be done in two ways, either by specifying the place of the term in a certain formula or network, or by stating a mathematical expression that can be substituted for the term. In other words, one can give either the context of the term or its component parts or both. For example, in a game model, C_1 can be defined both as a certain row in a probability matrix and as the sum of its component parts: $C_1 = \xi_1 C_2 + \omega_1(1 - C_2)$ (Rapoport, 1965, p. 68); C_2 in turn is defined in relation to C_1. McPhee, in his "Logic of Addiction" (1963, ch. 5) defines his three parameters by their mathematical context: s is multiplied by $1 - C$, r is multiplied by C, and a is multiplied by ΔC. Once the place of a parameter is specified, it can be moved around, of course, but only within the constraints set up by the definition. Many algebraic symbols have conventional formal meanings that specify their place in a network of relations: A_{ij} are any or all of the cells of the matrix A, A_{ii} is any cell on the main diagonal, A_{ji} is any cell across the diagonal from some other cell, j is any row or column after some other row or column, and A_{nn} is the corner cell in a square matrix. These are very general meanings valid for any use of matrix algebra. Boulding, following Richardson, defines hostility in a two-party situation as follows: "$h_1 = H_1 + (r_1 - m_1 h_2)h_2$. Here, h_1 and h_2 are the hostility levels of parties 1 and 2" (1962, p. 36; cf. also pp. 26, p. 169). This definition says that the value of h_1 is either independent of h_2 or dependent on it or partly independent and partly dependent. It also says that the degree of dependence may or may not vary as h_2 varies. If it does not vary, that is, if $m_1 = 0$, then h_1 is a linear function of h_2; otherwise it is nonlinear. Keynes defines the propensity to consume as the functional relation between consumption and income, $\dfrac{C_w}{Y_w}$ (1936, p. 90).

Relational definitions and formal meanings also occur in implicit formal theories, though their formal character tends to be obscured by the nonformal language in which they are expressed. Thus Neal Miller writes, "A response is any activity by or within the individual which can become functionally connected with an antecedent event through learning; a stimulus is any event to which a response can be so connected" (1959, p. 51). Miller is giving a relational definition $A = f(S)$ and adding that any rules of interpretation for A and S must satisfy the relational conditions it sets up.

A mathematically inclined reader will be sensitive to relational definitions even when they are expressed in ordinary language, but empirically inclined scientists may tend to overlook them. Indeed, a strong empiricist, used to operationalizing and to looking for empirical referents, may even misinterpret symbolic statements as a kind of shorthand empirical statement. This can lead only to confusion and to the hypostatization of relations. For example, it is a mistake to interpret Keynes' "propensity to consume" $(\frac{C}{Y})$ as a psychological entity, a habit or disposition, since it is simply a functional relation between consumption rate and income level, to which Keynes has given a heuristic name. Similarly, the "marginal propensity to consume" $(\frac{dC}{dY})$ and Domar's "marginal propensity to invest" $(\frac{dI}{dY})$ (Yamane, 1962, p. 158) are derivatives, not habits. Similarly, when Boulding interprets H as xenophobia and r as touchiness, he is simply being heuristic and is not defining real psychological entities. Again, when he says, "We may, perhaps, venture a hypothesis that the power of an ideology is made up of two factors, which we may call *intensity* and *appeal*" (1962, p. 281), the mathematical reader will notice the tautologous, relational character of the definition, but the empiricist may think that a genuine hypothesis is being proposed. Ashby warns against this sort of misunderstanding when he says "It must be appreciated that D,T,E, etc., were defined in S. 11/3 in purely *functional* [relational] form. Thus D is 'that which disturbs.' Given any real system some care may be necessary in deciding what corresponds to D, what to T, and so on" (1956, p. 216). By "that which disturbs" Ashby means an independent source of variation in T, including noise, which must be counteracted by a regulator R to produce a desired effect E.

$$D \rightarrow T \rightarrow E$$
$$\diagdown \quad \diagup$$
$$R$$

In their relational aspect, the terms of a calculus necessarily appear as components of propositions (or as components of a computer flow chart). There are two basic types of propositions in a calculus, initial statements and derived statements. Initial statements specify the set of relations to be studied; derived statements describe the characteristics of the structure produced by combining the relations under study.

Let us consider each of these two types of propositions in more detail, beginning with initial statements. Terminology here is not standardized; the terms *axiom*, *postulate*, *definition*, and *assumption* are used in a variety of ways, sometimes interchangeably and sometimes not. One reason for differences in terminology is that different models have different kinds of initial statements that cannot readily be fitted into any single classification. Another reason is that usage in logic and mathematics has varied from time to time; and in any case, the distinctions needed by a logician may not be the same as those needed by an ordinary model-builder. To avoid terminological discussion, I shall arbitrarily call initial statements "postulates." The reader can then substitute any term he chooses and can in addition make such further distinctions as are needed in particular cases. For instance, in many cases it is possible to distinguish a subset of definitions, or a subset of rules of operation on equations, or a subset of constraints on the values of variables, etc. The purpose of postulates, in general, is to specify a formal subject matter, a set of relations that is to be studied.

The terminology of derived statements is somewhat more standardized; they are generally called *deductions* or *derivations* or *implications*. Since all these terms mean approximately the same thing, I shall use them interchangeably. Theorems are an important subclass of derived statements which are more abstract and general and are used to make other, more particular deductions. Many models do not contain any theorems, but depend instead on standard theorems from the relevant branch of mathematics.

What sort of deductions does a formalist try to make? In general, he tries to find implications that follow from his postulates without regard to any empirical content they might have or might be given. In mathematical terms, he tries to derive implications from the *relationships* among his parameters and variables, implications that hold good in general and not just for particular values of the variables. Or, failing this, he tries to derive implications that hold at least for certain ranges of values or relative values. These implications will then be valid in any circumstances to which his initial postulates apply. The subject matter of these implications can be only the formal structure itself, rather than its empirical content, because the structure stays the same while the content varies. The formalist tries to discover implications that state the characteristics of the structure he is studying. Such implications may be called formal truths. Formal truths are truths about a model, a formal structure, and hold for the real world only insofar as the real world imitates the formal structure—in other words, only insofar as something approximating the formal structure exists in the real world.

Consider for example a simple formal structure, a zero-sum game:

$$
\begin{array}{cc}
 & B \\
 & 1 \qquad 2
\end{array}
$$

$$
A \begin{array}{c} 1 \\ 2 \end{array}
\begin{array}{|c|c|}
\hline
a & -a \\
\hline
-a & a \\
\hline
\end{array}
$$

In this diagram, A and B are the two players, and play consists of choosing either 1 or 2. A chooses either row 1 or row 2, and B chooses either column 1 or column 2. The two choices, which are made simultaneously, intersect in a cell, and the number in the cell is the payoff to A; the payoff to B is the exact negative of the payoff to A. In a non-zero-sum game the payoffs to A and B must both be listed in each cell. The formalist knows something about the structure of this game; he knows that there is no dominating strategy for either player. This means that when a person is playing the game against a shrewd, intelligent opponent, there is no consistent strategy he can use that will win. The best he can possibly do is avoid being beaten, playing for a draw by using a random strategy. This does not mean that actual players will use a random strategy. It may be that they are not smart enough to discover the optimum strategy or are smart enough to see that the opponent is foolishly using a non-random strategy. In either case non-randomness in actual plays does not mean the random strategy is "disproved" in some sense; it merely means one or both players are not completely rational or perhaps not concerned about winning or losing. The formal account of the game does not predict how actual players will play, only how they will play *so far* as both are perfectly rational and interested *only* in winning.

For another example, consider the neoclassical theory of the firm. The postulates of this theory define the firm as a rational decision-maker that tries to maximize expected returns and is able to perform the necessary calculations. This firm buys resources, combines them into new products, and sells the products. From these postulates it follows logically that the firm will continue buying, producing, and selling as long as there is some advantage in doing so, that is, as long as expected returns from selling exceed the costs of buying and producing. When the marginal cost of buying and producing equals the marginal benefit from selling, the firm will be "in equilibrium," will stop expanding. These postulates do not mean that any actual firm will act in this manner. Actual firms, we know, have many other interests besides money returns, including conflicting interests that reach compromises and form shifting coalitions; firms do not have adequate information on what they and their purchasers and suppliers will be doing; and they are unable to calculate down to the last unit anyway. The theory says only that actual firms will maximize expected returns *insofar* as they are rational, that is, insofar as they imitate or exemplify an ideally rational firm. Conversely, insofar as they do not maximize expected returns, they are not acting as an ideally rational firm would act.

We postpone the question of what use this sort of formal truth may have, but note the contrast with the truth sought by the empiricist. The empiricist looks for correlations that hold for the real world, not for ideal entities. These correlations do not state that there is a logical connection between two entities such that if one occurs the other must necessarily occur; they rather state that in fact when one occurs the other also happens in fact to occur. The empiricist is interested primarily in describing this factual correlation—the conditions under which it occurs, its probability and variance, rates of occurrence, and so on.

When an empiricist reads a formal theory he tends to regard it as describing and making predictions about the real world. He may overlook the logical connection between postulates and derivations and treat the derivations as hypothetical predictions about real entities, to be tested by experimentation or observation. When he tests these "predictions," he may find either that they are "false" or that they hold only in a very limited range and he will be confirmed in his belief that the formalist either is guilty of naive overgeneralization or is using a smokescreen of mathematics to conceal downright falsity and fraud. For example, Smelser misrepresents the neoclassicial theory of the firm when he treats it as a theory making predictions about the real world: "By a series of constructions, economists have built a model that predicts that the firm will produce that quantity of a commodity at which... marginal cost equals.... marginal revenue" (1963, p. 25). I shall discuss other examples of empiricist misunderstanding of a formal truth in chapter 4.

The contrast between empirical and formal truth parallels the distinction I made earlier between a quantitative and a relational conception of mathematics. The mathematically inclined empiricist will think of mathematics in quantitative terms. He will criticize a law in the form "B varies with A" as inexact and will ask for a quantification of the variables. But quantification does not change the kind of truth under study, beyond making it more exact; the validity of the law still depends on the empirical content of A and B. Thus a quantitative conception of mathematics is congenial to an empiricist, because quantification fits in with his basic aim, the pursuit of empirical laws or correlations. The deductive power of mathematics is of secondary importance to him because the empirical validity of a deduced proposition depends on the degree of empirical validity of the original proposition. So the empiricist will worry about the dangers of making elaborate deductions from a dubious, poorly quantified, or poorly verified initial set of propositions. First proper quantification, then maybe deduction later, he will say.

The formalist, in contrast, will criticize the "B varies with A" law because it is uninteresting. For example, Bush observes, "to a mathematician, Hull's theory is rather barren.... With a few exceptions, Hull did no mathematical analyses; he merely wrote down an exponential function to relate two variables" (1960, p. 129). In order to make an empirical law mathematically interesting, it is necessary to add more variables related to the first in such a way that deduction becomes possible. In other words, it is necessary to incorporate the law into a mathematical model. The empirical referent of the model will not be a simple pair of variables but a whole system of related variables. Interest shifts from the question of the empirical validity of a particular proposition to the question of how the whole system works, and verification is of the whole system as interpreted, not of separate equations. Thus when Coleman discusses the prerequisites for formal treatment of empirical correlations he begins by saying, "(1) The variables must constitute to some degree a 'system' of behavior; that is, there must be interdependencies, with at least one 'closed loop' or feedback. Otherwise, the propositions will remain a series of discrete propositions from which few or no deductions can be made" (1964, p. 48). In brief, the formalist's interest in making deductions becomes in practice an interest in analyzing the structural characteristics of formal models. The empirical referent of these models will be some "system" of relations, and the mathematical representation of the system will illustrate the relational rather than the quantitative power of mathematics. The implications deduced by the formalist will be formal truths, truths about the structural characteristics of the model or system.

Structural characteristics are those that control any empirical content entering the structure. For example, in process models where content enters the structure as initial input at time t_0, structural characteristics are those that determine the state of the system at equilibrium or its equivalent. This is the point at which all the variability of the initial input (content) has disappeared. In the game example above, the initial strategies will vary according to the personalities and experience of the players, but the final strategies will all be about the same—random. Not all processes move toward equilibrium; some oscillate around an equilibrium point, with the oscillations either diverging or converging or staying steady; some move away from equilibrium to infinity or minus infinity or zero, at either an increasing or decreasing rate; and some enter an area or zone of indeterminacy. Structural characteristics determine which of these final states the process moves toward, and what other properties (if any) the final state has.

In many process models, particularly those that move away from equilibrium, the final condition is determined partly by structural characteristics and partly by initial input (content). Thus in Simon's Berlitz model (1954, pp. 33-34) it moves to either of two equilibrium points. With such models the formalist tries to determine all the possible outcomes and to specify the range of initial conditions associated with each outcome.

In some models the structural characteristics determine the time path toward equilibrium or asymptote, as well as the conditions at equilibrium. For example, learning models, in contrast to some game models, prescribe a definite time path, the learning curve. Sometimes the structure determines a whole field of time paths, with a particular path dependent on initial conditions, as in Simon's lagged motivation model (1957, ch. 6) or some of Boulding's models (1962, pp. 27, 29, 115, 116, etc.). McPhee's addiction model (1963, ch. 5) has six different paths and outcomes, depending on the initial ratios of the three parameters of the model.

In summary, a formal theory is composed of a calculus and one or more interpretations; the calculus is a structure of relations, and each interpretation asserts that that structure exists somewhere in the real world. The calculus is composed of postulates and deductions. Postulates specify the relation or relations to be studied; when interpreted, they attempt to describe the essential structure of something real, usually in a simplified first approximation. The deductions are descriptions of the system that results when the postulates are combined.

I shall illustrate the points just summarized with an example, Riker's theory of political coalitions (1962). This is a specialized version of the theory of n-person games, to which Riker gives a political interpretation. Let us begin with the basic mathematical concepts of game theory, and then move to Riker's theory.

The basic relation in game theory is the conflict relation (Luce and Raiffa, 1957, p. 1), though one discovers as the theory is developed that conflict always implies cooperation (and vice versa) in the real world. A conflict situation is one in which some event is good for A and bad for B or vice versa.

The event is called an outcome, and the A, B, etc., for whom it is an outcome are players. Outcomes are good, bad, or neutral for the players—that is, they have value—and the value of an outcome for A is called its "payoff" for A. If the value of an outcome for A is the negative of its value for B, the two values add up to zero and the outcome is called "zero-sum." So far these are all relational definitions that together form a network of concepts.

We now add the postulates that at least two outcomes exist, and that these outcomes depend on the joint choices of each player. These postulates create a game described in the accompanying figure. Here A and B are players; 1, 2,

3...are alternative choices; cells 11, 12, 22...are outcomes; a, b, c...are payoff values to A; -a, -b,...are payoff values to B. For a game to have a solution, two more postulates are necessary. One is the rationality postulate: "given two alternatives, [each player] will always choose the one he prefers, i.e., the one with the larger utility" (Luce and Raiffa, 1957, p. 55). This postulate, as Luce and Raiffa point out, is a tautology since the preferred outcome is defined as the one that is chosen over the nonpreferred outcome. The other is the omniscience postulate, which is relaxed in more complex versions: "Each player is assumed to have full knowledge of the game...[including] the payoff functions of the other players" (1957, p. 54).

Note that these postulates have no empirical meaning (other than the heuristic meaning embodied in the English words) but only formal, relational meaning. A player is defined as one who chooses alternatives according to utilities, an outcome is an intersection of choices, a payoff is the utility of an outcome for a player, etc. We do not know what in the real world is a player —an individual, a group, a government, a programmed computer—or what things can be called alternatives and payoffs.

Riker adds several postulates to get a more specialized zero-sum game. (1) There are at least three players. (2) There are only two payoffs, W and L. (3) W is preferred to L. (4) Each player has a weight w, which is a degree of control over outcomes. (5) No player has sufficient weight to determine an outcome. (6) Coalitions are allowed; a coalition is defined as a combination of weights. From these and a few other postulates Riker deduces one derived statement, the size principle: "In n-person, zero-sum games, ...where players are rational, and where they have perfect information, only minimum winning coalitions occur. (Riker, 1962, p. 32). A winning coalition is defined as a combination of weights sufficient to determine the outcome, and since payoff W is preferred, a winning coalition will always choose W.

A minimum winning coalitition is defined as a winning coalition that becomes nonwinning when any one player is subtracted from it. Riker's deduction, which is lengthy (1962, pp. 247-278), may be summed up by observing that in a zero-sum game the value of W equals the cost of W to the loser; the larger the number of losers, the greater the value of W; a minimal winning coalition maximizes the number of losers and therefore the value of W; and all players desire to maximize utility.

The size principle is a formal truth, a statement about how rational players in a certain sort of game necessarily act according to the definition of the game. It describes the situation at equilibrium, when all the processes of coalition formation and breakup have come to an end and no more bidding or moving occurs, and in this sense it is a mathematical solution for a certain kind of n-person game. It does not describe the time path toward equilibrium, though Riker discusses some probable steps that can occur just before equilibrium is reached (1962, chs. 5,6).

To relate this formal truth to the real world, it is necessary to interpret some of the formal terms. Riker offers two interpretations, one for voting in a legislature and one for war. "Players" are interpreted as politicians that represent a constituency or a country; W is winning and L is losing; w is voting strength or military power. These interpretations imply that the politicians have no interest in anything but winning, since only two payoffs, W and L, are postulated. Nor do the players have any memory or foresight, since each voting or war encounter is treated as self-contained. With these interpretations, the size principle says that politicians try to win voting contests by one-vote majorities, and try to put together international alliances that can just barely win a war.

These interpretations serve to locate the size principle in the real world, but only very tenuously. Riker observes that verification of the size principle is "extraordinarily difficult" (1962, p. 48); I should call this an understatement. The empirical facts are that political combinations are continually fluctuating in size, from very large to very small, at varying rates of speed. As for specific votes, some are very close, some close, some not close, some overwhelming. If we consider specific cases, the best recent example of a minimal winning coalition was the British Labour Party's three-vote majority in 1964-1966; Labour's response to this was to try to increase its majority. As for wars, I do not even know what just barely winning a war might mean. Plainly the size principle is not a descriptive empirical generalization, not an empirical truth, though it could conceivably be an empirical falsehood.

What, then, does the size principle, as a formal truth, tell us about the real world? It tells us that *insofar as* politicians are interested only in winning a vote or a war and care nothing about anything else; *insofar as* they have no ideological principles, no moral scruples, no memories of past friends to be rewarded or enemies to be punished, no loyalty to anything or anybody, no foresight or interest in the next election (all this is included in Riker's rationality postulate); and *insofar as* they understand each other perfectly, *then* they will try to just barely win. They do not need any extra cushion of votes (as the British Labour Party did) because there is no uncertainty about anybody's vote; they do not want any extra cushion because it reduces the loot to be distributed and increases the number of people sharing in the distribution. Conversely, the size principle tells us that *insofar as* a winning coalition is larger than necessary or as it aims for a larger size than necessary, something other than omniscience and the pure desire to win is operating. It may be uncertainty, or ideological principles, or foresight about the next election, or loyalty to past associates, and so on. In short, if we call Riker's postulates p and his deduction (the size principle) q, his theory tells us that $p \supset q$ and $-q \supset -p$. It tells us these two things because he has deduced q from p. It cannot tell us q because p has been postulated, not proven.

What Riker's model does is differentiate out one aspect of the empirical manifold, the "rational" or "desire to win" aspect. The other aspects Riker calls "irrationality," "miscalculation," and "accident" (1962, pp. 48-76). It tells us about the dynamics of this aspect: desire to win a maximum necessarily leads to minimum winning coalitions. These dynamics are, however, always masked by the conjoint occurrence of other dynamics, so the surface appearance is chaotic.

For example, in 1961-1969 there were three parties in the West German Bundestag. The distribution of seats in the two elections was as follows:

	CDU/CSU	SPD	FDP
1961	242	190	67
1965	245	202	49

A minimum winning coalition would be SPD-FDP; actually, the other two possible coalitions were formed. Riker's formal truth, the size principle, tells us that these coalitions were necessarily based on something other than a pure desire to win a maximum during 1961-1969. It also identifies certain pre-coalition maneuvering as evidence of a "rational" or "desire to win a maximum" tendency.

Alternatively, one might interpret each party as a single player rather than as a coalition. In this case the weights are irrelevant, since any two parties can win over the third, and the model says that any of the three coalitions are equally likely. In other words, the model says that each specific coalition is the result, not of a desire to win a maximum, but of some other factor not included in the model. Thus any specific coalition, any deviation from randomness, must be explained by some other model. For instance, the movements of the FDP in and out of coalitions, as well as the party's various liberal-conservative-liberal shifts, might be explained by a Hotelling-Downs opinion model (Tullock, 1967, ch. 4) as an attempt to find a secure electoral base.

One could also say that the size principle does not apply to this case at all because asymptote has not been reached. However, this would merely be another way of saying that "nonrational" factors are still important in German politics, since asymptote is the condition in which nonrational disturbances have disappeared; and this statement throws one back to the two previous in-terpretations.

I do not claim that the size principle is a momentous formal truth as it stands, but I do think it has potentialities for development. I discuss in chapter 7 the question of the uses of such formal truths.

The preceding account applies most directly to mathematical models and must be qualified somewhat if it is to be applied to computer simulation. By "com-puter simulation" I mean a model that is conceived and written directly in a flow chart, and whose structural characteristics are adapted to the potentiali-ties of computer languages. Computers can also be used to make deductions from models that are essentially mathematical (for example, McPhee, 1963, chs. 2,3). These models consist of a set or sets of equations whose complexi-ty makes paper and pencil deduction unwieldy though (usually) not impos-sible. Similarly, when computers are used for data processing—constructing scalograms, analyses of variance, multivariate correlations, factor analyses, regressions, etc.—the underlying concepts are mathematical and the computer is used only to do the mathematical computations required.

Even with models that are conceived and written directly in a computer lan-guage, the basic similarity to mathematical models is apparent. The flow chart is analogous to a mathematical postulate set, and its outputs are the deductions or derivations; both types of languages are abstract-symbolic, and both types of model must be interpreted to be empirically relevant. But there are also differences. The "postulates" of a computer simulation are usually a good deal less abstract than the postulates of an ordinary mathematical model, in several ways.

First, individual postulates frequently refer to specific empirical entities. Def-initions are still relational in the model, but the empirical interpretation of the major terms is obvious and is continually present in the program. For exam-ple, the behavioral theory of the firm (Cyert and March, 1963) postulates specific organizational goals in five areas; profit, market share, amount of sales, production-smoothing, and inventory. Each goal is quite specific; the first three are specific levels of aspiration derived from previous performance, and the last two consist of maximum-minimum constraints. The names of variables in the flow chart remind one continually of the empirical referent: profit goal is PRG, market share is MSG, sales is SAG, production limits are LPRLIM and UPRLIM, inventory limit is INPROMAX. The neoclassical theory of the firm, in contrast, postulates no specific goals but assumes mere-ly that there are goals. This extremely abstract concept has no obvious or exclusive empirical referent and requires careful interpretation for any em-pirical application.

Second, the whole postulate set can be larger and more complicated than the postulate set of a mathematical model because of the computational capac-ity of computers. As a result one can include more aspects or characteristics of the empirical system one is simulating. A mathematical model is forced to limit itself to one aspect of an empirical system and to describe it *ceteris paribus,* sometimes in highly simplified fashion, while a computer model, with its multiple interacting mechanisms and nonlinearities, can more nearly approximate the complexity of real systems. Compare, for example, the computer models of firms, industries, or economies with the corresponding mathematical models, and consider how the computer models of personality venture to include aspects—emotions, neurotic processes, defense mechanisms, self-concepts—that have heretofore been impossible to model mathematically.

Third, the capacity of computers even enables one to model particular systems—a particular therapy patient, a particular industry or corporation, a particular group of voters—with all the complex interrelations, parameter values, and unique mechanisms that differentiate them from similar systems.

The empirical realism possible in computer models makes my previous distinction between a calculus and its interpretations nearly pointless. One can still say that the computer program is an abstract piece of logic that needs to be interpreted to have empirical meaning, but if the interpretation is obvious from the configuration and terminology of the program very little has been gained by making the distinction. Nor is there much point in speaking of alternative interpretations of a model that is obviously tailored to the peculiarities of one particular empirical system. Consequently it is more appropriate, in most cases, to describe computer models as abstract descriptions of the logic of some empirical system or process. Such models carry their one possible interpretation as an intrinsic part, and therefore do make a truth claim. This point has implications for the construction and verification of computer models which I shall discuss presently.

Consideration of computer models reminds us that an occasional mathematical model is so closely tailored to a specific empirical system that only one interpretation is inherently possible (see for example Weiss, 1956, p. 56, a sociogram). Such models, both mathematical and computer, are still formal inasmuch as interest is focused on discovering formal truths about an abstract structure of relations; only the structure is tied to a specific empirical referent. More generally, one could say that formal models are distributed along an empirical-abstract dimension, with the computer models clustered near the empirical end and the mathematical models distributed in the more abstract range.

3

The Development
of a Formal Theory

In chapter 1, I stated that this work treats scientific methods as methods of discovery or development, not as methods of hypothesis testing. A formal method is a method for developing formal theories, that is, models plus interpretations. Verification or testing is a subordinate part of a method; in formal methods it occurs throughout the process of development rather than after it. In this chapter we consider the main steps involved in developing a formal theory. Chapter 4 considers in more detail the special problems involved in experimental testing and development of mathematical models, and chapter 5 focuses on some special problems of computer models.

Although particular formal theories develop in all sorts of ways, several steps characteristically are necessary. First, it is necessary to have some conception of a distinct system or process to be studied—bargaining, deciding, a communication network, the forming of casual groups, a transportation system, a change of attitude or opinion, a kinship structure, the West Coast lumber industry. The system or process must be conceived abstractly, as an essential structure that stays the same in various temporal manifestations.

Next it is necessary to decide in general terms what sort of relation characterizes this abstract structure. This may be simply a matter of dividing the system or process into two parts and relating them, or it may involve a detailed probing to see which of various possible relations seem most important. For example, bargaining can be characterized as a conflict relation between two parties or as a transition from disagreement to agreement; deciding can be a preference between two alternatives or a transition from vague to clear preferences or from competing to harmonious preferences; a network is connections among points; groups form by adding and subtracting individuals; a transportation system takes on units at fixed entrances, moves them through fixed-capacity channels at some average rate, and loses them at fixed exits; attitude change is a transition from decided A to undecided to decided B; a kinship structure is composed of marriage, descent, and sibling relations; an industry is composed of firms with inputs and outputs, or of buyers and sellers exchanging.

One's choice of characterization determines the kind of theory that will result, and a change of characterization sometimes leads to great new theoretical developments. Thus the decision to characterize choice in terms of fixed competing preferences has been crucial in economics and ethics for well over a century, and the shift from a competition-exchange model of industry to consumption-investment and input-output models has led to great developments in economics. Similarly, note the radical shift of emphasis that occurs if one replaces the idea of perfect competition with the idea of an $n \times m$ Prisoner's Dilemma (Weil, 1966). Both ideas have the same empirical referent, but they point to quite different aspects of it. The $n \times m$ Prisoner's Dilemma focuses on the interdependence between individual welfare and general welfare. It shows how pursuit of individual gain destroys general welfare and with it the individual gain pursued, and enables one to investigate the circumstances in which individual sacrifices will serve the general welfare and thereby individual advantage. It also specifies the most important parameters governing the interdependence—number of individuals (n), number of alternatives (m), and relation between individual choices vector and payoffs (how many individuals must choose private gain before general welfare is damaged). The perfect competition model abstracts from this interdependence completely. It does this by making both n and m infinite, with the consequence that pursuit of individual gain automatically maximizes general welfare. This model focuses instead on the problem of how one maximizes individual gain. The Prisoner's Dilemma model cannot be used to investigate the problem of individual maximization insofar as m, the alternatives open to the individual, is made arbitrarily small for computational purposes. For other examples of alternative characterizations of the same subject matter, see Schwartz, 1961, pp. 214, 239; chs. 11-12, chs. 13-15; Coleman, 1964, ch. 4.

The next step is to choose the kind of formal language with which one will work. This step is closely related to the preceding step, and frequently will accompany or even precede it, since one's choice of basic relation determines the kind of language that is appropriate; conversely, the available kinds of languages limit the ways in which one can fruitfully characterize one's subject matter. Thus the fact that classical economists knew only calculus and analytic geometry undoubtedly limited their imagination; they could not, for instance, imagine a Leontief input-output model because matrix algebra was not yet available. The ideal procedure, I suppose, would be to decide first the basic characteristics of the subject matter and then to pick the appropriate language —and if no language exists, to invent one. This is the way some branches of mathematics (such as graph theory) came into existence, as well as some computer languages (such as IPL). However, few nonmathematicians have the ability to invent a whole new branch of mathematics.

The next step is to construct mathematical definitions of the relations one has decided to study. Here a range of possibilities is available, from empirical to abstract. At the empirical extreme, the formalist might examine his subject matter carefully and try to determine what sorts of relations exist in it. His statements would then try to capture the shape of these relations; they would be empirical judgments expressed as postulates. For example, in K. Cohen's model of the shoe industry, the postulates are descriptions of how retailers and wholesalers actually make decisions on buying, forecasting, and pricing. Cohen states, "We want to describe realistically the processes governing the behavior of a typical retailer, and then examine the extent to which these behavioral mechanisms could account for the observed behavior of all retailers as a group" (1960, p. 27). Cohen's postulates are based on direct observation of retailers and wholesalers by Ruth Mack. When an operations researcher constructs a model of a particular firm he proceeds in a similar fashion, observing the firm's various processes and then describing them mathematically. In general, the empirical approach to postulates occurs frequently in computer models but only rarely in mathematical ones.

At the abstract extreme, the formalist might select the mathematically simplest relationship for a start, intending to complicate it later to get a closer approximation to empirical conditions. Thus in explaining the predator-parasite model, Kemeny and Snell, speaking heuristically of rabbits, say, "The simplest assumption that can be made, and one that is quite realistic, is that the rate of increase of the rabbit population is proportional to the size of the population. . . $\frac{dx}{dt} = ax, a > 0$." (1962, p. 24). The neoclassical theory of the firm begins with many mathematical simplifications—complete knowledge, instant transportation, no policing problems, no irrationality of any sort, no taxes, no personal involvement, no breakage or spoilage, etc. Game theory also has developed in this fashion, beginning with simple games and moving toward complex ones. In general a person with a mathematical bent will tend to proceed in this fashion. Early mathematical models, such as those of Rashevsky (1951) and Richardson (Rapoport, 1957), tended to begin with extreme simplifications, while more recent model-builders usually have tried to combine simplification with some degree of realism.

Empiricists sometimes criticize formalists for basing their initial postulates on mathematical convenience, arguing that they should base them instead on empirical knowledge. However, there is an intellectual advantage in beginning with simplified postulates. It enables one to distinguish the basic structure of one's subject matter from confusing details and circumstantial variations. The basic structure is represented by the form of the equations and the way they connect with one another, while the details and variations are represented by the details of particular equations. By beginning with simple equations, the model-builder can first make sure he has the basic skeleton of his model working properly and determine that this skeleton is approximately correct empirically before he focuses his attention on details and variations. For example, Tustin (1953) first shows that a simple feedback model with lags and limits can produce time paths that are similar in shape to those of business cycles, indicating the possibility that business cycles can be described by some model of this kind. Having established this, Tustin turns to the kinds of modifications that are necessary to produce an empirically adequate model. These modifications, as Holland observes (1963, p. viii), force him to shift eventually from a mathematical to a computer model. The distinction between basic structure and details does not occur for the empiricist interested only in correlations, and so he may not fully appreciate the formalist's problems and procedures in this respect.

One of the disadvantages of computer models is that it is too easy to make one's postulates realistic in detail. The model-builder can thus avoid somewhat the intellectual labor of thinking through the structure of the system he is modeling to find its basic elements. Instead, he can simply put in everything he happens to find, trivial or not, and substitute the technical tasks of programming and debugging for the intellectual task of system analysis. The result is difficulties in analyzing and verifying the model, which I shall discuss later (ch. 5). For example, a behavioral modeler of a firm may find all sorts of goals operative in a short time period in the firm he is studying. It would be an easy mistake to put them all into his model in the interests of "realism," without inquiring what it is about the system that makes certain kinds of goals necessary and permanent; what other kinds of goals are permitted and why; which of the goals he happens to find are necessary and permanent, which are short-term fluctuating preferences, which are spurious, redundant, or special cases of more general goals. Similarly, the Gullahorns (1963) seem to have simply turned the theory they were studying into a flow chart without trying to find the logic implicit in the theory. As a result the flow chart is probably redundant, needlessly complex, and not as clear as it could be. This is a case where mathematical modeling would have been preferable to computer treatment, because it would have forced giving attention to the logic implicit in the theory. I shall discuss this example in detail later (ch. 8).

Another reason for beginning with mathematically simple postulates is that in many cases empirically adequate postulates would be too complex to permit deductions to be made. For example, in game theory a variable-person variable-strategy game with changing rules would be empirically more adequate than a zero-sum game, but would be mathematically forbidding. But the whole point of formal method is to make deductions, or as McPhee says, "to discover the unobvious consequences of some obvious assumptions" (1963, p. 188). A formal theory without deductions is no theory at all. This does not mean that one must choose between an empirically false theory and no theory; once one has constructed a calculus based on mathematically simple assumptions, it is possible to use devices that enable one to approximate to some degree the complex, mathematically impossible, empirical situation. Thus in game theory the straightforward theorems of the zero-sum game can be bent and qualified until they provide a basis for working with complex interaction situations.

After one's postulates are written down, the next step is to deduce implications. In practice this step is not completely separate from the formulation of initial postulates, because the attempt to deduce can reveal the need for changes of postulates. It may be that a simplification is necessary to permit deduction, or that an additional postulate which was tacitly assumed must be made explicit. In some cases where the theorist is intuitively expecting a certain result, failure to get this result may lead him to a re-examination of his postulates. Deducing implications is sometimes called "solving" the model.

The implications of mathematical models are found by straightforward deduction or by some approximative technique. Computer models, however, have too many parameters and variables for ordinary deduction—for example, the Cyert and March model (1963, ch. 8) has about 100 parameters and variables and another 24 output variables—and implications are instead derived by output sampling (cf. Churchman, 1963, p. 6). Output sampling consists of setting each parameter to some specific value, running the program, and collecting the output, including a trace of the internal process. Then one or more parameters are set to different values and the program is run again. After one has a sample of the possible outputs of the model, they can be correlated with the parameter values chosen.

Next comes a step that is often not mentioned in the written reports—the analysis of the model. First one examines the postulates for generality, simplicity, and redundancy. Is each definition and equation necessary for the result, or is one (or more) redundant? Is any definition a special case of a simpler and more general formulation that produces basically the same result? Do several postulates belong together as part of a single logical subroutine, or are they all equal and independent? Then one examines the derivations to see how they follow from the postulates. What kind of contribution does each postulate make to the derivations, and what effect would a change in the postulate have? For example, McPhee, in analyzing his addiction model, finds that of his three parameters, a produces oscillations in the time path, s controls the amplitude of oscillations, and r produces a gradual stabilizing effect (1963, pp. 188-192). In some cases the effect of a parameter on output is constant; in other cases output varies with changes in the value of the parameter. If the effect is variable, one wants to know what parameter changes are especially important in affecting output, and what changes, if any, have little or no effect. The investigation of parameter changes is called sensitivity analysis, since it determines the degree of sensitivity of output to changes in parameter values.

Analysis is a process of clarifying the logical workings of a model; its point is to put one in control of the model, so that one is ready to make any changes in it required by later developments. Analysis is also a necessary preliminary to some practical uses of models, as I shall indicate later.

At this point the model-builder has a skeleton of his model in working order; it describes in a very general way the essence of the structure or process he is modeling. It describes the basic component parts of the structure or inputs of the process, the basic relations or modes of transformation of input, and the basic output, time path, or equilibrium state. Through analysis the model-builder knows in a general way the kind of contribution each component of the postulate set makes to the derivations and how the postulates interact with one another.

The next step is to begin filling in the details of the model. This is done by a process of successive approximations. The simplified skeleton model is compared with the real system or precess being modeled, and the discrepancies between the two are examined. If the model-builder has analyzed his skeleton model well, he will know just what postulates are responsible for a particular discrepancy; he changes them and tests the revised model to see whether the discrepancies have been reduced. For example, if the time path produced by his model has oscillations of too large an amplitude compared with reality, he must revise those postulates or parameters or subroutines that control the amplitude of oscillations. This may involve adding an oscillation-damping subroutine, or correcting the feedback process that produces the oscillation, or perhaps merely revising a parameter estimate. For a second example, recall the Riker theory of political coalitions discussed in the previous chapter. The most obvious discrepancy between model and reality is the omniscience postulate, so a revision of this postulate will be a likely first step in improving the model. Revision may take the form of treating information as a commodity, as Downs does (1957, chs. 11-14); or it may take the form of adding decision rules for dealing with uncertainty (Borch, 1968, chs. 7, 8); or it may take the form of adding communication- and information-processing routines to the model, though these would lead to considerable complications. Another obvious discrepancy in Riker's model is the assumption that there are only two payoffs, winning and losing. To correct this assumption, players can be endowed with foresight, so they will take future plays of the game into account in their coalition bidding.

If the revision of the model reduces its discrepancy with reality, the model-builder knows he is on the right track and makes further revisions of the same sort. Then he examines some different area of discrepancy and makes revisions there. This process of alternate revision and testing continues until he has reached the limit of his mathematical ingenuity, or until the discrepancies are small enough for his purposes.

Note that the theorist's interest is always in *differences between the model* and what it describes, since the differences are the source of improvements in the model. If by any mischance the empirical data should conform exactly to the first version of the model, the model-builder would be baffled and would have to find new data. He knows that this model is a simplification, so that if the data conform to it they too must have been simplified and are failing to reveal the full complexity of the subject matter. They are therefore useless to him; they give him no new information. On the other hand, if there is too great a discrepancy between model and fact the formalist knows that he has somehow misconceived his subject matter completely. He will then either have to start over or search for a subject that conforms more closely to the model he has constructed.

Rapoport and Chammah emphasize the importance of discrepancies for the model-builder when they observe, speaking paradoxically: "Our main motivation for conducting these experiments was a conviction that the potentially rich contributions of game theory to psychology will derive from the failures of game theory rather than from its successes" (1965, p.11). "Every mathematical model in behavioral science should serve as a point of departure for investigations, not as a conclusive formulation of a theory" (1965, p. 150). So also Grant: "The theoretical scientist is not accepting or rejecting a finished theory; he is in the long-term business of constructing better versions of the theory. Progress depends upon improvement or providing superior alternatives, and improvement will ordinarily depend upon knowing just how good a model is and exactly where it seems to need alteration. . . .Therefore attention should be focused upon the various discrepancies between prediction and outcome instead of on the over-all adequacy of the model" (1962, p. 57).

The process of improving a model requires more varied and detailed empirical data than are needed for the initial stages of construction. The general outline of a structure or process is usually apparent to casual observation or ordinary experience, but the details of the mechanism usually must be searched out by careful experimental or statistical techniques, or in some cases by participant observation. For instance, if one is modeling a transportation system, the entrances, exits, and channels can be readily observed, but such details as the average processing time at entrances and exits or the changes in accident rates when channels are operating near capacity can be discovered only by collecting masses of data and manipulating them statistically. If one is modeling a bargaining process, the general outline is well known and can be modeled in a variety of ways; but the details—how an opponent's pattern of bids affects perceptions and counter-bids, how and when commitments are communicated, how and when salient features of the bidding space become relevant—can only be discovered by intensive experimentation or in some cases by extensive observation. If one is modeling managerial decision-making, the general outlines are apparent to casual observation and have long been known: the manager uses rules of thumb that rely heavily on past sales or production data. But to find out the exact rules and their hierarchical relation requires careful observation, questioning, and the study of written records. Consequently if the model-builder wishes to include this sort of detail in his model he will have to go to some trouble to collect the right kind of data. I shall discuss some of the problems connected with the collection of experimental data in the next chapter.

Let us consider the process of successive approximation in more detail. A formal theory connects with empirical reality at two different points, its postulates and its derivations. Its postulates describe the basic relations composing the subject matter, and its derivations describe what happens when those relations interact, either at equilibrium or through a time path. The postulates are analytic in the sense that they break up the subject into its presumed component parts, while the deductions are synthetic in the sense that they describe the operation of the whole system or process.

Initially either aspect of the subject matter—its parts or its total operation—

may be more accessible to the model-builder; in some cases they may be equally accessible. With small systems such as personalities or small discussion groups, the total operation—that is, behavior—may be accessible to observation, but the personality structures that produce this behavior may be relatively inaccessible. With large systems such as an economy, an industry, a formal organization, or a kinship system, the component relations of the system—buying and selling, entering or leaving a group, marrying and having children—may be accessible to observation while the long-run behavior of the system may be obscure. For example, in a typical operations research problem the researchers know the firm's structure and rules of operation; they must determine the effect of rule changes on performance. To be sure, the reverse may also happen; there may be large systems whose component parts are poorly understood but for which reliable performance data exist. For example, K. Cohen's simulation of the shoe industry is based empirically on reliable price and quantity data for the industry, while it treats decision-making in the firm as problematic. Finally, in some cases both the parts and the behavior of the system may be empirically accessible but the relation between the two may be obscure. For example, business cycle theories can build on aggregate data for the economy as well as on an understanding of how the component parts of the economy—banking and investment, production and consumption—are related. Their task is to connect the two and show how changes in ratios of investment, taxes, interest rates, exports, etc., produce cycles.

The theorist moves on the whole from the aspect that is empirically more accessible to him toward the one that is empirically more problematic. If he has reliable performance data for a system or process whose inner machinery is obscure, his task is to build up a model of the inner structure that will explain its visible workings. Such movement from performance to ·parts is called "explanatory" by Coleman (1964, p. 37) since its result is the explanation of system behavior. If the theorist has a clear understanding of how something is put together but does not know how it will perform in various circumstances, his task is to synthesize and predict its performance. Coleman calls this movement "synthetic" (1964, p. 41; cf. also Cyert and March, 1963, pp. 317-318, where the terms used are "analytic" and "synthetic"). The best-known example of a synthetic theory is neoclassical economics; economists thought they had a reliable subjective understanding of how individuals make decisions (for example, Von Mises, 1960, pp. 23-25) and on this basis constructed a theory of how an economy operates. The clearest example of an explanatory theory is stochastic learning theory, which tries to explain and predict experimental output data by means of a hypothetical reconstruction of the learning process. More recently the economist's supposedly reliable knowledge of how individuals make decisions has been pretty thoroughly discredited, and some economists have shifted their theory from a synthetic to an explanatory mode.

Both kinds of theory, explanatory and synthetic, move toward adequacy in a series of successive approximations, but the details of the movement vary. A person constructs a synthetic theory when the basic relational structure of his subject matter is immediately evident or available to him; for instance, he knows the explicit rules by which the firm or the kinship system or the communication net or the game officially operates. Consequently, he has considerable confidence in the correctness of his initial postulates, and his main initial concern may be to simplify them enough for mathematical purposes. On the other hand, output data for his subject matter may be obscure, complex, difficult to interpret, incomplete, and generally unreliable. When data and model output conflict, he is likely to dismiss the data as influenced by "friction" and random error, or to reinterpret them. Nevertheless he will somehow have to come to terms with the data, whether by gathering new data or reinterpreting the old. When he does, the discrepancies between data and model output will remind him of initial conditions that he had overlooked and omitted from his postulates. For instance, the game theorist knows in the abstract that rules must be enforced, but tends to omit policing arrangements from his model until puzzling data compel him to recall them. He knows people can sometimes leave a game unfinished, but he tends to forget to look for actual playing rules until impossible results force him to. Thus the main effect of output data is to compel a more thorough and detailed reformulation of initial statements.

A person constructs an explanatory theory when his subject matter is more or less a "black box" that readily emits data but cannot easily be opened for inspection. His task is to construct a model of what is in the box that will yield data closely approximating the actual set. He may base his initial postulates on hunches, tautologies, empathy, verbal theories, discarded physiological theories (Hebb, 1955), or what not, and should not have much confidence in them. Obviously, when discrepancies appear between deduced predictions and data, he will change his assumptions to conform to the data. However, it is a mistake to think of his aim as simply that of modifying his assumptions until he can deduce the data from them. This would be committing the fallacy of affirming the consequent.
This fallacy is as follows:

B. (A set of data to be explained)
If A, then B. (Discovering a set of assumptions A from which B can be deduced)
A. (Claiming that A has now been verified and is a valid explanation of B)

The error here lies in forgetting that the same consequences B can be deduced from any number of different assumptions, not only from A. For an example of multiple explanations of the same data, cf. Bales, 1951, 1953; Stephan and Mishler, 1952; Homans, 1961, pp. 302-307, 327-331; Horvath, 1965; Coleman, 1960, pp. 46-65. See also Cross, 1965. Multiple explanations are especially likely if the connection between model and data is statistical. In such a case Model A might fit the data in one fashion, Model M in a rather different fashion, and Model N in still another way.

What can one conclude about Model A if it fits data B reasonably well? It is possible that Model A does explain the data, and that those data which do not fit are accidental or random disturbances to be ignored. Or it may be that A explains some aspect of the data, perhaps peripheral, while other as yet unknown models would explain other aspects. Or the connection between A and B could be entirely accidental, due to some special characteristics of the particular set of data. In the latter case any further work that treated A as already verified could only mislead and confuse. Without further information, knowing only that B can be deduced from A, one cannot decide among these possibilities.

Consequently the theorist's aim in constructing an explanatory formal theory should not be to publish the first explanation that is statistically significant (or even worse, one that is not significant but merely leans in the right direction) but to select or construct one explanation out of the set of possible explanations. To do this, it is necessary to have an independent criterion of selection, an independent check on the empirical validity of one's assumptions. It is not enough to have more of the same kind of data—although this helps —because the fallacy of affirming the consequent is still there, though it may be less obvious. What is needed is some more direct access to the relational structure of one's subject matter, the structure described in one's initial definitions.

How can one do this if one's subject matter is a mysterious "black box?" There are several possible ways, though none of them is foolproof. One way is to instruct the box to report on its own working, that is, to emit a stream of responses as it operates so that the pattern of its activity can be tentatively reconstructed and embodied in revised definitions. For example, when Herbert Simon was working on a formal theory of problem-solving activity, he had subjects verbalize their thought processes while they solved problems and derived his postulates from the verbal protocols. Another way is to get "inside" the black box by participant observation of some sort; this is particularly appropriate when one is studying the working of a small group. In some cases physiology can provide suggestions for the structure of psychological mechanisms; thus Tomkins (Tomkins & Messick, 1963, ch.1) bases his definitions, in a formal theory of the emotions, on physiological analogies. Note, incidentally, that in a formal theory even emotions must be defined in relational terms; Tomkins defines them as reactions to changes in rate of stimulation.

None of these procedures by itself yields reliable knowledge, but that is not necessary. All that is necessary is a plausible picture of the inner structure of one's subject. The basic empirical reliance still is on the output data, and information about the inner structure is needed only to select from among the possible ways of deducing the output data.

For example, suppose one wished to revise the omniscience postulate in Riker's theory of coalitions or in some other model of rational behavior. Several ways of doing this are possible, but which one is best? Should one treat information as a commodity to be purchased, a signal to be processed, or a probability number in a "regret" matrix? Should one focus on communication channels, transmitters, and noise, on scarcity, or on ideological distortion? It may be that two or three alternative postulate sets can be made to fit ambiguous data. One selects among these alternatives on the basis of independent evidence as to how the players or decision-makers actually deal with uncertainty.

Notice that the path of empirical testing for explanatory theories moves in just the opposite direction from the path for synthetic theories. Explanatory theories move from basically reliable output data to the construction of a model from which those output data can be deduced. The theorist selects from alternative models and revises initial models on the basis of independent but less reliable information about the inner working of his subject matter. On the other hand, synthetic theories move from a clear understanding of the structure of some system or process to a deduction of possible outputs. The theorist revises his initial simplified model on the basis of questionable output data that remind him of structural factors he generally knew about but had overlooked or underemphasized. In both bases there is movement back and forth between the two points of empirical contact, but the main movement is from the more reliable to the less reliable information.

Finally, in some cases both inner structure and output are more or less empirically accessible, and both sorts of information are used to revise the theory. For example, the theory of the central nervous system is based on physiological research into the characteristics of nerve networks as well as psychological research on behavior. The former provides a basis for structural postulates and the latter provides output data. Theoretical work moves back and forth between the two, using each to suggest new investigations and interpretations in the other area. Thus a physiological theory that stresses different levels of organization in the brain has served to suggest new kinds of learning experiments (Bronson, 1965, pp. 22-23), while learning data have suggested ways of revising physiological postulates (for example, Milner, 1961) and also have brought out gaps in neurological knowledge to be filled in by physiological investigation (for example, Samuels, 1959). The revised physiological theories and research results in turn suggest new learning experiments, new interpretations of existing data, and so on.

It may seem that Milton Friedman's much discussed methodological pronouncement (1953, ch. 1) is opposed to the position taken above, since on the surface, at least, Friedman seems to reject the double contact of formal theories with empirical reality. He seems to say that in economics a theory should not be evaluated by the realism of its assumptions, but only by the accuracy of the factual predictions that can be deduced from it. All assumptions in science are more or less unrealistic, since science always simplifies or selects from the complexities of real life. Moreover, the best theories are not the most realistic, but those that predict most accurately. In our terms, Friedman seems to assert that the validity of a formal theory depends only on the empirical adequacy of its output predictions, not on the empirical adequacy of its assumptions or postulates. However, Friedman's remarks are open to varying interpretations and misinterpretations (Nagel, 1963; Simon, 1963; Samuelson, 1963; Rotwein, 1959; Massey, 1965; O. Davis, 1969; etc.), and I have tentatively concluded that the position Friedman opposes is different from the one I am advocating.

Friedman's intention was not to write a general statement about formal methods in the social sciences, though his argument is phrased in general terms. His interest was more specifically that of defending the marginalist theory of the firm against criticism by institutional economists. The marginalist theory is a mathematical model which says that a perfectly rational business manager makes his decisions about resource allocation and production on the basis of marginal utility, producing exactly the quantity at which the increased revenue from an additional unit of output equals the increased cost of producing it. The institutionalist critics said that empirical evidence showed that managers are not perfectly rational in their decision-making and, in fact, do not knowingly or unknowingly calculate margins and derivatives of curves in any sense. The marginalist theory is therefore false; its postulates about how a rational manager behaves are unrealistic.

Friedman's defense was to change the empirical interpretation of the marginalist mathematical model. In his reinterpretation the marginalist model is not a theory of how decisions are actually made by real managers—that is, it is not a behavioral theory of the firm—but a normative theory of what a firm must accomplish if it is to survive and expand (1953, p. 22). Those firms that survive do so because they somehow manage to make allocation and output decisions that approximate those prescribed by marginal utility criteria. In terms of decision-making, the theory states the ideal limit to which any effective set of decision procedures must approximate. As I interpret Friedman, his point is the same as that made by Harsanyi (1961, p. 194) in defending marginal analysis against a behavioral theory of the firm.

Friedman uses the example of a tree to illustrate his argument. A marginalist theory of the location of leaves on a tree might include the postulate that each leaf is located as if it were trying to maximize the amount of sunlight available to it. We know that this postulate is unrealistic: leaves, like business managers, are not smart enough to maximize. However, a process of natural selection is operative, producing approximately the same results as would intelligent leaves. Leaves cannot grow without sunlight and grow better in full sunlight, so over the years the leaves and branches of a tree grow toward sunlight and not toward deep shade. Similarly in business a process of social selection operates over the years to weed out the worst bunglers and reward those managers who by whatever means happen to approximate the formally correct decisions. So when Friedman argues that the postulates of a mathematical model need not be realistic if its predictions are correct, he is not arguing for any old postulates that happen to predict the right results. He means that the marginalist postulate of maximizing rational behavior need not describe individual decision-making realistically for the model to be correct. If there is a process of social selection that produces essentially the same result as individual rationality, the predictions of the model will be correct even though its postulates are unrealistic.

If this really is Friedman's argument, it is not opposed to my more general argument. This issue is complicated by Friedman's various qualifying statements (1953, pp. 20, 28, 29, 30), which I interpret to mean that he is not opposed either in general or in principle to the direct testing of formal postulates. Friedman's argument will be discussed further in chapter 21.

I have been discussing the formal theorist's method of successive approximation, by which he modifies an initially simplified calculus toward increasing empirical adequacy. I have indicated that this process depends on a twofold contact with empirical reality, first through the postulates of the calculus which describe the relational structure of his subject matter, and second, through the theorems which describe its behavior under various conditions (such as equilibrium). The theorist's method varies according to which of the two contacts with reality is the more reliable.

Another variation in method depends on the kind of subject matter the theorist has chosen to isolate for study. At the one extreme he may interest himself in a relatively concrete subject matter, such as the West Coast lumber industry (Balderston and Hoggatt, 1963), the U.S. shoe industry (K. Cohen, 1960), the U. S. economy in all its particular detail (Orcutt, 1961), or mass media entertainment in the United States (McPhee, 1963, ch. l). At the other extreme his interest may focus on an abstract process, such as continuous-time discrete state processes (Coleman, 1964, ch. 4), self-reinforcing activities (McPhee, 1963, ch. 5), a class of skew distribution functions (Simon, 1957, ch. 9), or the formation of random nets (Rapoport, summarized in Coleman, 1960). Or his subject matter may lie anywhere between these extremes. All the studies of psychological processes—learning (Bush and Mosteller, 1955), problem-solving and thinking (Feigenbaum and Feldman, 1963), perceiving and memorizing (Feldman, 1962), affects and neurotic processes (Tomkins and Messick, 1963)—deal with a process that is relatively abstract but still limited to individual human beings. Other studies focus on more specific processes—business cycles (Keynes, etc.), political coalitions (Riker, 1962), decision-making in small groups (Bales et al., 1962) —but still not limited to a specific time and place. In addition, a theorist's interest may move from specific to general or from general to specific. Thus he may begin with a theory of how music is composed (Hiller and Baker, 1962) and shift to a theory of how Bach composed music.

When the theorist is interested in a relatively concrete subject matter, his successive approximations move toward a more complex, detailed representation of its relational structure. He begins with a skeleton and adds details until he can match the specific performance of his subject. To do this he needs detailed data of his subject in operation, data of the kind provided by participant observation, as well as exact output statistics. It is not necessary for both sets of data to be equally reliable, as I indicated earlier. However, it is necessary to have data that are broadly representative of the system in operation in a wide variety of circumstances. The point of a system model is to describe the general structure and working of a system for a wide variety of inputs and contexts, and therefore the data on which the moded is based should be varied and representative.

All this empirical material must be matched by a very complex, detailed calculus in order to retain the information in the material. In recent practice this means that the calculus is likely to take the form of a computer simulation rather than a mathematical theory. Until the development of computers, the construction of formal theories of complex concrete systems was quite impossible because no formal language of sufficient complexity existed.

When the theorist is interested in a relatively abstract process, his successive approximations move toward capturing its essentials rather than the accidents associated with particular versions. To do this, he must be careful to distinguish between his calculus and a particular interpretation of it. He can then collect data for a wide variety of empirical exemplifications of his process, and by comparing these varying instances he can check the generality of his calculus, eliminate specialized details, develop variants, or generalize a too particular definition or postulate. For example, when Coleman was developing variants of the Poisson process (1964, chs. 10, 11), which describes a certain kind of randomness, he considered the following empirical exemplifications: deaths over a twenty-year period from being kicked by horses in the Prussian army, the number of calls in five-minute intervals from a group of six pay telephones, the learning of nonsense syllables, accident statistics, teen-age girls' purchase of phonograph records, population statistics, the number of nights a week teen-age boys go out with other boys, the distribution of friendship choices, sequences of purchase of coffee, voting in union elections, pedestrians meeting at street corners.

If the reader is by now somewhat confused by the variations in method I have mentioned, he has an accurate picture of "the model-building method." There is no rigid routine that all model-builders follow uniformly, only a series of similarities and variants in procedures that are themselves continually developing. The broad uniformities in these procedures become apparent only if one takes a rather detached position some distance from the range of particular cases. Nearly all model-builders begin by constructing a skeleton or first approximation model and analyzing it, later filling in the details and variants by a series of successive approximations. They construct their skeleton by letting their imaginations play over a series of heuristic illustrations, trying to locate the essential components and relations that characterize the structure or process they are modeling. This suggests a set of first approximation postulates, from which they deduce a few basic derivations. After that the details are worked in. The chief variations occur in the issue of realism vs. logical simplicity in the skeleton postulates; the issue of explanatory vs. synthetic emphasis in the testing and improvement of the model; in the degree of interest in moving beyond the initial skeleton, and in the question of whether one is modeling a rather complex, rather specific system or a rather simpler, more abstract structure or process. Other variations will be discussed in chapter 6.

4

Experimental Work
with Mathematical Models

1. The first stage in the development of a mathematical model, constructing a skeleton or first approximation model, is one in which formal clarity is more important than empirical adequacy. Consequently refined empirical data are not really necessary, and the model-builder can rely on common sense observation and introspection as a source of his initial postulates. But as he makes successive corrections in his initial model he needs more refined and reliable data about his subject matter.

The type of data collection that is appropriate depends on the kind of subject matter being modeled. If the model-builder is trying to simulate a complex real system such as a particular firm or industry, he needs complex and varied data, in some cases statistical and in others based on direct or participant observation (for example, Cyert and March, 1963, pp. 47 ff.). But if he is modeling a relatively abstract process or structure, one that appears in the real world in a variety of forms, experimentation is a more appropriate way to produce the necessary data. His subject matter can be experimentally induced, preferably without its ordinary disguises, and he can use the results to improve his model and test the improvements.

Models of abstract processes and structures usually, though not always, take the form of mathematical models, so most formalist experimental work is done in connection with the development of a mathematical model. The most common formal theories used in experimental work are game theory and stochastic learning theory. There is some experimental work with cognitive process models—memory, perception, cognitive balance, problem-solving—which usually are computer simulations because of the complexity that is necessary. However, in this chapter I shall concentrate on experimental work with mathematical models, particularly game theory and learning theory. The computer-oriented cognitive process models are developed in a similar fashion, except that they face additional problems that will be discussed in the next chapter.

2. Experimental work with formal theories is a meeting ground of two traditions, the experimental and the formal. Consequently one finds a great variety of practices as particular elements of one tradition are combined with elements of the other tradition. Some of these combinations seem at first glance to be felicitous and others to be more trouble than they are worth, but it is probably too early to name the most appropriate combinations. One also finds a great variety of pronouncements on method, as elements from the ideology of empiricism are combined with elements of formalist ideology.

A thorough understanding of this area requires an understanding of both traditions, the formal and the experimental. Unfortunately I cannot provide an adequate systematic account of this subject because I have not been able to make a systematic study of the cross-currents of thought and practice among empiricist experimenters, particularly as they have developed during the past ten years. As a holist I realize that one cannot understand this area adequately unless one understands pretty nearly all the methods of the social sciences in their historical context, but in practice I have fallen short of this requirement. Consequently the reader is warned that the following account is partial, perhaps somewhat distorted, and based primarily on a formalist standpoint and historical context. Much of what I describe and criticize might look different from an empiricist standpoint.

I shall begin by giving an account of experimental work with mathematical models from a formalist standpoint, and then add empiricist qualifications and reinterpretations one by one. I also ask that empirically inclined readers be patient and tolerant of an account that may at first seem somewhat peculiar to them.

3. A formalist uses experimentation in the later stages of developing a mathematical model, after the basic model has been constructed and analyzed. The postulates of his skeleton model determine the structure of the experiment, and the experimental results are supposed to correspond to the output or derivations of the model. In other words, the experiment is set up to imitate or exemplify the model.

The purpose of the experiment is not to test the skeleton model it exemplifies; indeed, it would be impossible to test a skeleton model experimentally. The model says that if its postulate set is exemplified empirically, then the solution or output deduced from those postulates must also occur empirically because it has been deduced from them. A game model says that a maximizing player will play in such a way as to maximize, whatever that may mean in a particular case; an operant conditioning model says that a reinforcer will reinforce if given a chance; and so on. If one sets up a gaming experiment by inducing some experimental subjects to act like maximizing players, and if one finds that they do indeed maximize, what does that prove? It does not prove that maximizing players play to maximize, because that is a tautology; insofar as it shows that the players were indeed maximizing, it proves only that the experiment was properly set up. Suppose now that the players do not maximize; what does *that* prove? It does not falsify the hypothesis that maximizing players play to maximize, but rather shows that these were not maximizing players. Suppose one knew from independent evidence that they really were maximizing players, regular gambling sharks, in fact, and lightning-fast calculators as well, but they still did not maximize; what would that show? That something was wrong with the experiment: either some interference was preventing them from acting normally, or they were maximizing in ways not intended or recognized by the experimenter.

The purpose of experimentation is not to test a skeleton model but to develop it further by adding details. The postulates of a skeleton are highly abstract, simplified, and unrealistic, and the deductions made from them apply only to the idealized situation they specify. Development makes the postulate set more complex and realistic, perhaps by relaxing some of the assumptions or by adding new postulates. Experimentation provides a basis for development by providing a set of empirical data with which the predictions of the model can be compared. The discrepancies between model prediction and data suggest specific changes in postulates.

If experimental data are to suggest changes in the postulates of a model, they must not be too close to the output predictions of the model; there must be discrepancies that are regular enough to suggest specific changes. On the other hand, if the discrepancies are too large and general, they cannot guide the search for proper changes in the model; there is too much freedom for the search process, which then becomes arbitrary and "creative." The trick in designing a formalist experiment is to produce results that diverge from model predictions somewhat but not too much. Sometimes the right amount of divergence appears automatically when one sets up the postulates of a model experimentally, but at other times divergence is the result of deliberate experimental design. The experimenter does not embody his postulates completely in the experimental design, but leaves out one restrictive assumption (such as perfect information or adequate calculating ability) or adds one variable not specified by the model (such as sex or age or foresight).

Hypotheses may or may not be used in the process of designing an experiment. The experimenter may have one or more hypotheses about what sort of postulate changes should be made to improve the model, and he can use them to suggest details of the experimental setup. Or he may simply wonder what would happen if he relaxed some restrictive assumption and thereby made his model more realistic. But even if hypotheses are used in the experimental design and tested by its results, the testing is a subordinate step in the larger process of model development. It is subordinate in the sense that the selection of hypotheses is determined by the shortcomings, the oversimplifications, of the skeleton model, as well as in the sense that the outcomes of hypothesis testing are used to correct and improve the model. The basic purpose of formalist experimentation is not hypothesis testing but model development, and testing is a means to that end.

I shall illustrate the above remarks with three examples. Consider first the Fouraker and Siegel series of experiments on bargaining (Siegel and Fouraker, 1960; Fouraker and Siegel, 1963). The formal theory of bargaining on which the experiments were based postulates two rational but not omniscient agents, "rational" here meaning "desiring to maximize expected utility, able to make the necessary calculations, and psychologically able to act on the basis of one's rational choice." Each agent has resources valued by the other; there is diminishing marginal utility of resources (that is, each additional unit of a resource is a little less valuable than the previous unit to a person); and exchange is permitted. From these postulates one can deduce that exchange will occur only if both agents are better off exchanging than not exchanging (since both agents, being rational, will do only things that leave them better off), and the amount exchanged will be such as to benefit both. One cannot, however, deduce from these postulates where in the area of mutual benefit the bargain will be struck.

Fouraker and Siegel wish to enrich the postulates of bargaining theory to specify more exactly the equilibrium location of a bargain in the bargaining space. They propose to discover the additional postulates in experimental data, and for this purpose set up bargaining experiments. The design of the experiments is specified by the postulates of the theory. They need two rational players, each with resources valued by the other, diminishing marginal utility of resources, and exchange permitted. To fulfill these requirements, they give one experimental subject a quantity of dummy resources, the other a quantity of play money, allow a fixed time period for bargaining, and promise to exchange the dummy resources and money for real money on a sliding scale. They attempt to cover the rationality postulate by making the necessary calculations simple.

Note first that these experiments cannot possibly test bargaining theory. The theory says that if its postulates are exemplified empirically, then exchange will necessarily occur within the area of mutual profitability; conversely, if exchange does not occur in this area, then one or more of the postulates, probably that of rationality, are not being exemplified. That is, if the experimental subjects are rational in the sense that they will do only things beneficial to themselves, then their exchanges will benefit them both; conversely, if the exchanges are not beneficial, this shows that the parties are not acting rationally, i.e., they are not acting to benefit themselves.

There is no way to test such a proposition because it is a tautology. If the experimental exchanges fall outside the area of mutual profitability, it shows that one or both of the experimental subjects were not acting rationally and that the postulates of the theory were therefore not exemplified experimentally. The experiments are not relevant to bargaining theory and therefore cannot falsify it. However, if the exchanges occur within the area of mutual profitability, as actually happened, this does not confirm bargaining theory; it shows only that the postulates of the theory were exemplified in the experimental set-up. The only thing that is tested is the ability of the experimenters to set up an empirical exemplification of the postulates.

The purpose of the experiments therefore cannot be to test the skeleton bargaining theory; they are intended rather to enrich the theory. The skeleton theory cannot specify where in the area of mutual profitability the exchange will occur, because its postulates are inadequate for this purpose. If the experimenters can discover a regularity in the location of the exchanges, this will suggest some additional postulates from which such regularities could be deduced. This is in fact what happened; the principles of equality (50-50) and of salience, which have appeared in other bargaining experiments, were shown to be implicit in the discovered experimental regularities. Such principles should now be added in some way to an expanded bargaining theory.

For a second example, suppose a person wishes to develop a theory of coalitions for three-person games. He begins with an elementary mathematical model, whose postulates are three identical players, each perfectly rational and omniscient; two payoffs, win and lose, win being preferred to lose; coalitions permitted, with a coalition of any two players sufficient to win; and each play of the game independent of all other plays—the players have no memory or foresight. From these postulates it is possible to deduce the proposition that at asymptote there will be a random distribution of the three possible two-man coalitions, each of them occurring about ⅓ of the time.

Here again there is no experiment that could either confirm or disconfirm such a theory. If one could find rational men of the sort specified in the postulates, then they could not possibly form regular coalitions because by definition the possible outcomes would provide no reason for them to do so. Therefore, if regularities occur in experimental conditions, it merely shows that factors not specified in the postulates are present to produce them. Either the players are not perfectly rational or they operate under additional constraints not specified in the game rules. In any case, the starkly parsimonious conditions specified in coalition theory are not present in the experiments, so the theory cannot be falsified.

The purpose of coalition experiments is thus not to test the original theory but to improve it. In this case improvement would take the form of relaxing the too restrictive assumptions embodied in the postulates. A theory describing people with no memory, foresight, personal attachments, or human feelings is not very useful in the real world; moreover, in the real world there are problems of game maintenance and policing about which the theory has nothing to say. Consequently the experimenter would set up some of the postulates but not all of them. He might allow for memory and foresight by specifying that a series of games will be played; the subjects would then look ahead and try to prepare favorable situations for later plays. He might bring in maintenance problems by allowing subjects to leave at any time and thus break up the game; and so on. In each case the experimental results would differ in regular ways from the prescriptions of game theory, and these discrepancies would suggest new postulates to be included in an enriched theory.

The various coalition experiments by Vinacke, Riker, Gamson, Lieberman, and others can all be construed as heuristic attempts to enrich coalition theory, though the experimenters did not always view them this way because of their empiricist beliefs. For example, when players were allowed to have foresight they regularly formed strong two-man coalitions that resisted tempting offers from the third man; the basis of these continuing coalitions was mutual trust (Lieberman, 1964; Vinacke and Arkoff, 1957, p. 414). This suggests that the notion of the rational man as having no sense of obligation to others is too restrictive; sometimes it is rational to pass up profitable short-run offers to prove one's trustworthiness to a partner and thereby ensure larger long-run returns. Riker has shown that this empirical regularity can be formalized very simply (1967, p. 55). If one postulates foresight, then as soon as two rational players have formed a coalition there is no reason to change it, because neither player could do better in an alternative coalition and could easily do worse. Consequently all coalitions between rational players will be permanent. This means that the empirical concept of trust was only the players' way of conceptualizing for themselves their discovery that a permanent coalition would maximize expected returns.

This formalization in its turn produces new experimental discrepancies, since in all continuous-play experiments known to me there were some coalition changes. One could argue that all these changes represented temporary lapses into irrationality, that is, that asymptote had not been approximated sufficiently. This would be a way of saying that nothing of formal interest could be learned from the remaining empirical discrepancies. Alternatively, one could locate a principle of fairness or equal treatment in the way the coalition changes sometimes produced approximately equal returns to all three players. A still more plausible interpretation is suggested by the discovery that permanent coalition partners occasionally let the third person win through temporary coalitions, to keep him interested in the game (Riker, Vinacke, unpublished). Goffman and Polsky could also comment on this tactic from a different standpoint (Polsky, 1967). This suggests that some coalition changes at least were for the purpose of game maintenance, that the concept of fairness is a way of conceptualizing game maintenance requirements, and that an adequate description of n-person games should include a statement of these requirements.

For example, Morton Kaplan includes three game-maintenance rules in his suggested set of rules for a balance-of-power game (1957, p. 686; cf. also Riker, 1962, pp. 161-162). The third rule says, "Permit defeated actors to re-enter the system as acceptable coalition partners." Kaplan's rules also bring out the conflict between the requirement of maximization and such game-maintenance requirements as fairness. If one wanted to model this conflict, it would come out as a three-person Prisoner's Dilemma. Kaplan's rules apply to games in which the interests of players occasionally change and in which occasional coalition changes are therefore rational. Future coalition experiments could profitably investigate such games, which are more realistic than games in which interests never change.

For a third example, suppose a person wishes to develop an incremental learning model, one which says that when a response is reinforced, its probability or its rate increases in a constant fashion. A reinforcer is defined as any stimulus that increases response probability or rate, making the model up to this point a tautology, neither true nor false. It would be pointless to try to test this model experimentally; if an experimental reinforcer did not increase response rate, this would show only that it was not acting as a reinforcer, either because some uncontrolled incidental variable was interfering with learning or because it was not really a reinforcer at all. In either case the experimenter would be at fault, not the theory.

The point of a learning experiment would be to enrich the skeleton model. As soon as one tries to construct such a model, one comes up against the question of what happens to the unreinforced response. If response A_1 occurs and is reinforced, its probability goes up by definition; but what happens to the probability of response A_2? Does it decrease toward extinction as though it were being punished, or does it stay the same? If it stays the same, how does one juggle the probabilities so they sum to 1? If it decreases, what happens if neither response is reinforced, and how do the probabilities still sum to 1? Another question is about the exact meaning of "constant increase": the most likely formalization is "constant proportion, θ, of the task remaining to be learned," but there are other possibilities. Various lines of learning experiments have explored these and other possible enrichments of the basic incremental model. It turns out that "learning" is a very abstract process that is interfered with by a host of variables which have been discovered one by one; or, speaking in terms of enriched models, there are many different forms of learning that occur in different circumstances. The task of the learning experimenter is first to construct complex variants of the basic models, and then to discover the empirical circumstances in which each comes to be exemplified in the real world.

4. Up to this point I have argued that the purpose of experimental work with formal models is not to "test" the basic models, which is impossible; it is the heuristic purpose of discovering suggestions for improved postulates to make the basic models more complex and realistic. Two distinct kinds of heuristic experiments are in use by formalists, boundary experiments and exploratory experiments (cf. A. Kaplan, 1964, pp. 149-150). A boundary experiment is one that attempts to determine the limits of relevance of a particular model; it tries to draw a boundary around the empirical area that exemplifies it. An exploratory experiment is one that attempts to discover, within this area or near it, additional empirical regularities that can be included in an enriched and more realistic model.

One sets up a boundary experiment by first providing an experimental exemplification of the postulates of a model. Next one selects a critical variable that either is mentioned in the model or may be relevant to it. Then one sets up a series of experiments—at least two—in which the value of this variable is systematically varied. In the first experiment the value of the variable should be such that the experimental results match the logical output of the model. This result does not "confirm" the model; it merely shows that it is relevant at that value of the variable. In later experiments the value of the variable should be changed until the experimental results no longer match the logical output. At this point one has discovered the limits of relevance—the boundary—of the model with respect to that variable. Another series of experiments can then uncover the boundary with respect to a different variable, and so on.

An example of a series of boundary experiments is provided by Lieberman (1962). The variable chosen for variation in the series is the complexity of the calculations required to select an optimum strategy. Perfect calculating ability is part of the rationality postulate, but we know this assumption is too extreme to be realistic in many empirical situations. Lieberman wanted to locate the situations in which the assumption is realistic and in which the simple game models do apply; beyond that he wanted to find the limit of complexity past which the models do not apply. His first experiment, a 3 × 3 zero-sum game with saddle point, was clearly inside the boundary, as more than 90 per cent of the subjects followed the minimax prescription on final plays. The second experiment, in which the optimum strategy was mixed, was clearly outside the boundary. Ideally, perhaps, later experiments could have explored the ground between the first two; but in any case, Lieberman succeeded in determining the general limits of relevance of minimax rationality for one type of subject. He found that mixed strategies are beyond the limits of these subjects' calculating ability.

A second example of boundary experiments is a portion of Vinacke's series of coalition experiments (Vinacke, 1959). Here the crucial variable is sex. Vinacke ran some games with male subjects and some with female subjects. He found that the prescriptions of coalition theory apply to men but not to women, or, more precisely, to subjects with exploitative motivation (usually men) but not to subjects with accommodative motivation (usually women). Gamson (1964) has also suggested various limits of relevance of coalition theory.

The deficiency of boundary experiments, even when they are properly carried out, is that they leave the model unchanged and clarify only its interpretations. It is important to clarify an interpretation and determine the extent of its relevance and, indeed, one of the chief errors in the use of formal method is a tendency to make hasty and uncritical applications of the model to reality. But the main aim of a formal method is not just to reinterpret existing models, but to construct new and improved ones. Boundary experiments are only a preliminary step, though an important one, in achieving this aim.

The improvement of a model is achieved by conducting exploratory experiments. In these, interest is focused on the discrepancy between model output and experimental results, as I have already mentioned. The experimenter sets up an experimental interpretation of a model, studies the discrepancies between theorems and data, and successively revises the model until he has sufficiently reduced the discrepancy. Or, alternatively, he locates regularities in the area of discrepancy and uses these to construct a new model. As questions come up about some part of the model, he devises a new experiment focused on that part. If he manages to achieve a good fit with a revised model, he introduces new complications into the experimental situation, by relaxing the strict assumptions of the model to produce new discrepancies. The complications are intended to make the experimental situation more nearly analogous to real life, so that the resulting model will be more readily applicable. For example, the coalition experimenter may shift from studying coalitions among three players to studying coalition processes among larger numbers of players with varying power distributions (Vinacke, in progress), or the game theorist may experiment with games with unknown payoffs and strategies (Shubik, 1964, pp. 307-310). Thus the process of alternate reasoning and experimenting continues until both experiments and model are complex analogues of real life.

Probably the two best-reported examples of exploratory experiments are B. Cohen's on conflict and conformity (1963) and Rapoport and Chammah's on Prisoner's Dilemma (1965). Cohen's aim was to construct a mathematical model of the conflict and conformity process, since he thought such a model would have very general applicability to life in society. No model of the process had previously existed, so this is an example of using experimentation to construct a model from the beginning, rather than to improve an existing skeleton model. In pursuit of this aim, Cohen begins by examining empiricist-motivated experiments on conflict and conformity and modifying their design to bring out more fully the dynamics of the conflict-and-conformity process. (I shall discuss formalist experimental design later in this chapter.) Next he runs the experiments, and then he must locate regularities as a basis for constructing his model. To locate the regularities he constructs three random-process models, including a learning model. These serve as null hypotheses, since each of them asserts that there is no underlying dynamic process. Consequently, if there are regular discrepancies between the null-model predictions and the data, they must have been produced by some non-random process, namely the process Cohen is trying to model. The regularities that do occur, therefore, point to the basic characteristics of the conflict-and-conformity process. Cohen uses these pointers, together with hints from verbal protocols of the subjects and from personality theory, to construct a first approximation of the postulated underlying process. Note that Cohen uses two kinds of data to construct this model: the verbal protocols (soft data) point directly to the postulates required, and the experimental data (hard data) point to the kind of output that is required of the model. Next Cohen compares successively more complex versions of the model with the data until he has a reasonably good fit.

At this point Cohen has used up the information provided by his first set of experimental data. He has eliminated the random elements from the data by means of the three null models, and then has constructed a model whose output matches the remaining data. This model has the double contact with empirical reality that was discussed in the last chapter: its postulates connect with the verbal protocols, and its output connects with the experimental output.

The next step is analysis of the model to determine its formal characteristics. The analysis reveals a new discrepancy: the last trial of the experiments, trial 36, is still far from asymptote. In this case the experimental data must be changed, not the model, so a new experiment with more trials (80) is run. Now the model can be compared with these new data to look for more discrepancies. However, it turns out that an uncontrolled incidental variable, the seating position of the subjects, is the source of most of the remaining discrepancy. This variable is part of the experimental situation rather than of the conflict-and-conformity process, so it can be ignored. The new data therefore provide no new information on how to improve the model —they match the model too well—and Cohen therefore returns to analysis of the model. This time he analyzes it by computer simulation, which runs the model far past 80 trials. The computer output reveals that there is an additional equilibrium state in the model; there are three final states, not just two as Cohen had thought. Sensitivity analysis of the computer output reveals that the time path is strongly affected by certain unsuspected, unobservable boundary conditions, and Cohen returns to the laboratory to devise experiments focused on these newly discovered parameters. Presumably these parameters will then be put into the model as further modifications.

In the case of Rapoport and Chammah's Prisoner's Dilemma experiments, a model of the experiments was already available, so their procedure was somewhat different from Cohen's. Prisoner's Dilemma is a mixed-motive game, in which there is conflict between the shared interest and the private interests of the players. The shared interest can be called heuristically "cooperation," and the private interests "defection" or "double cross." A player can improve his payoff by defecting (pursuing his private interest), but if both players defect both are worse off than if they had co-operated. Moreover, if one player co-operates while the other defects, the co-operating player receives the lowest payoff of all. It pays to co-operate only if the other player also does so, but if the other player does co-operate, it pays still better to defect—until the other player also defects. There are numerous real-life exemplifications of this game.

This situation can be expressed formally as a game matrix in which each player has two alternatives: co-operate (C) and defect (D).

The payoff values are arranged in the following order: $T > R > P > S$. This means that if the opponent plays C, the best response is D, since $T > R$. If the opponent plays D, the best response is also D, since $P > S$. The game theoretical prescription, therefore, is always to play D—always pursue private interest—since it maximizes payoff no matter what one's opponent does. The prescription to play D applies, by another argument, to any finite number of plays of the game. However, when both players follow this prescription they both lose with P payoffs.

The subjects in Prisoner's Dilemma experiments do not follow the game-theoretic prescription always to play D. They play C sometimes and D sometimes, receiving as a consequence all four possible payoffs, but mainly P and R. Since $R > P$ their total payoffs are larger than the total payoffs of the hypothetical rational player who always plays D and always receives P. The discrepancy between the formal model and empirical data is thus so great that it amounts to a paradox: rational players do worse than irrational players, which means that it would be irrational to act "rationally" in Prisoner's Dilemma. Plainly the game-theoretic definition of rationality does not apply to such situations. The solution to the paradox involves broadening or otherwise modifying the rationality postulate in such a way that it does apply, and this becomes Rapoport and Chammah's goal (1965, pp. 12-13). Their exploratory interest in modifying the definition of rationality begins just where Lieberman's boundary-locating interest in minimax rationality (1962) ends.

To modify the prescriptive concept of rationality it is first necessary to produce an accurate description of how the game is played. The game-theoretic account is plainly erroneous as a description: players are not minimaxing on successive plays. Therefore it is necessary to find out what they are doing to master the situation, and then bring out the rationale that is implicit in what the successful players are doing.

In undertaking this preliminary descriptive task, the authors first perform the basic experiments, then search the data for appropriate variables and parameters, and then construct a series of models based on the variables. The search for variables is systematic; it is based on the mathematical structure of the game. Each relation in the game structure suggests one variable, and each set of variables is put into appropriate hypotheses and tested against the data to see whether they bring out regularities. In other words, the basic search rule is, "Scan all the possibilities, looking for behavioral regularities." The possibilities are determined by the structure of the game, since the players' attempts to master the game must somehow be related to the characteristics of the game if they are to succeed.

There are five sets of variables. (1) Variations in the ratios of the four payoffs, T, R, P, and S. These variables are important if the players are responding primarily to their own payoff values. For instance, a player's choice of D might be an attempt to get T rather than R; if this were the case, there would be a correlation between D and the T/R ratio: the greater the value

of T relative to R, the larger the percentage of D responses. Or the choice of
D might be a defensive attempt to get P rather than S, and this would show up
as a correlation between D and the P/S ratio. The choice of C might be an
attempt to get R rather than P. These variables, incidentally, are those used
in the original game-theoretic prescription, and in view of the failure of that
prescription, it is unlikely they will tell the whole story. It turns out that
there is some correlation of set 1 variables with C and D responses.

(2) Concealing or revealing the matrix to the players. Revealing the matrix
produces better results, higher scores, suggesting that conscious strategy rather
than unconscious reinforcement is involved. In other words, a game model
rather than a learning model is relevant. There would have been other ways
to get this information, such as having the players talk about what they were
doing and comparing their verbalizations with their output, but this would
have involved changes in the search process.

(3) Relation between the simultaneous choices of the two players. These
variables would be important if the players' strategies somehow involved
either matching choices with the opponent (CC and DD) or cross-matching
them (CD and DC). Here two strong correlations occur, CC and DD, indicating that the players are indeed trying to match choices.

(4) Relation between a choice and the preceding choice of the same or
another player, and (5) relation between a choice and the payoff on the
previous play. To simplify considerably, two kinds of variables are included
in sets 4 and 5. First, relations between a choice and the preceding choice of
the other player, plus two set 5 variables, suggest a feedback process in
which a player is trying to match the other player's preceding choice. Here
again strong correlations appear. Second, relations between a choice and the
preceding choice of the same player, plus some set 5 variables, point to
personality characteristics of the player, including learning, which determine
a sequence of choices separate from what the other player does. The low and
inconsistent correlations of these variables indicate that personality factors
are not operating prominently in the experimental setup, except under certain
set 1 variable conditions. Note that the two groups of variables in sets 4 and
5 are contraries; the one group suggests that a player is matching his responses to those of the other player, while the other group suggests that the
player's responses are controlled by internal variables independent of the
other player.

The successive examination of all these variables has brought out a number of regularities, most prominently a tendency to match the other player's
response, both on the same and on the preceding play.

The next step is to construct a series of models of the underlying process
using variables from sets 1, 3, 4, and 5, and comparing model output with
the time paths in the experimental data. The information in the time paths
has not been used yet. The purpose is to obtain a better understanding of the
already observed regularities, especially the matching tendencies. The models,
including a learning model and some Markov chains, represent several

possible ways in which the matching tendencies could be produced. All the models fail, but a study of the discrepancies reveals what is happening: there is a lock-in effect in which the probability of continuing a CC or DD run increases the longer a run lasts (Rapoport and Chammah, 1965, pp. 172-173). This effect is the main explanation for the observed time path.

The next step is to investigate the lock-in effect to see what strategy is associated with it empirically. New experiments are run with contrasting populations, one with high lock-in on co-operation and the other with lock-in on non-cooperation. The search is for the strategy used by the co-operative population, since the set 2 variables have suggested that strategy is present. The dominant differential is the "tit-for-tat" strategy, discovered and described with set 4 variables. In this strategy Player 1 always matches Player 2's response on the preceding play. When Player 2 realizes what is happening, his best strategy is to play C steadily; at this point a lock-in on C occurs.

By now we have a pretty clear picture of what is happening. Successful players do not minimax, but rather use a tit-for-tat strategy to teach their opponent to co-operate (Rapoport, 1968). This teaching process begins about plays 30 to 50, when the structure of the game first becomes clear to the players. In many cases the teaching process is successful and pairs of players lock in on co-operation; in other cases it is unsuccessful and the players give up on each other and lock in on DD. Still other pairs bumble along through misunderstanding, double crosses, and renewed attempts at communication.

The final step is the prescriptive formalization of these results in a redefinition of rationality (Amnon Rapoport, 1967). Prisoner's Dilemma is formalized as a supergame with four component subgames: a co-operative game, a defensive game, and a pair of teaching games in between. Play begins in the teaching games. A rational strategy is one that moves the players into the co-operative game at least cost by means of tit-for-tat play or, if the price is too high in terms of set 1 variables, prescribes defensiveness. This strategy does not minimax, but it does maximize long-run expected returns. Included in this formalization is the element of conscience, the "he is like me" element that Anatol Rapoport has stressed (1964b, pp. 50-52; 1966, p. 100) and that is presupposed by the attempt to reach and teach. This element appears in Amnon Rapoport's third postulate (1967, p. 142).

If I were allowed to choose only one example to refute the absurd theory that there is no logic of scientific discovery, I would choose this series of Prisoner's Dilemma experiments. I do not claim that there is a deductive logic of discovery, which would be self-contradictory, but I do claim that discovery is a regular, systematic search process and not simply a matter of inspiration or "conjecture." Theories of deductive and inductive logic distort this search process and therefore are irrelevant to it.

5. So far I have argued that the purpose of formalist experimental work is the heuristic one of providing suggestions for revising and complicating a model. I have differentiated two kinds of heuristic experiments, boundary ex-

periments in which the limits of relevance of a model are discovered, and exploratory experiments in which regular empirical discrepancies suggest new or modified postulates for the model. I turn now to a persistent difficulty in formalist experiments.

Every formal model is composed of formal concepts that are defined relationally, that is, in terms of each other. In order to apply a model to empirical reality, as in designing an experiment, some of the formal concepts must be given empirical interpretations. This procedure looks something like the standard experimentalist procedure of giving operational definitions to theoretical terms, but there is an important difference. Operational definitions are translations into precise observation language of loose theoretical concepts like intelligence, morale, group cohesion. These concepts have no clear and distinct meaning, and one purpose of operationalization is to discover such a meaning. This is done by testing various operationalizations to see which of them produces regular correlations with other variables. When several different operational definitions produce equally good correlations they are treated provisionally as interchangeable, but a definition that produces poorer correlations is discarded. The test of an operational definition is located in the experimental or statistical work in which it is used, not in the theory from which the concept was originally taken.

The process of providing empirical interpretations of formal concepts is significantly different. Formal concepts are not loose and vague, but on the contrary have a quite precise formal meaning. This meaning consists of the various relations into which they are permitted to enter in an equation, and of the alternative formal concepts that can be substituted for them. An adequate empirical interpretation of formal concepts must carry over this relational meaning into the experimental design; that is, the relational structure of the experimental situation must match the relational structure of the mathematical model. If the two structures are not isomorphic the meaning of the formal model is not carried over into the experiment and the results cannot be used to modify the model. This holds even if the experiments uncover regularities or verify hypotheses; the hypotheses may be true, but they have nothing to do with the misinterpreted model that suggested the experimental design. The test of an empirical interpretation is its faithfulness to the formal model it interprets, not the experimental results it makes possible.

For example, in game theory *payoff* is defined formally as an outcome of value to a player; *player* is defined formally as a chooser of alternatives who is in a conflict or interdependence relation with another player, and *alternative* is defined as a choice that combines with the choice of another player or players to produce an outcome. If an experimenter is confused about the difference between an empirical interpretation and an operational definition he may simply operationalize these concepts, somewhat as follows: "Payoff: I'll define the payoff operationally as poker chips, since this is a game and poker is a game and chips are used in poker." Or: "Payoff: I'll make the payoff money. In view of my tight research budget, this will come to 3¢ per game." Or: "Players: Those are the experimental subjects. Since I am investigating three-person games, I'll hire three subjects." The trouble with these interpretations is that if the "payoff" does not have value to the players it is not a payoff, no matter what the experimenter may say. If the three players are in conflict with the experimenter over the possible outcomes, he is a player in a four-person game, no matter what he may say. Thus Lumsden (1966) has shown that in certain gaming experiments the actual payoffs were significantly different from the experimenter's official payoffs. Riker found to his surprise that in some of his experiments the three players were in a coalition against him; they were playing to maintain the game and keep his rather large payments coming in, with the distribution of payments a secondary question (Riker, 1962, p. 51).

Gaming experiments especially have been plagued by this problem of faulty interpretations of formal concepts. Too often experimenters have uncritically assumed an interpretation of their game model and have come to question the results only afterward, when puzzling experimental results came in. For example, various game experimenters have wondered in print whether comparative score, alleviating boredom or curiosity, or experimenter approval was the real payoff. Some experimenters have become sensitized to the problem and more careful in their interpretations; for example, Kelley (1966) tried a payoff of course grades, and Riker tried asking the experimental subjects to provide their own money. Others, I am afraid, have not adequately faced the problem. The question of what actual game rules the players are following came up for Vinacke et al. when they suspected that their subjects were slipping in an additional constraint of fairness (1966, pp. 181, 182). Rapoport (1966a) has also suggested that in some Prisoner's Dilemma games there are certain nonstrategic constraints that have not been recognized by experimenters.

The question of communication between players has proved to be tricky; experimenters announce such rules as "no communication allowed" and then find that players are signaling by various patterns of moves, and that signaling is in some cases the main feature of play. This discovery has suggested an important revision of bargaining theory to allow for tacit communication. Morton Deutsch got himself into much unexpected trouble when he put a gate into his experimental apparatus and defined it as an operationalized threat (Deutsch and Krauss, 1962, p. 55; Kelley, 1965, p. 81; Deutsch, 1966). As Kelley pointed out, a gate or any other experimental device is a threat only if the players use it to threaten one another; if they use it to teach or just out of curiosity, it is not a threat no matter what the experimenter says. The experimental exemplification of "asymptote" is another important question in formalist experiments, since many formal theories deal only with conditions that obtain at asymptote. The question of when asymptote is reached in a series of plays originally was settled by arbitrary time limitation or by the limits of the experimenter's patience, but many puzzling results led to increased caution and longer runs of plays. Early experiments settled for 10 or 30 or 36 plays; then the number moved up to 80, 210, 300, 700, and 1,000 in the search for an empirical asymptote.

When these questions of interpretation are not faced beforehand in the design of an experiment, they come up afterward in the form of inconclusive disputes over the meaning of experimental data (Kelley and Arrowood, 1960; Vinacke et al., 1966; Kelley, 1965; Deutsch, 1966). Interest shifts from the understanding of real phenomena to the interpretation of puzzling and ever more complex experiments. This sort of shift is always a danger signal. Shubik in particular has persistently called attention to the danger of an uncritical interpretation of formal concepts, not only in experimental work but in all work with game theory (1963, 1964, pp. 26-30; 1968). Unfortunately his warnings have not always been taken seriously, and the standard mistakes continue to be made.

Learning theorists on the whole have not had the same difficulty as game theorists, probably because of their much longer experimental tradition. Decades of learning experiments have produced many reliable examples of stimulus and reinforcement—flashing lights, buzzers, shocks, air blasts, bar presses, pellets of food, sips of water, etc. In the early 1950's Estes came to realize that other stimuli besides the official ones could be operating, and he allowed for them by developing the formal concept of stimulus sampling. This concept said in effect that the experimenter did not know what all the empirical stimuli were, so that "stimulus" became a partly uninterpreted concept. The formal concepts of self-reinforcement and implicit or internal response are other uninterpreted concepts that were developed in response to the problem of empirical interpretation.

It may be that uncritical interpretations of formal concepts have been especially serious in gaming experiments because these experiments represent a rather sudden merging of two traditions, the experimental and the formal. The experimental tradition includes a well-established procedure of setting up operational definitions of theoretical concepts. When experimenters trained in this tradition turned to gaming experiments, they applied their standard operationalizing procedure to game-theoretic concepts, not realizing that the procedure was inappropriate with formal concepts. In general, experimenters coming out of the formalist tradition have tended to be aware of the problem, as have some empiricists familiar with formal concepts and methods, like Kelley.

6. Apart from the kind of occasional confusion I have just discussed, the experimental tradition has made essential contributions to experimentation with formal theories. Its most important contribution has been the exploratory experiment, in the form that has been developed over the past thirty years or so; if formalists had to use instead the rigid and narrow hypothesis-testing experiment popular in the 1930's, they could not do anything with their models in the laboratory. The techniques of the exploratory experiment are still being developed further by empiricists, I am told, and future developments presumably will also be useful to formalists.

The exploratory experiment has several variants, of which I can distinguish three. First, for holists or semi-holists like Bales et al., the exploratory experiment is a way of getting as many different perspectives on a piece of behavior as possible, in order to build up a complex picture of what is happening. The experimenters are indeed busy in the Bales experiments: one observer sits behind the one-way screen, another perhaps is in the room but sitting at a different angle, another pores over the tape or movie recording, coding or doing content analysis, another catches the subjects before and after the experiment with tests and interview questions in hand, so that no interesting clue will escape attention. On the other hand, the traditional control function of the experimenter is mostly repudiated; the only controls on the experimental subjects are the assigned task and the rule requiring them to stay in their well-bugged room. This type of experiment is similar to the holistic techniques of direct and participant observation (chs. 11,12, below).

Second, there is the exploratory experiment of the searcher looking for statistically significant correlations, like Vinacke and Morton Deutsch. This experimenter sees his task as that of investigating a whole theoretical area step by step. He begins with a rather simple design and a few abstract variables, locates the main regularities among the variables, and then adds complications, each time searching for new regularities or perhaps testing hypotheses about the added complications. The experimental situation gradually becomes more lifelike and less like a laboratory, and the resulting generalizations or correlations become more complex and qualified. The process of adding complications one by one enables the experimenter to retain control of the many variables involved without having to control his experimental subjects; the latter are gradually freed to act in a relatively lifelike way. Third, there are the formalist exploratory experiments, like those of B. P. Cohen (1963) and Rapoport and Chammah (1965) that I have previously summarized. In these experiments the search process is controlled by the parameters and variables of the formal model being developed. Consequently it is a rather methodical process, and may even seem monotonous and unimaginative to the Vinacke-type empiricist. Whether these three types of exploratory experiment are individual variants of a single tradition or parts of relatively distinct traditions I do not know.

7. Up to now I have described the general characteristics and purposes of formalist experiments. I wish now to contrast them with empiricist experiments that use mathematical models. I shall illustrate the contrast by comparing some empiricist Prisoner's Dilemma experiments with Rapoport and Chammah's formalist Prisoner's Dilemma experiments, and also comparing empiricist conflict-and-conformity experiments with Cohen's formalist experiments on the same topic.

The ultimate aim of the empiricist experimenter is still the discovery of statistically significant correlations that will withstand varied and rigorous experimental tests. Exploration may be an essential preliminary to the discovery of important rather than trivial correlations, but sooner or later the correlations will have to show up if the enterprise is to be justified. From this ideological standpoint, experimental work with mathematical models must be justified by the kinds of correlations it produces. This means that even when the empiricist is exploring, he is on the lookout for potential correlations. Models do not particularly interest him except as instruments of control or as means of graphically representing an experimental design.

When this type of empiricist uses mathematical models in his experimental work, he treats the constraints of the model as a means of operationalizing a dependent variable he wishes to study. The purpose of his experiments is to locate independent variables that correlate with his dependent variable. For example, Morton Deutsch's experiments have been focused on the question, "What factors, personal and situational, induce co-operation between human beings?" Co-operation has always been his dependent variable. He has used two experimental designs to study it: Prisoner's Dilemma, which he calls "the trust problem" (1965, p. 517; 1962, p. 296), and the trucking game, which he calls "the bargaining problem" (1965, p. 519; 1962, p. 297). These two, together with a Schelling-type game he calls "the co-ordination problem" (1965, p. 521; 1962, p. 301), represent three common human situations in which co-operation occurs, and Deutsch uses them to investigate what factors produce co-operation in those situations. The problem of empirical interpretation of formal concepts appears in Deutsch's assumption that these formalized experimental situations are isomorphic with real-life situations.

Deutsch's Prisoner's Dilemma experiments (1962, pp. 309-312) are typical of a large number of empiricist Prisoner's Dilemma experiments, including those of Lave (1965), Oskamp and Perlman (1965), and Sampson and Kardush (1965). In these experiments the game model is used to operationalize the dependent variable, co-operation, which appears as the C response. The purpose of the experiments is to discover correlations between co-operation and some independent variable—communication, F-scale score, various induced motivations, age and sex differences, or personal backgrounds of the players. The primary theoretical and experimental interest, therefore, is the various independent variables external to the gaming situation.

The formalist, by contrast, is interested in the dynamics of the gaming situation itself, not in the influence of external factors. By the "dynamics" of the gaming situation I mean the way in which the conflicting pressures work themselves out through a time path and approach a final solution at asymptote. He does not include any independent variable in his experimental design and tries to control or eliminate the effects of variables external to his model. The gaming situation is the whole experiment, not just one operationalized variable. In a Prisoner's Dilemma experiment the dynamics consist of the players' first discovering they are really in a dilemma, then somehow trying to master the dilemma, and finally either succeeding or giving up. In a conflict-and-conformity experiment the dynamics consist of the subject's attempt to resolve the conflict between the pressure to conform and the pressure to be independent.

The contrasting interests of formalists and empiricists express themselves in contrasting experimental designs. Since the formalist is interested in dynamics, in time path and asymptote, he needs a long series of identical trials so the structural dynamics can work themselves out. The empiricist does not need a time path; he needs only statistically reliable data about the behavior of the dependent variable, and for these a few trials per experimental subject are enough. Thus Deutsch's subjects first played one trial and later ten trials (twenty trials in his trucking game), while Rapoport and Chammah put their subjects through 300, 350, and 700 trials. The effect of multiple trials is to wash out the personality factors, induced motivations, and preconceptions that the subjects bring to the game—the independent variables in which the empiricists are interested—and to bring out the effects of the game structure itself. Another difference in design is that Deutsch chose only a single version of Prisoner's Dilemma, one that minimizes structural barriers to cooperation, thereby minimizing the effect of the rational paradox in which a formalist would be interested. Rapoport and Chammah used a variety of versions covering a wide range of payoff ratios to bring out the full range of the paradox. Still another difference, mentioned before, is that Deutsch always used an independent variable while Rapoport and Chammah did not.

The same contrast appears between Asch's empiricist experiments and B. Cohen's formalist experiments on conflict and conformity (Cohen, 1963, pp. 8-12, 15-23). Asch treated the experimental setup as a way of operationalizing the concept of conformity; his aim, and that of later empiricist experimenters, was to obtain correlations between conforming behavior and various external and independent variables such as personality. To this end these experimenters used total frequency of conforming as a measure of conforming behavior. Their experiments consisted of eighteen trials divided equally between correct responses by the stooges, moderate errors, and extreme errors, and the three types of responses were carefully distributed. This distribution is a control; it serves to wash out any cumulative effect of the conflict-conformity situation and produce instead a kind of average response suitable for correlation with external factors. Cohen's formalist aim was to study the dynamics of the conflict-conformity process itself, the very process that Asch's controls excluded. Consequently he eliminated the control that Asch put in to get rid of the process; in Cohen's experiments there was an unbroken run of extreme errors by stooges. Also he needed a longer run of trials so that the process could work itself out to asymptote if possible. In Asch's 18-trial series there were 6 moderate and 6 extreme errors; Cohen's experiments ran for 36 and later for 80 trials, each one identical, and could in some cases have profitably run still longer. With 80 trials Cohen obtained a good time path and some approximation to asymptote, while in Asch's experiments no time path appeared. If one had appeared, it would have indicated a failure of experimental control over some "sleeper" variable.

Another contrast between the empiricist and the formalist experimenter is in the line of development, the logic of progression, of a series of experiments. Since the empiricist is interested in discovering independent variables that correlate with his chosen dependent variable, development in his experiments usually occurs in the area of the independent variables. (An exception is in cases of wide-ranging preliminary exploration, when anything in the experimental design may change.) Once the game—the operationalized dependent variable—is properly set up, the experimenter's work with it is finished; it stays the same from one experiment to the next, while the independent variables change. The experimenter's ingenuity is devoted to the search for independent variables, and his sensitivity is focused on the performance of the particular variable he is studying. Its performance raises theoretical issues which may suggest that a different variable would be worth studying; an uneven performance suggests modifications in a particular area, perhaps a new control or better operationalization of the independent variable, which might improve performance. For instance, when Vinacke found that sex correlated significantly with coalition behavior, it suggested to him that further refinements of the sex variable were appropriate. Perhaps some personality characteristic associated with sex might make a better independent variable, or perhaps different life experiences of the two sexes gave incidental aspects of the game different meanings, for which the experimenter should control (Vinacke, 1959; Uesugi and Vinacke, 1963). The dependent variable, coalition behavior in a three-person game, stayed the same. Similarly, the various empiricist Prisoner's Dilemma experimenters have tried one independent variable after another, always with the same dependent Prisoner's Dilemma variable.

The development of the formalist's experiments is determined by the deficiencies of the model he is developing. Most of his developmental work is theoretical, not empirical, in contrast to the empiricist who tends to alternate between theory and new experiment in a regular way. Once the formalist has his basic set of data, he has a great deal of theoretical analysis to do. He may apply a whole series of partial models to his data, looking for discrepancies, trying to improve fit, and using the results to modify his basic model. Only when he has used up the information in the data and cannot find any more new ideas in them does he need new data. The design of the new experiment is determined by the remaining questions he has about his model. Thus Rapoport and Chammah ran a new experiment only after they had a general theoretical explanation of the Prisoner's Dilemma time path, focusing this new experiment on a detail of the time path that remained unexplained: what strategy did the successful pairs use to achieve a lock-in on CC during the period between approximately trial 50 and trial 200? Even this question might possibly have been answered from their original data. Cohen ran a new experiment when the model he had developed told him he did not have a long enough time path in his data. Still later, sensitivity analysis of his model pointed to new boundary variables whose relation to the model needed to be investigated experimentally. In still other cases a formalist may want to relax some restrictive, unrealistic assumption of his model, and so devises an experiment to suggest replacements for the restrictive assumption.

A third contrast is in the kind of theorizing used and whether it comes before or after experimentation. The empiricist's theorizing tends to be loose and nonformal, and occurs prior to his experiments; for example, Deutsch's theorizing was substantially complete by 1949 (Deutsch, 1949), while his experimental reports have been appearing since 1957. Models are used, if at all, only to illustrate or diagram a theoretical point (cf. the use of game models in Thibaut and Kelley, 1959; Deutsch, 1962, 1965). The formalist's theorizing prior to experimentation is confined to basic deductions from his model, if he has one, and conjectures about empirical interpretation. His main theorizing comes after experimentation, as he tries to make formal sense of his data. The reason for this contrast is that the empiricist uses experiments partly to test his conclusions and partly to explore the effects of variables he has already speculated about, while the formalist uses them to provide information about a structure or process he is studying and trying to model.

To appreciate the importance of whether theorizing comes before or after experiment, consider what happens when a hypothesis is verified $p < .01$. For the empiricist it is the successful conclusion of one experiment; his theorizing has been correct or at least is on the right track. For the formalist it is only a beginning. What has happened is that the null hypothesis has been falsified, in the sense that the experimental results could not have occurred by chance as often as one time in a hundred. We now know that the process is not random—but nobody ever supposed it was random, as Forrester complains in criticizing some empiricist decision-making experiments (1961, p. 123). Consequently we have not learned anything new about what is really going on. We have learned that a certain regularity happens to occur; but for a formalist, regularities do not simply occur, they are produced by some mechanism (or are a part of some mechanism), some bit of logic or rationality that is operating in the world. Moreover, the same empirical regularity can be produced by a variety of different logical mechanisms. The task of the formalist is to uncover the particular mechanism at work and reveal it in all its abstract purity. To do this, he must learn much more about the situation: what other regularities occur in it, what the constraining boundary conditions or controls are, what the dynamics of the process are as it moves toward equilibrium or away from it, how the process changes with parameter changes, and so on. To find these things out, he must examine the data carefully with the help of all the mathematical tools he has available. All this work begins at the point where the empiricist claims to have verified some hypothesis.

To be sure, from the empiricist standpoint the proper order of things is exactly the reverse: one first formulates a model and then tests it experimentally. To complicate matters, some experimenters hold both of these beliefs. They resolve the contradiction by first making a ritual bow toward the received empiricist philosophy and then adding apologetically that they are not yet in a position to test their model; they are still developing it. So the definitive experimental test is postponed to the indefinite future, which never arrives, and practice proceeds in the standard formalist fashion, in which testing is a continuous part of the process of model development.

My contrast between formalist and empiricist experimental work with models is not intended invidiously. Each type of experimentation is equally valid and each has its own advantages and dangers. The purpose of my distinctions is merely to clarify, hopefully, a confusing and rapid developing field.

Having made a distinction, I shall now endeavor to eliminate it. From an empiricist standpoint, the various formalist experiments are still tests of hypotheses, or preliminary explorations aimed at some eventual tests, since these are the purposes of all experimentation. The experimental designs of some people I have called formalists may be rather stiff and mechanical, perhaps because of their debilitating training in mathematics, and they certainly run on much too long (1,000 trials! Fantastic!), but that does not make the experiments worthless. They need merely to be supplemented by more skillful, short, focused experiments on the same topic. Consequently the distinction I have perversely tried to draw between empiricist and formalist experiments is essentially arbitrary, no more important than three or four other distinctions one could draw in experimental work. Nor does the use of a mathematical model make that much difference in experimental work, since experimenters use all sorts of devices nowadays. In fact, all the experimental work I have discussed in this chapter is an integral part of the experimental tradition, and it is misleading to single it out for special attention just because there are some matrices and graphs in evidence here and there. Experimental work is simply getting more mathematical these days.

In support of this argument the empiricist can point out that Fouraker and Siegel (1963) were actually testing hypotheses about bargaining behavior, that these hypotheses were used in the construction of the bargaining space and were not just window-dressing, that one hypothesis was confirmed and the rest disconfirmed, and that the diagram of intersecting marginal cost and marginal revenue curves, etc., was only the experimenters' way of describing the experiments for themselves.

Now if we shift to a formalist standpoint the distinction I have been making also disappears, but in a different way. For a formalist all the various experiments in, say, Prisoner's Dilemma or bargaining or coalitions are simply preliminary explorations that will eventually be used to construct better models. To be sure (the formalist will add) all this concern with X^2, degrees of freedom, etc., is wasted precision, and all the dubious correlations with the F scale, MMPI, etc., are essentially irrelevant; but if we take all the contradictory experimental results from many experimenters we have considerable suggestive material for constructing a good model. In this sense nearly all the various experiments I have discussed in this chapter can be seen as part of the model-building tradition, though some, such as the 1000-trial one, are undoubtedly better conceived and more directly valuable than others.

As for the Fouraker and Siegel experiments, it is unimportant whether hypotheses were involved. These experiments are important because they are a big step away from the old, simplistic, highly abstract bargaining model of the economists toward the new, more complex and realistic models we are now developing. The old model assumed rational bargainers who tried to maximize and who had better calculating abilities than any computer, and at that it gave indeterminate results. The newer models assume limited rationality and realistic information-processing capacities, and include such concepts as salience, change of aspiration level, signaling, tacit agreements, and bargaining dilemmas. Fouraker and Siegel did not complete the construction of one of these newer models, but science is a co-operative enterprise and they made their contribution to it.

From these arguments I conclude that apart from varied interpretations and misinterpretations due to ideological differences, formalists and empiricists can each make use of the other's experimental results. The boundary I have tried to draw between the two kinds of experimentation is more a matter of difference of interpretation and of ultimate aim than of substance, though differences of substance do remain.

8. The co-operation I have just described occurs, from a formalist standpoint, in the process of improving and complicating a skeleton model. It is concerned with details to be added to a model, not with a whole model. For a formalist it makes little difference whether one conceives that hypothesis testing is occuring during this process; what matters is not the hypotheses but the improved model. From an empiricist standpoint it makes little difference whether there is a model somewhere in the background as long as important generalizations about human behavior are eventually discovered, tested, and qualified as to their range of applicability.

There is, however, one encounter between the empiricist and formalist traditions that is disastrous. It sometimes happens that an empiricist will treat a whole model, not just the detailed improvements, as a hypothesis to be tested experimentally. The empiricist proposes to test his model by setting up the conditions specified in the postulates, as near as practicable, and then seeing whether the "predictions" of the model, its derivations, agree with the experimental data.

The error here lies in supposing that there is merely a hypothetical or contingent connection between the postulates of a formal theory and its predictions. This is indeed the case with empirical generalizations, which assert that a connection merely happens to exist between two empirical facts. It may also sometimes be the case in implicit formal theories expressed in verbal language, since it is very hard to be sure just what a verbal statement implies or assumes. But in a formal theory the connection is not hypothetical or contingent; it is necessary. If the conditions described by the theory's postulates are set up experimentally, the results described by its theorems must necessarily occur, because the theorems are deduced from the postulates. That is, they are contained in the postulates and assert nothing that has not been implicitly asserted by the postulates. Conversely, if the results described by the theorems or derivations do not occur, this shows only that the conditions specified in the postulates have not been exemplified in the experiment. Consequently, if an experimenter finds that his results agree with predictions, he has shown two things: (1) he has demonstrated his skill in interpreting and setting up the conditions postulated by the theory; and (2) he has demonstrated that no mathematical errors occur in the portion of the theory tested. He has not verified the theory, because there is no possibility of falsification in the circumstances; once the postulated conditions have been set up, the deduced results must follow of necessity. The only thing that could disturb them would be additional conditions not stated in the postulates, but disturbing conditions are precisely the sort of thing a good experimenter will have eliminated.

Frequently an additional complication enters in, when the experimenter is unable to set up all the postulated conditions himself. This is notably the case with formal theories in which rationality of some sort is postulated, and in general with theories that postulate some specific psychological condition or process. The experimental subjects may or may not be in the condition postulated, and the predicted results accordingly may or may not occur. If they occur, the experimenter has demonstrated his skill or luck in setting up the conditions postulated by the theory; that is, he has shown that the theory is exemplified by his experimental set-up. If the results do not occur, he has shown that the theory does not apply or is not exemplified because the conditions it postulates have not occurred. But in any case his results will neither verify or falsify the theory.

Coleman (1964, pp. 50-51; 1960, p. 144) has discussed and illustrated the disastrous consequences of supposing that a mathematical model can be tested experimentally; I shall merely add two examples. The first is a famous one: Vinacke and Arkoff (1957). These experimenters decided to test two alternative coalition theories yielding contrasting predictions. One was the formal theory of coalitions developed by game theorists. This theory states that in a three-person zero-sum game played by rational players who desire nothing but to maximize their expected returns in each separate game, if any two players can win by forming a coalition and if there is nothing to distinguish the players in this respect, then at asymptote of a long series of games no discernible regularity in coalitions will occur. The other theory was that of Caplow (1956), who argued that in real life people are usually interested not so much in immediate rewards as in an improvement of their relative power position. Consequently the important conflicts in society are not over specific rewards but are long-term continuing struggles to improve one's position of dominance relative to other people. This is essentially the same point Hobbes made long ago when he argued that man's chief desire was not for immediate pleasure but for power and more power. On the basis of this argument, Caplow examines six possible power distributions in three-person groups and deduces predictions as to what coalitions will form if each person is trying to improve his relative power position. Thus where the formal theory of coalitions predicts random coalitions at asymptote, Caplow predicts certain regular coalitions depending on relative initial power positions.

Vinacke and Arkoff, being empiricists, are not particularly interested in the lines of speculation that led to these contrasting predictions. In their view the purpose of theory is to suggest operational definitions and experimental designs, and the payoff is the empirical regularities that are discovered and confirmed. Consequently they focus on the predictions and try to design an experiment that will determine which one is correct.

Their experiment consists of a board game in which each of three players is assigned a weight at the beginning of the game. For instance, player one might get a weight of 4, player two a weight of 3, and player three a weight of 2. Coalitions are permitted. The largest weight or combination of weights always wins the game; in the 4-3-2 distribution, player one wins if no coalitions are formed, but any coalition of two players can beat the third player. Each set of players goes through three series of plays, arranged in a Latin square. This means that in each separate play the weights are redistributed so that each play is different from every other.

The results are a triumph for Caplow's predictions. Caplow-type regularities appear in the coalitions, so Caplow wins and formal coalition theory loses. Vinacke, in his successive articles from 1959 through 1966, states with ever-increasing finality that he has confirmed Caplow's theory and disconfirmed formal coalition theory. Caplow, in turn, was reportedly happy that his speculations had been empirically confirmed.

Actually Vinacke and Arkoff have not tested either of the two theories they set out to test. The game-theoretic "prediction" of random coalitions holds only under the specific conditions listed in the postulates, and Vinacke and Arkoff did not set up those conditions. Specifically, game theory assumes perfectly rational men, and the experimental subjects were not perfectly rational and not even very bright. They were fooled by irrelevant differences in weights: in the 4-3-2 distribution the apparent differences are irrelevant, since any two players can win over the third, but the players acted as though they thought the differences were important. Nor did the experimenters determine whether the poker-chip playoff was the real payoff or whether the subjects had other interests during play. And in any case, three series of plays cannot possibly get to asymptote, and the "prediction" holds only at asymptote.

Nor are Caplow's hypotheses tested. Caplow interprets "payoff" as "change in relative power position" (1956, pp. 489-490), while Vinacke and Arkoff, as well as later experimenters, interpret it as "winning the game." Thus in a type-3 game, A=B>C (2-2-1), payoff to an AB coalition is zero for Caplow and 100 for Vinacke. Caplow himself notices this contrast in a later article (1959), in which he distinguishes "continuous" and "episodic" payoffs. He notes that he was thinking of continuous payoffs in his 1956 article, while the Vinacke and Arkoff experiment was intended as episodic.

On this basis Caplow should have concluded that the experiment was irrelevant to his 1956 theory, but he avoids this result by assuming that the
subjects "regarded the game situation as continuous even though the experimenters regarded it as episodic" (1959, p. 492), overlooking the Latin-
square design that makes continuous play impossible, and supporting his
ad hoc assumption by very dubious reasoning. Caplow also theorizes that
in episodic payoff situations, coalitions should be based on actual rather
than perceived weights, which is exactly the hypothesis that Vinacke thought
he had disproved.

I conclude that nothing at all has been tested by Vinacke and Arkoff
(1957), and that the strength of this renowned experiment is in its heuristic
suggestiveness.

Another example is provided by Suppes and Atkinson's *Markov Learning
Models for Multiperson Interactions* (1960). These experimenters wish,
among other things, to determine the comparative validity of learning theory
and game theory, and to do so have devised a series of crucial experiments
(1960, p. 2). They begin "by staying close to some thoroughly investigated
learning setup" (1960, p. 2), a setup only remotely resembling a game,
and then make a series of changes in the setup that cause it more and more
to resemble a game. At each step they make sure that game theory and
learning theory will yield differing "predictions," so that if the predictions of
one theory are always verified experimentally and the predictions of the
other theory always fail, the one is verified and the other falsified. For example, when two responses are rewarded with differential probability, say 60
per cent and 40 per cent, learning theory "predicts" that the two responses
will be chosen with the same probability (this is called probability matching)
while game theory "predicts" that at asymptote the more frequently rewarded response will be chosen every time, *given adequate information about
reward probabilities*. Both "predictions" are equilibrium predictions. The
experimenters find that the learning theory predictions are approximately verified and the game theory predictions not verified, and conclude that learning
theory has scored a validity point over game theory (1960, pp. 33, 92).
But has it? No; the experiments have nothing whatever to say about the validity of the two theories.

Consider an experimental setup in which two responses are differentially
rewarded in some constant proportion such as .60 and .40; this is, in general, the Suppes-Atkinson setup. Suppes and Atkinson's learning model
states that if learning as defined in the model takes place, that is, if a response probability is increased by reward at some constant rate, then at
asymptote probability matching *must* occur; thus the statement "if learning
occurs, probability matching will occur at asymptote" is a tautology, not a
prediction. A game or decision model states that if maximizing takes place,
the response that is rewarded with highest expected probability will always
be chosen at asymptote; thus, the statement "if maximization takes place,
the response with highest expected reward will always be chosen" is also a

tautology, not a prediction. Consequently, if probability matching occurs, this tells us nothing more than that learning has occurred and maximization has not occurred. Similarly, a result somewhere between probability matching and choice of highest expected reward (as happened in the Suppes-Atkinson experiments) tells us at most that some combination of learning and maximizing could be occurring. Now learning theory applies only to learning situations, and game theory applies only to maximization situations. Consequently, if maximization does not occur, game theory is not relevant, and if learning does not occur learning theory is not relevant. But a theory that is not relevant to an experiment cannot be falsified by it. Consequently this sort of experiment will tell us, at most, only what sort of theory is relevant to interpreting and explaining the results.

Thus Suppes and Atkinson have not invalidated game theory; what they have done is to demonstrate their skill in setting up a learning situation. Let us consider their setup to see how they have produced learning. Their subjects are run through a series of 210 trials, which continue without a break. Each trial lasts ten seconds; during that time a signal flashes, a button must immediately be selected and pushed, a reward light flashes, and the subject is given three seconds for rest and reflection. (In one experiment these three seconds also are pre-empted by flashing lights.) These are not conditions conducive to gathering and interpreting information, making calculations and predictions, and reaching decisions, though perhaps some expert mathematicians may succeed in doing so. They are conditions for learning, for the change of response rates through time, because the constant commotion on the signal board inhibits thought processes or attitudes that would interfere with learning. Estes and Straughan, discussing an earlier version of the Suppes-Atkinson setup, state explicitly that the signal board commotion was a control put in to inhibit rational thought: "The high rate of stimulus presentation was used in order to minimize verbalization on the part of Ss" (1954, p. 346); "verbalization" is the learning theorist's term for "thinking." Consider in contrast a game theory experiment with a similar signal board (Radlow, 1965). Here the game was preceded by elaborate instructions to make sure the subjects understood the game structure and the outcome of each strategy; when the results indicated some possible residual confusion, a second experiment with even more elaborate instructions was run. Thus the rational thought processes of the subjects were deliberately mobilized, with results appropriate to game theory, while in the Suppes and Atkinson experiments they were inhibited. Cf. also Rapoport, 1963, p. 573, and the instructions in Edwards' game-theory-oriented experiments (1961, p. 386): "You will find that you can improve your performance in the test if you pay attention and think what you are doing." Similarly, in binary choice experiments related to a hypothesis-testing model, the hypothesizing ability of subjects was stimulated by the experimenter's constant "Why? Why?" until the subject settled into a constant hypothesis-testing process (Feigenbaum and Feldman, 1963, pp. 339-340). Riker, in one of his coalition experiments, even welcomed campus gossip about his experiments and discussions among the subjects about how best to beat the game, because they helped to get the subjects into the proper rational-maximizing mood. "Since this was not an experiment in learning but rather one to determine behavior among relatively sophisticated subjects, this discussion was welcomed by the experimenter" (Riker, 1967, p. 59). In each of these cases the experimenter's activities or his experimental design were intended to provide an empirical exemplification of the postulates of a model with which he was working. In each case the experimental results conformed to the chosen model. Suppes and Atkinson's design was one appropriate to a learning model, so there is nothing remarkable in the fact that they got a learning output.

Another difficulty in the Suppes-Atkinson experiments is the question of whether asymptote was reached in 210 trials. Since both theories involved deal only with response probability at asymptote, this question is important. If one looks at the response curves, it does seem that they flatten out shortly before the end. However, Ward Edwards found in his 1000-trial game-theory-oriented experiments that with $\pi = .30$ or $.70$ and with game-theory-oriented instructions, the response curves were still sloping at the very end (Edwards, 1961, pp. 387, 392). Asymptote is a formal concept, an ideal limit, which can only be approximated in experiments. The question of whether it has been approximated sufficiently is one of interpretation and judgment, thus providing an easy entry for experimenter bias.

If the Suppes and Atkinson experiments have nothing to say about validity, do they at least tell us something about relevance? That is, do they clarify the conditions in which learning theory and game theory are relevant to the empirical world? In the case of learning theory, yes, a little. The initial setup adds nothing to our knowledge because, as the authors point out, it has already been thoroughly investigated by other learning theorists. We already know that a flashing light can be a reinforcer, given the proper experimental instructions, and that a button press can be a response, so in certain experimental conditions the formal terms "A" and "R" can be given the interpretations "button press" and "flashing light." What the experimenters have shown is that these interpretations are not invalidated by certain changes in the experimental instructions, and continue to hold even when two more lights are added to the signal board. In other words, they have extended the range of relevance of learning theory by two lights. Beyond this, they have suggested changes in learning models that would make them applicable to more situations—situations involving small monetary rewards, social conformity experiments, and perhaps even oligopoly conditions. These modifications make the models considerably more complex—one needs to speak of self-reinforcement, reinforcement by memory of the last i trials, and complex patterns of stimuli located in "the nuances of social communications" (1960, p. 265). At some early point the models become so complex that they are no longer mathematically workable. This situation does not invalidate learning theory, as the authors correctly observe (1960, p. 182), but merely shows that it is not useful to apply learning theory to ordinary, complex empirical situations at the present time.

Thus the authors have made a trivial contribution to our knowledge of the range of applicability of learning theory. For game theory they have done nothing. They recognize that game theory is relevant to some situations and have carefully avoided those situations (1960, p. 182); they show that game theory is not relevant, in its simplest forms, to other situations. But they have not explored the intermediate ground, as, for instance, Lieberman has done (1962). It is instructive to contrast the authors' approach to game theory with that of Deutsch and Krauss (1962). The latter introduced factors that inhibit rationality in order to explore the conditions of rational behavior; Suppes and Atkinson also introduced inhibiting factors, but illegitimately concluded that theories of rational behavior are invalid.

The situation now seems to be that learning theory and game theory are both formal theories and therefore neither true nor false in general; both have areas of obvious applicability, which in both cases can be extended greatly by constructing more complicated models; at some point the models become too complex to be mathematically tractable or practically useful. The purpose of experimentation should be to locate further areas of applicability and to suggest further modifications of models, not to verify or falsify. Incidentally, Suppes and Atkinson are inconsistent in rejecting as "little more than an ingenious attempt" (1960, p. 94) a modification of a game model that is much more simple and direct than the ambitious complexities they cheerfully propose for learning models.

My impression is that Suppes and Atkinson are not alone among learning theorists in their tendency to treat a mathematical model as an empirical hypothesis to be tested. The way in which mathematical learning theory experiments are conducted suggests that the intention usually is to test the validity of a hypothesis. The experiments are very carefully controlled, and statistical analyses are made of the results. The ideal result is a complete fit between model and data; if statistically significant discrepancies appear, the experiment is treated as a disconfirmation and in that sense a failure. There is no interest in analyzing the discrepancies, except perhaps to suggest some new experimental control that would eliminate them. Thus progress consists of developing ever tighter controls in "tests" of essentially the same models, instead of developing ever better models through the experimental production and study of discrepancies. If a model is "validated" it becomes available for further testing in somewhat different experimental conditions. Sooner or later it is disconfirmed, and takes its place among the other models that may or may not be "true." The results of all this experimentation so far are discouraging (as of 1966). A deluge of models has flowed over us, each with some experimental validation of $p < .01$ to its credit, and some with disconfirmations as well. Apparently some models apply to some situations and others to other situations, but the basis of applicability is not clear. Thus nothing definite is being accomplished by these carefully designed and controlled and analyzed experiments. Models are being "verified" at a great rate, but not really; the limits of relevance of a model are generally not being uncovered by boundary experiments, and most important, there is little exploration to find bases for improved models. As Harrison White complains, "They control so many things that there is no possibility of finding out interesting things about human interaction" (1963b, p. 306). The alternative is not to omit all controls, but to leave just enough looseness so the results can suggest new ideas for improved models.

It may be that this situation is only temporary and that some invincible model will presently appear; indeed, one occasionally hears rumors that the long-awaited perfect model has just been discovered. But my impression is that learning theorists are attempting the impossible, as well as the useless, when they try to verify a formal model experimentally.

The explanation for this state of affairs is probably historical. Mathematical learning theorists see themselves as carrying on the unbroken tradition of scientific experimental learning theory that goes back to Pavlov and beyond. The experimenters of the 1930's and 1940's—Hull, Spence, Guthrie, Tolman, etc.—were empiricists both in their ideology and in their learning theory. Their theories were substantive propositions about organisms, not mathematical structures subject to multiple interpretation. For instance, for Hull a stimulus is a physical impact on physiological receptors; it sets up an electrical impulse that travels along the nerves and, after much interaction and many intervening adventures, ends up in a muscle (Hull, 1943, ch. 3 ff). The physiological receptors are all known and the kind of physical impact that will stimulate them is also known, so there is nothing mysterious about a stimulus. Propositions about stimuli are substantive propositions about definite physiological and physical events. Experimental interest is focused on testing specific propositions stating that a certain physical input is connected to a certain muscle movement. The propositions are are expressed verbally at first, and reasoning is verbal and fallible (Hull, 1943). Mathematics is seen as quantification, a way to make propositions more exact (cf. Hull, 1952); if diagrams are used, they are illustrative only and nothing can be deduced from them (cf. Tolman, 1951).

There are implicit formal elements in Hull's theorizing, but they remain far in the background. Skinner, in contrast, is obviously an implicit formal theorist. In his work the whole substantive physiological basis of earlier learning theorists drops out, and with it the testing of substantive hypotheses; interest shifts to the discovery and exploration of regular, reproducible mathematical relations, that is, smooth curves. Skinner is not interested in finding out what exact physiological and physical entities are stimuli, responses, and reinforcements—in this sense he is not interested in "theory"—but in exploring the formal characteristics of the equilibrium systems created by various schedules of reinforcement. These systems are composed of a schedule of reinforcement, that is, a ratio of reinforcement to response; a response frequency rate or pattern; a resulting reinforcement rate or pattern; and a rate of weight loss or gain that feeds back on response frequency (1959a, p. 100 ff). Some systems are stable, others unstable in that they move either toward zero—"nothing but starvation lies ahead in that direction" (1959a, p. 108) —or toward satiation. Skinner tells how one can explore the unstable systems to find the exact critical ratio that produces equilibrium. Note that in these experiments Skinner has made the crucial shift away from the empiricist correlation of variables to the formalist study of whole equilibrium systems.

Skinner's terms are also implicitly formal or relational. For example, in his article "The Generic Nature of the Concepts of Stimulus and Response" (reprinted in 1959a; originally 1935) he argues that one chooses the exact specification of S and R by seeing what correlates regularly. Thus an uncorrelated S or R cannot, by definition, exist. Similarly, in his first book he states, "A reinforcing stimulus is defined as such by its power to produce the resulting change. Some stimuli are found to produce the change, others not, and they are classified as reinforcing and nonreinforcing accordingly" (Skinner, 1938, p. 62, quoted in Meehl, 1950). Thus a reinforcer that does not increase response rate cannot exist.

Learning theory becomes formal, in principle unfalsifiable, and therefore neither true nor false. Interest lies not in testing particular S-R hypotheses but in exploring the mathematical characteristics (Skinner calls this "order") of various types of learning, which is a typical formalist approach to experimentation. Learning theory is applied to real life by showing that some relational structure studied in the laboratory also occurs in real-life—for example, a variable-ratio schedule of reinforcement is exemplified in gambling (1959a, p. 106)—and that the real-life output is therefore determined and explained by the formal structure, the schedule of reinforcement, etc., implicit in the activity. The parallel between Skinner's reinforcement models and McPhee's formal addiction model (1963, ch. 5) is striking.

With Estes, Skinner's pupil, and the mathematically trained Bush and Mosteller, the formalism implicit in earlier learning theory becomes explicit. S, for instance, is now explicitly formal; it stands for a set of unknown entities (Estes, 1959, pp. 399, 424-427; Suppes and Atkinson, 1960, p. 3), and is defined relationally rather than operationally. Propositions are formulated initially as equations, and reasoning is rigorously mathematical.

But alongside this shift to formal theory the empiricist ideology has apparently remained unchanged, so that the experimental method properly used by the empiricists is applied to a formal theory unsuited to it. This conflict could be creative, as I believe it has been in much experimental work with formal theories in that new types of experimentation and new theories have been developed. Estes' innovations in experimental design are an example. But with statistical learning theorists this has happened only infrequently, as far as I can tell.

If practice elsewhere is a proper guide, statistical learning theorists should stop working toward the perfectly controlled experiment that will verify the perfect model. Instead, they should determine the limits of relevance of existing models, by boundary experiments, and beyond this they should use learning models as baselines for exploration, as for example Bush and Mosteller have suggested (1955, pp. 235-236), and Rapoport and Chammah (1965, pp. 84-86) and Cohen (1963, pp. 41-43) have done. In these exploratory experiments learning theory becomes a kind of null hypothesis; if it is verified, nothing else of interest is happening and the experiment is a failure. Experiments should be so devised that the null hypothesis fails, so that we can learn, from the way it fails, "interesting new things about human interaction." Or, alternatively, researchers can follow the lead provided by Skinner's interesting formalist experiments.

Now look at this question from the standpoint of the empiricist. He would say, I imagine, "We know about this distinction between a model and its interpretations, but it isn't all that important. We want truths about the real, everyday world, not formal truths laid up in a Platonic heaven. If a formal theory, that is a model and an ordinary, plausible interpretation, does not apply to the everyday world, we are not interested in it. You may think you are saving the model by reinterpreting it so it doesn't apply to anything recognizable or real, but you are merely making it irrelevant to the real world. Take specifically game theory. If you claim that game theory applies only to perfectly minimax-rational people, and it is agreed that there are no such people alive, then game theory applies to nothing and is worthless. Either it applies to real human beings or it is useless. Perhaps learning theory does not apply to real people either—it hasn't been conclusively proved that it does—but we want to find out whether it does by treating it as an empirical hypothesis and testing it."

There are two answers to this objection. One is provided by Luce (1959, pp. 133-134), who argues that it is appropriate to reinterpret a formal model if this is not done ad hoc or arbitrarily and if the result is to find some way in which the model does apply to the real world. The other answer is that a simple law or model of the sort developed by learning theorists rarely applies directly to everyday behavior outside the laboratory. Even granted that we are trying to capture only the logical "essence" of a system or process and not all the empirical details, still such essences are likely to be more complex than a 2 x 2 game or an incremental learning model with two response possibilities. The point of such simple models is to serve as a skeleton or a module of more complex, more adequate models, and these cannot be developed by constructing ever more elaborate tests of the simple models.

In any case, I have argued in this whole chapter that the purpose of experimental work with mathematical models is not to test the "truth" of simple, abstract skeleton models. It is to explore experimental situations similar to those postulated in the models and to locate possible modifications that will make the models more complex and realistic. Testing can occur intermittently during this search process, but a model is never tested as a whole; that would be pointless. What one does instead is determine the conditions of relevance of an interpreted model, and then make improvements that expand its area of relevance.

5

The Analysis and Verification of Computer Models

The special problems of computer models have only recently begun to appear, because the method is still new. For some years the primary concern was, first, to demonstrate the theoretical feasibility of simulation and, second, to construct models that would actually run. The concern with theoretical feasiβility manifested itself in discussions of concepts to show that they could be formalized in terms of some computer language, and in the development of appropriate languages. The second concern manifested itself in discussions of technical problems, such as debugging routines and error traps. But once these problems had been solved and working models constructed, the problems of analysis and verification began to loom up as the really difficult ones.

The goal of analysis is to determine exactly how output follows from a program. One wants to know what each part of the program contributes to the output, and what changes in output would result from a change in each part of the program. The difficulty lies in the complexity of most computer programs. The whole point of using computers rather than mathematics is that computers make possible more complex and therefore more realistic models, but this advantage brings with it a corresponding increase in the difficulty of analysis (cf. Hoggatt and Balderston, 1963, pp. 186-191, for a discussion of the problem of analysis, and pp. 275-286 for an illustration).

The most straightforward analytic technique is to assume that each parameter or subroutine is substantially independent in the sense that it produces its own unique effect on output. The effect is then discovered, in the manner of an experiment, by holding everything constant except one parameter and seeing what output changes correlate with changes in that parameter. If there are a considerable number of parameters and crucial subroutines, each one must be studied separately, and the result is a large set of outputs. This technique works insofar as parameters actually are independent, but it fails to locate interdependences. In principle these too can be discovered by expanding the output sample sufficiently. For example, if three parameters are interdependent it is not enough to hold two constant while varying the third; it is also necessary to hold them constant at varying levels and varying ratios. As the number of parameters increases, the number of runs required increases rapidly and soon becomes impossibly large. Consequently it is necessary to devise output sampling strategies, and devising a good strategy depends heavily on hunch and intuition.

Another technique is to use a multiple regression procedure on the output sample. This technique will locate the most important parameters of the model and show how the influence of each is distributed over the output variables. For instance, a particular parameter might be especially important in controlling three output variables, have a lesser influence on six others, and show no appreciable influence on the rest. However, this technique also fails to take account of interdependences, since the regression procedure assumes that each input factor is independent of all the rest (cf. Hoggatt and Balderston, 1963, pp. 190, 281).

To locate interdependences, one can follow the trace of a run in detail to see just how the effect of some parameter or subroutine is modified by the successive routines of the model. One can even see how the effect of an earlier routine is completely eliminated by later routines (cf. McPhee, 1963, p. 183: "A lot of dynamics went nowhere"). The disadvantage of this technique is that it is laborious and unsystematic. It works well for locating a few basic interdependences, but as the varying traces of a complex model pile up, one rapidly gets lost in a maze of contingencies and alternatives.

A more radical solution is to construct one's model out of a series of basic mathematical processes. The GPSS language is especially suited to such a tactic, since each statement in the language is actually a whole standard subroutine. Since each mathematical subroutine is already well understood, the only remaining problem is to see how they interact, and this can be done by studying output traces. The basic difficulty of this solution is that it radically limits the amount of flexibility possible in a model (cf. Newell, 1962). Since each mathematical subroutine is isolated from all the others, one is limited to making detailed changes within a subroutine or changing the sequence of subroutines; intercommunication between subroutines immediately produces difficulties.

Other techniques of analysis continue to be developed, for example, spectral analysis, which factors out oscillations in time-path outputs. One or another of the available techniques may well be adequate for the analysis of a specific model, but as models become still more complex, analysis will continue to be a problem. The main point of analysis is to facilitate the improving of models through successive approximations; difficulties of analysis compound the difficulties of working out reliable improvements. This is the real problem in computer modeling—not simply constructing a model that runs, but knowing how to make it run better.

The process of empirical testing and improvement consists in setting parameters according to observed values where possible, guessing the other parameter values, collecting an output sample, and comparing the sample with empirical data. The discrepancies between output and data are supposed to suggest model changes that will reduce them. Insofar as the model-builder knows through prior analysis what routine or parameter of the model produces the discrepant ouput, he also knows where the error is located and can take steps to remedy it. The proper procedure is to re-examine the specific subprocess that was erroneously modeled to see what correction should be made. This can be done by directly observing the real system being modeled, by experimentally isolating the process for more careful controlled examination, or by some other technique. Then the corrected model is run again to see whether the discrepancy has been reduced. For example, K. Cohen mentions two cases in which odd or discrepant outcomes led to re-examination of the system being modeled. In one case the model had no special mechanism for dealing with large price changes, mainly because such changes had not occurred during the period of initial observation of the firm; an extensive search was necessary to discover the mechanism. In another case remarkably long delivery delays appearing in model output made the modelers realize they had neglected to include any function for losing customers because of delivery delay (Cohen and Cyert, 1965, ch. 8).

But this process of correction is possible only insofar as the model-builder knows the source of any particular output error through prior analysis of his model. If analysis has been inadequate, a discrepancy can serve only as a general error signal, since the model-builder does not know what part or parts of the model are responsible for it. Consequently, if he wants to improve the model he must re-examine almost the entire system he is modeling. Since this would be prohibitively difficult, the temptation is to take the easier path of "tinkering" with the model, changing this and that on hunches or at random until the discrepancy is reduced. Unfortunately the same output changes can be produced by a variety of model changes, particularly in view of the many degrees of freedom of a computer model with its many parameters, and so tinkering is most unlikely to lead to substantive improvement. The model may eventually be made to reproduce a given set of empirical data, but there is no assurance that the data are produced by the same process that occurs in the real system, and therefore no assurance that simulation is occurring. Tinkering is analogous to curve-fitting in empirical work; it enables one to summarize data but not to describe the process that produced them. But if one gives up the aim of describing underlying substantive processes there is no reason to use a computer at all; data can be summarized more simply with a few equations.

A second difficulty in verification is that the empirical data (and not the model) may themselves be in error or misleading. The point of a simulation model is to describe an empirical system or process with some degree of detail and from a particular standpoint. Output data help by providing information about what the system has produced, but any given output datum may be unrepresentative and misleading because it was produced under un-usual circumstances. Econometricians are familiar with this problem in deal-ing with economic statistics, and routinely allow for unusual circumstances such as wars, depressions, seasonal variations, and strikes. Similarly, a par-ticular price or production decision may have been made in the absence of a regular administrator, or experimental responses may have been based on mishearing or misunderstanding (Feigenbaum and Feldman, 1963, p. 346), or meters may have been read incorrectly (Greenberger, 1965, p. 149). To be sure, if there are large masses of output data the few misleading items will disappear in the mass; but data are not usually available in large masses, and may in some cases be quite sparse. Large masses of data can be produced when one is modeling a simple abstract process that can be repeated again and again in the laboratory; but when one is studying a complex system that labors mightily to produce a single output, one must be satisfied with relatively sparse data. The same is true when one is study-ing a relatively complex but reproducible process like problem-solving, where it may take fifteen minutes to produce a single output. When output data are sparse, direct observation or controlled experimental study of the empirical system is necessary to reveal which output data are reliable, which unrepresentative, and which probably erroneous.

These two difficulties together make model improvement a difficult and complicated affair. A discrepancy between model and data may be due to defects in the model, or to unrealiability or error in the data, or some combination of the two. A defect in a model, even a well-analyzed one, may consist either of a misestimated parameter or two, or a sub-stantive error, or both; and a defect in a poorly analyzed model may be almost anything.

To sum up, the empirical difficulties involved in testing and improving computer models seem to center in difficulties with output data. First, when one is simulating complex systems or processes, output data are likely to be relatively sparse and unreliable. Second, when one reasons backward from output discrepancies to possible model changes, the large number of parameters and postulates in a computer model give one much too much freedom in deciding what changes to try. Any number of possible changes might reduce output discrepancy more or less, one way or another, and one cannot tell from output data alone which changes are correct. The fal-lacy of affirming the consequent is serious in simulation.

The implication seems to be that when one is improving a simulation model, one should place primary reliance not on output data but on direct observation of the component parts of the system being simulated. In other words, one should where possible construct a synthetic rather than an ex-planatory model (cf. ch. 3). A synthetic model is constructed when one knows and understands the individual components of a complex system or process but not how the whole system operates. During construction the main reliance is on direct observation of the component parts, and output data are used only as a less reliable secondary check. A discrepancy between model output and empirical data is treated mainly as a warning to re-examine the relevant part of the system and to recheck the relevant postulates; if the discrepancy persists the empirical data are treated as doubtful, and new data are collected if possible. Because of the difficulties in interpreting output discrepancies in computer models, they are especially suited to this method. In contrast, explanatory models, with their primary dependence on reliable and intelligible output data, are likely to maximize the difficulties of verification.

Synthetic models are most appropriate in studying systems or processes whose component parts are directly observable or knowable: firms, organizations, economies, communication and transportation systems, mass behavior, neural nets. Individual cognitive processes and personalities, with their relatively unobservable components, are more suited to explanatory modeling. Consequently it seems likely that the strength of computer simulation will lie in the modeling of large, readily observable complex systems, and that personality models are going to be difficult to develop properly. And further, even in the development of personality models it will be important to devise better ways of getting directly at the personality processes being modeled. The simulation of cognitive processes has pointed the way here by developing the technique of collecting verbal protocols. But these protocols are not reliable indicators of underlying mental processes and therefore are more suitable as a source of hypotheses than as a basis for verification. Personality and small group models could depend, analogously, on clinical observation; but clinical observation is not highly reliable either, once it is taken out of its active and continuing clinical context. Another difficulty with clinical observation is that it involves continuous participation in (and changing of) the system being observed. Clinicians are aware of this problem and know how to deal with it, but it is one more problem added to all the others that occur in the simulation of personality. No doubt these problems will eventually be solved, but it will not be easy.

In the construction of synthetic computer models, one promising tactic is to build the model up from individually verified modules or microcomponents. Orcutt (1963, p. 222 ff.) and McPhee (1963, pp. 8-17) in particular have commended this tactic. Each module is built up and verified separately, and is improved and modified until it is adequate; when the whole model is put together all that remains is to see whether the interrelations are correct. In this way analysis and verification of the total model are reduced to a minimum, and most of the work is done with small, more easily analyzable and verifiable components. Unfortunately this tactic is not always feasible.

A more basic tactic is to give up some of the technologically possible complexity for the sake of greater analytic clarity. This means avoiding complications that are introduced solely to provide greater realism, as well as complications added to allow for empirical variants, and perhaps even some useful complications. It may be advisable to construct a skeleton model whose workings can be easily analyzed (flow charts sometimes perform this function informally), and then to add only a few variants and details as they are needed. This tactic implies a repudiation of the earlier claim that computers have made simplicity unnecessary in scientific theory. Simplicity, though of a different order than needed in mathematical models, is still necessary to enable us to maintain analytic control over our computer models.

An extreme example of the difficulties that result when one ignores the requirement of simplicity is the proposed Orcutt model (Orcutt et al., 1961), which proved to be so impossibly complex that, I hear, it had to be abandoned before completion. A similar fate, I hope temporary, seems to have overtaken the proposed Bales model (Bales et al., 1962), which also ignored the requirement of logical clarity and simplicity in favor of empirical realism of postulates (Philip Stone, personal communication). Computer simulation has not made mathematical thinking obsolete, as may once have seemed possible; it represents rather a chance to combine the analytic clarity of mathematical thinking with at least a reasonable amount of empirical complexity and realism.

6

Types of Formal Theories

Formal theories have been classified in a variety of ways, each typology bringing out some distinctions and emphasizing some similarities. I wish to mention a few distinctions briefly here, chiefly to indicate some of the ranges of possibility open to a formal theorist.

From economics I take the useful distinction between *aggregate* and *structural* models. This is a continuum rather than a sharp division, and movement in a structural direction is called *disaggregation*. A structural model claims to represent or describe the actual structure of some empirical system or process, while an aggregate model deals only with averages, totals, or main outlines of a system or process. The Keynesian model is a typical aggregate model; it deals with total consumption, investment, and income in a whole economy. Relations between these categories are either total or average relations; thus total income in one time period is either consumed or invested in the next time period (note the relational conception of all these terms), investment at t_1 produces income at t_2 at an average rate, and there are average rates of profit, production costs, and time lags. Later econometric models are considerably more disaggregated: the Klein-Goldberger model (Goldberger, 1959, Hoggatt and Balderston, 1963, pp. 177-180) distinguishes farms, households, businesses, and government, each with its own type of assets, wage bills, income, profit rates, and output; there are five kinds of taxes, two kinds of interest rates, and so on, amounting altogether to 38 variables and 21 equations in the model. The proposed Orcutt model of the U. S. economy (Orcutt et al., 1961) is still more disaggregated. The household sector, for example, consists of a representative sample of more than 2,300 households. Each one is characterized by over two dozen status variables and over twenty output variables, and the distribution of initial values of each of these variables is supposed to be representative of the actual U.S. distribution in some year. Each household goes through a complex decision-making process to determine the value of its output variables. Outputs are distributed and collected as inputs to a

101

large set of "markets," of which some of the outputs become inputs to households while others become inputs to banks, insurance companies, firms, farms, etc. Thus there are many types of decision-making units, each with its own decision procedure; many types of markets, each with its own pricing mechanism; and many variables to characterize each unit. Each type of unit and of market is represented by a large number of individuals serving as a representative sample of the corresponding units in the U.S. economy.

McPhee's "campaign simulator" (1963, chs. 2, 4) is an example both of disaggregation and of formalization of empirical attitude surveys. In the empirical surveys a sample is drawn from a population, data generated by the sample are summarized, and the results are extrapolated to the whole population. Theoretical interest is focused primarily on the empirical reliability of the sample, rather than on the structure or process that produces opinions. While the campaign simulator is still based on samples of a population, each person in the sample is represented by a simulated process of opinion formation: The person meets a given opinion with a probability based on his position in a communication net, discusses it with a probabilistically selected close acquaintance, makes up his mind through a process of cognitive balance, encounters new opinions, and so on. Further disaggregation in this model can proceed in two directions: Either the sample can be enlarged until it approaches identity with the total population being modeled or the microstructure of communication and opinion formation can be modeled in greater and greater detail. For the model's purposes, however, further disaggregation would be a mistake, as it would introduce unnecessary complexity (cf. ch. 5).

Another example of an aggregate model is the group of so-called social gravity models, of which Zipf's is the best known (cf. Catton, 1965, for a gravity model, and Huff, 1965, for a criticism from a structuralist standpoint). These models treat people as molecules whose aggregate motions in social space can be described by a few simple equations. The corresponding structural model might be based on utility theory or something analogous; the movements of individuals would be explained or predicted in terms of their utility spaces, and the total change in population distribution would reflect the interaction of changing opportunity and utility spaces. Intermediate models would deal with population samples rather than with individuals.

Stochastic learning theory is all aggregative; it deals with classes of stimuli sampled probabilistically, with probabilistic response classes, and with average learning rates; and it seeks to correlate the average changes of response ratios over time with stimulus ratios. The two- and three-stage models make a beginning at disaggregation, since they seek to describe at least the main structural steps of a learning process. However, even here the steps remain hypothetical and they seem more like arbitrary constructs —epicycles—than serious attempts to chart a process. In contrast, the aim of Hull and his contemporaries, in their theorizing at least, was thoroughly structural; they wanted to describe the exact physiological way in which behavior was generated and learning took place.

It is difficult to imagine a structural counterpart for some aggregative models. These are models of random processes in which the underlying microstructure, if any, is unknown: the statistical models such as Poisson, Yule-Greenwood, and others, which describe the average outcome of some sort of random process; the Coleman-James model of random groups, which is a truncated Poisson model (Goodman, 1964); and many of the random process models in Coleman's work (1964). There is no obvious way to disaggregate these models, and if one is interested in microstructure one must turn to an entirely different sort of model, such as a utility model or a game-theoretic model.

Structural and aggregate models differ both in the kind of formal language they use and in the kind of empirical work required to develop them. Aggregate models are almost always probabilistic since they deal with masses of events distributed over one or more dimensions, while structural models are more nearly deterministic since they deal with determinate structures. However, even a detailed model of a structure can be aggregative for its still finer microstructure, so probabilities may still appear. Recent structural models often are computer simulations because complex structures are beyond the power of mathematics to model, but simpler structures such as communication nets and some input-output systems can be described mathematically. Aggregate models tend to use complex mathematical equations, including random variables, and if computers are used it is usually in their role as calculators, to solve the equations.

Empirically, initial construction of aggregate models requires little knowledge of their subject matter; all that is usually required is a superficial knowledge of its main features and their relations. However, improvement of the initial model (here, not disaggregation) through successive approximations requires elaborate statistical data, suitably analyzed, factored, or scaled, according to the requirements of the model. Model development often involves parameter estimation and curve-fitting techniques, since the details of the model must grow out of the latent structure to be found in the data. Structural models require more intimate knowledge of their subject matter than is afforded by output statistics; they require process records, reports based on direct observation of process, questionnaires designed to bring out sociometric patterns of interaction and preference, or departmental records within a firm.

Extreme aggregate models are difficult to distinguish, on first glance, from empirical generalizations such as regression equations or the outcomes of factor analyses. Consequently the question may arise as to whether these are formal models at all, that is, representations of some logic or necessity to be found in fact. How does a formal model of a random process like the formation of groups at a street corner or the lines at a post-office window or the flow of money or traffic differ from a plain factual report of what usually happens? To be sure, for an empiricist who conceives his only function to be testing models statistically, say an empirically minded econometrician or survey researcher, the distinction is not important (as Coleman observes, 1964, p. 291). He will take any plausible hypothesis available without regard to its source or nature and will be concerned primarily with operationalizing and measuring the variables. Thus the distinction between empirical and formal is sometimes a matter only of how a model is used or treated; nevertheless the distinction can also be expressed in terms of what is there. A formal model, even an aggregate one, describes in outline those constant characteristics of a structure or process that constrain its output, its time path, or in general the data it emits. These constant characteristics represent a necessity or "logic" that constrains the data and from which certain features of the data can be deduced a priori. An empirical equation ("empirical model") contains little or no such logic; it merely describes distributions or correlations of data that have in fact occurred and says nothing about the structure that produced them. Consequently nothing can be deduced from them, although they can be juggled and sifted for clues to some hidden underlying structure, as in latent structure analysis.

The distinction between empirical and formal equations (or "models") is important to a formalist, since he cannot perform his deductions and analyses unless there is something there with which to work. In the case of aggregate models, the "logic" or necessity consists of statements of necessary steps in a process and of logically complete classifications of alternative paths or outcomes. For example, in a post-office queue people must enter the line at a random rate and leave it at an average rate determined by the various possible transactions at the window. This may seem like a flimsy, trifling bit of necessity, yet all the formidable mathematical apparatus of queuing theory is built on it. Similarly, a traffic flow must move along streets, entering or leaving at definite points; each point and each street has a maximum capacity and an average rate of use. Income must be either consumed or invested, and output must go either to "households," "government," "export," or other firms; there are no other logical possibilities. For a formalist these are all logical categories relationally defined; for instance a "household" is defined by its distinctive inputs, transformation processes, and outputs, rather than by the daily drama that goes on inside a house. The question of what empirical entities should be treated as households is a matter of interpretation, not of logic.

Another distinguishing characteristic of a formal aggregate model is that its logical categories and relations are open to alternative empirical exemplifications. Thus queuing theory applies not just to physical lines of people but to any process that has a random input, no internal transformation, and an average output. The economic theory of the firm can be applied, not only to automobile manufacturers but also to municipal politics, professional associations, and college fraternities. In contrast, as I mentioned earlier, the empiricist is not interested in the possibility of alternative interpretations; he is interested in describing his particular subject matter, and asks only whether his model describes it accurately. Consequently he may uncritically assume a particular interpretation of his model and ignore the possibility of alternative interpretation, just as the formalist ignores the details of a particular case in his search for a generalizable piece of logic.

The distinction between structural and aggregate models is not intended invidiously; each has its own appropriate uses. However, the usual line of development for formal models has been from aggregative to structural (except, of course, for those random process models that cannot be disaggregated). I think the reason is that structural models are more "thoroughly" formal than aggregative models. The point of a formal model is to describe some relational structure, some piece of logic, that is exemplified in reality, and while both kinds of formal models do this, structural models are likely to do it more thoroughly. Consequently, whatever uses and advantages formal models possess are likely to be found to a greater extent in structural models. Here again the major exception is stochastic learning theory, where the line of development has been from the structural models of the 1930's to the aggregate models of the 1950's. The explanation again is probably historical; the structural models were in difficulties (cf. Osgood, 1953, chs. 9, 10).

Cutting across the aggregate-structural continuum is a second continuum that ranges from models of some limited, abstract segment of behavior to models of a total, relatively self-contained system or process. The limited models deal with the dynamics of a bit of behavior under highly specified conditions, with other things assumed to be equal. The classical model of rational choice and the stochastic learning theories are both limited models, since both specify limiting conditions in some detail. In general, any model of experimentally induced behavior will be limited, since the point of experimentation is to isolate a specific bit of behavior for study. For example, Cohen's conflict and conformity model (1963) deals with behavior in a specified situation that was originally induced experimentally. In operations research the so-called sub-optimization models are limited; they deal with an inventory problem, production programming, or a selling campaign, but not with optimization for the whole firm.

Total models deal with relatively self-contained systems, such as a whole economy, a whole industry, a whole firm, a whole personality, or a whole discussion group. The modeler's primary interest is in the internal relations between parts of the system; in limited models there is also inescapably an interest in the relation between parameters, which represent the specified external conditions, and variables. Total models obviously cannot use experimental data unless they are derived from holistic Bales-type experiments. Instead they depend on official statistics, surveys, or direct observation of the systems. Limited models are all mathematical or logical, while total models, because of their complexity, are usually associated with computers, except for some general equilibrium and business cycle models in economics.

The terms *total* and *limited* should both be taken relatively, since every formal model deals with a somewhat isolatable, self-contained system or process, but no system is completely self-contained. Nevertheless, there is a characteristic difference between, say, a queuing model and a model of an economy. And more important, there is usually a range of options open to the model-builder with regard to the number of things he wishes to assume as parameters and the number of things he wishes to include as endogenous variables.

The usual line of development, when there is one, is from limited toward total models. It is obviously simpler to begin by studying some sharply delimited phenomenon, and when one has come to understand that well, to go on to more and more complicated phenomena containing the first one. Experimental work in game theory illustrates this sort of development nicely; the earliest experiments specified payoffs, players, and strategies quite sharply, while later experimenters have introduced ever more complicating factors —communication, uncertain payoffs, unequal power, indeterminate strategies, policing, and so on. The complications make the game less artificial and more like some real, relatively self-contained system, say, an oligopolistic industry or a bipolar international system or a small legislature. Nevertheless the development from limited toward total models is by no means continuous, universal, or rapid, since there are many limited models that are useful just as they are.

A third continuum of options for the model-builder is from the general to the specific. His model can describe either a certain type of system, or one specific system at a specific time, or something in between. The former models are called norm-descriptive and the latter case-descriptive. For example, one can work with a model of a generalized economy, or with a model of an underdeveloped economy that resembles the economy of India (Holland, 1963), or with a model of one specific economy (Orcutt, 1961) or industry (K. Cohen, 1960). The builder of a generalized (norm-descriptive) model needs information of a variety of examples so he can distinguish essential elements from accidental variations, while the builder of a case-descriptive model needs detailed structural and time-series information about his specific case. Both types of model-builder can work closely together and use each other's work; the general models provide a framework that can be particularized, while the specific models can provide a check on the generality of the general models. Thus the operations researcher carries a battery of general models in his kit as he approaches a specific problem, adapting one of them to the case at hand; the case in turn may provide a clarification, generalization, or special variant of the general model.

Case-descriptive models have usually been relatively total models of the computer simulation type, describing a complex system in some detail. However, one can also construct a limited mathematical model of a particular system; for instance one could construct a sociogram of a particular communication net, or a payoff matrix of an international system at a particular time. In such a sociogram the theorems of graph theory could be brought to bear in analyzing the logic of the system, namely the possibilities and limitations of communication in it. In the second case the conclusions of game theory could be used to analyze the pattern of forces operative in each cell of the matrix to produce a time path, and also to discover the time-path effects of changes in payoff values.

One may question whether and in what sense case-descriptive models are formal at all. Is it not essential to a formal model that it be distinguished from its various possible interpretations? But a case-descriptive model can have only one interpretation, because it is of one specific thing. Is this not history, then, or naturalistic description, rather than formal science?

The formal element of a case-descriptive model is located in its modules (McPhee, 1963, pp. 8-17) or component parts. Each module describes the structure of some general system or process, some general bit of logic that has multiple exemplifications. For example, each component of the Orcutt model is, or should have been, a general type of input-output system. The total model is made unique by the particular combination of modules used, the particular connections among them, and the specific parameter values assigned. This means that the logic of the model's component parts is already known and can be directly brought to bear on the analysis of the model.

7

Uses of Models

The aim of formal theories is to give us an understanding of a relational structure that exists somewhere in the world. Once this aim has been achieved by developing an adequate, well-interpreted, and well-analyzed model, the model can be used in various ways.

1. A model can be used to summarize data. A good experiment yields an output of thousands of numbers, which by themselves mean nothing. If the experimenter has a model that adequately describes his experimental setup, he can reduce all his numbers to the two or three parameters of the model. The thousands of numbers then become instances of the probability distributions described in the model, and some numbers become errors or random disturbances due to uncontrolled experimental conditions. For example, Bush and Mosteller observe that their learning model can at least be used to reduce their experimental output of about a thousand numbers to just three numbers without a loss of information (1955, pp. 235, 333-336). The three numbers are parameters of an equation, and the equation describes the form of a curve, with variances, that covers nearly every one of the individual items.

This descriptive use is normally preliminary to some other use, since few scientists are content simply to report data. Once the data have been summarized and made manageable, they must be used for something—to test, to make inferences, to diagnose, to predict, etc.

2. A model can be used to explain data by deducing them. Here interest lies not in the data but in the system or process that produces them, and the theorist tries to discover the inner structure of this system and describe it in his model. The process of explaining data by deducing them can also be regarded as a verification of the hypothesis that the model adequately describes the system or process being studied. Strictly speaking, of course, what is verified is not the model but an interpretation of it, since it is the interpretation that ties the model to a specific subject matter.

Sometimes appropriate models are already available, and the theorist has

108

only to adapt them to his particular data; in that case what he has discovered is a new interpretation of a model. At other times he must construct a model almost from the beginning, or out of parts of other models; in that case his task proceeds in the fashion I have indicated earlier (ch. 3). Note, however, that a theory that was originally developed synthetically may be put to an explanatory use. For instance, marginal utility theory, originally synthetic, can be used to explain the output data of small groups (Homans, 1961).

3. In the explanatory-deductive use described above, the interest moves from reliable output data to dubious postulates. A successful explanation increases one's confidence that the postulates as interpreted actually describe the subject matter under study. We turn now to a synthetic use, in which interest moves in the opposite direction: the use of a model to interpret or make inferences from data. The terms of a calculus can be treated as place-holders for empirical content, and data can be substituted for them. If the data are reliable and if the calculus correctly describes the real relations existing in the subject matter from which the data were gathered, the theorems of the calculus will yield valid inferences from the data. For example (see Coleman, 1964, pp. 254-255), suppose we have the following data for a population: birth rate, total population, total population for each age in years, and death rate for each age in years. Of themselves these numbers imply nothing; they must be placed into a deductive calculus to have implications. But the implications will be valid only if the calculus used represents the relations that really exist between birth, aging, death, and birth and death rates. We know fairly well what these relations are; aging is a continuous process in time, birth and death are transitions between discrete states. So the model we need is a continuous-time, discrete-state model, and in this case we select a model with three discrete states in sequence. This model has terms for the three states and the two transition rates included in its definitions, as well as theorems for deducing the relative number present in any state at any time. Now we substitute the data for the terms and deduce the population at some future time. If both the data and the interpretation of the model as a population model are valid, the prediction will also be valid.

To be sure, the matter is not this simple. We know, for one thing, that the relations are more complex than I have indicated: birth rate is not an independent variable but is related to numbers of female population in certain age brackets, and perhaps to death rate and many other factors; the data may not be equilibrium data, though the model is an equilibrium model; or they may represent a temporary or limited equilibrium; and so on. The "ifs" of the preceding paragraph are big "ifs." But all they mean is that the model must be complicated if we want a closer approximation, and more data are needed for the more complex model. It does not change the basic procedure.

The use of formal theories for data interpretation can be generalized to include all branches of mathematics, including statistics. In a sense, as Brodbeck (1959, pp. 386-389) has pointed out, any branch of mathematics can be thought of as a calculus or model and used to make inferences from data. For example, matrix algebra can be used to derive cliques and liaison individuals from a list of sociometric choices (Weiss, 1956). The procedure in all cases is the same as the one I have indicated. First, a branch of mathematics is selected whose relational structure is the same as that thought to exist in the subject for which there are data; then the data are substituted for the terms in the mathematical definitions, and the desired implications are deduced. The only difference between a branch of mathematics and a formal theory is that the latter is more specific; but as some branches of mathematics are more specific than others, even this is not a sharp distinction. Matrix algebra is more specific than algebra, Markov chain theory is still more specific, and a four-state Markov chain with two absorbing states is more specific yet. Nor does a difference lie in the fact that mathematics already exists, while formal theories were invented. Mathematics too was invented and is being invented, and the invention of game theory or graph theory is not essentially different from the invention of a very general formal theory.

4. The two previous uses treat calculi primarily as bridges for connecting two aspects of one's subject matter, or two sets of data. We come now to exploratory uses that treat a calculus more as a representation of a system or process and use it as a map or guide for exploration. The exploration can be either theoretical or practical, or both combined.

Every formal theory, even the most complex, is a simplification of the subject matter it intends to describe. Consequently there is always some discrepancy between its predictions and what actually happens. If we are interested in studying the discrepancy, then we are using the theory as a baseline for exploratory purposes. We know that we already have an explanation for part of what happens, namely the part predicted by our theory, and therefore need concern ourselves only with the remainder.

For a simple example (Allen, 1938, pp. 80-82), suppose there are two firms that produce the same product at the same price. Transportation costs are paid by the consumer, and are lower for firm A. Knowing this, we can deduce a circle, which is the equilibrium line at which transportation charges

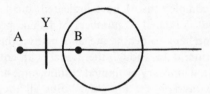

of the two firms are equal. Firm B is inside the circle, and its transportation charges are lower to all points inside the circle. The radius of the circle is related to the ratio of the two transportation costs. (If the two costs are equal the circle becomes the straight line Y.)

The empirical distribution of sales will not be bounded by a perfect circle, but will be irregular. We explore the irregularity, the deviation from a perfect circle, and try to find some pattern in it. Of course one pattern we will find is the pattern of transportation routes, since the model assumes a homogenous transportation space rather than specific routes. If the remaining deviations are slight and randomly distributed, we can dismiss them as random error or friction. The model becomes an ideal type that essentially describes the system, apart from unintelligible empirical details. But if the deviations are considerable, then some other process or system is operating to produce them, and the task is to locate that process, describing it in a formal theory and thereby explaining the deviations. Note that this task is made possible by the original model, since the deviations to be explained exist only with reference to that model. They do not appear directly in the data.

After exploring discrepancies in sales distribution, we can turn to another discrepancy. The existence of differential transportation costs is itself a deviation from the predictions of some larger equilibrium model, some variant of a perfect competition or game model; these differentials represent a disequilibrium relative to the larger model. This means that some process is operative to maintain the disequilibrium, and we can search for it. Here again we are alerted to the existence of a hidden process by the discrepancy between actual data and the predictions of an abstract model.

This exploratory use of formal theories is the one Martindale rejects, if I read him correctly (1959, pp. 87-88). It is the same as the heuristic use Machlup defends against Samuelson's insistence that only explanatory uses are valid (1964).

5. In the use just described, our interest was focused on what was in the subject matter but not explained by the theory. One can also be interested in what is not there but could be, and what would happen if it were there. That is, one may ask, "What would happen if I did X?" Or more generally, one may ask, "How can I act within this system?" This is a practical exploratory use of a model.

The basis for this use is the fact that an adequate formal theory describes the whole working structure of a system or process. It shows why the system acts as it does, and how it will respond to various ranges of initial input; it describes the necessities, possibilities, and impossibilities of the system. The necessities of the system are the structural characteristics that derive from its initial defining conditions and cannot be changed as long as the initial conditions hold. The possibilities of the system are the ranges of input, the critical inputs, that have an effect on system output. The impossibilities are the ranges of input that are absorbed by the working of the system and have no lasting effect on its output.

For example, in the simple game referred to earlier, (p.39) necessities of the game are its rules and payoffs, which determine how it works and, in particular, determine that there is no dominating strategy for either player. This necessity produces an impossibility, the impossibility of devising any strategy that will guarantee a win for either player. All positive strategies are absorbed and counteracted by the system; they are punished by losses and eventually disappear. There is only one possibility, that of avoiding a loss by playing the minimax strategy.

Recent theories of economic growth provide another example. These theories characterize economies as essentially Berlitz systems (Simon, 1954), in which any level of resource input below a critical ratio is absorbed by the system as it returns to equilibrium or zero. Any input above the critical ratio becomes self-reinforcing and moves the output path of the system into a growth curve. The necessities of the system derive from such initial conditions as the current state of agricultural technology in the economy, or a population growth rate that rises with increased economic output up to a point and thereafter levels off. The possibilities of the system are provided by the critical ratio with the choice it provides of moving the system into two different output paths. The impossibility range is the whole input range below the critical ratio, where variations in input have no effect on output. Incidentally, if one adds a second and lower critical ratio to the model, it applies also to formal organizations, to personalities, and to any system that uses resources to maintain itself. At input levels between the two ratios, the system maintains itself in equilibrium; above θ it grows, and below ζ it declines and disappears.

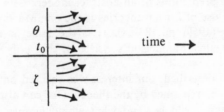

Detailed formal theories permit prediction of the effect of specific actions as well. For example, business cycle theories provide ways of determining the effect on an economy of tax cuts, changes in government spending, tariff changes, and the like. The proposed action is formalized as a change in the value of some parameter, and the effects of the change are calculated and interpreted. Note, however, that these theories predict the relative rather than absolute effect of a change; they do not predict the absolute effect of a tax cut on output, but only the change from what output would have been otherwise. To make an absolute prediction one would need a model of all the factors influencing output, economic and noneconomic, and no such comprehensive theory exists. A relative prediction allows for unknown effects of unknown factors on output and adds merely that a tax cut has an effect of a certain magnitude in a certain direction, assuming other variables stay within certain ranges.

The practical exploratory use of models is most common in political economics and in operations research and also occurs in international diplomacy. In operations research a model of a firm or organization is constructed and used to explore the ranges of possible action and the effects of various policies on the firm's output. In international relations, games simulating an international situation are constructed and played to determine the consequences of various diplomatic and military moves (Shubik, 1964, chs. 18, 19, 21).

6. Closely related to the exploratory use is the normative use of formal theories. In this use, a person's or an organization's goals are postulated in the initial definitions; rationality of some sort is also assumed. Then the range of possibility is located in the model, and within that range the optimum input is located. The result takes the following form: If you want X and Y you should do a^1 or a^2 but not b or c.

Here again the validity of the recommendation depends on the adequacy of the model, and in particular on whether all of the person's or organization's relevant goals and constraints have been included. As with other types of models, adequacy is achieved by a series of successive approximations. The researcher examines the discrepancy between his recommendation and the action that is taken and tries to construct a goal or constraint that will account for it. Then he puts the new goal into the model, works out the implications, and tries a new recommendation. For example (Churchman, 1957, p. 109), an operations researcher constructs a model of an organization, including the goals that management states explicitly and those that can be inferred from management's behavior. The firm is about to expand, and the researcher infers that the best location for a new plant would be town A. His advice to locate in town A is not taken; on inquiring why, he hears that management does not want to work with a certain union official there. He must then add this antipathy to his model as a constraint on management and work out a new recommendation.

Alternatively, the researcher can modify his rationality postulates to account for the discrepancy. By now it is clear that the concept of rationality is capable of being formalized in a variety of ways, so the researcher need not be limited by a priori concepts in adapting his model to the data.

7. The two previous uses were normative uses of essentially descriptive models, and together they constitute the two basic practical uses of models. In addition, a few models are directly normative in the sense that they prescribe what a person ought to do in certain types of situations, or how a perfectly rational person would act. Examples are the mathematicians' treatments of game theory and Amnon Rapoport's discussion of optimum strategies for Prisoner's Dilemma (1967). Normative models can also be used as baselines for the experimental exploration and construction of more complex descriptive models.

8. Two incidental uses of computer models deserve mention. First, they can be used for teaching the characteristics of a system or process (Guetzkow, 1962, p. 92; Rome and Rome, 1962; Haldi and Wagner, 1963). A model of the system is constructed but one or more control points are left unsimulated. For instance, if a formal organization is being simulated the

top management positions are left open. The student is then placed at one of these control points and the model begins to operate. Information, advice, and requests come in to the student from the model, and he must make decisions. The effects of the decisions are simulated by the model and come back to him as new information, advice, and requests. At the end of the simulation period, the total effects of his decisions can be examined and evaluated in comparison with alternative decisions. The possibilities of constructing man-machine systems of this sort are endless, since any desired part of the system can be left unsimulated. It is also possible to use a man-machine system to study the man rather than the machine, as in some game theory experiments where most of the calculation, communication, and playing is done by machines, and the experimental subjects are called on only to make the key decisions. The advantage of a man-machine system is that it provides a perfectly controlled experimental environment, should that be desired.

Second, computer models can be used as robots. Here the output of the model is substituted for the output of the human system simulated. Robots are a direct continuation of industrial technology; the latter simulates human muscles, while computers simulate mind.

9. A special use of the simpler mathematical models is for propaganda purposes. Since the simpler models are composed of highly abstract, highly selective postulates, they can be used to focus attention on those aspects of reality that are embodied in the postulates. By selecting his postulates, the propagandist can call attention to desirable (or undesirable) aspects of his subject and draw attention away from other aspects. If he is using an implicit formal theory, he may in addition be able to pass off his model as an empirical description, thereby idealizing his subject. I shall discuss this use briefly in the next chapter, which deals with implicit formal theories, though an adequate treatment would really require a separate volume.

8

Formalization

Formalization is in the first place a process of translating a verbal theory into a mathematical or computer language. It involves locating the terms and propositions of the theory and substituting symbols for terms, and equations for propositions. Complex concepts must be symbolized by a set of related terms, and complex propositions become a series of equations.

The effect of translation is to make the potential advantages of a formal language available to the theory. These advantages include clarity and exactness in the statement of propositions, ease in making and checking deductions, and a clear distinction between empirical and formal elements in the theory. Such things can indeed be accomplished in a verbal language, but not as easily and not as thoroughly. The whole point of translation is to make it possible to do them thoroughly.

Translation is thus just a preliminary step. The main part of the formalization process is the ensuing transformation of the theory. Once propositions have been stated clearly, they can be checked for incompleteness or redundancy. Incompleteness occurs when one of the assumptions used in the development of the theory has remained implicit, and redundancy occurs when one proposition can be deduced from another and thus is not an independent assumption. More often propositions expressed in words have never been thought out clearly, and formalization forces one to clarify them. It also makes it possible to distinguish the empirical or postulational aspects of the propositions from the self-evident or logical aspects and thus to specify exactly what is being assumed. I shall later give examples from verbal theories of each of these difficulties.

After the initial propositions of the theory are checked and corrected, the next step is to check the deductions and make new ones. This is the most obvious advantage of formalization. Clearly defined concepts, explicitly stated propositions, and explicit rules of inference make deduction a more dependable affair and extend its range far beyond the capacity of ordinary intuition and insight. In particular it becomes easier to work out the dynamics of the system created by the set of postulates, that is, to work out the totality of interactions among all the postulates. It becomes possible to see the direction or directions in which the system is moving, what keeps it moving in that direction, and what system changes would be needed to change its direction.

The completion and systematization of deductions usually enables one to see the theory more abstractly, as a formal structure relatively independent of its particular embodiments. Its original empirical content is seen as one possible interpretation, and a search is made for other interpretations. Variations in formal structure from one interpretation to another can be noted and included in the propositions of the theory as variants of more general propositions. The effect of this is to generalize the theory and free it from association with particular empirical content.

Let us consider these points in more detail. One important weakness of verbal theories is the difficulty of working out a clear and complete postulate set. By this I mean a set that states exactly what is being assumed with no ambiguity, a set in which all assumptions are made explicit, a set in which there is no redundancy and each postulate is needed, and a set in which the logical status of each postulate is clear. By logical status I mean the fact that some postulates are tautologies of various sorts, some are definitions that serve to specify the type of relation being studied, and some are empirical statements of various kinds. The difficulty of working out a clear and complete postulate set in a verbal theory is well known. Verbal propositions are notoriously ambiguous; their implicit assumptions are hard to detect, and it is difficult to distinguish a logical, analytic statement from an empirical, synthetic one. To be sure, these things are difficult enough to do even in a formal theory, and complete success is probably impossible even there, but they are still more difficult in a verbal theory.

Boulding provides a minor example of confusion about the logical status of a proposition when he says, "We may, perhaps, venture a hypothesis that the power of an ideology is made up of two factors, which we may call *intensity* and *appeal* " (1961, p. 281). By *intensity* he means the power an ideology has for its believers, and by *appeal* he means the number of believers. This is not an empirical hypothesis and it need not be hesitantly ventured; it is simply a classification of two possible dimensions of variation in power. If it had been stated as a mathematical definition, its empirically vacuous nature would have been immediately evident. Boulding himself undoubtedly realized what he was saying, since he is a clear thinker who works mathematically even when he chooses to express himself verbally for rhetorical purposes. A mathematically inclined reader would be able to spot the logic through the empiricist rhetoric, but an empirically inclined reader might take the rhetoric seriously and start imagining the statistical surveys and factor analyses that would be required to verify the hypothesis.

A minor example of redundancy, the least serious logical error, occurs in

Schubert's Hughberts Game (1959), a three-person zero-sum game with variable weights. Schubert postulates two goals for Hughberts: (1) maximize the number of unanimous coalitions, and (2) maximize his own power. Goal 2 implies a strategy of participating in a minimal winning coalition whenever possible. It also implies a strategy of always participating in a winning coalition, since the rules make that possible. Thus Hughberts will never be in a minority, will never be in a minority of one, and will never act to prevent unanimity by being a minority of one. Consequently the first goal is redundant, since it produces no strategy or change of strategy (if one excludes preplay communication). Another example of redundancy is one Samuelson found in his own earlier work: Samuelson, 1966, pp. 13-14.

A more serious example of confused postulates occurs in Homans' *Social Behavior: Its Elementary Forms* (1961). Homans' theory consists of five basic propositions from which corollaries and implications are deduced. Each proposition is stated as a correlation between two variables, and Homans thinks of them all as empirical generalizations for which he proposes to give evidence in the rest of his book (1961, pp. 83, 111). It will be sufficient for our purposes to examine propositions 2-5, which are:

2. The more often within a given period of time a man's activity rewards the activity of another, the more often the other will emit the activity (p. 54).

3. The more valuable to a man a unit of the activity another gives him, the more often he will emit activity rewarded by the activity of the other (p. 55).

4. The more often a man has in the recent past received a rewarding activity from another, the less valuable any further unit of that activity becomes to him (p. 55).

5. The more to a man's disadvantage the rule of distributive justice fails of realization, the more likely he is to display the emotional behavior we call anger (p. 75).

Proposition 3 is incomplete as it stands, because it omits reference to cost. Homans defines the cost of an activity as the value of the foregone alternative, and plainly does not intend to say that when the cost of an activity is greater than its reward the activity will still be emitted (pp. 62-64). He means that proposition 3 holds when cost is kept constant. But if the phrase "given constant costs" is added to 3 the proposition can be deduced from a more general proposition that appears a few pages later: "the greater the profit of a unit-activity, the more often it will be emitted" (p. 69; cf. p. 63), which according to Homans "sums up the facts." "Profit" is defined as "reward less cost" (p. 61), and "more valuable, given constant costs" thus is a special case of "more profitable."

This proposition in turn probably can be deduced from a still more general assumption that slips into the argument on p. 62, to the effect that a person will choose the most profitable alternative available: "if at the moment

I saw any better use for my dollar I shall presumably not have bought the coffee" (p. 62). Homans comments later on this assumption: "On reflection he will find that neither he nor mankind has ever been able to offer another [explanation of behavior]—the thing is a truism" (p. 79). He is pointing out that the assumption is true a priori (in some fashion) rather than empirically, since there is no alternative to it. But then the empirical evidence is irrelevant to the assumption's truth or falsity and therefore also to the truth or falsity of propositions deduced from it, including number 3. The empirical materials appearing in the rest of the book do not serve to verify this "truism"; they serve only to provide interpretations of the formal terms occuring in it, the terms "reward," "cost," and "alternative."

We turn now to the phrase "more often" appearing in propositions 2 and 3, which at one point becomes "more likely" (p. 63). This phrase is ambiguous; it may mean either response probability or response rate over time, and "response probability" may in turn mean either the ratio of response to stimulus or the ratio of response 1 to total response. Each of these meanings can be found in the text, but the most frequent meaning, I think, is response rate. Homans introduces a new term, "rate of exchange," which he defines as the ratio of response rates in an exchange. If we remember Homans' warning that his propositions hold good only when other things are equal, proposition 2 becomes: When profit rates are held constant, the rate of exchange will be constant ("more often" divided by "more often"). But the proposition is deducible from the more general proposition that "the rate of exchange of approval for help . . . should equal the proportion profit per unit-approval bears to profit per unit-help" (p. 68). This proposition in turn Homans seems to deduce from propositions 3 and 4, but I have difficulty following the argument (pp. 64-68). In any case, number 2 is not a primitive proposition and is not an empirical generalization; and if it is deducible from numbers 3 and 4, it is also redundant.

Proposition 4 seems to be a tautology. On pp. 42-43 Homans proposes as a measure of the value of A the inverse of the quantity of A received in the recent past. If we substitute this measure into 4, it reads: The lower the value (per unit) of a rewarding activity, the less valuable any further unit of that activity. The meaning of "any further unit" is not clear, but it seems to mean "the next unit."

Finally, proposition 5 looks like an empirical generalization, the only one of the set. Anger, as Homans defines it, is a substantive concept, unlike profit, cost, reward, punishment, and exchange rate, which are all formal and relational. Also the connection between anger and unfairness is not logical but factual for Homans, as near as I can tell.

The Gullahorns, in their computer simulation of Homans' theory (1963), have not explicitly raised the question of the formal adequacy of Homans' propositions but I believe some of the points I have made can also be illustrated from their flow chart. They find it necessary to include profit, cost, and expected profit considerations that are omitted from the propositions; they "are experimenting with different means" of measuring reward frequency (1963, p. 380); and they find that proposition 5 is much more complex than the others. The other questions, redundancy and tautology, cannot be answered from the Gullahorns' poorly conceived flow chart (cf. ch. 5 above).

Plainly Homans' theory is badly in need of formalization, to clear up the confusions in his postulate set. Or more accurately, postulates 2, 3, and 4 have already been formalized long ago; they are nothing more than the old theory of marginal utility, which Homans has dressed up in words to look like empirical generalizations. A plain mathematical treatment of the three propositions would have exposed the confusion immediately.

We turn now to a second weakness of implicit formal theories, the difficulty of making dependable deductions. Verbal theories tend to be rich in shades of meaning, suggestions, and subtle innuendos, but it is difficult to pin the meanings down and see what they strictly imply rather than what they suggest associatively. Consequently, drawing implications is more a matter of intuition (and perhaps wishful thinking) than of strict logic. Rhetorical considerations influence the choice of words and shading of emphases, and the theory is often carried along on a rich tide of suggestiveness, emotion, and intuition. Indeed the present work, being verbal, is undoubtedly subject to this tendency.

In contrast, formal languages are free of rhetoric, emotion, and intuition, and are exact in what they imply. The penumbra of suggestiveness found in verbal theories is eliminated, and strict implications are made explicit. As Simon and Newell observe, a formal theory is less rich in implications than its verbal counterpart, but its implications are more readily available for use (1956). Here again, computer languages are a compromise between verbal and mathematical languages. They allow for a wide variety of ways of drawing implications. For example, in some simulations each word is defined by a list of words with which it is associated to some degree of probability, and each of the associated words is in turn defined by another list. The computer, in its search procedure, can move among these lists and locate subtle implications for testing. Thus a computer program can approach verbal theories in complexity and creativeness, while retaining, perhaps, the exactness and accountability of mathematical theories.

Homans' work (1961, ch. 4) is a good example of the difficulty of deducing the consequences of several interdependent verbal postulates. Another example, which serves also as a happy instance of the use of formalization to correct an implicit formal theory, is provided by developments in Hebb's theory of the central nervous system. Hebb's theory (1949) consists of a set of postulates that describe the operations of nerve cells, plus deductions as to how the resulting system would operate to produce behavior, learning, memory, etc. Hebb deduced, among other things, that regular stimuli operating on a random network of cells would produce cell assemblies. A cell assembly is an organized set of cells that continues to reverberate for a while through self-stimulation, once it has been set in motion, and that develops regular connections to other assemblies. These assemblies, Hebb supposed, were the neurological basis for short-term memory (in fractions of a second) and also for learning. However, when Rochester et al. formalized Hebb's postulates as a computer program, they found that cell assemblies did not develop (1956). Through analysis of the program they also figured out what sort of postulate changes would be needed to get the desired results. They communicated their conclusions to Hebb and Milner, and the latter suggested new postulates based on recent physiological discoveries and fitting the specified requirements (Milner, 1957). The new postulates dealt with short-axon inhibitory cell connections. When they were added to the computer program it was found that cell assemblies did develop. This example illustrates the fruitful combination of experimental physiological work to provide realistic postulates, formal computer simulation to synthesize the consequences of the postulates, and psychological experimentation to provide the behavioral output data to be explained or synthesized.

The most serious deficiency of implicit formal theories is that the verbal language disguises the abstractness of the theory. A theory expressed in terms of A_{ij}, Σ, $\int_{\infty}^{\infty}$, and other forbidding symbols is obviously abstract, and all the assumptions it makes are also obvious because they must be made explicitly. But a theory that uses ordinary, familiar words moves along so smoothly that one tends not to notice the underlying logical machinery—the relational definitions, the exhaustive classifications, the tautologies, the hidden assumptions. One tends to treat the theory as a simple discription of the facts or as a low-level empirical generalization rather than as an abstract bit of logic in disguise; this is the fallacy of misplaced concreteness.

The consequence of this mistake is that the theory looks too convincing to its proponents. Tautologies, neat distinctions, implicit deductions from hidden assumptions already look very convincing when dressed up as factual descriptions. Further, since all possible facts can fit into any complete set of logical categories or any set of tautologies, there is no way of falsifying the "descriptions." Consequently as the theorist looks around for evidence to support his theory, he finds to his delight that the evidence is overwhelming. There is no contrary evidence! Everything in the world falls into place, and he comes to see that the theory is really a deep, fundamental statement of the most essential principles of human behavior. As a result he becomes the prisoner of his own logical model and is rendered incapable of seeing reality from any other standpoint.

The implicit formal theories of Homans and Skinner provide good examples of this sort of error. Homans does not realize that his book mainly provides new exemplifications for the terms of a venerable formal theory that is neither true nor false; he thinks he is providing empirical evidence for the truth of empirical generalizations. He finds that the evidence is overwhelming and that the generalizations are therefore true. His theory, he feels, gives us a true account of what social behavior really is: It is exchange (cf. Homans, 1961, p. 80: "The new economic man is plain man"). Similarly, Skinner finds schedules of reinforcement wherever he directs his attention (Skinner, 1966). But the most widespread example is provided by the neoclassical economists, such as Frank Knight, Ludwig von Mises, Henry Simons, and their present-day followers. These people seemed to think they had penetrated to the very essence of rational human action, and that they knew whatever was knowable about it (cf. von Mises, 1960). They believed, for instance, that "choice among available alternatives so as to maximize expected returns" was what rationality really is and always will be; they believed that perfect competition is approximated in the United States, or would be if government would remove obstacles to competition instead of creating them; they believed that labor is a commodity like other commodities (see, for example, the quote in Schwartz, 1961, p. 197). In other words, they believed that their abstract postulates were concrete descriptions of empirical reality. Consequently, at a time when the theory of the firm under perfect competition is useful chiefly as a propaganda device for corporate management, the followers of these economists, the Buchanans and McCord Wrights, are still teaching it as empirical truth about the economy. In this respect they are using their implicit formal theory as a propaganda device to support the present capitalist social order. They describe the U.S. economy as essentially competitive, apart from inept government interference, and demonstrate that the wishes of consumers necessarily determine what is produced, while the laws of supply and demand insure that the distribution of products is fair and just. This fantasy serves as a façade behind which corporate managers, government officials, and the military can continue their interlocking power maneuvers and their plundering, polluting, wasting, and destroying without fear of punishment.

In general, implicit formal theories in economics and political philosophy are well suited for propaganda purposes. The abstract formal model implicit in such theories is an idealization of one facet of a complex reality, while the verbal language of the theory disguises the abstractness of the model and makes it look like a simple empirical description. Thus the theory can readily perform the essential function of all propaganda, which is to pass off an idealized picture as a true account of reality. The effect is to draw attention away from less savory events not fitting the model; or if such events are inescapable, they can be dismissed as temporary empirical aberrations or as details in need of reform, or even as the price we must pay for our wonderful institutions. The disguised formal theory also enables the propagandist to satisfy another requirement of good propaganda, which is that a propagandist must be deeply and sincerely convinced he is telling the truth. It is amazing how deeply some of these economists and political philosophers are convinced that their abstract postulates are not only simple empirical descriptions, but also the only reputable type of description possible of economy or government. One reads of isolated, self-generated individuals with fixed preference schedules, near-perfect information-processing capacity, and perfect law-abidingness, in a society of perfect laws interpreted by impartial judges, where individuals' preferences are impartially aggregated by voting, logrolling, or the brokerage activities of precinct politicians; but these postulates are so hidden and disguised by verbiage that the account passes for factual description.

I do not mean to imply that the perfect competition model and its variants, or democratic theory for that matter, are useless; far from it. The perfect competition model has been and is very useful as a baseline for exploration, both theoretical and practical. It becomes pernicious only when it is treated as the empirical truth about an economy. The effect is to exclude from consideration alternative formal theories that focus on other facets of empirical reality. The alternatives I have in mind are not the imperfect and monopolistic competition models, which are simply variants with the same basic assumptions; I mean, rather, such models as the *n*-person Prisoner's Dilemma model of an industry; or Shubik's games of economic ruin, K-R stability, and other ideas for oligopoly (1959); or Boulding's theory of viability (1962, ch. 4); or the various behavioral models of the firm (Cyert and March,1963; Cohen and Cyert, 1965, ch. 17) growing out of Newell and Simon's General Problem Solver; or the Leontief input-output model. And even these are just bare beginnings of the possible ways of modeling a firm or an industry; for example, a piracy and racketeering model would bring out characteristics of the U. S. economy hidden by other models but well known to businessmen.

The effect of formalization is to make explicit the logical machinery, tautologies, and hidden assumptions that help to make an implicit formal theory convincing. Once the logic is made explicit, it becomes obvious that alternative assumptions or postulates are possible and can be made to sound equally convincing, and that an equal amount of empirical "evidence" can presumably be marshalled to support them. The formalist knows, and continually uses in his work, the distinction between logic and fact, calculus and interpretation. He knows that any piece of logic can have multiple empirical exemplifications, and every empirical system exemplifies (or can be operated on by means of) a multiplicity of logical structures. Consequently he is unlikely to make the mistake of supposing that any single theory can capture the essence of concrete reality.

It may be an exaggeration to claim that formalization and formal methods are a complete cure for narrow-mindedness; one may find an occasional bit of narrow-mindedness even among formalists. Indeed, this quality is so pervasive among men that it can hardly be called a weakness; it seems more like an essential defense mechanism. But it is the case that constant work with formal languages produces flexibility of thinking *in logic*. The formalist knows that logic is an infinitely rich and variable instrument, that any model can be changed in a great variety of ways, and conversely, that no model can ever express completely the equally rich variety of empirical fact.

The main problem and the most important step in formalization is that of picking an appropriate formal language. A language is appropriate insofar as its central concepts, its semantic structure, match the concepts and logic of the theory to be formalized. By the central concepts of a formal language, I mean the essential relations out of which a language is built. Thus, game theory is built out of the relations of conflict, interdependence, and alternativeness; graph theory is built out of connectedness, and Markov chains are composed of transitions. If the concepts of the empirical theory to be formalized are complex combinations of some such set of relations, then there is a match between empirical concept and formal language. The empirical concepts can be translated into formal concepts without substantial loss of meaning, and the formal rules of transformation can be applied to the concepts to yield significant deductions. Conversely, a mismatch would mean that much of the content of the empirical concepts would be lost or distorted in translation, and the formal deductions would yield implications different from those of the original theory.

Among formal languages the main distinctions is between mathematical and computer languages. The various kinds of mathematics, and symbolic logic as well, all deal with relatively simple, abstract relations, while the computer languages, especially list-processing languages, are suitable for more complex empirical concepts. If a concept is analyzable into a set of simple relations, it can probably be formalized as a mathematical model; such concepts as casting a vote, ascribing higher status to, rewarding, responding to, getting divorced, all are expressible as mathematical operations. Concepts more suitable for computer languages include search, applying a rule to a case, committing oneself, repressing, recognizing, self-concept, humanistic conscience. Search, for instance, consists of testing successive items on a list according to some criterion that can be revised according to a rule. A rule might be a set of conditional sequences—"if A then X, if B then Y . . . if X then E, F, G, or H, if E then . . ." —in which each successive statement is compared with a given state of affairs until a match if found; the sequences can be revised according to another rule. Defense mechanisms, self-concepts, and conscience can be analyzed into a set of rules, criteria, and the like.

There may be concepts and theories that cannot be adequately formalized at present either mathematically or by computer languages. The proper tactic with these theories is not to condemn them as bad or to force them into some misleading mathematical transformation, but to devise an appropriate formal language for them. For example, I very much doubt that dialectically related concepts can be translated into any existing formal languages, because the dialectical rules of transformation appropriate to such concepts are not present in existing languages. However, Kosok (1966) has sketched a possible formalization for such concepts by means of a one-valued logic, though the details have by no means been worked out. Also the possibilities of many-valued and modal logics are just beginning to be explored, and new modes of formalization may come out of these explorations.

9

The Implicit Ontology
of Formalists

An ontology is a conception or theory about what sorts of things make up the world, how they are related, and how they act. It serves to organize and explain the otherwise disorderly flow of experience by suggesting the basic realities that underlie the flux of appearance. Thus for some people appearances are reducible to the orderly growth and change of things or substances—trees, blades of grass, people. For others, people are abstractions from systems of action; for still others, they are confused aggregates or hypothetical entities mistakenly thought to hide behind the realities of behavior or habit. Every culture includes a set of ontological principles that organize thoughts and action and that are expressed in myth, ritual, technology, and social organization. They are called variously "eidos" by Bateson (1936, pp. 32, 218-256; cf. also Nadel, 1951, pp. 392 ff), "philosophy" and "world view" by Kluckhohn and Leighton (1946; Kluckhohn, 1949), "world view" by Krasnow and Merikallio (1964, p. 254), and "dominant ontology" by Feibleman (1956). The ontologies in cultures are generally implicit and not fully developed to philosophical consistency and clarity of detail, or to explicit affirmations and negations.

The culture of science also includes various ontological principles, which perform the usual functions of ontologies. These are transmitted and maintained by the usual means—socialization, interpersonal contacts, and the teachings of moralists—and are reinforced or modified by the pressures of day-to-day scientific work. Consequently, differential contacts as well as differences in daily practice lead to variations in ontological principles. Each major method tends to develop its own dominant ontology, which serves to systematize, explain, and justify the method. However, there is never a complete one-to-one relationship between method and ontology. For one thing, widespread contacts among scientists diffuse ontological beliefs far from their natural homes, just as scientific techniques and tactics are spread widely in the same way. For another, an empiricist ideology dominates present-day science. Particular empiricist beliefs are widely diffused, appearing in the oddest places, and alternative ontological principles are sometimes expressed in empiricist terms or combined incongruously with empiricist principles. Consequently, individual scientists (including methodologists themselves) affirm a bewildering variety of ontological and methodological beliefs, which conflict with their actual practice in a variety of ways and degrees. Nevertheless, one can still find a dominant ontology associated with each main method, underlying the variations.

The dominant empiricist ontology runs somewhat as follows: "We think of reality as composed of various things, or entities, which have various traits, attributes, or characteristics" (Stephens, 1968, p. 3). The superficial disorder of appearance consists of continuous change in the characteristics of things, from fat to thin, Republican to Democratic, having two children to having three children, ethnically mixed to ethnically homogeneous, agricultural to suburban, and so on. These continuous changes are not really disorderly; they occur in regular sequences, and what looks like disorder to the casual observer is really a multiplicity of sequences, each set in motion by its own proper set of conditions. There are many such regularities all intertwined, masking, distorting, and disguising one another, so that the result for the untrained observer is confusion. However, the scientist can disentangle this surface disorder; he locates the real constants and regular variables within the flux of appearance and untangles and lays them bare one by one. Mistakes occur when the scientist fails to find a real variable and is deceived by some temporary combination of real variables, or when he is deceived by some accidental pseudo-regularity, or when he overgeneralizes the conditions in which a regularity occurs.

Empiricists differ on whether the regularities are to be thought of as cause-and-effect laws or merely regular sequences, on whether the real variables are quite different from appearance or lie close to the surface of appearance, and on whether all reality is regular or a bit of irregularity exists here and there. For example, it could be argued that although everything that exists is regular, the regularities themselves sometimes intersect in a haphazard way, so that there really is some chance and free will in the world. Metaphysical issues of concern to empiricists include the nature of causation, the reality status of such "things" as families, cities, groups, and the global variables associated with them, and the issue of determinism and free will. Methodological individualism, for instance, is the doctrine that only individuals are real, societies and groups are not, and therefore all explanation must be based ultimately on statements or laws about individual behavior (cf. Nagel, 1961, pp. 535-546).

The implicit onotology of formalists is characterized by a sharp distinction between two aspects of reality, the empirical and the logical (or mathematical or rational). In its logical aspect reality is orderly, systematic, and general, while in its empirical aspect it is haphazard and particular. The logical aspect of reality is what makes it knowable, intelligible, explainable, while the empirical aspect is what is apparent to our senses here and now.

The achievement of dependable knowledge requires the separation and isolation of the logical component of reality so that it can be studied in its pure form, uncontaminated by the everchanging appearances of things. Ordinary common-sense knowledge, by contrast, is an indiscriminate mixture of the logical and the empirical; it notes experienced regularities, sequences that occur frequently or usually, but it is content to describe these regularities as they happen to occur. It accepts the vague, gross entities of ordinary experience—people, dollar bills, stop lights, legislatures, bargaining sessions—just as they appear and describes the regular changes that seem to occur in them. Empirical science is not far removed from common sense; it too produces empirical generalizations, though these are stated more exactly and cautiously and the entities described may have some logical clarity. But the true (formalist) scientist must penetrate into experience to locate the underlying logical order that produces the surface regularity, and must replace the vague entities of sense with clear and distinct logical ideas. Only in this way, by clearing away the confused pandemonium of sense, can he achieve dependable knowledge.

Consider, for example, a pond or a low, marshy area in a forest. A profusion of colors, sound, and smells is apparent to sense: wild grasses and flowers, bushes, birds, insects, frogs croaking, rotting vegetation, algae, snails, a fringe of small trees. The display is always changing, going through the cycle of the seasons but becoming a little different each year. How can one understand all this? Common sense and empirical science can note some regularities in the riotous display of sensations. For one thing, they group themselves into kinds—the grasses, the croaking frogs, the water, etc. These are species. Then each kind goes through a characteristic cycle: the living species sprout, flourish, grow old, die, and rot, becoming food for other living things, each in its own regular way. The other kinds of things also go through regular changes. The total scene is a combination of all these regularities, each sequence proceeding at its own rate of speed, with a haphazard total effect.

The formalist develops the idea of an ecosystem. This is a relatively closed system in which balanced internal exchanges of various components occur and in which exchange takes place through a neutral medium, critical variables regulate or maintain the whole system, departures from equilibrium are controlled by negative feedback, and irreversible changes produce a gradual ecological succession. The components of an ecosystem are mathematical entities consisting of inputs, transformation processes and transformation rates, and outputs (Boulding, 1953, introduction). Once the scientist has abstracted a pure mathematical idea, such as "ecosystem," from its empirical embodiments, he can study the idea and describe its dynamics. He can describe the equilibrium state or states, locate the critical ratios or variables, trace time paths toward or away from or around equilibrium and locate the factors that produce the paths, and so on (Kemeny and Snell, 1962, ch. 2). Finally, he makes this knowledge useful by reuniting the logical and the empirical without, however, confusing them. Both the particular sensations and the observable regularities now become intelligible as exemplifications of a single mathematical idea. Instead of a riot of sensations we now see mathematical processes occurring—exchanges, transformations of input, surpluses and shortages, the reaching and exceeding of critical limits.

Further, the same mathematical idea can be found exemplified in quite different parts of the world. "Society is a great pond," observes Boulding (1953, p. xxi); that is, the multifarious sounds and smells of the city are all manifestations of another ecosystem, in which money rather than water or air is the neutral medium of exchange, and in which all the mathematical processes and components of an ecosystem are appropriately exemplified. Both the society and the pond are intelligible as exemplifications of the same idea. (Note that Boulding's statement is nonsense for an empiricist, but literal truth for a formalist.)

Not everything in a society or a pond can be made intelligible as the exemplifications of an ecosystem, but only those facts and regularities that contain or exemplify some logic. The regular cycles of pork prices, the regular cycles of tree parasites, or the regular sequence of species in the history of a pond can be explained; but the variations and spread of pork prices on a particular day or the eating of a particular insect by a particular frog cannot be explained in terms of the logic of ecosystems. These are empirical facts, particulars, and therefore unknowable, unintelligible, arbitrary.

The ratio of logical to empirical is not constant throughout nature. Some parts of reality may be rather strongly logical and therefore quite intelligible, while other parts may be characterized mainly by random variability. For example, the logical structure and dynamics of a highly developed economy may be readily apparent, while the shifting likes and dislikes of individuals or the delusions of psychotics are in comparison relatively unintelligible. However, it may be that in particular cases the underlying logic has simply not yet been uncovered, and unintelligibility lies only on the empirical surface.

The ratio of logical to empirical may also change over time. Thus the development from a primitive to a modern economy is in part a process of rationalization in which the idea of production and exchange has been progressively realized, developed, and purified of irrelevant encumbrances. Similarly the development of money from cattle to gold to paper to computer numbers represents the freeing of the idea of a neutral medium of exchange from irrelevant material connotations. In such cases the logical idea immanent in some piece of reality is also a rational ideal that constitutes the limit of the reality's development or change. Consequently when one uncovers the logic of this sort of system one can both describe the dynamics of the system and prescribe an ideal for it; the good and the true become identical. This identity appears, for example, in decision theory and in game theory. To be sure, if the reality is still strongly encumbered with nonlogical elements both prescription and description may appear unrealistic to the empiricist concerned with immediate appearances.

Take, for example, the minimax rule in game theory. The empiricist (cf. Messick, 1967) finds that in the short run people follow all sorts of shifting strategies and that these vary with personality factors and the like. The formalist notes a long-run trend toward the minimax strategy, and he also finds empirical evidence of the stability that he knows a priori must exist when the minimax strategy is followed. Consequently he knows that at the limit, when all the shifting, arbitrary, particular strategies have run their course and been dissolved, when all the personality factors have been counteracted by other factors, the minimax strategy will survive and dominate play. He also knows that this strategy will yield maximum returns to both players. In other words, the good and the true are identical *at the limit*.

The same piece of reality may exemplify more than one logical idea and therefore be knowable in more than one way. Sometimes the ideas are supplementary in the sense that what is unintelligible chaos relative to one idea exemplifies a different logical idea. For example, if one thinks of a pond or an economy as an ecosystem, the eating of particular insects by particular frogs or the particular range of pork prices during a day appears as random, unintelligible events. However, perfect randomness is itself a logical idea or, more properly, a set of ideas, so that these events may be statistically intelligible as exemplifying to some degree some idea of randomness. The deviations from randomness may in turn point to still other ideas. It would be possible to carry the idea of multiple exemplifications to the limit and argue that reality is completely logical through and through, that everything that is unintelligible from the standpoint of one logical idea *must* exemplify some other idea. However, I have not come across any formalist statement of this sort; all the formalists I have known or read allow for the existence of nonlogical residues.

Sometimes multiple ideas are contradictory rather than supplementary; the exemplification of one may exclude others. For example, a random net cannot become organized into trees with minimal sources or sinks or into a set or reverberating loops without losing its randomness. Similarly, these two types of nonrandomness are themselves incompatible. An ordinary net may fluctuate between these two limiting ideas or may shift cumulatively from one to the other. A well-developed kinship system, which moves toward the ideal that everyone in a society is a relative of everyone else so that all transactions are controlled by particular kinship obligations, is incompatible with a well-developed market economy, which moves toward the idea that everyone in a society regards everyone else impersonally so that all transactions are controlled by considerations of personal advantage. The two ideas, interpersonal obligation and impersonal exchange, are contradictory. An ordinary society may fluctuate between these two limiting ideas or may shift cumulatively from one to the other. When, as in the previous case, the two contradictory ideas are also rational ideas, the society that exemplifies them is caught in a dilemma or an antinomy or a logical paradox. Prisoner's Dilemma is another example of such a paradox.

The primary instrument for studying the logical aspect of reality is mathematics, including mathematical logic and the logic built into computers. By mathematics is meant not counting and measuring—these are the empiricist uses of the *results* of mathematics to work with the empirical flux—but, as Whitehead describes it, "the study of abstract patterns of order" (1941). Each branch of mathematics studies and describes some type of order. The order may have been originally found in or suggested by some empirical occurrence, as for instance the staggering of a drunk may have suggested the idea of a random walk, but the mathematician frees the idea from its empirical embodiment and studies it in its pure form. Mathematics can therefore be called the language of nature, as well as the basic language of science.

This does not mean that scientists must necessarily write and talk in equations and flow charts. What is necessary is that they *think* in mathematical modes and perceive mathematical forms in the flux of experience. Thus to a mathematical thinker an imperceptibly small deviation is an epsilon, a cafeteria line is a Markov chain, a bunch of gabbling relatives is a kinship tree, a pronouncement about shipping in the Gulf of Aqaba is a move in a game of chicken, and so on. Once the basic ideas are clearly conceived, they can be expressed in ordinary language or in mathematical symbols, though for careful work the symbols are more helpful.

All these ideas may seem mystifying or perverse to the empiricist, just as the empiricist's metaphysical outlook may seem superficial and commonsensical to the formalist. For one thing, the empiricist is bound to be puzzled by the glorification of mathematics as the language of nature. Mathematics to him is just an instrument for counting and measuring real things, but when the instrument is taken to be real and the things it measures are treated as appearances, surely the natural order of things has been reversed. Nor will the empiricist accept the supposed connection that Whitehead makes between mathematics and order. For the empiricist, mathematics is primarily numbers and potential numbers, and he knows many kinds of order that have nothing to do with numbers—constitutions, legal codes, dramas, ceremonies, and personality itself. The formalist, conversely, will take this attitude as another example of the empiricist's superficiality, of his accepting the surface appearances of things for reality and thereby missing the underlying logic of these complex appearances. He will also take it as further evidence of the empiricist's superficial knowledge of mathematics, logic, and computer languages, in which numbers play an insignificant part.

Most of all, the empiricist will be puzzled by the distinction between a logical and an empirical aspect of reality. We experience things as single items; why double them? The "logical aspect of reality" is nothing more than a way of looking at things that we adopt for convenience and simplicity, and to transmute this way of looking into a kind of reality is surely a mistake. For the holistic empiricist, whose standpoint I shall take in Part 2, this dualism is already sufficient evidence that the formalist standpoint is partial and therefore inadequate.

So far I have stated that, for a formalist, reality is composed of empirical and logical or rational components in varying degrees and combinations. The logical component is the knowable part of reality and mathematics is the instrument for studying it, since mathematics deals with pure forms abstracted from their empirical exemplifications. Let us next consider what these forms look like. What kinds of entities are there in nature?

The most frequently discussed entities are systems. These are defined in different ways, but Rapoport's definition (1966b, pp. 129-130) is as good as any:

> A fully rigorous definition of *system* would single out from all classes, aggregates, or phenomena those which can satisfy the following criteria:
> 1. One can specify a set of identifiable elements.
> 2. Among at least some of the elements, one can specify identifiable relations.
> 3. Certain relations imply others.
> So much constitutes a static system. Dynamics is added by including a time dimension:
> 4. A certain complex of relations at a given time implies a certain complex (or one of several possible complexes) at a later time.
>
> A complete specification of the elements and the relations among them defines a *state* of a system. A dynamic theory of a system is therefore one which enables us to deduce certain future states from a given present state.

Systems may be primarily closed or primarily open or somewhere in between. Some systems preserve their states within limits by means of negative feedback or other equilibrating mechanisms, while others expand or shift continuously until checked by outside forces. Some system dynamics are related in determinate ways to an equilibrium state or states, while others are ergodic, that is wandering indeterminately. Every system is composed of subsystems and is in turn a part of some larger system, and so on indefinitely.

Another type of entity that is formally determinate enough to be worth studying is a *process*. Processes are the dynamic aspects of systems. A queuing process or a branching process or a random walk or a Markov process, for example, has a beginning or initial state (though not necessarily an end), a finite or infinite set of possible changes, and rates of change. Processes differ from systems in that they are composed of states rather than of elements and relations. To be sure, states are of elements and sets of elements, but this merely means that processes are the dynamic aspect of systems. For example, if one thinks of a queue as a set of elements ordered in a list, one is thinking of a system. If one thinks of the dynamics of this system, namely entering and leaving at certain rates, waiting certain average times and lengths, one is thinking of a process that the elements go through.

Are there other aspects of systems that are also worth studying by themselves? Specifically, if all systems are composed of elements, do elements have important characteristics of their own? One type of metaphysical thought holds that the elements of things are likely to be the ultimately real entities and that relations between elements are usually secondary, derivative, fluctuating, superficial. For example, if societies and groups are composed of individuals, then individuals are real, while groups are derivative and perhaps even imaginary entities. The characteristics of individuals, their motives, beliefs, energies, purposes, give groups whatever characteristics they possess. To claim that a group is real is to claim that there exists somewhere an element, a group mind; and since such an element cannot be discovered apart from individuals, groups are not real apart from the individuals who compose them. Similarly, if ecosystems are composed of plants, animals, and chemicals, it is these elements that are real, and the ecosystem is simply the set of relations that these real things happen to have with one another. The characteristics of the ecosystem are derived from the characteristics of its constituent parts and how they are related. If the parts were scattered around into other favorable environments they would still be alive and basically unchanged in nature, while the ecosystem would have disappeared, thus indicating its derivative character. Such "system" concepts as *society* and *ecosystem* are, therefore, at best, concepts we have invented to work with elements in the aggregate, but there is nothing real that corresponds to them.

This type of thinking is rarely shared by a formalist. To him the elements of a system have no determinate formal character of their own; they are simply the terminals or connecting points for relations. They are like points in geometry. Even if an element has no relation to the rest of the system that contains it, it is still characterized negatively by these absent relations; it is not adjacent, it is unreachable, its row has all zeros, it is in no coalitions, etc. If an empirical entity that is represented as an element in a model is to be studied seriously in its own right, it must be seen as a system, not as an element. For example, if a person is to be studied in abstraction from some social system, he becomes a system—a personality system, a cognitive system, etc. As for the argument that the elements of systems, the plants and animals, etc., can survive the disappearance of the system, this is a shortsighted view. In the long run the dynamics of a continuing system determine the states of elements and their relations. The dynamics of an ecosystem determine how many of a particular species can exist at once and what their characteristics must be to maintain system balance. At a particular time this balance can be disturbed and the elements scattered every which way, but this is a random empirical disturbance that does not affect the basic system dynamics. In the long run such random disturbances cannot maintain themselves. In general, a preoccupation with the elements of things rather than their relations is a preoccupation with what is obvious to sense, the bulky, colorful, wriggling things that loom up here and now. Elementalism is a form of empiricism; it locates its real entities in the short-run sensible flux.

What about structures? If one can abstract process from a system and study its characteristics, can one also abstract structure? Such a notion would be puzzling to a formalist. The structure of a system *is* the system seen as static. There is nothing else.

The basic entities, then, for a formalist are systems and processes. Processes are the dynamic aspect of systems, but have their own independent formal characteristics. Systems are composed of subsystems and are ingredients in larger systems. In the real world systems are always embodied in empirical instances. The empirical finery in which systems appear makes them visible, sensible, real, but also serves to obscure the formal characteristics that make them knowable. Mathematics is the instrument that brings out the formal characteristics of things and reveals the hidden dynamics of nature.

Formalists differ on the question of how many basic logical ideas there are, though this is more a difference of personal emphasis than a sharp ideological disagreement. At one extreme one finds a tendency to believe that there may be one basic idea from which all others are derived. This tendency appears among social gravity theorists like Zipf and Dodd, and also among some devotees of the principle of marginal utility like von Mises. The latter's view is that all human, rational conduct must eventually be explained by means of the maximization of utility principle, and all other phenomena of the social sciences must eventually be explained in terms of the laws of human conduct. The social gravity view is somewhat similar.

Other formalists hold that there is a relatively small number of basic ideas which, in their many variants and combinations, underlie the great empirical complexity of social life. For example, McPhee asserts, "But give me only 50 to 100 really distinct *logical* ideas about elementary social processes. . .and I will bet they can be reinterpreted and recombined in the 50,000 ways that are necessary, I agree, to cope with social diversity" (1963, p. 21).

Other formalists seem to believe that the number of logical ideas is indefinitely large. This amounts to believing that ideas, or models, are our own invention, and so we can go on creating new ones indefinitely. To be sure, nature must have some logical character, since otherwise we could not be successful in using our models to work with it. But the logical character of nature may be extremely complex, as complex indeed as its empirical aspect. In this case there is not much point in distinguishing between logical and empirical, since both are of approximately equal complexity, and the distinction becomes one between two ways of dealing with nature. This type of formalism is closer to empiricism than are the other two types I have mentioned.

Metaphysical issues that arise in a formalist ontology include the questions of how the empirical and the logical aspects of reality are related and how sharply they are to be distinguished. There is also the question of the existential status of logical and mathematical entities, a question that has traditionally been summed up by the mysterious word "subsistence." One could also ask whether models have any dynamic effect on reality (and, if so, how?) or whether they are simply abstract descriptions of what happens. Is there really something magical about the number 7 ± 2, or is its regular appearance in information theory simply a coincidence? Are triangles the real building blocks of nature, as Plato and Buckminster Fuller have surmised? Do some ideas of equilibrium, such as the sphere, the circle, the principles of minimax and marginal utility, act as final causes that gently attract behavior by their sheer simplicity and mathematical beauty? Or are they simply prosaic descriptions of the final battlelines after the combatants have done their best? In the physics of fluids the sphere represents the solution to a minimum-maximum problem—minimum surface tension and maximum enclosed volume—and the minimax and marginal utility principles are quite similar. Are these ideas final causes, then, or simply records of what will necessarily happen at the limit? I list these issues, not in the expectation that formalists will have discussed them, but to point out connections between the implicit ontology of formalists and some explicit ontological positions in the history of philosophy.

The ideas described above are found most typically among mathematical thinkers and appear less frequently among practitioners of computer simulation. My impression is that those who have come to computers from mathematics and regard simulation as an extension of mathematical modeling ("experimental mathematics," for example), as I have treated it in this book, are likely to have a formalist outlook. Those who regard computers as a substitute for mathematics and as a way of overcoming the weaknesses of mathematical modeling (for example, Cyert and March, 1963) are not likely to be formalists. They are not likely to make a sharp distinction between the logical and empirical aspects of reality; and in a simulation the distinction does indeed lose most of its point. A simulation can be said to describe the logic of some real system, but this logic is so particularized that it can hardly be distinguished from the empirical particulars of the system. Also they are likely to treat models as human inventions which can be indefinitely multiplied in number; and simulations are such complex things that it is easy to treat them as artificial constructions.

This difference in outlook between mathematical and computer models, while not large enough to hinder communication, supports the idea that computer simulation may eventually form the core of a new method somewhere between the present formalist and empiricist methods—and retaining the advantages of both, simulation enthusiasts would say. Or it may be that formalist methods will simply expand and diversify by combining various empirical methods—experimental, statistical, clinical—with various types of formal languages and modeling techniques in a variety of new ways.

II

Participant–Observer and Clinical Methods

10

The Holist Standpoint

In Part II we deal with the various ways of studying a whole human system in its natural setting. The system may be a little community, relatively self-sufficient emotionally and perhaps economically as well (Redfield, 1960a). It may be a whole nonliterate society composed of a number of villages, bands, or clans (Malinowski, 1922). It may be a complex kingdom or state combining several races and cultures in a loose political unity (Nadel, 1942), or it may be a factory (Gouldner, 1950, 1954) or firm (Jaques, 1952) treated as a relatively self-sufficient community. It may be a small informal group (Whyte, 1943) or a family (Handel, 1967) or even an individual. Moving in the other direction, it may be a small modern city (Warner et al., 1941, 1942, 1945, 1947, "Yankee City Series") or some subculture or social stratum within the city, treated as a semi-independent community (Polsky, 1967). It may be a mass movement or large bureaucratic organization within modern society (Gusfield, 1963) or even a whole civilization or historical period, as in the work of Werner Sombart.

The various kinds of human wholes differ greatly in size and complexity, and these differences lead to important variations in method which I shall discuss later. They also differ greatly in degree of self sufficiency and in their relationships to the larger wholes that include them. But all can and have been studied from a holist standpoint, producing a similarity of method that is worth noticing.

The holist standpoint includes the belief that human systems tend to develop a characteristic wholeness or integrity. They are not simply a loose collection of traits or wants or reflexes or variables of any sort (cf. Blumer, 1956); they have a unity that manifests itself in nearly every part. Their unity may be that of a basic spirit or set of values that expresses itself throughout the system—the spirit of capitalism, the apollonian way of life, the Navaho philosophy—or it may be that of a basic mode of production and distribution that more or less conditions everything else—slash-and-burn agriculture, tapping and trapping, irrigation, feudalism—or perhaps that of a basic personality that shapes all cultural institutions to its own needs and drives. Or the unity may not have any focal point, but may consist merely of myriad inter-weavings of themes and subsystems in a complex pattern. Holists disagree on whether the organic unity of human systems, the complex interweavings of relationships, derive from some basic source—religion, ethics, technology, per-sonality—but they agree that the unity is there.

This means that the characteristics of a part are largely determined by the whole to which it belongs and by its particular location in the whole system. Consequently, if two superficially similar parts of different systems, say, folk tales or marriage practices, are compared carefully, they will be found to differ in characteristic ways. They will differ even if they have obvi-ously been borrowed from the same source, because a borrowed culture trait or practice will be changed to fit its new surroundings. For example, the Ghost Dance which spread rapidly through the Plains Indian tribes in the 1890's took on a different form and meaning in different tribes ac-cording to their particular configuration of strains, defense mechanisms, and ceremonies. Among the Dakota Sioux it became a war dance (Mooney, 1896, pp. 816-828); among the Pawnee it became amalgamated with a group of traditional games (Lesser, 1933, pp. 58-118); among still other tribes it became involved in tribal traditions of individual trances and sorcery; while the California tribes rejected it entirely.

The contention that human wholes exist and determine their parts is not unusual and could be accepted by most social scientists. But some scientists who agree that a particular culture trait is different in different cultures see the variation merely as a problem of measurement and correlation. The dif-ferences can be described as different values on a set of dimensions, and they can be explained by correlating these values with the values of other culture traits. For example, why did the Ghost Dance become a war dance among the Sioux and not among all the other Plains Indian tribes? Mooney explains it in terms of the particular configuration and history of Sioux culture, but a survey researcher could explain it by discovering laws or multiple correla-tions in which "belligerency" is the dependent variable. The independent variables must be such that the Sioux would score high on them and all other tribes low, and the high score would explain why the Sioux made it a war dance. Consequently for a survey researcher there is nothing wrong in speaking of traits, factors, variables, or other "atomic" entities; they are simply vehicles for describing and explaining the manifold differences among human wholes.

The holist, however, believes not only that wholes exist but that his ac-count of them should somehow capture and express this holistic quality. As Redfield says, it should be "a knowledge that will preserve some of the holistic qualities of the things compared" (1960a, p. 2). By "holistic quality" is meant not only the manifold interrelations among parts that ap-pear in the original but also some of the unique characteristics, the distinctive qualities and patterns that differentiate this system from others. This is the point at which many social scientists part company with the holists; it seems to them that an emphasis on uniqueness makes generalization impossible, and without generalization there can be no science (cf. for example, Rapoport, 1966b, pp. 138-139).

One preserves a measure of holistic quality in a description partly through the choice of proper concepts and partly through the kinds of descriptive statements used. The concepts used must be relatively concrete and particularized, close to the real system being described, rather than abstract mathematical concepts developed in some other science and imposed on the subject matter a priori or concepts that grow out of a testing instrument and get their meaning from the instrument. As many of the concepts as possible should be derived from the subject matter itself, from the thinking of the people being studied; and the other concepts should at least not be foreign to their way of thinking. Consider, for example, the careful way in which Radcliffe-Brown (1922) tries to understand and explain the Andamanese concept of *ot-kimil*, or the way Malinowski works on the Trobriand concept of *mana*; these concepts are taken from the subject matter being studied, and the investigator tries to remain faithful to the native meanings. Contrast these concepts with the way the typical survey research concept of intraception was developed (chapter 1); this concept was not taken from the thinking of the people being studied, but came out of a series of testing instruments including the F scale and various intraception indicators. It is not particularized to any special group of people, as *ot-kimil* is, but applies indifferently wherever the testing instruments can be used. The topic of concept formation will be discussed further in chapter 15.

Equally important, each description of a segment of the system should refer to the many connections of that segment to the whole system. Even if the investigator is focusing his interest on one segment only, say, the latent functions of Navaho witchcraft or the biculturation of Mesquakie teenage boys, his study should always have as background a detailed knowledge of the whole system so that he never loses sight of it in his investigations.

It may be possible to capture the holistic qualities of a human system by means of an apparatus of variables and indices, but no such thing has in fact occurred. In practice, investigations of this sort have been confined to a few variables of interest to the investigator. The variables have been selected in advance, and observation has been mainly confined to them. Even if enough variables could somehow be assembled to produce some approximation to the complexity of the real system, the resulting avalanche of numbers and arbitrary operational definitions would have no recognizable resemblance to the original. Variables, indices, and operational definitions are in current practice selected to meet such requirements of scientific method as measurability, controllability, verifiability, and above all, general applicability, rather than for their faithfulness to the particular subject being described. Consequently they are likely to be highly abstract and general, applicable in some way to many human systems but not expressing the unique qualities of any particular system.

The disagreement here is over the relative importance of subject matter and of "science" in determining one's concepts and procedures. The holist believes in the primacy of subject matter; he believes that whatever else a method may be, it should at least be adequate to the particular thing described and should not distort it. This belief in the primacy of subject matter over method is perhaps the most striking characteristic of the holist standpoint.

The opposite standpoint is characterized by a belief in the primary importance of being "scientific." A person who holds this belief will argue that whatever else his procedures are, they must at least be scientific. If the requirements of scientific method are ignored or changed radically to fit the supposed requirements of some subject matter, or worse yet, if a radically different method adapted to the subject matter is invented, then the result is not science. It is permissible to adapt methods to unusual subject matter to some extent but only if the basic requirements of scientific method are not thereby violated. Conversely, the holist does not object to attempts to make a method "scientific" in a traditional sense only so long as the results do not distort the subject matter beyond self-recognition. The requirement of self-recognition will be discussed in ch. 11.

The holist is likely to emphasize the differences between the natural and the social sciences because their subject matters are different. He will object to the idea of applying natural science methods directly to human subject matter and will argue that the social sciences can develop their own methods, which may or may not differ from natural science methods. Some holists have even emphasized the similarities between the social sciences and the humanities, since they have the same subject matter (for example Redfield, 1962, p. 47 ff). A person who holds the opposite point of view will take seriously the question whether it is possible to have a natural science of society and, however he answers the question, will recognize that it reduces to the question whether natural science methods can be applied to social subject matter.

To be sure, the holist has a method too and presumably is also a scientist, so the question of whether subject matter or "science" should have priority makes no sense. It is merely a matter of choosing among different methods. However, I am reporting the holist standpoint here and therefore must put the question in the way it appears to the holist. He sees himself confronted on the one hand with a subject matter and on the other with received and philosophically approved canons of scientific method, and he feels a certain incompatibility between the two (cf. Rogers, 1961, ch. 10; Kroeber, 1948, p. 328). He thinks also of the pioneers—Freud, Rorschach, and Malinowski—who dared to experiment with new approaches to human subject matter rather than continuing to use received practices.

The holist's belief in the primacy of subject matter is closely related to his more general attitude of respect for human beings. Human beings, he feels, are not things and should not be treated as things; they should not be experimented upon, controlled, duped, and generally used in the name of science. Even a scientific reduction of a person to a set of variables is in a way disrespectful because it mutilates integrity. The holist's attitude of respect is not often expressed explicitly (but cf. Kardiner and Ovesey, 1951, pp. 80, 168; Herskovits, 1948, p. 77) but one feels it again and again in the way he goes about his work.

Accompanying this attitude is a feeling that the only instrument that is good enough for studying human beings is man himself. Only the human observer is perceptive enough to recognize and appreciate the full range of human action; only the human thinker is able to draw the proper implications from the complex data coming from human systems. Mechanical recording devices are sensitive only to the specific, isolated facts for which they have been programmed, and the mechanical reasoning associated with mathematics, symbolic logic, and computers cannot transcend the static, abstract formulas with which it must work. The only acceptable mechanical devices are those that assist the human observer, like cameras and tape recorders, rather than pretend to substitute for him. And if a model is to be constructed, the only adequate one is the scientist himself, who in the course of his observations turns himself into an analogue of his subject matter. No machine, no computer, can be complex enough to replace the human personality as a model of some other human system.

The holist standpoint I have described above is an ideal type. Not all holists share these views in every detail, and not all clinicians and participant observers think of themselves as holists. Holists agree that one should study a whole living system rather than just one part taken out of context, but there are varying conceptions of how whole the system has to be. For some, it is enough to study a whole political system or kinship system; for others, politics and kinship must be understood in the context of other institutions; for still others, the detailed daily functioning of all these institutions must also be studied if possible. (This topic will be discussed further in ch. 19). For some holists an account is not adequate unless the subjects described can understand and approve it, while for others this requirement is desirable but not essential. Also there are various attempts to combine holist attitudes with the belief that science is the verification of hypotheses or general laws. However, the attitudes I have described are widespread and important because they justify the use of participant-observer and clinical methods; consequently an appreciation of the holist stance helps one understand these methods.

11

Main Steps of a Case Study

Field and clinical methods exhibit a great deal of variety depending on the peculiarities of the subject matter and the particular objectives of research. Consequently, any step-by-step account of these methods should be treated as a general guide rather than an exact statement.

Prior Preparation

Whenever possible, the prospective field worker acquaints himself with his proposed subject before going into the field. He reads published reports about the area or related areas and talks to people who have been there. Similarly the clinician may have available the results of tests and interviews before he sees a patient. The field worker also begins to learn the language he will be using in the field, if this is possible and appropriate. He may try to assure himself of entry into the area by securing letters of introduction or other messages from former visitors or officials.

Theoretical preparation is also important prior to beginning field work. The prospective field worker will acquaint himself with a variety of theories (the more the better) that may be applicable to his case. He may also develop check lists of things to look for, such as an index of dream characteristics (Erikson, 1959a, p. 82) or a table of culture traits (Herskovits, 1948, p. 89); the various theories he has considered will, of course, also suggest a large number of things to look for. In addition, the field worker may have specific theoretical issues or questions that puzzle or interest him, and he may even have hypotheses he wishes to test or clarify. These interests can serve as the basis for a formal research design that the field worker may write to get support for his work. The research design may say, in effect, "I wish to study the relation between A and B in this culture" or "I wish to compare these two cases with respect to A" or simply "I wish to study area A." Various possible hypotheses may also be specified for each topic.

142

In the field the research design serves as a place to start, an initial focus of attention, and perhaps as a point of reference or departure for later explorations. In any case, unless it is very general, it is usually transcended, supplemented, or left behind as the developing field work suggests new topics and hypotheses. It is important, therefore, that the design be loose enough to allow for developments in the field; too strict a design ties the research down and inhibits the changes in concepts that are characteristic of field work. In some cases the field worker can proceed without any design at all and find an arbitrary starting point in the field; and in some cases a research design turns out to be a hindrance that is discarded as soon as possible. The best-known example of the latter is Radcliffe-Brown's study of Andamanese culture (1922). Radcliffe-Brown went to the Andaman Islands in 1907 to reconstruct a historical process of culture diffusion but found instead that the facts seemed to require a functional treatment (Radcliffe-Brown, 1922, preface).

Activities in the Field

The field worker's activities may be divided into two categories, which we may call scheduled and unscheduled. The scheduled activities are rather easily identifiable and describable, may be routine and impersonal, and can be programmed in advance. These are the things that the worker is officially "doing"; he points to them when asked to explain his activities or justify his presence. A great deal of routine data collection may be included in the scheduled activities—mapping a village, taking a census, collecting genealogies, measuring food intake or listing diet items, clocking a villager's daily schedule, administering questionnaires or projective tests, cataloguing market exchanges, and so on. These data are relatively external and disconnected, meaningless by themselves but capable of taking on meaning for a person who knows the village intimately.

Another type of scheduled activity is interviews with informants. These are necessary whenever some sector of the subject matter is inaccessible to direct observation, such as history, specialized techniques, esoteric knowledge and beliefs. Informants are also valuable in testing interpretations (to be discussed later). Since different informants will have different perspectives on the community being studied, the choice of informants is an important phase of the research. Indeed, in extreme cases the selection and cultivation of informants is the researcher's most important task; for example, the thoroughness of Dalton's remarkable work (1959, 1964) is due to his skillful work with informants. Dalton's subject was that most closely guarded of inside secrets, the actual politics of a factory, so large numbers of strategically placed informers were essential. This work, however, could hardly be called "scheduled," since the interviews were necessarily private and his informants remained secret.

Sometimes the researcher has an official assignment in the community, and this too is part of his scheduled activity. For instance, Dalton worked for a time in the plant he was studying. In Bettelheim's school the participant observers have various scheduled tasks—teaching, feeding the children, putting them to bed, etc. (1955). Sometimes the researcher will be assigned regular tasks by the people he studying, and these will constitute his official activity.

The heart of field work, however, consists of the unscheduled activities in which the researcher is constantly engaged, no matter what his official activities may be. His first and continuous task is to become part of the community or group he is studying. This task imposes an essential requirement of permissiveness on the researcher: he must make himself acceptable, allow himself to be socialized, accept the point of view and ideology of his hosts. Making himself acceptable involves avoiding actions and expressions that would seem alien or threatening to his hosts. As Geer observers, "He should not have the manner or appearance of any group which his informant group distinguishes sharply from itself" (Geer, 1964, p. 325). For example, Blau reports that he made the mistake early in his field work in an office of taking out pencil and notebook and recording interactions on the spot (Blau, 1964, p. 27). This made him seem like a time-and-motion study man to his hosts, who did not regard themselves as factory workers whose every move is subject to scientific measurement.

To be sure, the field worker cannot make himself acceptable to everybody, since he cannot change his personality or identity, and these may irresistibly suggest alien or hostile roles. For example, my access to at least one experimental psychologist was closed off as soon as I used the words "philosophy department" to identify myself. He wasn't having any of that abstract speculation about angels dancing on a pinpoint; he was a scientist and I was not. Similarly, a white man cannot readily gain access to Negro youth, or a woman to a man's organization or a patriarchal community. Since the field worker cannot pretend to be something he is not, he may as well not even try to study a community in which his personality or identity will not be acceptable. In group research, part of the preparation necessary before entering the field is to select researchers who are likely to be acceptable to the community under study; it is often a good policy to send a varied group so that each field worker will be acceptable at least to a segment of the host community.

Though the field worker must make himself as acceptable as possible without deception, he may not necessarily accept every role that is offered him. Some role to which he is being assigned may not be suitable for his thorough participation in the community, and he will have to refuse it, if possible, and try to take a more centrally located role. For example, in a community split into factions it is dangerous to become identified as a close friend of one faction because that will make other factions inaccessible (cf. Gusfield, 1960, p. 101). Here again the simplest solution is to have a group of participant observers, so that some can "join" the congenial factions and some may remain neutral (cf. Gearing et al., 1960, pp. 242-244). In psychotherapy also, the importance of refusing therapeutically unpromising roles is well known. Nevertheless the host community ultimately decides what roles the worker is allowed to take, and he must make the best of them (cf. Herskovits, 1948, p. 85).

Note the contrast between the field worker's and the experimenter's approach to his subject matter. It may be that one universal requirement of scientific methods is for the scientist both to act and to be acted on by his subject matter, but experimentation and field work meet this requirement in opposite ways. The experimenter acts first and is acted on much later. He begins by developing hypotheses about his subject matter and refining them until he knows exactly what he has to look for. Then he takes his subject matter, ties it up, puts it in a cage, "motivates" it, instructs it, and in general controls it so thoroughly that it can only act within the narrow range that he leaves open. Finally he stimulates or signals it, and only then becomes passive as he watches it react. The reaction is the unique contribution of the subject matter to the experiment; no bias, hypothesis, perceptual distortion, on other experimenter activity should be allowed to interfere with it. In contrast, the participant observer is first acted on and only much later active. He is acted on in the sense that he allows his subject matter to impose admission requirements on him, indoctrinate him with its categories and values, assign him roles, and share with him its troubles and aspirations. No prior hypotheses or bias should be allowed to interfere with this socialization process, since otherwise the objective of studying the human community in its natural setting will be blocked. Only much later, in the stage of testing interpretations and searching for limits, does the researcher begin to act on his subject matter.

Discovery and Interpretation of Themes

As soon as the participant observer has begun to be socialized he can begin observing, though not as yet participating. His observations and his scheduled activities together produce a steady stream of data, though in a haphazard and helter-skelter fashion. He does not wait for masses of data to be collected, processed, and analyzed, as in survey research methods, but begins immediately to develop his case. His first step usually is what has been called "engaging in free-floating attention" (Erikson, 1959a, p. 80) or "listening with the third ear" (Reik, 1949). It is a process of waiting to be impressed by recurrent themes that reappear in various contexts. His waiting is not entirely passive; it may involve running over his check list and noticing that something is recurrently absent, or noticing that a hypothesis one has taken into the field is continually supported or disconfirmed, or noticing a regular contrast with some other situation. Frequently, however, it is simply a matter of being surprised by something. Some themes are major in that they appear frequently and in many different contexts, while others are minor.

For example, Geer notes that among the major themes she discovered in her first few days of studying entering freshmen were the notions of bigness —KU is a big place—and seriousness about school; the latter was contrary to her expectations (Geer, 1964, pp. 337-340). The theme of seriousness appeared in three different contexts: academic, social, and career.

Once a theme is identified it must be interpreted: what does it mean? Here the hypotheses and theories taken into the field can be used to suggest interpretations, and other interpretations can be developed by observing the context in which the theme appears. For instance, Geer noticed that "seriousness" was often connected to a "real life" theme—college, unlike high school, is part of real life. This suggests the interpretation that "freshmen are serious *because* they regard college as part of real life." The researcher does not rest satisfied with his first interpretation but thinks up as many as he can, sometimes quite rapidly (as Meehl notes with regard to clinical interpretation; 1954, p. 120). Each interpretation is tested, and those that survive are tested some more. Testing and revision of interpretations is a continuous process.

Clinical Evidence

Themes and interpretations are tested by comparing them with evidence, either evidence that is already available or new evidence. This brings us to the nature and uses of evidence in the clinic and in the field.

In statistical surveys investigators are concerned with both reliability and validity of evidence. By "reliability" they mean roughly the extent to which different investigators using the same data-collecting instrument on the same population will agree in their results. In other words, the reliability of a data-collecting instrument is the extent to which its results are independent of the person using it. An instrument that depends heavily on the intuition, empathy, or judgment of the investigator or on his personal relationship to the people he is studying is unreliable because different investigators will get different results with it. Conversely, the ideally reliable instrument is one that is wholly automatic and impersonal. Reliability is measured by having different investigators use an instrument on the same population and measuring the extent of their agreement.

By "validity" survey researchers mean roughly the extent to which data are in some sense "true." In practice this means the extent to which different data-collecting instruments or different parts of an instrument will agree when applied to the same event (cf. Cronbach and Meehl, 1955). For instance, if a person is asked the same question six times, each time in different words and different circumstances and different sequences, and if he gives the same answer each time, this agreement suggests high validity for the testing instrument. Measures of validity can be built directly into the instrument, and there are standard procedures for doing this (cf. Kendall and Lazarsfeld, 1950, pp. 169-181).

The holist is interested neither in reliability nor in validity in this sense.

Reliability implies the ideal of an impersonal, automatic investigator; but in case studies, the personality of the investigator and his relations with the people he is studying are an essential source of understanding. Validity in all four of its officially (American Psychological Association) approved senses is in the relationship between a test response, profile, or pattern and some real attribute or quality; but to the holist such isolated data are nearly meaningless because they have no context (Erikson, 1966, pp. 157-158).

The holist uses evidence to build up a many-sided, complex picture of his subject matter. He accomplishes this by using several kinds of evidence, each providing a partial or limited description that supplements other partial descriptions. Similarly, complex studies will often employ two or more investigators, each providing a partial perspective that supplements the perspective of the other investigators. When several kinds of evidence are available, any particular bit of evidence can be interpreted in the context of other bits to determine its meaning. For instance, a Rorschach test might provide evidence that a person is prone to use a certain kind of defensive tactic, say dissociation of affect; a Thematic Apperception Test might specify the kind of interpersonal situation that the subject sees as threatening and requiring defense; direct observation might yield evidence on the behavioral manifestations of the defensive tactic; and a life-history interview might suggest the latent meaning of the tactic for the person. Taken separately, these bits of evidence mean little; combined, they tell a good deal about the person and about each other. Or again, statistics might reveal a significant shift in grievance rate or material spoilage in a factory; interviews might reveal a pattern of verbalized discontent; direct observation or participation might locate work situations producing discontent, showing that the verbalized grievances had been rationalized in a certain direction to make them sound legitimate; and company records might reveal a shift of operating rules that led to frustrated illegitimate expectations.

But evidence can be used to build up a many-sided description in this way only if it is true in some sense. The holist is not concerned with reliability because his method is not impersonal, but he must be concerned with something analogous to validity in the sense discussed above. He need not be concerned with the atomistic validity of an isolated test response or profile predicting a single character trait or attribute; his concern is rather with contextual validity. Since the participant observer or clinician always has several different kinds of evidence available, he can always assess the validity of a kind or piece of evidence in the context of others.

Contextual validation takes two main forms. First, the validity of a piece of evidence can be assessed by comparing it with other kinds of evidence on the same point. Each kind, as I shall indicate presently, has its own characteristic ambiguities and shortcomings and distortions, which are unlikely to coincide with those of another kind. Consequently, when several kinds of evidence agree on some point, the result is assumed to be relatively dependable. Manning Nash provides an example:

When I say, for example, "the family considers taking a meal together as a nearly sacred occasion," this statement reflects the dozens of meals I have taken with Cantelenses, seeing them keep silent during eating, noticing the formality with which the food is served, hearing accompanying thanks to the deities, and remarking the general attitude of ceremony surrounding the eating. I have also asked them what they think the meal means, and why they do the things they do. And they have told me in part that the meal is akin to the mass, that the food is a token of the beneficence of nature, and that they are thankful to fill their stomachs, and similar kinds of remarks. Each man and woman says something akin to, and yet different from, his fellow villager; just as each meal is like and still different from the one which preceded it and the one which will follow it. My report of the meaning of the meal is a summary of the regularities in meals. It is a blend of things seen and things explained, and becomes a social fact to be reported when I feel that I am able to act in a Cantel meal on the same general premises as do the people of the community (Nash, 1955, p. 2).

Here three kinds of evidence—observation, informant statement, and participation—all converge on the same theme. (cf. also Spence, 1968, for a discussion of how evidence is cross-validated in psychotherapy.)

This sort of validation is commonly used in testing a theme or interpretation. When a theme is discovered in informant statements and questionnaires, it is tested against observation on the same point; themes located by observation or participation are tested by questioning informants; regularities in official records are checked against interaction counts by observers; and so on.

The second form of contextual validation is to evaluate a source of evidence by collecting other kinds of evidence about that source. The objective here is to locate the characteristic pattern of distortion in a source, so that it can be taken into account in using later evidence from that source. For example, the characteristic distortions of a particular informant can be determined by observation and by comparison with other informants (cf. Llewellyn and Hoebel, 1941, pp. 29-32); observer bias can be estimated by checking observations against test results and informants' opinions; test results can be checked against observation, opinions, and behavior in crisis situations. Churchman has emphasized the importance of this sort of validation. Its advantage is that once the characteristic distortions of a source of evidence has been determined, its output need not be checked again point for point but can be immediately corrected or interpreted.

The techniques of contextual validation enable the holist to use types of evidence whose independent validity might be middling to low, since the different types of error are presumed more or less to cancel each other out. When a psychometrician or survey researcher finds that a testing instrument has low validity, he discards it or tries to redesign it; but the holist simply reinterprets the results. For instance, if an informant brags or idealizes, his remarks can be discounted or he can be consulted only on certain topics. If a testing instrument is ambiguous rather than consistently off by a certain amount, its output can be compared with other equally ambiguous instruments in a convergent process.

Of course, this technique of cross-checking various middling to weak kinds of evidence will never produce certainty, but only varying degrees of plausibility. When only one or two sorts of evidence are available on a point, the researcher's interpretation must remain hypothetical; if many kinds of evidence substantially agree, he can be fairly sure of an interpretation. The reader must remember, however, that I am discussing the use of evidence in a method of discovery, in which a test is always a check point that serves to tell the researcher whether he is moving in the right direction. Every scientific method I have studied has check points built into it, each checking some detail of the developing theory or description against some sort of possible error. When there are many check points no one need be infallible and conclusive, since later checks can catch errors that escape earlier ones. The researcher builds redundancy into his checks as a substitute for individual infallibility. Consequently there is no need for a single grand test of a whole product. The philosopher's dream of a crucial experiment in which a laboriously developed scientific theory stands or falls as a whole is a myth for the social sciences, whether or not it is true for physics.

In the present context this means that a test of a particular theme or piece of evidence against other available evidence need never be conclusive, since later tests are likely to catch errors that pass earlier ones. A theme is tested during its initial formulation against the evidence then available; it is tested against as it is being built into a model of a case; and it may be tested again when the case is compared with other cases. A different kind of testing occurs at each stage, since the theme is examined in a different, broader factual context each time. A source of evidence is tested by comparing its output with the output of other sources; it is tested again as it itself is being built into the model of the case being described. An informant, for instance, is tested both by checking what he says and by finding out what he is in the community being studied. The two quite different contextual checks supplement each other.

To distinguish contextual validity from the kind of validity important to the psychometrician and survey researcher, I shall venture to call it *dependability*. The dependability of a source of evidence is the extent to which its output can be taken at face value relative to other sources of evidence, in the process of interpreting manifold evidence. None of the evidence used by clinicians and participant observers is absolutely dependable; none is ever completely free of the need for cross-checking and reinterpretation. The techniques of contextual validation must be used more or less continuously on nearly all the evidence gathered.

Let us consider these points in more detail. I have argued that the essential characteristic of evidence in case study methods is the use of several kinds of evidence for cross-checking and reinterpretations. I can distinguish seven kinds of evidence, each with its own strengths and weaknesses.

Informant Statements

Informant statements are valuable because of their great range and variety. One can get statements about many events that no one person could ob-

serve by himself, and one can get reports on the same event from many informants, so that the statements of one informant can be checked against
those of others. The range of a theme across situations and across informants can be readily discovered, and hypotheses about the theme can be
checked over the whole range. Does the hypothesis apply whenever the theme
appears, or are there negative cases? If so, what explains the range of applicability? Does this answer also explain why the theme does not appear in
certain circumstances or in the statements of certain informants? Would a
modification of the hypothesis take care of the negative cases?

A further advantage of informant statements is that one can usually
come back for more to fill in gaps or recheck puzzling points. Thus if the
answers to the previous questions are not clear, the researcher can continue
checking against new statements and can solicit statements in the specific area
being studied. He may even try to predict how an informant will answer a
certain question, as a check on his hypothesis.

Informants' statements are biased in various ways, depending on the topic,
the circumstance, the informant, and his relationship to the researcher. To a
newcomer an informant is likely to give an idealized version of what happens
or how he feels; a co-operative informant may report what he thinks the researcher wants to hear or would find interesting; esoteric material is likely to
be simplified to the researcher's presumed level of comprehension; in politics,
the informant will repeat official versions of the doings of his friends and
nasty rumors about the doings of his opponents; perceptual and cognitive
distortions may occur in material in which the informant is personally involved and important details may be missing in material in which he is not
involved; and so on. (Cf. Vidich and Bensman, 1960; Llewellyn and
Hoebel, 1941, pp. 29-37.)

This means that informant statements cannot be accepted as plain truth,
but must be checked against other evidence where possible. The purpose of
cross-checking is not to find the true statements and dependable informants
and to discard the rest; there would be little, if any, material left. The purpose is rather to estimate the probable direction and amount of bias and to'
interpret the statement accordingly. If the statements of a particular informant are consistently biased in a certain way, they do not have to be
checked individually but can be interpreted as soon as they appear. More
usually, deviations form a more complex pattern that cannot easily be
predicted.

The pattern of bias itself may be of interest. A particular informant's pattern of distortions can help to locate him sociometrically in relation to other
informants with other patterns. If other evidence indicates that a particular
report is idealized, the pattern of idealization and the relation between ideal
and actual reveals something about the defense mechanisms of the institution or personality being reported on. Nasty rumors about the political
opposition can be interpreted as projective statements revealing the infor-

mant's fears and hostilities, or perhaps his judgment about the fears and hostilities of the public who might overhear his statement. In short, informant statements are not to be treated as quasi-objective descriptions of a subject by an outsider, but rather as part of the subject being studied. They are the subject's report about itself.

Documents

The same cautions apply to written records and documents—autobiographies and memoirs, memos and reports, official records and minutes. Autobiographies and memoirs are obviously biased by the writer's need for self-esteem and limited by his perspective, and so must be checked against others' statements and reports. Unofficial memos and reports must be interpreted in their organizational context, and official records give only an idealized public version of what happened. Often the omissions are more interesting than the inclusions in such records; for example, Dalton's chief interest in his firm's records was in the pattern of falsification he found in them (1964, pp. 77-78, 81).

Observation

Personal observation is a most important kind of evidence, chiefly because it is cheap and readily obtainable. There are areas in which it is not easily come by, such as history, folklore, personal beliefs, and deep personality factors; and there are circumstances in which it is expensive, for instance, if an ethnologist becomes famous and too high-paid to have much time for field work. But for ordinary behavior and overt personality factors, observation is usually the best evidence. The main problem with observation is observer bias. All the theories and hypotheses the observer takes into the field affect his perception and interpretation; personality and cultural differences are further sources of bias; and his position and mode of involvement provide a bias of perspective. This does not mean that observations are to be discarded as invalid; they must simply be interpreted. Biases of perspective can be located, interpreted, explained, and allowed for on the basis of comparison with observations from different perspectives. Personality biases can be located, interpreted, and allowed for on the basis of self-knowledge. Where personality bias is important, as in the intimate interaction of psychotherapy, the achievement of greater self-knowledge is an important part of training for clinical work. Theoretical biases can be located by having one's theories made explicit to oneself, and by consciously searching for evidence that contradicts one's theories and hypotheses (though I doubt whether anyone actually does this). And, most important, observations can be checked against other kinds of evidence.

Self-observation is a special source of evidence that is sometimes overlooked. When the observer has been well socialized, or when the clinician has established a substantial relationship to his patient, his own reactions are part of the system he is studying. Consciously and intellectually he is

still the detached observer, but emotionally and subconsciously he has become an active part of his subject matter. Consequently his intuitive reactions provide evidence as to the covert meaning of actions or statements. For
example, Erikson was able to treat his own anger as evidence that his patient was trying to make an unreasonable demand on him and, in combination with other kinds of evidence, this led to an interpretation of a dream
report (1959a, p. 93). Evidence from self-observation is reliable only insofar
as the observer is really a socialized part of his subject matter; since no one
is ever completely socialized this sort of evidence by itself is not completely
dependable either.

Tests, Mappings, and Counts

A different sort of evidence is provided by the tests, mappings, and
counts the observer may have collected as part of his scheduled activity.
Some of this evidence may extend into areas not otherwise covered; for
instance, one may engage in intensive direct observation of a small sample
area and then use questionnaires to survey the rest more superficially. The
questionnaire should then alert one to the existence of variations limiting
the generality of conclusions about the sample area. Tests and mappings
more usually provide additional evidence on points already covered. For
example, a village map provides evidence of the degrees of geographical
closeness of factions or clans, supplementing more direct evidence of their
political unity or emotional closeness; and projective test evidence on defense
mechanisms can supplement direct observation of defensive behavior.

The evidence provided by tests is no more dependable by itself than any
other kind. Answers to tests can be regarded as a kind of informant statement, and as such are subject to all the distortions and inaccuracies of any
such statement (cf. Vidich and Bensman, 1960, pp. 201-203). In addition, the impersonal or otherwise unfamiliar testing situation may produce
its own pattern of distortion. The field worker tries to estimate the pattern of
distortion by discovering the meaning of the test questions and the test situation to the people involved. He does this by direct observation, by picking
up casual comments, and by comparing the situation with other situations
in which he has participated. He also evaluates and interprets particular
responses against observed behavior and other test results. For example,
Turner finds that "certain regularities that emerged from the analyses of
numerical data, such as village genealogies and censuses . . . became
fully intelligible only in the light of values embodied and expressed in symbols at ritual performances" (Turner, 1969, p. 8).

Informant's Opinion

Hypotheses or interpretations derived from direct observation and informants'
reports can be tested by asking informants' opinions about them. For some
British ethnologists this is said to be the ultimate test of an interpretation,

and nothing that fails this test is acceptable, no matter how strong the other evidence for it may be (R. Needham, in conversation).

Nevertheless it seems to me that this type of evidence is no more dependable than any other, and that informants' opinions are as much in need of interpretation and evaluation as any other bit of information. An informant may agree with an interpretation because he wants to be agreeable, or because he is not interested in the topic and does not want to get into an argument about it, or because he is momentarily persuaded by the verbosity or the status of the participant observer. He may disagree and correct an interpretation because he wants to show the researcher that the latter is still an outsider who does not understand, or because the style of theorizing is unfamiliar or disagreeable to him, or because he wishes to protect esoteric knowledge. Consequently it is necessary to evaluate his opinion in terms of his relationship to the observer, his style of thought and expression, and his interest and involvement in the subject being discussed. If all these factors are just right, the informant becomes a kind of collaborator and his opinions are most valuable, but this does not often happen.

Informants' opinions are especially unlikely to be reliable in studies of covert culture and in depth psychology. For example, Kluckhohn's study of the latent functions of Navaho witchcraft (1944) could not rely on informant opinions of his interpretations, since his informants would have been preoccupied with the manifest dysfunctions instead. Similarly, a sexual interpretation of the Hopi corn fertility ritual, which involves putting a hoop or ring around an ear of corn, is not necessarily discredited by informants' rejection, though the alternatives presented by the informants may provide leads to other interpretations.

Acting on an Interpretation

The participant observer can also test an interpretation or hypothesis by acting on it and observing the reactions of those observed. For some American ethnologists this seems to be the ultimate test: they understand a culture when they are able to act as a regular member of it (cf. Nash, 1955, p. 2). But evidence that one is acting as a member is provided by others' reactions, which must be interpreted in turn. If someone laughs, he may do so because the behavior he observes is incongruous, or because he is nervous and laughter is a defense, or because he is surprised at how quickly the newcomer has caught on. Nevertheless, the researcher who has become well socialized will be able to interpret others' reactions to his behavior and to correct his mistakes, so this kind of evidence is probably the strongest available.

Challenge

In some cases the researcher becomes still more active—he provokes or arranges challenging situations in order to see how people will deal with them.

For instance, one of Clark's tactics was "to plan confrontations and conflicts among individuals within groups and between groups in order to draw forth deep feelings and ambivalences, and to see how these individuals responded to and interpreted and resolved those conflicts" (Clark, 1965, p. xix). This tactic provides evidence about deeper psychological factors, as Clark indicates, and so will be used mainly by researchers with an interest in depth psychology. Though the evidence it provides may not be obtainable in any other way, it presents both theoretical and ethical difficulties. Action in challenging situations is difficult to interpret theoretically because it mobilizes layers of personality that are not ordinarily active and visible. Few samples of such behavior may be available, compared with the large quantity of more normal behavior that can be observed. Some of a person's possible modes of dealing with challenge may never appear in the samples, and those that do appear may not be representative, since they may be evoked by unusual characteristics of the challenging situation. Consequently the participant observer should prepare himself in advance to interpret responses to challenge. He can predict probable responses on the basis of projective test evidence, observations of more normal behavior, and a tentative model of the whole personality, and he can develop alternative possible interpretations for various possible responses.

Ethically, the challenge may be more severe than expected or may get out of control and damage the personality. Consequently it would be wrong to provoke challenges lightly, without considerable evidence and thought about how well the subject person or group is equipped to deal with them. The challenge tactic is most frequently used by psychotherapists who already have a tentative picture of their patient's capabilities and who also are in a position to extend immediate help if something goes wrong. In the therapeutic situation the tactic serves simultaneously for research, testing a tentative model of deeper layers of the personality, and for therapy, exposing those layers to the consciousness of the patient. It is a borderline tactic belonging simultaneously to science and to action.

A single case study will usually be based on three or four kinds of evidence, since these are sufficient to provide a considerable degree of cross-checking and cross-interpretation. Some complex studies of culture and personality use more kinds, and occasionally one may find all seven kinds. But the objective of the researcher is not to use as many of the seven kinds of evidence as possible; it is to use those kinds that are appropriate to the subject being studied. The holist chooses his data-collecting techniques not for their reliability and validity, as the survey researcher does, but for their appropriateness to the subject matter. He tries to select those techniques that will fit the characteristic modes of expression of his subjects and that will bring out the particular facets of their lives that he wishes to study. This is part of what the holist means when he calls for the primacy of subject matter over method.

For instance, if the people he is studying are used to expressing themselves in action, the researcher will not impose long verbal interviews on them, but will rely more on participation and observation (Nash, 1955, p. 2). In studies of the Plains Indians, old people made good informants because they were expected to sit for long hours by the fire, telling stories and giving advice, while others listened. Young people, on the other hand, were more likely to open up in situations of active participation. In interviewing, one would not ask about rules and obligations if the informants did not think in those terms (Llewellyn and Hoebel, 1941, p. 22), but would instead ask them to tell stories. In studying Harlem residents, Clark found that the tape-recorder microphone seemed to be a symbol of respect that encouraged free expression, while "standardized questionnaire and interview procedures would result in stylized and superficial verbal responses or evasions" (Clark, 1965, p. xix). When Polsky was studying criminals in their native habitat, he dared not use a tape recorder or pencil and notebook or even direct questions; he could only listen appreciatively (Polsky, 1967, p. 128). Nor would participation be appropriate, as this would have marked him as a dupe. In general, the extent of participation is a difficult question whenever deviant subcultures are being studied; sometimes it is essential, sometimes quite the reverse. What is always essential is that the researcher preserve his integrity and not pretend he is something he is not, since dishonesty would spoil the close relationships essential to the method.

In chapter 1 I suggested that holistic historical research can be regarded as a deficient form of participant observation, and I can now elaborate on that statement. The historian who is making a case study of a particular organization or institution or sequence of events can use neither observation nor participation. He is limited to two or three kinds of evidence: written documents, statistical data, and sometimes informant interviews. However, he can treat his limited stock of evidence in the same fashion as the participant observer, checking sources of evidence against each other, combining one-sided or partial accounts, looking for recurring themes, and interpreting them by finding a network of connections among them. Because of the deficiency of evidence, there is much more room for error in this process than in participant observation.

Building a Model

As soon as several themes have been discovered, interpreted, and tested, the researcher moves on to the next step. This step is to build a model, first of some restricted segment of his subject and eventually of the whole system. A model is built by connecting themes in a network or pattern. The connections or relations may be of various kinds: they may be causal or functional; they may involve the relation between a belief and its exemplification or the expressive relation between a symptom and its underlying source, a triadic communication relation or a means-end relation, or various logical relations in belief systems, and so on. Among the functional relations are those of compatibility and incompatibility, that of a tension reliever or outlet to a source of tension (this is also an expressive relation), that of a conflict resolver or manager to a conflict, those of functional alternatives and substitutes, and other more complex relations. Each of the relations or connections in the model is developed as a partial interpretation of a theme. The fact that no interpretation is by itself completely reliable is what forces the model-builder to push on to new interpretations, new relations. Each of these in turn raises further questions and doubts, and so the model expands.

The various relations are discovered empirically in exactly the same way that themes are discovered; they are discovered along with the themes and in some cases are included in the statement of a theme. However, the attempt to construct a model always reveals missing connections, which must be sought in existing or new data. In many cases relations are directly observed; for example, in therapy and in projective testing, relations appear as continually recurring free associations.

> He made clay worms. Snakes. Guns. But always something had to happen to them. . . He had to turn them into eggs or cookies or cakes; boats, canoes, or what not . . . Inevitably he would put cracks or holes or hollows in these from which water would drip or splash (Baruch, 1952, p. 65).

The relation observable here is a sequence of themes in time, from the clay-worm theme through the something-happening theme to the hole-with-water theme. In studying families, small groups, city governments, or organizations, one can similarly observe recurrent sequences of action and counteraction.

Frequently connections appear as recurrent sequences in interview data and written records:

> The political heads will ratify almost any proposal upon which the principally affected interests agree, and they will postpone as long as they can a decision upon any proposal about which they are not agreed. Knowing this, the interests try very hard to reach "out of court" settlements . . . The principal civic leaders are therefore constantly engaged in negotiations with each other (Banfield, 1961, pp. 271-272).

Here the first sentence summarizes two recurrent sequences in interviews and records: civic leaders (the interests) agreeing on a proposal and the mayor (the political head) accepting it, civic leaders disagreeing and the mayor postponing action. The other two sentences presumably report Banfield's hypothesis about a further connection between what civic leaders know and what they do. Such a hypothesis would be confirmed if an informant were to say, "I knew the Mayor would approve the plan if we could get X, Y, and Z to agree to it, so we went and talked it over with them." It would be disconfirmed by a failure to turn up any such statement even with "why?" questions.

Occasionally connections are discovered by statistical analyses of quantitative data; for an example of a holist using statistics in this fashion see Epstein, 1967, pp. 44-45.

Since connections are discovered empirically rather than inferred logically, they are not *necessary* connections as in formal models. Each connection, therefore, is as dubious as the data in which it is found. When a connection is directly observed, the observations are always subject to observer bias, including theoretical preconceptions, personal needs, expectations, and the observer's standpoint. Connections appearing in interviews, records, quantitative data, and other sources are subject to the shortcomings of those sources. Consequently, observed connections must be subject to the same continuous testing against other kinds of evidence as are themes. Note that the participant observer does not follow the mistaken advice of Hume and Kant, who argued that since empirical connections are not absolutely indubitable it is necessary to call in nonempirical apparatus to guarantee them.

Subsystem models can take a variety of shapes because of the many kinds of relations available as possible components. For example, Redfield discusses four kinds of patterns that he noticed during his work in Yucatan (1960a, pp. 20-24). One was the annual cycle of agricultural activities, a series of links in an endless means-ends chain. A second was a maplike organization of human activity around four prominent geographical characteristics, which themselves were related like terms in a mathematical proportion; a similar four-focal point map of human activity occurs in Leighton et al. (1960). A third pattern was radial, with corn in the center of human life and other things grouped around it and connected to it in different ways. A fourth pattern, that of variations on basic themes, appeared in the beliefs of the people. Still other patterns appeared as Redfield continued his work; he observed that the patterns "do not connect themselves one to another by any rule or principle that I can see. And they crosscut or overlap one another; things seen in one systematic context are later seen again in another" (1960a, p. 24).

When all the subsystem patterns are combined, the result is a model or account of the whole system being studied. Such models again take a variety of shapes. Redfield's model, by his own account, is irregular and bulky. The Kardiner-Linton models, in contrast, are simple and streamlined: the two primary institutions of technology and family structure cause basic personality, which in turn expresses itself in secondary institutions. The absence of such a primary causal locus (the two primary institutions of society) is what makes Redfield's model so irregular. A Freudian personality model is likely to focus on conflicts and defenses among the main personality factors, with different factors emphasized by different theorists. A Kelly-type all-cognitive personality model consists of the more or less coherent set of beliefs or constructs that make up the person's perceived world, together with his main ways of dealing with this world (Kelly, 1955, vol. 1; cf. Mischel, 1964).

Explanation

A system model serves both to describe and to explain. The whole model describes the activity of the whole system, and any part of the model taken by itself describes some part of the system. The relations between that part and other parts serve to explain or interpret the meaning of the part. As Radcliffe-Brown observes, "We have to explain why it is that the Andamanese think and act in certain ways. The explanation of each single custom is provided by showing what is its relation to the other customs of the Andamanese and to their general system of ideas and sentiments." (1922, p. 230; cf. also Beattie, 1968, p. 118-121).

This type of explanation is what A. Kaplan has called the pattern model of explanation (1964, pp. 332-336). A theme, and also a relation, is explained by specifying its place in the pattern. For example, Becker and Geer (1960, p. 278) give the following explanation of why interns in a certain medical school use the term "crock": The interns see themselves as gaining valuable experiences by treating actual cases. Certain cases exhibit routine symptoms but no recognizable underlying organic disease. Examination of these cases yields no experience in treating disease, since the cases have no disease. The interns perceive these cases as a waste of their valuable time and express their resentment by a derogatory term. In this case the pattern consists of a conflict between expectations and actual tasks, with the resulting emotion expressed in the term "crock."

If further explanation of other phases of the same theme is desired, one traces more relations between the theme and other things. Thus Becker and Geer explain the use of the term "crock" further by noting that these patients were also disliked because they gave the student no opportunity to assume medical responsibility. The term is thereby connected to another theme, the desire to assume responsibility, and to another conflict, that between students and faculty over the allocation of responsibility.

If these new themes and relations in turn prove puzzling, one explains them by tracing out more and more of the pattern. If one wishes to explain the students' expectations of gaining experience and assuming responsibility, one traces the development of these beliefs in the earlier years of medical school. They appear as solutions to the problems facing medical students, problems that are set by the curriculum, the hierarchical organization of the school, and patterns of communication among students (Becker and Geer, 1960, p. 278; Becker et al., 1961, chs. 12-13).

The objectivity of this sort of model and of the explanations based on it lies not in any one component but in the whole. As I have indicated earlier, the sorts of evidence on which a holistic model is based are not highly reliable, considered in isolation. Consequently any particular interpretation of a theme is questionable, in the sense that plausible alternative interpretations can be developed using much the same evidence. A larger network based on a greater variety of evidence is not so readily questionable; it is more difficult to imagine an alternative that manages to include all the same themes. The larger and more complex the pattern, the more difficult it is to imagine an alternative, and a time comes when no plausible alternative is imaginable. At this point one stops.

Pursuit of objectivity, or verification of a model, consists therefore of expanding it further and filling in more details. The model-builder tries to set up a plausible connection between themes that seem independent or whose relation is unclear, and he tries to bring into the model items that have stubbornly refused to fit. The latter process may involve considerable recasting of the model to make room for the difficult item, may lead to a re-examination of dubious themes and interpretations, and may even lead to ejecting some theme that formerly fit comfortably. Thus the model and its component themes may be considerably and frequently recast in the process of verification. The model-builder cannot stop recasting as long as any considerable cluster of themes remains outside the model, because these themes could serve as the nucleus of an alternative explanation. Nor can he be satisfied if any considerable number of detailed connections remain puzzling, because as these connections are filled in they may call other parts of the model into question.

The process of setting up plausible connections and of recasting a model is not a matter of arbitrary speculation or logical inference but rather one of observation and search. Puzzling connections and independent themes indicate the need for further observation in those specific areas, or for cross-checking existing data. When this cross-checking fails to turn up a connection, it may be necessary to try a new kind of data collection. In any case, the search must continue until the connections are found or clarified.

Objectivity can also be pursued to some extent by increasing the dependability of a particular interpretation, for instance by re-examining a source of evidence or bringing a new kind of evidence to bear. However, this is also a process of developing and extending a small pattern, as I have indicated earlier. A source of evidence is authenticated by explaining how it operates, including how it distorts or focuses, and this explanation consists of building a pattern around it. For example, the dependability of an informant is clarified by locating his role in the community, namely, the kind of information, stories, and advice he is regularly expected to provide; by describing his personality, namely, the pattern of anxieties, defenses, values, and ideas that determine his perceiving and thinking; and by determining his relation to the participant observer, including possibly the way it recapitulates his other relationships. Each of these is a pattern. Similarly, two or more kinds of evidence support each other when the differences between them can be explained by their respective biases. For instance, the difference between an informant's account of a ceremony and direct observation of it may be explained by the informant's tendency to idealize, by his special interest in some part of the event, and by the observer's ignorance of certain symbolic meanings. If such an explanation is possible, the two accounts reinforce each other. In all of these cases the degree of objectivity depends on the size and complexity of the pattern involved.

Abraham Kaplan sums up the matter of objectivity nicely when he suggests, "For the pattern model, objectivity consists essentially in this, that the pattern can be indefinitely filled in and extended: as we obtain more and more knowledge it continues to fall into place in this pattern, and the pattern itself has a place in a larger whole" (1964, p. 335). To be sure, it is rarely the case that new facts fit directly into a pattern without changing it, but Kaplan is stating the ideal. Note also that the pattern model of explanation is somewhat similar to the coherence theory of truth; in both cases truth comes in large packages.

There are several characteristic differences between the pattern model and the well-known deductive model of explanation, in which a particular occurrence or regularity is explained by deducing it from a general law. First, in the deductive model there is always a sharp distinction between the *explanandum*, the thing to be explained, and the *explanans*, that which does the explaining. The explanans is always more abstract and more general than the explanandum, and can be used on other occasions for an indefinite number of other explanations. Thus the explanandum may be a particular occurrence, an empirical regularity, or a low-level law, while the explanans is always a general law or system of laws. The explanans can even belong to an entirely different discipline, as when a historical fact is explained by psychological laws or an empirical regularity in political behavior is explained by an economic or sociological theory.

In the pattern model both explanandum and explanans are on the same level of generality, and the relation is that of part and whole. Both are equally particularized to the system being described, and no general laws appear anywhere. The whole explanation is a description of a particular personality, social, or cultural system, and no statement within the explanation need be generalized beyond that system. This does not mean that the statements necessarily refer to particular facts; they may also refer to a general practice, a widely held belief, a standard type of defense mechanism, a cultural norm or law.

General laws are used to suggest practices or tendencies that may be operative in a particular system. For example, if there are laws of dream and symbol interpretation, they cannot be used to explain directly a particular dream symbol: one cannot say that climbing a staircase symbolizes sexual activity; this dream includes a climb up a staircase, and therefore this dream is about sexual activity. Such an explanation would take the particular symbol out of its context, the dream and the dreamer. Instead, the general law should be understood as a statistical generalization: "usually, for most people most of the time . . . ." Then the particular circumstances of this dream and this dreamer can be examined to see whether the generalization holds in this case. If it does hold, the generalization has served to direct attention to the specific factors that provide the real explanation. To the holist, generalizations and general laws do not explain; only specific circumstances do.

Devotees of the deductive model of explanation can argue that every case is a member of an implicit class of cases, that every explanation of the case depends on implicit statistical generalizations ("covering laws") about the implicit class, and that a pattern explanation is therefore an implicit deductive explanation in disguise. Though this may seem like an absurd bit of hocus-pocus in which imaginary laws and classes are conjured up ad hoc, there are some case studies in which it makes sense. However, it is of little practical value because (1) implicit statistical generalizations do not in fact exist in most cases; (2) where tentative generalizations exist, they are in most cases not as well verified as the model of the particular case; and (3) even if a well-confirmed statistical generalization were available, it would give only a list of possible outcomes, each with its associated probability number, and would not explain the specific outcome that is in question. Consequently, if a pattern explanation were to be transformed into a deductive explanation by an overenthusiastic logician, some of its information and most of its validity would be lost in the process. It would be a case of the dog dropping his real bone to snap at the imaginary logical bone he saw reflected in the water.

Consider, for example, Baruch's case study, *One Little Boy* (Baruch, 1952). The explanation of the boy's poor schoolwork and of his asthma looks like this when diagrammed:

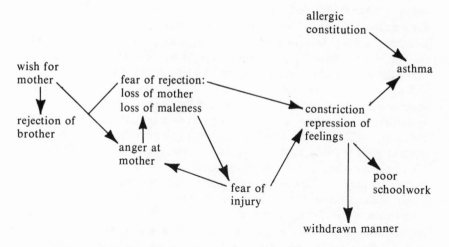

One center of dynamism in this pattern is the vicious circle of reinforcement between anger and fear of rejection; asthma and poor schoolwork are explained as symptoms of this circle. The pattern as a whole seems arbitrary until it is seen as part of a larger pattern of vicious circles involving the mother and father; this pattern in turn is explained by fitting it into a still larger one involving grandparents, brother, employer, and friends.

The deductive version of this explanation would bring in an implicit statistical generalization about the causes of asthma, in the form of a long list of causes, each with a number stating the amount of variance that is explained by that particular cause. One can also imagine a statistical generalization about the symptoms or behavioral consequences of fear of rejection, each with a number stating the probability of that particular consequence. Neither of these potential generalizations is now known, except perhaps vaguely; and even if one of them were known, it would explain this boy's asthma only by stating the probability of its occurrence in this class of cases. The more restricted the class, the larger would be the probability; but restricting the classes would also make the generalization more complex and more difficult to discover and verify. At the limit, the generalization would be limited to this one case and would be a pattern explanation.

A pattern explanation shows the direct connection *in this case* between asthma, anger, and fear of rejection. The connection is directly observable as a regular sequence in the clinical evidence and does not depend on any implicit general law. Similarly, most of the other connections in the pattern are better known through direct observation than through the potential general laws that would replace them. Only the more remote elements of the pattern are not directly observable and so must be conjectured on the basis of general laws. Consequently a transformation of the pattern explanation into a deductive explanation would greatly weaken it.

On the other hand, there are cases in which such a transformation seems appropriate. Take, for example, Nadel's explanation of the aspects of Nupe witchcraft that differ from Gwari witchcraft (Nadel, 1952). The two cultures are very similar, but differ in some respects; Nadel supposes that any one difference is to be explained in terms of some of the other differences (the method of difference or of concomitant variation). His assumption drastically limits the area in which the search for an explanation must take place.

The differences to be explained are the Nupe beliefs that witches are always women and their victims usually men, that the head of the society of witches is also the head of the society of women traders in real life, that men have the power to block witchcraft but occasionally betray their own sex and cooperate with witches. Explanatory factors include stress and mutual hostility in Nupe marriages; the superior economic position of Nupe wives who, by leaving their families to become itinerant traders, take over the financial responsibilities that husbands think they should have; the husbands' expressed resentment of their wives' immorality and domineering behavior; and a general dualism or polarity in Nupe beliefs and values. These factors provide material for a psychocultural pattern explanation. However, Nadel (1952, p. 207) chooses instead a deductive explanation, as follows:

1. When people believe in witchcraft, the particular content of their beliefs expresses their frustrations, anxieties, and other mental stresses.

2. Nupe men believe in witchcraft.

3. Nupe men have certain frustrations, anxieties, and stresses.

4. Therefore, the content of their witchcraft beliefs is such that it expresses their frustrations, etc.

The focal element in this explanation is point 1, which is a place-holder for a future general law about the causes of the content of witchcraft beliefs. This law is treated as the source of explanatory power, and other factors in the situation are treated either as conditions that make the law applicable or as background factors that need not even be mentioned. But if such a law is so important in the explanation, it becomes necessary to discover it, state it clearly, and verify it. Consequently Nadel's explanation points away from the specific case toward a world-wide comparative statistical study of witchcraft.

A pattern explanation, in contrast, would put together the particular factors listed above in a detailed account of Nupe family life and personality structure. The account would immediately be seen as superficial and incomplete, and it would become necessary to collect more facts to fill in the pattern. What meaning for the men does their wives' immorality and financial dominance have? What sort of threat is it? What beliefs and values are available for interpreting such threats, and what defense mechanisms do men use in dealing with them? What are the women up to with their trading? To what extent is the witchcraft accusation a kind of blackmail used to redistribute wealth along channels of political influence? The pattern explanation thus points back to the case and shows the need for a deeper and more extensive study of it. Nadel did not make such a study because, as a member of the British structuralist school, he believed in focusing on social structure and avoiding depth psychology and belief systems. His accounts of Nupe life do not contain such material (1935, 1942), nor did he have available the projective and clinical techniques that would uncover it. In addition, he views all explanation as properly deductive (1951, p. 234). I conclude that in this case the apparent pattern explanation is psychologically incomplete, and really reflects an implicit appeal to a (nonexistent) general law. (Cf. also Radcliffe-Brown, 1952, ch. 1 (1924) where the explanation is clearly deductive.)

In general, the emphasis in a deductive model is on laws, while in a pattern model it is on facts. Facts are included in a deductive model, but only as circumstances that condition the applicability of laws. Laws are sometimes used in a pattern model, but only as suggestive guides in the search for directly observed particular connections. Consequently, to devotees of the deductive model, pattern explanations look like descriptions, since they cannot find the laws they like to use as sources of intelligibility. Sometimes they dogmatically assert that there *must* be laws hidden in the explanation somewhere, since otherwise it would not really be an explanation.

The pattern model seems appropriate when an explanation involves many diverse facts or factors of approximately equal importance, when the pattern of relations between these facts or factors is important, and when the relations can be rather directly observed in the particular case. The deductive model seems more appropriate when one or two basic factors or laws determine what is to be explained, and when these laws are better known than the individual instance. In the latter case it is the laws rather than direct observation that guarantee the connections or correlations explaining the situation.

A second difference between a pattern and a deductive explanation is that in the former it is not possible to deduce an unknown part of a pattern from a known part. (I exclude consideration of deduction by computer simulation, in which the meaning of "deduction" is expanded somewhat, and where such "deductions" may become possible in the future.) Most of the relations in a pattern are not those of logical implication, and one cannot know in advance which will prove to be logical. A symptom is not logically implied by nor does it imply any particular source, since the same tension can express itself differently in different circumstances, and the same symptom can point to different tensions in different people. An ideological element does not imply any particular exemplification, and an end does not imply any particular means. None of the functional relations is necessary or exclusive, since functional alternatives are always possible. Causal relations are usually not sufficient for deduction either, because the kinds of causes discovered in participant observation are dependent on circumstances for their operation. Even the logical relations in a belief system, though at times suitable for deduction, are not dependable, because belief systems can be irrational and inconsistent at any point.

A corollary of this point is that one cannot deduce specific predictions of future behavior in novel circumstances from a pattern explanation; the symmetry of prediction and explanation that occurs in a deductive model is not present. In a deductive explanation one can with equal facility explain the past and predict the future, but in a pattern explanation one can only explain. To be sure, if there is no novelty one can predict that the pattern will continue unchanged, but one does not need science to make that sort of prediction. In novel circumstances one may be able to say that a certain range of behavior is likely and another range unlikely, but not that any specific thing must occur.

Prediction is important for devotees of the deductive model, and an explanation that does not predict does not seem at all like an explanation to them. For instance, the core meaning of "explanation" for Hempel (1965) seems to be the phrase "it was to be expected," which he keeps using as a touchstone, and predictability is part of this core meaning. For devotees of the pattern model, explanation consists essentially of bringing out the connections of a puzzling item with other items. Beattie states it in this way:

> But what every kind of explanation has in common, what in fact makes it an explanation, is that it relates what is to be explained to something else, or to some order of things or events, so that it no longer appears to hang in the air, as it were, detached and isolated (Beattie, 1968, p. 118).

Beattie's way of putting it collapses the distinction I have been making between a pattern and a deductive explanation by making deduction a special kind of pattern. This particular pattern is hierarchical, uses laws or principles as connectors, and yields predictions.

A third characteristic of a pattern model is that a pattern is rarely if ever finished completely. The model-builder always has loose ends to work on, points that do not fit in, connections that are puzzling. The reason lies partly in the method and partly in the subject matter. The participant-observer method involves taking data as they come, and they usually come in scattered, disconnected fragments. Unlike the experimentalist, who can demand evidence on a specific question from his subject matter, the participant observer must adapt his thinking to what his subject happens to be doing. He has to observe each casual interchange as it happens, participate in the ceremony of the day since it may not occur again for two years, talk to the informants who are available, and get involved in whatever problems and controversies are prominent at the moment. At the end of the day he comes home with a wealth of information on a variety of points, but nothing conclusive on any one point. Over the weeks and months his evidence on a given point gradually accumulates and the various points start to fit together into a tentative pattern. But there are always pieces of evidence missing, because the occasion for them did not occur. There are always themes whose meaning remains unclear or ambiguous and alternative interpretations and patterns that cannot be conclusively rejected. The researcher gradually becomes more active and tries to fill in the gaps, but he never quite finishes.

The nature of human subject matter also produces incompleteness of pattern. Human systems are always developing and always unfinished; they always retain inconsistencies, ambiguities, and absurdities. Belief systems never achieve complete rationality and consistency; personalities and groups are always in the process of resolving old conflicts and sharpening new ones; accumulations of power are always crumbling and being rebuilt; ceremonies are being elaborated or simplified. Consequently a faithful model of a particular system at a particular time will itself include inconsistencies, ambiguities, and exceptions. How many of these are due to the inconsistencies of the subject and how many to the looseness of the method is difficult to say.

The participant observer can respond to these twin difficulties by building an idealized model in which exceptions and variants are ignored, developmental dynamics either ignored or frozen at a moment of completeness, ambiguities arbitrarily resolved. This is particularly easy if the subject matter lies in the indeterminate past, as in the case of the ethnographic reconstructions of cultures as they existed prior to Western influence (cf. for example, Fortes and Evans-Pritchard, 1940). These cultures continued to develop during the extended period in which Western influence gradually appeared, and some of their development was in response to aspects of Western culture. Consequently the ethnographer could select items from a period of perhaps sixty years, incorporating earlier items because they were pre-Western, later items because they represented a fuller development of earlier tendencies, along with some Western items (like trading posts) that had been thoroughly absorbed into the culture. The result was a static idealization that understated the amount of change and disorganization in non-Western cultures.

The same idealizing tendency occurs in secondary accounts, such as Benedict's *Patterns of Culture* (1934). Here the author's bias has full play in determining the selection and organization of the primary material, because there is no alternative source of evidence against which it can be checked. Secondary accounts are useful for teaching purposes and for popularization, since they bring into focus aspects of a culture that illustrate a particular theoretical point.

The researcher who does not want to idealize his model can respond to the problem of incompleteness by reworking his model endlessly. This is particularly tempting and easy to do if one is working with contemporary subject matter. New data are continually coming in and clarifying the meaning of old data; the participant observer's position is becoming more secure and his own biases are becoming clearer; and the shortcomings and advantages of all kinds of evidence become better known. Consequently the model becomes continually more detailed, complete, and reliable. In addition, the continuing development of the subject produces further clarification. The meaning of an ambiguous tendency becomes clearer as it develops to fruition or disappears; deviations reveal themselves as either fruitful sources of novelty, harmless sports, or sources of destruction; crises that once seemed all-absorbing turn into minor disturbances or variations on a continuing theme. So even if the researcher is forced to leave the field and publish his incomplete data, he tends to return when opportunity permits, revisiting Chan Kom or Ramah or Boyowa or Mexico City or Tama or New Guinea or Harry for another look and another and another.

Some case-descriptive computer models may also be interpreted as pattern explanations and may remain incomplete for the same reasons. However, this type of modeling is still too new to allow for an adequate judgment on the possibility of completeness. Deductive explanations are also difficult to complete, but there the difficulty is that of conclusively confirming a general law. There are many deductive explanations, particularly in the natural sciences, whose general laws are sufficiently well-confirmed to warrant confidence that they will not be appreciably changed. The standard works on deductive explanation by Nagel, Hempel, etc., are full of examples, where the explanation can be.called substantially complete. The possibility of completion is due partly to the experimental method, which allows the researcher to focus his efforts, and partly to the physical subject matter, which has no noticeable history.

A fourth characteristic of pattern models of explanation is that any or all of the pattern is subject to change in the course of its development. In a deductive explanation the sharp distinction between *explanandum* and *explanans* enables each to be developed and tested separately. In a pattern explanation there is no such distinction, and any part of the pattern may be affected by changes in another part. The process of developing a factual description of a situation is thus quite different from the process of developing a general law that will deductively explain a single aspect of the situation.

Because of the nature of evidence in clinical and field studies, we can be sure that changes will be necessary as new data come in. As I have indicated earlier, no particular bit of information or interpretation is absolutely dependable. Information gains dependability from the convergence of several kinds of evidence, and interpretations become dependable as they gain support from more and more items of information from different contexts. But as new evidence comes in, even well-established facts can be called into question and well-established interpretations modified. Although this happens most frequently in the early stages of an inquiry, even a well-developed model must at times undergo major recasting.

As a consequence, field workers are often advised in their training not to discard any of the raw data on which their developing interpretations and descriptions are based. The time may come when they must recast their account partially or entirely, and at such a time old data may be seen to have new and different implications. And since memory is not a good place to store data, field workers are urged to write everything down as it happens. In particular, they are often urged to keep a diary in which they record everything that happens in the field, even things that seem insignificant or puzzling at the time, because these insignificant facts may later provide clues or support for new interpretations and patterns. Unfortunately "everything that happens" means (in practice) "everything that seems important," and this depends on what concepts and hypotheses are in the air at the moment. Consequently when a model is recast, old data sometimes lose their relevance and the same empirical ground must be covered again.

These four characteristics of the pattern model of explanation are the methodological basis of holism. Holism is not, in the participant observer method, an a priori belief that everything is related to everything else. It is rather the methodological necessity of pushing on to new aspects and new kinds of evidence in order to make sense of what one has already observed and to test the validity of one's interpretations. A belief in the organic unity of living systems may also be present, but this belief by itself would not be sufficient to force a continual expansion of one's observations. It is rather one's inability to develop an intelligible and validated partial model that drives one on.

Writing a Report

Two tasks remain for the participant observer once he has developed and tested a model of his system. One is to draw theoretical implications that will carry over to other cases; I shall discuss this topic in later chapters. The other is to write a report that will be intelligible and plausible to an outsider. In many clinical cases the clinician makes direct therapeutic use of his model, and no written report is necessary. But if one's knowledge is to be used by others, it must be communicated.

This means not only setting down the completed model one has constructed, but also providing enough evidence and reasoning to make it plausible.

The problem is that part of the evidence is intuitive, namely the reactions and interpretations of the observer. These are valid and important data insofar as the observer has become an active part of the system he is studying; but when they are communicated directly to others, they look like dogmatic assertions devoid of factual or logical basis. Consequently it is necessary either to avoid using this sort of evidence in one's report, or if it is used, to make explicit the evidence and reasoning underlying it. This involves a kind of probing of one's own subconscious to see why one reacted in a particular way and why one reached a particular conclusion. The manifold interrelations between observer and subject—mutual expectations, shared understandings, shared experiences—have to be brought into the open; the implicit values, beliefs, and commitments underlying one's reasoning have to be made explicit. This is not easy.

Another difficulty is that some of the evidence is located in the observer's memory, particularly if he has not followed the rule of writing down everything that happens to him. This makes it necessary to search out supporting evidence in the available written documents. A good deal of my own time in preparing this book has had to be spent in this fashion, searching for references that would document statements I had heard orally or remembered vaguely.

The process of making explicit the basis of intuitive judgments and of finding documentary evidence serves as an additional check on the objectivity of one's model. Intuitions can be based on all sorts of things, and memory is notoriously subject to distortion by long-term biases and recent hypotheses. In addition, the discrepancy between memory or intuition and more objective evidence can help reveal the observer's biases to himself so that he can correct his own future judgments. (Cf. Becker and Geer, 1960, pp. 279-289, on the problem of making out a plausible report of one's observations.)

12

Holistic Uses of Statistics

The interaction in recent decades between case study and survey research methods is of considerable methodological interest, especially from a point of view that tries to distinguish the two. If one defines the boundaries of a method empirically in terms of differential rates of interaction among scientists, the interactions between holists and survey researchers raise questions: How distinct are these methods, after all? Are they perhaps parts or variants of the same method, or are they in process of combining into a new method, or is the clinical or participant observer method perhaps gradually becoming statistical? To be sure, there is ample evidence of differences between the methods. Apart from the obvious differences in procedure, there is a tradition of polemic and diatribe (for example, Meehl, 1954; Blumer, 1956; Lazarsfeld, 1959, pp. 67-77; B. Moore, 1958, pp. 93, 129-132) that suggests the existence of sharply different values and beliefs. However, it may be that these polemics are now out of date and that harmony and co-operation are becoming dominant. Indeed, at one time I thought that the holist-survey research distinction was entirely artificial, resulting from some compulsion of mine to separate and classify; or that at any rate, if the distinction did exist it was in process of disappearing. The original title of this chapter was "The Holist-Survey Research Continuum," which reflects that belief. I have since come to feel that the distinction is still sharp and real and not likely soon to disappear, for reasons to be given below. The various combinations and compromises that occur are to be interpreted as frequent borrowings between two essentially different methods rather than as points on a continuum or as forerunners of a new combined method. (To be sure, I may be mistaken in this judgment also.)

Borrowing between the two methods occurs in both directions, but since our main interest here is in participant-observer and clinical methods, I shall describe the borrowings by survey researchers only briefly. The most obvious borrowing of this kind is survey researchers' inclusion of field work as one of many available research methods. Each of the standard texts on survey research methods has one chapter devoted to field work, in which one reads that field work, though imprecise, disorganized, and highly intuitive, is sometimes the only method available for gathering some kinds of data. Because of its many weaknesses, it is not good for verifying hypotheses, but may be used heuristically for a preliminary survey of a problem, for the suggestion of initial variables, indices, and hypotheses, and for a preliminary screening of plausible hypotheses.

Apart from such well-meant but rather patronizing treatment of field work, survey researchers have also borrowed some helpful ideas for use in their own work. For one thing, holist theories and descriptions have reminded them again of the importance of subjective perceptions and attitudes as determinants of behavior, and they have tried to pick up these factors in their scaling and indexing operations. For another, the holist emphasis on the uniqueness and integrity of the individual case, the person or the community, has sometimes been taken seriously by statistically minded scientists, who have responded by devising global and contextual variables and even a holistic type of factor analysis, Q-technique. This technique has occasionally been used by holists (for example, Rogers, 1961, pp. 256-257). In addition, the holistic insistence on the importance of context in determining the meaning of a variable is sometimes taken seriously, leading some survey researchers to define variables according to the context in which they appear rather than according to some constant internal characteristic (cf. for example, Janowitz and Segal, 1967). This tactic is tricky and must be used with caution; the coders of the Human Relations Area Files have accumulated much troubled experience on this point. Finally, the idea of collecting several kinds of evidence on the same point and cross-checking them seems also to be catching on among survey researchers (for example, Webb et al., 1966, pp. 173 ff), though this may be an independent and parallel development rather than a borrowing.

We turn now to borrowing in the other direction. Perhaps the most common instance is the use of sample survey techniques as a source of additional data. The participant observer, as I indicated earlier, may use a wide variety of data-collecting techniques, including various kinds of interviews, questionnaires, census data, village mapping, photographs, tape recordings, projective techniques, content analysis of essays and stories, participation in rituals, joining a fishing expedition, and even sitting and looking at the moon while listening to someone play a flute. He endeavors to adapt his data-collecting to his subject matter and in any case tries to collect several different kinds of data so they can be used to check and supplement one another. For example, Mills' *White Collar* was based on census data and other government statistics, interviews, participation, and direct observation (1951, pp. 356-363). Gans' study of Levittown was based on questionnaires, interviews, and participant observation (Gans, 1967). Karsh, in his study of a strike, used structured interviews that were subjected to content analysis, and also files of correspondence, photographs, newspaper clippings, songs, court transcripts, outlines of speeches, notes, and personal memos; in this case direct observation was not possible because the event being studied was in the recent past, so these data were used to reconstruct it (Karsh, 1958, pp. 161-168). Hess and Handel's study of whole families used interviews (both questionnaire and open-ended), projective tests, essays, and observation (Handel, 1967, pp. 50-52). In general, any new data-collecting technique that the survey researchers invent is regarded as a welcome addition to the holist's repertoire, to be used when appropriate.

The distinguishing characteristic of the holist is not so much the kinds of data he collects as the kind of treatment he gives his data. Both holist and survey researcher can use questionnaires, interviews, essays, census and other official data. But the survey researcher subjects his data to statistical manipulation, while the holist interprets it holistically.

By "holistic interpretation" of quantitative data I mean the following: 1) Any particular number can be revised up or down, or discarded, or given a greater or lesser confidence rating according to other (qualitative) data that the researcher has about the same material. For example, Leighton et al. (1960) make many revisions of their questionnaire data:

> Although the fishermen may answer the questionnaire so as to call time not spent fishing as "unemployed" they are as a rule attending to the maintenance of boat and gear, matters essential to their occupation (p. 263).
>
> Our own observations in the Areas makes it impossible to believe that almost one quarter of the people attend church once a month (p. 276).
>
> Judging from the context . . . it may be that what appears to be permissiveness [on an index] is actually indifference or neglect (p. 293).
>
> Car ownership is down to 22 per cent. This, of course, is to be expected in terms of its insular position and the use of boats [in a fishing community on an island] (p. 264; cf. p. 181).

2) The data are searched for recurring themes. A theme, to be genuine, should show up in several kinds of data, not just one. Once a theme is found, it is checked for distribution, intensity, and variants.

3) Themes are combined into a consistent pattern that describes the dynamics of the system; each part of the pattern is checked in the manner indicated in 2.

4) Where possible, the case is compared with some standard or normal pattern, described quantitatively, and significant deviations are investigated and explained.

This process, I believe, is essentially the same process used in interpreting nonquantitative data. The use of quantitative data adds greater variety to the holist's stock of data—and variety of data is important to him—but does not otherwise change the method.

Note that the holistic interpretation of quantitative data is not possible if most of the available data are derived from statistical surveys, as, for example, in W. Mitchell (1962). It is not possible to cross-check and thus interpret information, to search for recurring themes, and especially to locate internal connections and system dynamics in purely quantitative data. Instead, connections appearing as correlations must be found by the use of statistical techniques. It is possible to conjecture a functionalist pattern of relations among the data, as Mitchell does, but there is no holistic way of testing this pattern. Functionalist theory in this case becomes a static set of categories for classifying facts rather than a heuristic set of concepts and questions to guide new observation.

A second holistic use of statistical techniques is to control a sampling process. This use is appropriate whenever a participant observer selects a sample of his case for study instead of trying to observe everything that happens. One could argue that all participant observers necessarily study only a sample, since the complete study of anything is impossible. However, I am concerned now with a conscious, deliberate, controlled sampling process, and this is relatively uncommon in holistic work. Ordinarily the participant observer takes a passive stance toward his subject matter; he accepts data as it comes and continues to accept it until he has enough to construct a model of his whole subject. Only as the model begins to take shape does he become more active, searching for missing evidence, testing details of his construction, provoking crises to observe his subject in unusual or extreme situations. This generally passive stance is effective in studying small subjects—isolated communities, families, individuals—but when the subject is large, heterogeneous, and complex, a researcher using such a tactic would never finish. In such a case it is necessary deliberately to sample one's subject. Instead of studying every family, every occupation, every legal case or political dispute in a community, one studies a number of representative cases.

The necessity of sampling introduces an element of chance into one's method, and whenever chance appears it can in principle be controlled by statistical techniques. There are several ways of doing this. One is to select one's area or areas of study on a nonstatistical basis but to check the representativeness of the results statistically. For example, one could select a neighborhood in a city for intensive study on the basis of its availability and apparent representativeness, and later survey the whole city by questionnaire to determine the representativeness of one's results. If the questionnaire turned up significant variants, these also could be studied intensively. This seems to have been the method used by Schwab (1960) and by Vidich and Bensman (1958).

Another type of control is to use statistics in the first place to locate the sample that is to be studied intensively. For example, in the Hunter-type studies of community power structures, rating scales are used to locate the power elite, who constitute the focal points of the political structure. Similarly, Gladwin used a crude popularity index to locate a representative sample of cases (Gladwin and Sarason, 1953, pp. 210-212). If the community to be studied is complex and heterogeneous, it may be necessary to select a representative sample of areas, and this can also be done statistically; for example, in the Stirling county study (Leighton et al., 1959, 1960, 1963), a set of six areas was selected. The authors describe their method as characterized by "samplings, or studies of aspects here and there in different parts of the society and with regard to different topics as a means of achieving some grasp of the totality and of different components within the totality" (1960, p. 60). The six sample areas were selected by constructing two indices of sociocultural disintegration and applying them to census, questionnaire, and key informant interview data. This enabled the researchers to choose communities that varied in level of disintegration, in ethnic composition, and in degree of homogeneity (1960, pp. 58-89). Unfortunately the authors do not seem to have finished carrying out their research design by examining the interrelations among the sample communities sufficiently; some relations—those between ethnic groups—are examined but others are not. For example, it seems possible from the data that one condition for the maintenance of integration in some Stirling county communities is the availability of discard areas for failures and rejects, so that the integration of one community depends on and promotes the disintegration of another community. At any rate, once an area has been broken up for study into a set of representative subareas, it is necessary to put the parts together again in a model of the total system.

A third and still less frequent use of statistical techniques is their direct application to one's data. A participant observer or clinician will collect a great quantity of data during his months or years of studying a single subject; his field notes, for instance, may have 5,000 or more entries. If he has used projective tests, surveys, or interviews as well, the quantity will be still greater. It may well be that quantification destroys the qualitative uniqueness of human life, but this truth is academic if one's field notes, written or in memory, have 5,000 entries. In such a case quantification has already occurred. But whenever this has happened, it is possible in principle to subject the results to mathematical treatment such as counting, comparing, and ordering on a scale, and even to tests of significance and factor analysis.

This does not mean that voluminous field data must necessarily be given mathematical treatment. Participant observers and clinicians have regular techniques for interpreting data, as I have shown, which accomplish some of the same purposes as mathematical treatment, but in a nonmathematical way. In place of statistical correlation the field worker or clinician can often directly observe the association of two items; in place of tests of significance of a correlation he notes the recurrence of a theme and then searches for the same theme, or its absence, in other types of data. At the same time, these standard techniques depend heavily on the sensitivity of the field worker, and it would be helpful to provide a more impersonal check on his sensitivity and memory. Quantitative techniques can be useful here, not as a substitute for clinical intuition but as a supplement to it.

The simplest quantitative technique is counting, and the simplest use of counting is to check the importance of a theme. Becker et al. (1961) report on their use of such a technique. After a theme had been identified, each of its occurrences in field notes was tabulated according to various characteristics —date, circumstances, type of person involved, etc.—and the entries in each cell were counted. This enabled the authors to confirm the importance of a theme quantitatively; it also enabled them to map its extent over time, persons, and situations, and to define boundaries between it and other themes. Where two conflicting themes overlapped, it was then possible to define a boundary probabilistically by means of a test of statistical significance (for example, X^2 appears in Becker et al., 1961. p. 151). For another example of the quantitative mapping of a theme, see Kluckhohn (1944, p. 59).

Counting can also be used to locate a theme. Instead of waiting to be impressed by a recurring theme, the observer can simply tabulate his data and discover his theme at the top of the list (see for example, Kluckhohn, 1944, pp. 85, 94; Becker et al., 1961, p. 78; Weiss, 1956, p. 42 and passim). This is a standard use for projective test scores; the quantities, ratios, and profiles suggest general characteristics of the person being studied. A more complex technique for discovering a theme or characteristic is to construct an index and apply it to the data; for example, Becker et al. use an index to discover and map the "latent culture" of their students (1961, p. 144). See Epstein (1967) for extensive discussions and illustrations of the uses of statistical techniques in anthropological field work.

When we consider these various holistic uses of statistics we are led to wonder (as I have suggested) whether they are the forerunners of a new combined method, one that will combine the faithfulness to human subject matter of the participant observer with the precision, objectivity, and reliability of the statistical researcher. In fact, it may seem that the new combined method is already here. All of the objective survey research techniques that Lazarsfeld (1959, pp. 67-77) commends as a substitute for holistic mysticism, and more, have already been used by holists. These techniques may have made them less mystical but have not spoiled their holism. Consequently it may seem that with a few more years of practice and development the new method will become firmly established.

To check this possibility we turn to the oldest holist use of statistical techniques, namely the Rorschach test. This test is now fifty years old and has used statistics extensively from its very beginning. If the development of a combined method is only a matter of time, it should have advanced farthest in this area.

The result of this examination is disappointing. I shall argue that (1) it is possible to distinguish sharply between two theoretical approaches to the Rorschach, one holistic and the other statistical, each adequate and good in its own way; (2) this distinction has been and perhaps must be blurred in practice; (3) the result is often likely to be not a synthesis of the best from each approach, but rather a hybrid that is defective both holistically and statistically.

The Rorschach, and projective tests in general, have provided the most common as well as the most ancient meeting ground between the two methodological traditions under discussion. The sheer quantity of test responses makes some sort of quantitative treatment of data unavoidable, while the test situation is in many ways an ideal setting for the intimate interpersonal encounter that the participant observer and clinician prize.

The holist approach appears in the works of Schafer (1954), Shneidman (1965), and Schachtel (1966), to take recent examples, while the statistical approach is exemplified by Lindzey (1961) and most of the contributors in Hirt (1962). The two approaches are not completely exclusive; each has accepted and incorporated some ideas and techniques from the other, and each shows some understanding and appreciation of the other. This is particularly true of Lindzey's sensitive and judicious work. Such an exchange, after all, is to be expected in a situation of continuous contact and interaction lasting over decades. Nevertheless a clear distinction can still be made between the two—unless the distinction I find is the result of sampling error.

The holist sees the testing process as a complex interpersonal situation similar to a clinical interview, in which the subject is responding to a number of things besides the ink blots themselves. The subject responds to the tester, both as a person and as a transference symbol; he responds to the blots in terms of his interpretation of the test situation, including his interpretation of the tester's expectations and implicit constraints; and he interprets the test situation in terms of its institutional setting—clinic, school, home, ethnographic interview. In addition, the tester's interpretation of the situation, of his own role and the role of the subject, helps to structure the situation and affects the subject's responses. Finally, the personality of both tester and subject affect their interpretation of the situation. Some clinicians emphasize the importance of the immediate experiential situation and others emphasize more the underlying personality dynamics, but beyond these small differences there is agreement that the test responses are set in a large interpersonal context.

As a consequence the meaning of the responses must be understood in terms of their situational context, and the clinician must get an understanding of the particular test situation before he can interpret the responses properly. This means that he must be alert to all possible situational cues—to gestures, tones of voice, handling of the cards, sequential changes in behavior, his own actions and reactions, indeed, everything that is happening. For instance, the way a response is given, the particular words chosen or the comments made about it, may reveal more about the subject's attitudes than the response itself. In addition, any other available data about the subject—case history, other test results, interview protocols—are helpful in understanding his personality and thereby clarifying the meaning of his actions and responses. The holist does not believe in shunning this other evidence by engaging in blind interpretation, "blind fortune-telling" as Rosenzweig calls it (1949, p. 188). Indeed, he may insist on collecting other types of evidence to supplement test scores. Schachtel concludes his account with the following warning:

It cannot be stressed sufficiently that Rorschach's test—and any other test—should not be used as the only diagnostic tool, but always in connection with other tests and a diagnostic interview. Only such a variety of perspectives permits us to gain a reasonably complete and rounded picture of a person and compensates for the distortions that the meaning of the situation created by a single approach and the view from a single perspective may create. If such a multiple approach does not yield data sufficient for diagnosis and insight into the essential personality dynamics, a retest by another person different in personality type and sex from the first tester may elicit a fuller and richer performance (1966, p. 328).

As for the responses themselves, their relations to each other, both sequential and spatial, are often more revealing than their scorable characteristics. Sequences of responses give information about unconscious associations and about how the subject copes with the impulses expressing themselves in his response. Spatial relations or lack of them give information about associations or incompatibilities and about the subject's way of coping with both. For example, if the Blessed Virgin and a church are seen in a usual sexual area and no sexual responses are given even under questioning, this omission suggests a certain incompatibility and also a certain type of defense.

The interpretation of the test responses and of the situation proceeds in much the same manner I have described in chapter 11. The tester notices recurring themes (cf. Schachtel, 1966, pp. 18, 42; Schafer, 1954, ch. 4); he searches for more instances or counterinstances of the themes in several kinds of data (the test responses being only one kind); he checks his statement of each theme against each instance or counterinstance; he combines themes into a model of the personality; difficulties in fitting together parts of the model send him back to look for new evidence or to recheck old evidence. New evidence is produced by questioning the subject about what he meant by a response, "testing the limits" by asking the subject to find a specific and difficult image in the blots, and in some cases by changing the test format. entirely.

Statistical elements occur in scoring and in standard response profiles. Scoring consists of classifying a response according to a great number of standard criteria: whether it refers to a whole card, or a part, or a small part; to white, or black, or shaded, or colored areas; to the form of the blot, or its colors, or combinations of the two; whether movement is reported; and others. Then the content of the response is classified, both according to standard categories—animal, human, anatomical—and how common that response is to that blot. When each response has been classified, the number of responses in each category is added up. The subject's score is then reported, partly as totals for each category, and partly as ratios of certain categories. A standard response profile is a mean score derived from a large sample of some population—schizophrenic, normal American, children.

The holist has little use for scoring and sometimes ignores it entirely (for example, Sarason in Gladwin and Sarason, 1953). A score, such as WFA (whole, form, animal), takes the response out of every sort of context and thus is nearly meaningless. Even the standard scoring categories may be objected to because they are imposed on the data a priori rather than derived from the subject's own way of classifying the world (cf. for example, Schafer's objection to content scores; 1954, pp. 117-119). A response score not only loses most of the information in a response, but it may even distort what little information is left, classifying together heterogeneous things and scattering homogenous items into artificially distinct categories. The main search for themes and their interpretation should ignore formal scores and focus on particular responses and response sequences. After a preliminary interpretation has been worked out in this fashion, total scores can be used as a partial check on the frequency of some themes, a partial summary of some response characteristics, and perhaps even a source of suggestions, though the latter will rarely occur. The basic reason that scores are limited to these relatively trivial uses is that scoring categories are mechanically given in advance rather than worked out by the tester to fit the categorizations made by the individual subject.

The other use of statistics is in reporting standard response profiles, and here statistics are of considerably greater use to the holistic test interpreter. The profiles are treated as types, described quantitatively, and the types are used to facilitate interpretation in a standard holistic manner. If a particular protocol looks similar to a particular profile, it is tentatively classified as an instance of that type. This classification produces a hypothesis that the other characteristics of the type will also be found in the case, which is used to direct further study and interpretation of the protocol. If a contrast is found between the type and the individual protocol, the question arises of why this particular case is different. The answer throws a light on the individual dynamics of the subject. For example, if a subject gives a W response on a card where W is unusual, or fails to give a particular P (popular) response, this indicates that something special is going on that is worth investigating. To be sure, if there are many contrasts the case has been misclassified and must be first assigned to a different type. I shall discuss the holistic use of typologies in more detail in later chapters.

Since the Rorschach types are described statistically, an individual case cannot be assigned to a type or compared with it in detail unless it is scored. This is probably the only reason scoring can be defended from a holistic standpoint.

Statistically inclined scientists generally express one of two different attitudes toward the Rorschach. One group takes the position that since the test is not yet adequately validated scientifically, the clinical psychologist would do well to avoid it and use a validated test such as the MMPI. For example, Rotter (1954, p. 288) concludes his discussion of the Rorschach with the emphatic warning that the test is still subjective, "subjective" in this statement clearly meaning "unscientific." The other group takes the position that though the test has not yet been validated there is no reason why it cannot eventually be validated. Since all or nearly all human behavior is probably lawful in some statistical fashion, and since test responses are behavior, these responses probably are governed by laws which in principle can be discovered. The task of the social scientist, then, is to discover the laws governing Rorschach test responses. These will take the form of a correlation to some high degree of probability between some personality variable and some response variable. The problem is to find the right variables and to measure the degree of correlation.

Discovering laws in this way is no easy task; the statistically minded scientist does not agree with Skinner's formalist view that if one can only control an experiment sufficiently one will see order directly, right there in plain view. He expects rather to have to search carefully for the order hidden beneath surface chaos.

The first part of the task is to locate and strip away the contaminating factors that disguise and distort the sought-for order. How does one locate these factors? The purpose of the test, after all, is to diagnose the testee's personality on the basis of his responses; it is not to diagnose the tester's personality, the testee's mood or interpretation of the situation, or the interaction between tester and testee. Consequently, everything other than personality and test response is contamination. The statistically minded scientist can agree with the holist that test responses are affected by the context in which they occur; but if his purpose is to find correlations between response variables and personality variables, all contextual influence is contamination (cf. on this point Lindzey, 1961, ch. 5).

For example, it has been established that the tester's personality affects test results (Lord, 1950; Masling, 1960). Consequently, before searching for personality response correlations it is necessary to control for the tester's personality variables. This cannot be done by standardizing the tester's behavior, because personality factors leak through even a standardized administration procedure (Lord, 1950). Statistical control, involving the use of a large number of different testers, would be possible but expensive; a simpler control would be to adjust test scores by subtracting the presumed effect of the tester's personality.

Once the main contaminating factors have been discovered and controlled, it is possible to search for the response variables that will correlate validly and reliably with personality variables of some sort. It is important to remember that these variables, both response variables and personality variables, are not given to the researcher; they must be discovered. The essence of statistical research methods is the systematic search for variables that will behave lawfully and can be reliably measured. One begins with the obvious surface variables, the W (wholes), D (details), C (color responses), and others, even though it is highly unlikely that these will prove to be the correct ones. When one finds that these do not behave lawfully (Wittenborn, 1949, 1950a; Knopf, 1956), one moves on to more complex variables—ratios such as M to Σ C, clusters of scores or entirely new scores (Wittenborn and

Mettler, 1951), or total profiles. Then there are possible latent variables to be discovered by factor analysis, such as III' or IV' (Wittenborn, 1950b, pp. 172-173). These are complex response profiles which occur with statistically significant frequency in a sizeable number of tests. They also look familiar enough to suggest hypotheses about the personality factors with which they may correlate; III' suggests the hysterical or extroverted personality, and IV' suggests the ruminative, obsessive, compulsive personality. It may even be necessary to bring back some factors previously excluded as contaminants, though this would complicate the laws. A law would then take some such form as "Personality factor P combined with tester's personality factor T or U will produce response profile R $\pm$ r with probability Π ."

Once plausible variables have been isolated, measured, and correlated, it is possible to refine and purify them, to specify variants and ranges of variation, and to specify relevant circumstances and contaminants to be controlled. The end result of all this research would be a set of laws that would make possible automatic statistical inferences from test scores to personality. Insofar as these laws have not yet been discovered, interpretation must still depend on subjective intuition—and to the statistically minded, this includes a large component of plain luck.

The statistical researcher's endless troubles with the Rorschach reinforces his suspicion of the holist who continues to use this dubious testing instrument. "These holists," he thinks, "do not seem to care about Science. They ignore all our negative findings and go on using this dubious test in their mystical way, depending on intuition rather than verified principles. Are they scientists or fortune-tellers?" However, incomplete and negative statistical research results do not invalidate a holistic interpretation of the Rorschach test. The holist does not make statistical inferences by applying a general law to a score; instead he uses an inductive procedure to discover and check particular themes, and then builds up a particular model. He uses previously established results, such as standard profiles or types, not as a basis for mechanical deductions but heuristically as a source of suggestions to be checked in the individual case. Consequently the type itself need not be statistically validated, though of course the more arbitrary it is the less useful it will be. For the holist the primary locus of validity is not the general law or even the typology but rather the individual case. Laws and types can be validated too, but the process depends heavily on the presumed validity of individual case reports, not vice versa.

Both holistic and statistical interpretations of the Rorschach have borrowed from each other. The holist uses statistics to control the collection of samples, to summarize, to check, to suggest themes, and to compare with other cases, as I have indicated. The statistical researcher in turn has learned from the holist the importance of the subjective meaning of a test response to the testee, and he endeavors to score and study this subjective variable rather than outward behavior. He also has learned the importance of contextual and global variables, as Lazarsfeld calls them, and is willing to investigate complex ratios and patterns rather than simple "atomic" variables. But there is still a clear difference between the two interpretations.

We turn now from the Rorschach theorist to the harried and hastily trained Rorschach practitioner, the clinical psychologist or ethnographer. The psychologist is likely to be called on to administer any one of many different projective tests and a variety of other kinds of tests, between conferences, supervision of trainees, and consultations. The ethnographer has probably taken a hasty course in projective tests before departing for the field; there he tries to administer as many tests as he can manage amid his other activities. Both types of researchers are probably inclined to be holists and are familiar with the requirements for a proper holist interpretation. But this sort of interpretation takes time, care, intimate familiarity with the testee, and broad familiarity with standard response profiles, few of which requirements are likely to be available. Consequently shortcuts are in order. I depend here mainly on Lindzey's review of ethnographic use of the Rorschach (1961). Lindzey states in summary: "The anthropologist often appears to have accepted the projective technique as a relatively immutable device that can be administered in a standard manner and scored in an objective fashion, with the consequence of specifiable results quite independent of variation in the surrounding world" (1961, p. 298). In other words, the anthropologist, who is a holist, administers the test under the pressure of circumstances in a standardized, objective fashion, though without controlling contaminating influences; he then makes statistical inferences from test scores using generalizations that are not validated. The resulting dubious interpretations are then holistically combined with other types of field evidence. This sort of combined procedure is defective from both holistic and statistical standpoints, since context is neither controlled nor used to interpret scores.

To be sure, "defective" does not mean "worthless"; shortcuts may decrease the value of the test but do not destroy it. From a holist standpoint, a reliance on superficial test scores and artificial combined scores means that most of the valuable information obtainable from the test is lost, but the remainder can still be worth something as a supplement to other kinds of data. From a statistical standpoint, it may not be objectively clear what the various test scores correlate with, but we do have a general notion of what they may predict; with the help of hunch and intuition we may get a somewhat useful prediction out of the test, which will do if the more thoroughly studied MMPI is not available.

More important, by taking care, it is possible to avoid most of these defects. For example, in Sarason's interpretation of the Truk Rorschach protocols, a variety of information was used—sequences, especially content sequences, other relations between successive responses, expressed attitudes toward oneself and toward the test and the test responses, interaction with the tester, responses to further inquiry, elapsed time, and so on. The ethnographer was consulted for the cultural meaning of response content and in turn used some of the test interpretations as leads to discover and interpret ethnographic data. Scores were used holistically as leads to discovering themes—"Why so many minuses on this card?" "Why does he do so much better on that card?" rather than as the basis of a mechanically deduced interpretation. Total scores for each person were not even computed. Instead of constructing an artificial "average profile" for Truk by adding scores together, Sarason located the "typical" or modal pattern and used individual deviations as leads to the interpretation of a particular protocol (Gladwin and Sarason, 1953, pp. 465-572). Altogether there is very little that either a holist or a statistical researcher can object to in Sarason's procedure (cf. Lindzey, 1961, pp. 269-273).

Nevertheless, even the best clinical performance with the Rorschach does not represent either a synthesis of the best in clinical and statistical methods or an improvement over either method used separately. It can at most aspire to be as good as a good clinical performance. The statistical elements of the test enable the clinician to enrich but not to transcend his own method; they serve to provide additional leads and checks, to summarize and simplify, but not to change basic procedures. And the more ordinary Rorschach interpretation must cope with the danger of combining the defects rather than the advantages of clinical and statistical methods.

I conclude reluctantly that in this area, at least, the holistic use of statistics is not developing into a new and superior synthesis, or even into a moderately good combined method. My former hope of finding such a synthesis has had to be temporarily inactivated. Each method has borrowed concepts and techniques from the other during their decades of interaction, but each still retains, at least for the time being, its own unique character. It also follows that those theorists who foresee an eventual conversion of clinical into statistical method (cf. for example Hempel, 1965, pp. 151-154) are operating completely on faith; I find no evidence of such a development in the area of projective techniques. However, the development of a combined method is not impossible, and it may well be occuring or about to occur in some other area. Specifically, I still think it possible that a more careful examination of recent work by symbolic interaction theorists would reveal signs of a developing synthesis. This is an area in which interaction between the two methods has been extensive and sometimes friendly, in contrast with the rather strained and acrimonious relationships in psychology. And I think it even more likely that new combinations are developing in political science, where the most heterogeneous techniques are being enthusiastically adapted and mixed together, sometimes with skill and ingenuity. If I were to investigate this area, I would begin with the work of James Barber and Robert Lane at Yale and work outward in all directions from there. But traditions are changing too rapidly in this area to allow me to speak more firmly of the future, for a method is not something that exists in an individual work, but only in a tradition.

13

Comparative Methods
and the Development of Theory

Up to now I have discussed only the methods of describing a particular human system in its particularity. Field workers and clinicians are also interested in the development of general theory, and indeed the two interests are inseparable. Without some theory or theories in mind there is no way of developing the many low-level hypotheses that guide observation by suggesting things to look for. Conversely, if theory is removed from contact with empirical reality, it rapidly degenerates into sterile deductive exercises and abstract speculation. Holist theorizing should always proceed in intimate contact with particular cases, so that each theoretical step can be immediately checked against a range of examples.

The classic works in anthropology and clinical psychology combine general theory with particular description in this fashion, and later works have continued the practice. Freud's early theorizing grew directly out of his attempts to understand his cases, and Malinowski's and Radcliffe-Brown's descriptions of the Trobrianders and the Andamanese were simultaneously expositions of functionalist theory. Mead's empirical studies in Samoa and New Guinea were also theoretical examinations of how sex roles affected personality development; Redfield described four settlements in Yucatan in order to apply and study the *Gemeinschaft-Gesellschaft* typology. For some holist scientists the primary interest is in using theory to enrich the understanding of the particular case, while for others the case is primarily an instrument for the development of theory, but both interests are always present.

The basic problem in combining particular cases with general theory is the disparity between the two. How does one move reliably from the particular to the general and back again? Generalization from a single case or a few cases is always a haphazard affair, since one cannot tell which characteristics are general and which are unique. Ethnologists have learned the dangers of overgeneralization from some notable examples: Malinowski's occasional generalizations to all of "savage societies" from his one case, Mead's dubious generalizations about sex and temperament based on three questionable case studies (cf. Bernard, 1945; Zelditch, 1955, esp. pp. 321-324, 336-337; Harris, 1968, pp. 408-414), Redfield's overgeneralizations about the folk society (Redfield, 1941, p. 358), Holmberg's generalization to hunting-and-gathering societies from one case (Holmberg, 1950, pp. 93-94, 98; Needham, 1954). Ethnologists in turn have exposed the overgenerality of theories based only on Western culture.

The reverse difficulty occurs in the application of theory to case. A theory that states what is true of all men or societies at all times is not of much help in untangling the unique complexities of a single case, while a more particularized and detailed theory might not apply to the case at all.

The basic solution is to move from the particular to the general and back in small steps rather than in one grand jump. One first compares one's case with a similar case, then to another and another, then to one somewhat more different. Potential generalizations discovered in the first case can be tested against the other cases. The generalizations that survive these tests are not claimed as universally valid, but valid only for cases similar to those studied. Gradually one moves to still wider generalizations and a more heterogeneous range of cases, though the scope of previous generalizations may also be narrowed in this process. This is the comparative method, which is always used in case studies to produce or to apply generalizations. Comparison is not postponed until the individual case study is completed, but occurs continuously during study and is an essential part of it. For the purpose of consecutive exposition I have split the method in two, but the reader must remember that the split is artificial.

The present chapter deals with the use of comparisons in case studies. Comparison of some sort probably occurs in all social science methods, taking different forms in different methods. The form used in case study methods is sometimes called "the method of controlled comparison," particularly among anthropologists (cf. Eggan, 1954), and I shall use this name. Another name that has appeared in sociology more recently is "analytic induction" (Lindesmith, 1968). In order to bring out some of the unique characteristics of controlled comparison, or analytic induction, I shall contrast it with another comparative method, the cross-cultural or hologeistic method. This comparison is appropriate because both methods use the same data, namely case studies, and differ only in the way data are compared. Other comparative methods, including cross-polity surveys (such as Almond and Verba, 1963) and the cross-national comparisons (Hopkins and Wallerstein, 1967; Marsh, 1965) use survey data and thus differ in more complex and fundamental ways from controlled comparisons.

The method of controlled comparison developed as a solution to problems that arose in comparing cases. Consequently, to understand the method one must see why and how one compares cases, what difficulties appear in the process, and how the various attempted solutions relate to these difficulties.

Comparison provides a bridge between the variability and uniqueness of a case and the uniformity and generality of theory. The bridge is two-way: It makes theory available to guide and control observation, and it makes observation available to test and improve theory. Let us consider the guidance of observation first.

The greatest need for guidance occurs in the early stages of a case study when everything is still strange and confusing. The newcomer to a strange culture or organization or personality is overwhelmed by movements and sounds that make no sense and therefore cannot be described. The idiosyncratic cannot be distinguished from the typical for that culture, and the meaning, the connections, of an event are not apparent. When a man seems to be punching another on the left arm while smiling ("binging," Homans, 1950), is he being his usual quarrelsome self under a smiling front, or is this a personal feud, or a standardized expression of contempt for inferiors, or a casual greeting, or a mark of respect and acceptance as an equal? Many meanings can eventually be sorted out and clarified by long observation and participation, but this is a slow and uncertain process. The process can be speeded up if the observer has a set of reliable guides that suggest things to look for and possible interpretations of what is found.

Guidance is provided by a parallel case that has already been interpreted and explained. The observer asks himself what a puzzling event would mean in his parallel case, and the answer provides a suggestion for interpreting the event and deciding what to look for next. The clinician's rapid interpretation of behavior is based on such comparisons with parallel cases he has experienced. The parallel case brings theory to bear, not in an abstract and universal form, but in a particularized form suitable for making specific suggestions for observation and interpretation. For instance, a general theory might say, "Every society has some kind of law, including rules, judicial decisions, and enforcement; look for these." This is too general to be of much guidance. A case might say, "Study plaintiff-defendant fights carefully. In this case what looked like a fight was probably a standardized form of law enforcement in which the plaintiff was administering a prescribed punishment" (cf. Llewellyn and Hoebel, 1941, p. 59). Another case might say, "Pay attention to relatives of the plaintiff, especially which relative gets involved in a case." These lower-level theoretical statements provide more guidance than the injunction, "Look for law enforcement."

Parallel cases also provide guidance in later stages of a case study by suggesting less obvious things to look for—phenomena that are obvious and well-developed in a parallel case but hidden and disguised in the case being studied. For instance, studies of ceremony and ritual in nonliterate cultures have led to the suggestion that these phenomena are more prevalent and more important in Western culture than had been suspected; studies of repression, projection, etc., in neurotic patients have suggested that these are present in some form in normal people too.

Theory is tested and improved by seeing whether a generalization that fits a parallel case also is valid for the case being studied. If it is valid, this provides confirmation and clarification; if it is not, this suggests limits to the generalization and perhaps a re-examination of the evidence for it. The new case can then be examined to find modifications of the generalization that would make it valid, and these can be tried on further cases. Note that here as elsewhere in science testing is always a step in a larger process of theory development. However, in contrast to other methods of theory development, the case-by-case method is piecemeal—or should be, as we realize from examining rash attempts to jump from one case to a universal generalization.

The effectiveness of a process of comparison, both for guiding observation and for developing theory, depends very much on what sort of case is being used as a parallel. As a guide to observation, the wrong case may not only fail to provide guidance but may lead the researcher into misinterpretations. Areas that are important and well-developed in one case may be unimportant or embryonic in the other; connections and influences that occur in one may be absent or entirely different in the other. Even if the same institutions are present in both, they may take quite different shapes, and their differences may be more significant than their similarities.

For example, Malinowski pointed out the errors that resulted when earlier anthropologists used Western society as a guide for observing a "savage society" (1926, pp. 1-15). Students of primitive law looked for "central authority, codes, courts, and constables" (p. 14); students of primitive economics looked for commercial transactions based on money or barter (Malinowski, 1922, pp. 84-85). As a result they not only failed to find the Western institutions they were looking for, but they also failed to see the institutions that were present. Consequently we got reports of societies that had no law, or no economy, or no politics, or no family, and of course no morality (for example, see Murdock, 1949, p. 264).

When used in developing theory, the wrong parallel case may provide generalizations that cannot be applied to the new case for testing in any clear way. Suppose we are applying generalizations derived from Western society to the Trobrianders: what sort of generalizations shall we apply to what? Is Trobriand agricultural magic a primitive form of science, suitable for testing generalizations about the history of science? Or is it a kind of nonscientific superstition, perhaps a form of magic that, unlike much Western magic, is dissociated from religion, or conversely perhaps an unusual kind of religious practice? Or is the proper comparison a legal one—when the Trobriand farmer puts a mark on a tree to indicate that a curse has been placed on any future thief, is this similar to our "patent pending" mark? (Riesman, in lecture). Or consider the yam distribution system, which centers on the chief. Is this a type of economic exchange, as Polanyi suggests by his classification of types of economy (1957, pp. 250-256)? Or is it a form of taxation and welfare redistribution, both oddly limited to the chief's relatives? Or is the proper comparison political, the yam exchanges being symbolic of political ties like strategic marriages among royal European families and the strategic exchanges of assistance among ward politicians? Such questions leave room for much speculation without any obvious criteria for a correct answer. Consequently, comparison becomes a kind of parlor game with prizes for the most imaginative and unusual comparisons, but little in the way of reliable results.

Even if a series of proper points of comparison were to be found, a second difficulty would occur. Suppose that a generalization presumably valid for one case were tested on a second case and disconfirmed—what next? The two most likely steps, apart from re-examining the first case, would be to find out why the generalization did not apply and to change it so that it would apply. The former would lead to a statement of the conditions of applicability of the old generalization, and the latter would lead to a new generalization of presumably broader applicability. In both steps the search would have to focus on the differences between the two cases; but if the two cases were haphazardly selected—for instance, the Trobriands and Western society—the differences would probably be so great that one would not know where to start looking. There would be too much freedom for the search process. If one were seeking to learn why a generalization did not apply, any of a dozen differences or combinations of differences might provide a plausible reason; and if one were looking for changes in the generalization, any number might be suggested. The process would no longer be an orderly search, but a guessing game of the kind some philosophers of science have imagined science to be.

For example, Malinowski (1927) claimed that the Trobriand case disconfirmed various Freudian propositions about the Oedipus complex. The Trobriand boy's hostility was directed against his maternal uncle while his relations with his father were friendly, contrary to Freud's generalizations from Viennese cases. Malinowski also offered a modified generalization that would fit both the Trobriands and Vienna: in both cases hostility was directed against the authority figure, who in the Trobriands was the maternal uncle, rather than against the sexual intimate of the mother. However, the differences between the two cases are so great that a number of other and equally plausible modifications are possible, and Malinowski's suggested improvement seems arbitrary. For one thing, authority in the Trobriands is exercised by the father till a boy is seven or eight, so that up to that age the predictions of the two theories do not differ. For another, the content of authority is very different; in the Trobriands, by Malinowski's account, it centers much more than in Vienna on complex and interesting incest prohibitions. Then also, the whole shape of sex life and its place in society is different; matrilineal descent and patrilocal residence change the whole basis of masculine identity, and so on. Plainly some changes needed to be made in Freud's generalizations, particularly with regard to how oedipal feelings are expressed after age seven or eight, but what they should be is difficult to determine from this single case.

Suppose now that a generalization derived from one case were to be confirmed by a second case—what then? This confirmation would be significant only if we knew that the second case was significantly different from the first. If the apparent differences were superficial or irrelevant, we would not have learned anything new about the generalization from the fact of its applicability. The comparable problem in survey research is that of the biased sample, in which the same kind of case is unwittingly sampled too many times so that the resulting correlation may be spurious.

The solution to all these problems is to set up a control over the parallel case chosen for comparison; hence the term "controlled comparison." The factor to be controlled is the degree of similarity of the two cases being compared. If a case is to be used to guide observation it should be similar—but with enough difference so something new can be observed. If our primary interest is in testing generalizations, we need a series of cases distributed along a similarity-difference continuum in the area of the generalization being studied, while similar in all other respects if possible. This is a large order; if it cannot be filled one needs at least a case similar in all but a few relevant respects.

The problem is that similarity is a very elusive and deceptive thing to pin down, especially when dealing with complex wholes. Two culture traits that look superficially similar may actually be quite different because of their different context, and two superficially different traits may be actually similar. Further, two cases may each be similar to a third in different ways; which should one use for comparison? Worst of all, one must determine similarity before the new case is studied in detail, if comparison is to be of any use. What is needed are reliable indicators of over-all similarity that can be observed early in a case study.

The survey researcher can see this as a familiar problem of quantification, scaling, and development of indices; and indeed this may be the most desirable way to deal with the problem. However, I am here reporting not what may seem desirable but what has been and is being developed. The method of controlled comparison is essentially a series of attempts to solve the problem of similarity or comparability and thereby provide a dependable basis of control.

The simplest principle of control is geographical contiguity. One compares cases that live as close to each other as possible and that have been close together for a long time. The supposition is that these cases will be similar in many ways because of their contiguity; their economy, their history, their language are likely to be similar, and they will have borrowed many culture traits from each other. When a number of cultures or communities are contiguous one can select the pair with the greatest similarities in language, economy, and history. For example, Nadel selected two pairs of contiguous African societies for his comparative study of witchcraft (1952); Dozier compared the Hopi and the Hopi-Tewa who live on the same mesa (1954); Eggan and others compared several Plains Indian tribes (Eggan, 1937;

Linton, 1940); Redfield compared four Yucatan communities, varying in size from large to small (1941).

The ideal limit of this type of control is to study and compare *all* of the cases that live in a given region, as Schapera proposes (1967, pp. 61-63); one can then observe the full range of variation that occurs against a common background. An example is the Rimrock study, which dealt with all five cultures of the Arizona-New Mexico region (various works, including Vogt and Albert, 1966). In this study, unlike those cited above, the cultures were known to be widely different in historical background, and the focus of interest was on the effect of the common geographical setting. More often than not, however, it is difficult or impossible to isolate a definite region and study all the cultures present in it.

The main difficulty with geographical contiguity as a control is that contiguous cases are not necessarily similar at all. So one must check even contiguous cases to see whether they really are similar; one must, in fact, compare cases before comparing them, which reduces the usefulness of the method. In addition, if two contiguous cases prove to be similar, this may have been due not (or not only) to contiguity but to some other cause (perhaps subsistence technology). Consequently, the real basis for control cannot be mere contiguity, but something else that is sometimes associated with it. Contiguity is only the starting point in the search for this other, more dependable basis of control.

A second type of control is historical. One selects a society that split into two or three parts some time ago, with each part now located in a different environment. Thus the original culture is similar in each case while the environment differs. For example, Spicer compared three Yaqui communities in Sonora, Arizona, and southern Mexico (1940, 1954); Linton compared the dry-rice Tanala with the wet-rice Betsileo who had the same origin (Kardiner, 1939, pp. 329-351); Dozier compared the Rio Grande Tewa with the Tewa living in Hopiland (1954); Hallowell compared the Berens river Ojibwa with the Flambeau Ojibwa and with the related Wisconsin Menomini (1955); Thomas and Znaniecki compared Polish peasant communities in Europe and America (1920). These are usually acculturation studies, since they deal with a single society that has been subject to one or more acculturative influences. They do not really compare two cases, since only one original society is involved; instead, they examine one case under two or more conditions. Consequently they can suggest generalizations but cannot test them without bringing in really different cases. However, they do provide excellent control over observation. One can see how a society deals with a variety of environmental challenges; the coping mechanisms must have all been present in the original society, but their operation and the limits of their capabilities have been made more visible. For example, the ceremonies that Spicer regards as the principal coping mechanism of the Yaqui were present in the original Sonora communities, but the power and range of their effects were certainly not visible there. The various changes that later occurred must all have existed in the original society as potential changes, as paths of growth, accommodation, and breakdown.

Ordinary acculturation studies fall short of these controlled studies inasmuch as the original (nonacculturated) society is not available for comparison. Consequently one cannot determine how much of the observed change is due to culture contact and how much is due to internal strains and disequilibriums. Consider, for example, the Plains Indian tribes or the Zulu kingdom in the eighteenth and nineteenth centuries. Both were highly unstable, the Plains tribes economically and the Zulus politically, and both were changing rapidly and continuously. One source of change was indirectly European—the horse, the gun, population pressure by displaced tribes; another source was direct culture contact; and other sources were indigenous. It is difficult to separate these sources to see what changes were due to each, but one can begin to do this in a controlled comparison.

The difficulty with historical control is that it is possible only rarely. Indeed, in clinical work the only good analogue is the clinical study of identical twins. Further, it is not always clear that the communities compared were originally identical; for example, the Polish peasants who emigrated to America may have differed systematically from those who stayed home. Finally, culture contact is a complex process, and since in all these cases of controlled comparison the contact has occurred in the past, its detailed development cannot be directly observed but must be reconstructed.

A third kind of control is by typology. There are several kinds of typologies that will be distinguished in the next chapter, but for present purposes, a typology is a set of types, and a type is a group of cases that are basically similar. The question of what similarities are basic rather than superficial is theoretical, and typologies must eventually be controlled by theory of some sort to be reliable, even if they are originally developed empirically.

Insofar as an adequate typology is available, the researcher can tentatively assign his case to a type and then compare it to others within the type. He can either select a case that has the similarities he wishes, or he can compare with the mode for the type. For example, the holist interpretation of a Rorschach protocol depends heavily on comparison with a quantitatively defined standard response profile for a type. If the researcher is interested primarily in the development of theory rather than in observing his own case, he can run each possible generalization through a series of cases within the type. Then if the generalization is still standing, he can try it on cases from a different type to see how broad its range of validity is. For example, Apter developed generalizations about the modernization process in political systems by comparing two groups of cases at the opposite ends of the modernization continuum (1965, p. viii).

In either case, comparison within a type means that there are many similarities and relatively few differences to examine. It also means that residual, unobserved factors are likely to be similar and therefore under control. Consequently the problems inherent in the comparison of unique cases are solved relatively well. First, comparability is not difficult to achieve because the basic pattern of both cases, or the case and the standard profile, is the same, and therefore any pair of traits is likely to have a similar context and a similar meaning. Second, controlling differences is not difficult because there are not many differences to control. Furthermore the old case or the standard profile should be a reliable guide to observation of the new case, since most of the standard factors will be present in some form, and the occasional differences will be worth investigating; if too many differences turn up, the case should be reclassified.

Control by type is the commonest basis for controlled comparison because it solves the problems of comparison rather well. Indeed, in clinical work it is the only regular basis of comparison that I know of. Unlike geographical and historical controls, it can be used on any case since it does not depend on fortunate geographical and historical accidents. Also, unlike other controls, it can be indefinitely improved by improving the controlling typology —and this improvement is consequently an important theoretical result of case studies. Each new case can add something to the understanding of its type, by adding an alternative exemplification of a typical mechanism, by suggesting a new variant or subtype, or by confirming or disconfirming the previously accepted mode for the type. For example, Nash (1955) showed that peasant culture, or some subtype of peasant culture, is not incompatible with industrialization of some sort, and that the basis of peasant culture is therefore not entirely technological and occupational. He did this by showing that the factory in Cantel was not a source of disorganization or rapid change but had been absorbed into the relatively stable local culture.

As typologies are improved, they move toward ever greater precision in delineating the boundaries and the mode of the type and toward increasing detail in the form of variants and subtypes. Also, the basis for classification moves from superficial or symptomatic characteristics such as geographical location to more fundamental functional characteristics such as technology. Consider, for example, the development of the "schizophrenia" type (Wolman, 1965, ch. 34). Early scientists described a type of disease characterized by mental degeneration in adolescence. Later Kraepelin classified the various observed forms of this disease, listing them all under the general heading of dementia praecox, or premature degeneration. This name made the disease a type of senility and suggested that metabolic and other somatic factors were essential to it. Bleuler observed that many cases with the same outward symptoms did not lead to degeneration; nor did they all develop during adolescence; nor was the disease irreversible, like senility. He suggested that emotional disturbances, including discontinuity of affect and autism, were central, and thus classified it as a type of psychic disorder. Freud suggested that the underlying mechanism of paranoid schizophrenia was projection, and that regression was an important mechanism in other types. These explanations focused attention on underlying defense mechanisms and suggested that classification should be based on psychodynamic

processes and problems rather than on outward symptoms. Later classifications were based on these factors, on problems and attempts at solution
rather than on symptoms. It also became possible to classify stages of development, or degeneration, each representing a more complete failure at
solving the original problem. A developmental typology makes possible a
much more exact prognosis of the individual case and enables one to chart
the progress or failure of treatment rather exactly.

Control by typology has the additional advantage of enabling one to move
toward the development of general theory in a way that is not possible using
contiguity and historical controls. By a "general theory" I mean one that is
intended to apply to all types of men and/or societies and does more than
simply classify them into types. Conclusions based on contiguity and historical controls cannot be general in this sense, but must be limited to the particular area or particular society or particular type of case being studied.

The construction of a general theory is the most risky and difficult of projects for a case study method, because general theory is farthest from the
individual case. To achieve real generality, it is not enough to base one's
theorizing on many cases, because they may not be representative. For
example, the early formulations of functionalism can now be seen as overgeneralizations from a biased sample of cases, resulting in overemphasis on
stability, consensus, and the integration of institutions.

What is necessary is to find some way of getting a really representative
sample of cases that is still small enough so each one can be examined in
detail. Typologies provide a basic solution to this problem; insofar as the
typology is adequate, a case from each type and subtype constitutes a complete representative sample. With a complex typology, even such a sample
would be too large for intensive study of each case, but one could at least
use the typology to outline a research program. In practice, the general
theorists are more likely to begin working with a few cases as widely diversified as possible, with diversity determined by their typology, and later fill
in the gaps where possible. For example, the initial formulation of the
four-function theory of Parsons et al. was based on studies then in process
of personality development in childhood, the therapeutic process, the American family, interaction in small groups, occupational mobility, "McCar-
thyism" and social tensions, and other problems (Parsons, Bales and
Shils, 1953, pp. 10-12 and passim), against a background of previous
studies of the medical profession, kinship structure, aggression and deviant
behavior, etc. Later studies have gradually filled in some of the remaining
gaps.

This method of developing general theory is necessarily slow and piecemeal. The validity of the result depends on the adequacy of the controlling
typology as well as on the adequacy of the separate case studies. As the
typology is modified, new studies become necessary and old studies may
be called into question and reexamined; and such a process could go on
indefinitely.

The difficulties and the disappointingly slow pace of the method may make some scientists wonder whether controlled comparison is worth the trouble it takes. However, there is no easy solution to the problem of comparing human systems. Other comparative methods avoid the difficulties of the controlled comparison method but have their own compensating difficulties. To illustrate this point and to illuminate further the problems of comparative method, I shall consider briefly another comparative method, the cross-cultural or hologeistic method (cf. F. Moore, 1961).

The use of the cross-cultural method may be traced back at least to E. B. Tylor in the late nineteenth century, but the present phase began in 1937 with the establishment by Murdock and others of the Human Relations Area Files and with the publication of Murdock's *Social Structure* (1949). The HRAF is a data bank consisting of coded information about a sample of societies from the whole earth throughout history; hence the name "hologeistic." The information consists of case studies, in fact the same case studies used in controlled comparisons; the two methods use the same data but subject it to a different kind of treatment. While a controlled comparison begins with two similar cases (where "similar" means "belonging to the same type and subtype") and adds new cases to the comparison one at a time, cross-cultural comparison begins immediately with a sample of cases from throughout the world. While controlled comparisons of a pair of cases are holistic, cross-cultural comparisons are statistical, involving both random and representative sampling, statistical manipulation of data, and statistical controls over the results. Consequently, a comparison of these two methods should illuminate somewhat the problems of comparing case studies.

The problem of comparability is handled in the cross-cultural method by the HRAF data bank rather than by the researcher using the data. The researcher cannot check the comparability of his cases because he has too many of them; for example Whiting and Child (1953) use 75 cases, and Udy (1959) uses 150 cases. The researcher can examine an occasional doubtful or negative case in slightly more detail (for example, Homans and Schneider, 1954, pp. 40-50), but any really careful examination, one that included positive cases also, would take too long. The HRAF deals with this problem during the coding process, when a new case is being added to the files or an old case is being updated. The coder is supposed to read all the literature on a case before coding it, which enables him to get a pseudo-holistic "feel" for the case and also to check different ethnographic reports against each other. His knowledge of the whole case gives him a background for interpreting the meaning of any particular item, so that he can code it according to its real contextual meaning rather than its superficial appearance. In addition, his coding categories are supposed to be culturally neutral so they do not force the meanings of one unique case into a mold provided by some other case. (A controlled comparison, in contrast, can use the concepts and categories of the two cases being compared, because these are likely to be very similar.) The HRAF way to achieve cultural neutrality has been to break items down into smaller and smaller components until one finds, if possible, items that have identical meanings in all cultures. These cultural atoms supposedly are combined in varied ways in different cultures to yield the observed uniqueness of each culture. Holists are accustomed to this atomizing procedure in the technical area of kinship—for example, one speaks, not of a second cousin, but of Mother's Brother's Son's Daughter, or MBSD, breaking the relationship down into its atomic components—but in the HRAF it is applied to all of a culture.

This solution to the problem of comparability—using atomistic categories and contextual coding—brings its own difficulties. For one thing, the ethnographers who collected the data did not know their work was going to be coded, and so they collected the data they thought were important for their own theoretical interests. Consequently, when the coder confronts an ethnographic report with his list of 800 or more items he finds to his dismay that the report is silent on many of them. His first recourse is to curse the participant-observer method for its vague and careless results; then he proceeds to code as well as he can. Some doubtful items he cross-classifies, others he guesses at, and others he leaves blank. These question marks and blanks later reappear in the cross-cultural researcher's data matrices, where they louse up his Guttman scales and throw doubt on his neat multivariate correlations.

Apart from "gaps" in the ethnographic report, one may argue that errors in coding are bound to occur when a case is coded by someone not intimately familiar with it, using categories different from those of the original reporter. For example, Köbben (1961, pp. 188-189) shows that Horton's supposed correlation (1943) between alcoholism and premarital sexual freedom depends on a mistaken coding of three or four cases; when these are corrected the correlation disappears (cf. also Washburne, 1961). Needham (1962, pp. 59-60, 65-66) argues that Homans and Schneider (1954), among other mistakes, have misclassified several of their cases, and argues that only by an intensive study of each single case can one really understand and properly code kinship rules. However, the holist's high regard for the uniqueness of each case here leads him astray. The cross-cultural researcher is not interested in a thorough understanding of a single case, but is searching rather for statistical generalizations; for this purpose he does not need absolutely correct coding of every case. If he has a large enough number of cases, a few errors of coding will make little difference; thus Horton's error was not miscoding but using too few cases. In addition, the researcher can estimate how much difference coding errors would make and use this estimate to evaluate his result. He can even control statistically for errors in the original ethnographic reports by using data quality control techniques (Naroll, 1962).

Another difficulty is that the 800-item coding list is essentially unchangeable. A few new items can be added to it for new cases, but any substantial change would necessitate recoding the whole 250-case file. Consequently no advance of scientific theory can be applied to the improvement of the list, and no theoretical issues not reducible to the categories of the list can be studied by means of the files. The list constitutes a complete and closed observation language, and the philosophical discussions about the possibility of such a language apply. However, this philosophical difficulty may amount to very little in practice, since the cultural atoms on the list are of very general applicability.

One may also object in principle to the use of a list of cultural atoms for coding. No matter how well the coder knows the context of an item he is coding, once he has coded it the context disappears and the item therefore loses its cultural meaning. The meaning that is lost is the set of connections within a case, connections that are usually directly experienced by the participant observer. However, the cross-cultural researcher is looking for a different sort of meaning, a nomothetic meaning that goes well beyond immediate experience. Even the variables with which he is concerned may be inaccessible to direct observation, appearing instead as scores or profiles on indices. Consequently the loss of contextual meaning is irrelevant to his interests.

Hologeistic comparisons have other problems which Naroll has discussed and studied in detail (Naroll, 1968) and which I need not therefore repeat. Some of these problems disappear in cross-polity and cross-national comparisons and are replaced by others. Cross-polity and cross-national researchers do not depend on coded ethnographic data; they collect their own data by questionnaires and other survey techniques and so can generate exactly the kind of data they need. They do not have to depend on a rigid list of cultural atoms, but can use variables, some quite complex, discovered through previous research and theorizing. The main compensating problem is the extremely high cost of generating data; to meet this problem, international data banks are now being set up, which in turn will produce problems already familiar to HRAF coders and researchers.

There is no point in estimating whether the problems of controlled comparison are greater than the problems of cross-cultural comparison or some other comparative method; speaking as a cultural relativist, one can say that each method has its own characteristic problems and solutions. Speaking as an absolutist, one can say that the basic problem of all comparison is that of relating the general and the particular, the One and the Many, so that each can enrich the other. There is no complete and permanent way of doing this at present.

Variations in the solution to the problem of comparison result not from differences in scientific ability but from the varying uses to which comparison is put. Specifically, controlled and hologeistic comparisons use comparison for quite different purposes, which determine the kind of comparison that occurs. In controlled comparison the parallel case is used first of all to guide and control observation. The parallel case presumably has already been theoretically explained and interpreted, so one knows what is important about it and what is superficial. This knowledge is used to direct observation specifically to the important characteristics of the new case. The differences between two cases, if they belong to the same type, are also illuminating, since they reveal the alternative possibilities that are rejected or lost in the new case and raise the question of why these alternatives are absent. Consequently the strict control of differences that Naroll expects and fails to find in controlled comparisons (1968, pp. 240-241) is neither necessary nor desirable; all that is needed is a basic over-all similarity. The new case is also used to test and modify limited generalizations embodied in the parallel case. Thus the parallel case is treated as a combination of fact and particularized theory, and both aspects are used.

The cross-cultural researcher is not interested in using comparison to guide observation, but wishes only to test and modify generalizations. His cases are treated only as factual descriptions, and he makes a sharp distinction between facts, collected in the HRAF, and theory. He can even assign the two tasks of collecting facts and developing theory to different people working at different times, while for the holist this division is hardly possible.

Even more important in determining differences between the two methods is the kind of theory one hopes to develop by comparing cases. The cross-cultural researcher is interested in abstract generalizations that apply over all the earth and perhaps even throughout history. For example, Murdock's classic study (1949) centers on his postulate 1 (1949, p. 138), which says that kinship terminology is determined by kinship relation; that is, the greater the similarity between two kinship relations, the greater the likelihood that the same kinship terms will be applied to them. The meaning of "similarity" is spelled out in thirty theorems and propositions. To test this kind of generalization one needs a representative sample of cases from the whole earth throughout history; and the problems of controlling error in such a sample require a still further increase of sample size, as well as a variety of statistical controls.

The holist is usually not interested in this kind of generalization. His ultimate interest always returns to individual cases, and if he makes long ventures into theory it is for the eventual purpose of understanding cases better. But a universal generalization is not of much use in understanding specific cases; one needs instead a rather particularized kind of theory that will say a great deal about a few cases rather than a very little about all cases. And even this particularized theory cannot consist simply of statistical generalizations, statements about regularities that happen to occur in a case. For a holist an isolated regularity represents a puzzle to be investigated and explained, material for theory rather than theory itself (cf. Kluckhohn, 1967, p. 39). The regularity is explained by connecting it with other regularities and themes in a complex pattern that describes the structure or dynamics of the case.

A type provides this kind of particularized "theory." It describes a typical pattern, variants and alternatives, ranges of variation on specific points, probable courses of development, and so on. Consequently the holist's primary theoretical interest is in the development of more complex and detailed types. When he ventures beyond types to still more general theory, its purpose—as I shall argue later—is to control and explain a typology by organizing it in some sort of pattern.

Controlled comparison is suited to the development of particularized holistic theory and unsuited to the development of statistical generalizations. If the researcher is to learn more about a type, he has to engage in intensive, detailed investigation of examples, which means that he must limit himself to two or three examples at a time. Differences among the examples tell him more about variations within the type, while similarities tell him more about the basic pattern constituting the type. If he is interested in more general theory he must somehow broaden the range of his examples, but never so far that he can no longer examine each case in detail.

If we now ask why the holist is interested in this kind of theory, which always returns him to the study of individual cases, we are moving beyond questions of methodology. A partial answer is provided by the unique practical uses of holistic theory, as I shall indicate in chapter 18. This answer is especially important for clinicians, who need holistic theory for their practice. However, some holists have no particular interest in the practical uses of their theory, and for them the answer will probably be found in personal predispositions, personal history, and other nonrational considerations.

14

Typologies : Real and Ideal Types

The simplest and probably also the most important kind of theory coming
out of controlled comparisons is typological. A set of types is used in every
case study to direct observation and suggest interpretations and is the most
common basis of control in controlled comparisons. Consequently the improvement of typologies is an important basis for the improvement of case
studies and the general theories that come out of them.

The present discussion of typology is based primarily on the following
examples: Redfield's "folk society" type (1947) and his commentary thereon
(1960a, ch. 9); Redfield's "peasant" type (1960b) and the various contributions and comments on it, for instance, in the special *American Anthropologist* issue on Latin America (June 1955); the classification in *Industrialism and Industrial Man* by Kerr et al. (1960, ch. 2); Gouldner's types of
industrial bureaucracy (1950); K. Polanyi's classification of economic distribution systems (1957, pp. 242-269) and Kapp's commentary thereon
(1961, pp. 194-199); the multilinear evolutionists' classification of primitive
economies—irrigation (Wittfogel, 1957), slash and burn, etc.; the typing of
kinship terminology—Omaha, Crow, etc.; the various psychoanalytic typologies of Rank, Fromm, H. Deutsch, etc.; Fallding's typology of families (1967);
and Rorschach's concept of *Erlebnistypus*. My procedure has been to examine
one instance, usually Redfield or Kerr; to check the characteristics I find in
that instance against all the others to see whether they also share them; and
if there are one or two negative instances to study them to see what they
suggest about themselves or the other instances. I have also rechecked my
results against various examples that later came my way. Throughout I
have in mind a comparison and contrast with formalist ideal types (of the
sort Kapp suggests).

Real and Ideal Types

Kapp calls the types coming out of empiricist case studies "real types" and contrasts them with the "ideal types" constructed by mathematical model-builders. This terminology will perhaps confuse those for whom the term "ideal types" suggests Max Weber, particularly since Weber's types become, in the present account, an atypical combination of formalist and empiricist elements. (Cf. Kapp, 1961, p. 195: "Weber's 'ideal' types were essentially real types.") Nevertheless I shall use Kapp's terminology as a point of departure.

A *real type* groups a number of cases together because they have many important characteristics in common. It is thus more like a mode than a formal construct. The type has no reality apart from the cases it summarizes, and might have been called a *nominal type* rather than a real type. The cases, not the type, are real; they are distinct, independent entities and not merely instances or exemplifications of an abstract universal, as cases are in formal typologies.

A description of a type lists the common characteristics and shows the pattern of their relations to one another. It also states areas in which variations are found to exist and lists either all or the most common variants in each area. There may be an explanation of the variants; perhaps they are all essentially the same in that they perform the same function, or perhaps the differences among them result from differences in external circumstances, and so on.

In contrast, the type a formalist constructs is an abstract system or process based on a few postulates, for example, pure monopoly, a random net, one-trial learning, the game of chicken, a bipolar international system, a queue, a block, a normal distribution, matrilineal descent. Such a type is an idealization in the sense that one does not expect to find any pure empirical examples of it. On the other hand, the type is a real entity in the sense that it has a dynamic of its own, one that operates even in its impure empirical exemplifications. The basis of the dynamic is the set of relations between the postulates defining the type. Once these postulates come to be empirically exemplified, the situation in which they appear has a dynamic tendency described by deductions from them. For example, if one-trial learning is really occurring, the learning curve will take a certain form whose detailed characteristics depend on the learning probability and the initial guessing ratio. Whenever there is a queue, its average length, average waiting time, standard deviations, etc., will depend on entering rate and leaving rate; insofar as these characteristics deviate from the prediction, other factors are operating that may be part of some other dynamic. Types of this kind, though they are idealized abstractions to the empiricist, may be called *real types* by the formalist in contrast to the empiricist's *nominal types*, and the difference between the two kinds of typology is a version of the old realist-nominalist disagreement. To an empiricist, talk of the dynamics of an abstract system such as "monopoly" sounds spooky, since he knows there are no pure monopolies in the world, for they are mathematical inventions. To the formalist, on the other hand, empiricist types like "the peasant society" are not really types at all, merely collections of instances in which a real type may eventually be discovered by the techniques of formalization. And, as with all disputes, the issues are stated differently by the two sides. The empiricist (Kapp) calls his types *real* (because they remain close to empirical reality) and disparages the formalist's types as *ideal*, while for the formalist *his* types are real and the empiricist's merely nominal.

Typologies

Since formalist types are always constructed from a few basic postulates, one constructs a formalist typology a priori by systematically varying the postulates. Thus, beginning with monopoly one can move on to monopsony, duopoly, oligopoly, oligopsony, cartels, etc. Similarly, Rapoport constructed a typology of the four possible mixed-motive games (Chicken, Prisoner's Dilemma, Hero, Leader) by systematically varying payoff ratios (Rapoport, 1967), as well as a typology of all possible 2 × 2 games (Rapoport and Guyer, 1966). In contrast, the empiricist must construct his typology empirically by discovering a new grouping in his remaining cases, or by finding subtypes in his original type. Nor can the empiricist deduce additional characteristics of a type, as the formalist can; every characteristic that he lists must actually be found in his group of cases. He can, if he likes, make guesses or hypotheses about what other things might be found there, but if he cannot actually find them they must not be included in his account.

The classic example of a shift from a formal to an empirical type is Max Weber's reinterpretation of neoclassical economic theory. The economists thought that in their model of perfect competition they had an abstraction that applied to some extent to all action; Weber reinterpreted the model as an idealization of a particular case, European capitalism. The question for Weber then was, how are other cases similar and different from this one, and what explains the similarities and differences? This is a typical empiricist question; its answer leads to a fuller characterization of the type by clarifying some of the interdependencies in it, and perhaps also leads to the discovery of additional types. Weber's typologies of bureaucracy and of law are also empirical, though bearing traces of their formal origin in the formal concept of rational behavior.

The empiricist uses a typology to bring general knowledge to bear on his particular case and thereby help him understand it better. If he wishes to compare his case with another similar case, the typology tells him which cases are similar enough to make comparison worthwhile. If he wishes a more generalized comparison, the type itself provides a quick summary of a number of cases. Controlled comparisons of this sort suggest a list of characteristics to look for and thus help to sharpen his observation. They also call his

attention to unusual, atypical aspects of his case that require further observation and special explanation. The deviation may prove to be a variant
in an area where other variants are already included in the description of
the type, or it may be a real exception or negative instance; if several negative instances are clustered together, his case may be a new subtype or some
combination of two types. Or it may be a mistaken observation. Finally, the
typical aspects of his case find a ready-made explanation in the standard
explanation of the type, if an explanation has been worked out. The explanation can be checked to see whether it fits the new case, and any modifications
required by the unusual aspects of the case can be added.

The use of a type to illuminate a case also serves to test and refine the type
itself. Complete or nearly complete agreement would be a corroboration of
the hypothesis that a type or grouping of the sort suggested actually does
exist. Partial disagreement may suggest modifications in the description of the
type: a new variant may be added, or certain factors once thought to be
essential may be reinterpreted as variants, or certain typical factors may begin to stand out as essential characteristics or determinants.

There is some danger, however, that the application of a typology to a
particular case may narrow and limit observation rather than broaden it.
Since a type gives the observer a list of things to look for, he may find just
what he is told to seek and nothing else. One finds this occasionally, for example, among young and enthusiastic Marxists for whom Marxism is more
an abstract typology than a dialectical procedure for examining concrete
problems. In this typology the world is divided into peace-loving nations,
imperialist aggressors, and colonies. Every occurrence in the latter two is
either part of a complex imperialist plot or evidence that oppressed people
are struggling to free themselves; every occurrence in the peace-loving group
is either part of a defense against imperialist aggression or an attempt to
assist the struggling oppressed peoples. One also finds this tendency among
amateur Freudians, who discover inferiority complexes, death wishes, and
guilt feelings everywhere.

This misuse of typologies, in which a type becomes a stereotype, is the
result of inadequate empiricism. Types are treated as already completed and
verified theories, rather than as tentative groupings useful for illuminating
particular cases. The intimate connection between observation and theory that
is characteristic of case study methods is broken, and theory becomes self-
sufficient and dogmatic. A person falls into this misuse of typologies when
he has too much theory and not enough experience, and tries to make his
theory substitute for the careful empirical study of cases. The way to avoid
misuse is to be more empirical, that is, to insist on checking every single
characteristic of the type to see whether it is present in one's case. It is not
enough to check just a few characteristics and then assume that the rest are
also present, because one's case might be different; it may have variants or
combine two types or even be a new type or subtype.

Note that the procedure for misusing an empiricist's "nominal" type looks
superficially very similar to the procedure for properly using a formalist's

"real" type. When a formalist applies his type to a case he needs only to find empirical interpretations of the basic relations or postulates from which his type is constructed, and from there on he can proceed deductively if he wishes (depending on the use he is making of his model). This deductive procedure is a mistake with a "nominal" type because such a type is found empirically rather than constructed a priori, and the deductive nexus is therefore not present in it. This similarity perhaps helps to explain the empiricist's suspicion of formalist ideal types, which seem to provide a substitute for observation rather than an aid to it.

Polar Ideal Types

One occasionally finds a slightly different kind of empiricist typology which, following Redfield (1960a, pp. 139-147), might be called "polar ideal." The investigator constructs for himself a pair of opposite types to serve as the two extremes of a continuum, by abstracting some aspect of the case before him and idealizing or purifying it by imagining a whole system composed of just that aspect; then he negates that aspect to get its polar opposite. For example, Maine's status-contract typology is constructed by imagining a society composed only of contractual relations and then deriving by negation the idea of a society based on pure status. Parsons' pattern variables are also polar idealizations of this sort, as are Redfield's folk-urban continuum and Gusfield's reworking of the traditional-modern types (1967).

According to Redfield, such a typology enables the investigator to describe the case before him more exactly by placing it at some point on the continuum. He first describes the ways in which his case is like the first extreme, then the ways in which it is like the second; two cases also can be compared simply by comparing their locations on the continuum. Further, if he has reason to suppose that one type is historically older than the other, the position of that case on the continuum is also a position in a time scale. Thus Maine supposed that status relations are more ancient than contractual ones and that, therefore, he could range societies along a scale of historical development by determining the relative ratio of status to contract in each.

The use of polar ideal types involves dangers that are not present in ordinary empirical typologies. For one thing, polar types are supposed to represent tendencies that are present in all societies or even in all human systems, so they must be based on study of a great number of varied cases or on very general theoretical considerations. For another, we know from the fate of Maine's proposition that any broad historical use of polar types is extremely dubious; if both poles represent tendencies present in all or nearly all societies, then a given society cannot move indefinitely in one direction along the scale. Sooner or later the suppressed pole must reassert itself in a reversal of movement, as did Maine's status elements in the legal developments of the last century. (Cf. also Apter, 1965, pp. 56-59, for a similar argument on the traditional-modern developmental typology.)

Polar types differ from more usual holist typologies in that they are extremes on a continuum rather than modes of a distribution. Since the number of extreme cases may be small or nonexistent, the types are constructed by exaggeration or idealization rather than by simple description and summary. In this respect they are more like formalist typologies, which are also constructed by abstracting and idealizing. One may even wonder whether some polar ideal types are not implicit formal theories, suitable for formal systematization. Is not the idea of a pure contractual society a formal idea, one that, moreover, bears a strong resemblance to the idea of a perfectly competitive economy?

The difference lies in the dialectical relation that is present in polar ideal typologies. A formalist who constructs the idea of a purely contractual or a purely competitive society is interested in studying the intrinsic dynamics of his model, its time paths, equilibrium states, critical ratios, etc. When he applies his model to an empirical case he tries to show how the intrinsic dynamics are exemplified in that case—how, for example, the element of competition that is empirically present forces a tendency toward a certain pattern of distribution of goods. He is interested primarily in those empirical elements that correspond to his model and sees other elements either as unknowable empirical residues or as potential exemplifications of some other model. In contrast, the dialectically minded holist is interested primarily in his whole particular case. He uses his two types as a "pair of lenses" (Redfield, 1960a, p. 139) for studying his case; each type rescues him from the abstractness and one-sidedness represented by the other. Thus if he gets too involved in the abstract idea of contractual relations, his typology reminds him that status also exists in every society, probably in the very relations he has been seeing as contractual. Nor does he suppose that his types have any intrinsic dynamics, since he knows they are pure fictions. If he does study dynamics, they will be the dialectical dynamics of conflict between the opposing elements present in his case. Thus if he finds that the element of contract, or of secularism, or of achievement values is localized mainly in one class or region, while the element of status, or sacredness, or ascription is localized mainly elsewhere, he expects to find class or regional conflict; if he finds both elements loosely mixed within the family or the individual he expects to find internal conflict.

In spite of the characteristic difference between the formal and empirical approaches to ideal types, they are a potential meeting ground between the two methods. The formalist can contribute his theoretical clarity and ingenuity by systematizing types, locating their essential postulates and their dynamic tendencies. The holist can contribute his empirical sensitivity by bringing out the complex interplay between opposed principles or types in particular cases. There have been border crossings at this point; Max Weber and Parsons borrowed types from formalists, and more recently, Kemeny, Snell and Thompson (1957, pp. 343-353), Harrison White (1963a), and Russell Reid (1967) have borrowed kinship types from the empiricists. Nevertheless such contacts have been rare, and the two methods remain quite distinct.

15

Some Characteristics
of Holist Theories

We turn now to a consideration of the general theories that have come out of case studies. By a "general theory" I mean one that is intended to apply to all types of men or societies and does more than simply classify them into types. A general theory is developed by comparing cases of widely different types and seeing what they have in common, by seeing what characteristics of the first case are present in all other cases. Its generality depends on the adequacy of its associated typology, which determines what cases can be regarded as representative.

The chief general theories coming out of case studies, and used in them, are the psychoanalytic and psychodynamic theories, the functionalist theories, the theory of multilinear evolution, and the theory of symbolic interaction. These theories overlap somewhat: as Hempel has observed (1965, p. 306), psychoanalytic theory is really functionalist; some functionalists have borrowed psychoanalytic concepts and some have discussed evolution (Parsons, 1966a; Apter, 1965); and symbolic interactionism uses some psychodynamic concepts and shares some concepts with functionalism. Nor are the boundaries of any of these theories clear, since some people define them narrowly and others broadly. My concern, however, is not with boundaries but with characteristics that all these theories have in common because of common origin in case studies.

I find four common characteristics: (1) they are holistic; (2) they are concatenated rather than hierarchical (Kaplan, 1964, p. 298) and therefore involve little deduction and no mathematical or symbolic logic; (3) their concepts are empirical—Bruyn calls them "sensitizing" (1966, p. 31 ff)—close to ordinary experience, and frequently include emotive and subjective elements; and (4) their concepts are frequently related dialectically. I shall discuss each of these characteristics in the present chapter.

Holism

By "holistic" I mean here that the theories are about whole societies, communities, persons, organizations, groups, or processes. They deal with part-whole relations, or stages of development of a whole, or essential subdivisions of a whole and their relations, or classifications of wholes, and so on. A holistic theory is an appropriate guide for participant observation because it continually reminds the observer that his particular, immediate observation must be understood and interpreted by reference to a larger background, and it provides a general account of the background that can illuminate the particular observed fact. It also reminds the observer that his investigations must continue until he has surveyed the whole system, and it provides a general framework to guide his investigations and to remind him when he has overlooked something. Even if the observer is primarily interested in some more limited hypothesis, the hypothesis will contain some reference to the larger background. For example, Kluckhohn's hypothesis that Navaho witchcraft provided certain adaptive and adjustive responses (1944, p. 76 ff) is a derivative part of functionalist theory. As such it directed him to search for sources of tension in childhood socialization, adolescent culture contact, and adult farming technology and social structure; to search for the culturally determined ways of dealing with frustration; and to search for alternative patterns of hostility, aggression, and withdrawal. His understanding of these institutions and practices in turn depended on knowing their social and cultural context. Thus the holistic character of functionalist theory called for an investigation of nearly the whole culture in order to understand and explain one institution.

Hypotheses that relate pairs or sets of variables are not suitable for guiding holistic observation because they focus the observer's attention on a few things and allow him to ignore the rest. For example, Festinger, Riecken, and Schachter's guiding hypothesis for a case study was that under five specific conditions the empirical disconfirmation of a belief would be followed by increased proselytizing (1956, p. 4). This hypothesis focused the attention of the observers first on the five conditions that would make their hypothesis empirically relevant to the case, and second on the two variables of disconfirmation and proselytizing behavior. Other events could be ignored, and if they were noticed, no attempt was made to interpret them or develop their theoretical relation to the two main variables. Consequently, although the authors did observe and participate in a single case they did so in the spirit of experimental method because of the kind of theory that guided them. Their interest was in the measurement of variables and the verification of a hypothesis rather than in the unities and conflicts of a particular system. Note also that such hypotheses, if confirmed, produce deductive explanations rather than the pattern explanations characteristic of participant observations.

Concepts

The concepts of holistic theories are usually complex and rich in content, and their content is close to ordinary experience with its emotive and subjective emphasis. Consider such well-known concepts as myth, ritual, authority, kinship, role, ambivalence, identity, apathy, community; or think of Freud's fruitful and suggestive concepts, I (*das Ich*), it (*das Es*), the higher I (*Über-Ich*), censor, repression, etc. All these concepts have some immediate meaning drawn from our own experience, yet all are complex enough to require long study.

To the practitioners of other methods, such concepts seem vague and anthropomorphic, too close to common sense to be scientifically useful. For example, Osgood (1958) ridicules Freud's concepts as being hopelessly anthropomorphic; Freud's account of mental processes seems to imply there are several little men hard at work inside the subject's head, demanding, censoring, and compromising. Truly scientific theories for Osgood are those that explain mental processes in terms of S and R concepts, and the scientific problem is one of arranging S's and R's in the right combination. Similarly, Simon and Newell (1956) observe that the concepts of ordinary language are rich in implications, but these implications are not available for dependable deductive work because the concepts are so vague and fluid.

But the concepts of holistic theories are appropriate for the methods used by holists, just as the different concepts used by practitioners of other methods are suitable for those methods. In field and clinical methods, theory and observation are closely connected; observation is continuously guided and clarified by theory, and new low-level and limited hypotheses are continuously developing out of observations. This connection requires concepts that are vague and open enough to be capable of continuous modification. In a method that demands that observation range widely enough to include the whole of a human system, the concepts guiding observation must also be complex enough to lead it on rather than restrain it. Thus the many vague and fluid implications that are useless for Simon's rigorous deductive purposes are suggestive enough to guide the holist observer. Finally, a method that requires the observer to involve himself empathically in his subject matter requires concepts that mobilize his experiences, emotions, biases, and sensitivities, and point to similarities between his experience and that of his subject. Anthropomorphic, subjective, and common-sense concepts do just that; they emphasize similarities and make the observer feel at home rather than (like Osgood's S and R) emphasizing differences between the rational, detached scientific technician and his subject matter. Consider 'kinship,' for instance. We all know what relatives are like because we have them; the concept tells us how to look for relatives in our subject matter and reminds us of our similarity to the people we are studying.

In experimentation and statistical surveys the distinction between theory and observation is somewhat sharper. Theorizing is a rather loose kind of verbal speculation, which may involve a survey of the literature and a balancing of various pro and con arguments about a hypothesis, while observation is precise and detailed. Theorizing and observing can be done separately and by different people, though some experimenters object to such a separation. The main function of theorizing is not to guide observation directly but to suggest new and plausible concepts and hypotheses; the main function of observation is to locate promising lawlike correlations under controlled conditions.

Corresponding to this difference between theorizing and observing is a difference between theoretical and observation concepts. Theoretical concepts are vague and suggestive, to facilitate the creative task of devising new hypotheses, while observational concepts must be precise enough to focus attention on the exact variables being measured. Observational concepts (but not theoretical concepts) also should be behavioristic enough to close off the experience, emotions, and biases of the experimenter and thus help him approach his ideal of scientific objectivity.

Theoretical concepts, because of their vagueness, cannot be applied directly to controlled observation; one does not directly observe group cohesion, morale, syntality, n achievement, authoritarianism, or intraception. Instead, these concepts are related to observation indirectly through the medium of operational definitions. The indicators, indices, and scales used in operational definitions are composed of observational terms, and it is these that are related directly to observation.

Theoretical concepts as viewed by experimenters and surveyers are not much different from the concepts used by holists. Both are complex, vague, and suggestive, and both can contain subjective and emotive elements. Consequently the surveyer and experimenter can accept such holistic concepts as those of psychoanalytic theory (Sears, 1943) or functionalist theory (K. Deutsch, in Jacob and Toscano, 1964, ch. 4) as suggestive theoretical concepts, ignoring their observational aspect. But for purposes of controlled observation the holist concepts are useless.

For example, consider the contrast between the holist concept of latent function and the experimenter's concept of response latency, an observation concept. A latent function is a certain kind of effect of which the people involved are not aware. This concept focuses attention on people's awareness and its limits and thus forces the participant observer to learn the point of view of his subjects. How much are they aware of in this area and how does it appear to them? The concept also reminds one of the various defense mechanisms that prevent awareness—repression, projection, etc—and raises the question of which one might be operating. And if a particular one is operating, why? In this way the concept of "latent" first puts the observer directly into the middle of his subject matter and then leads him into ever-widening areas of investigation. "Response latency," on the other hand, is the amount of time (usually in hundredths of a second) between stimulus and response.

This concept focuses attention on the experimenter's measuring instruments and recording apparatus, since that is where response latency is to be found. The experience of the animal during latency, its doubts and fears, are closed off as irrelevant, and the experimenter's possible empathy with his subject matter is also closed off by the strict behaviorist nature of the concept.

Formal methods make the sharpest distinction between observation and theory. To the formalist the functions of theory are to construct abstract logical systems and to study their logical characteristics; the functions of observation are to locate empirical exemplifications of the systems and to suggest modifications of them. Consequently the needs for precision and suggestiveness are located in a manner exactly opposite to that of experimental method. Here it is the theoretical concepts that must be precise, to make deduction dependable, while observational or interpretive concepts can be loose and suggestive.

Theoretical concepts are made precise by eliminating all empirical content and leaving only mathematically defined symbols. Such concepts focus attention on permissible logical operations, on the rules and theorems of a particular branch of mathematics. Contrast, for example, Erikson's concept of identity with mathematical identity. The one is rich in subjective and emotive elements, complex and suggestive; it begins in one's own immediate experience and leads into the complete life-world of one's subject. The other is bare self-relation. Or consider what happens when the concepts of authority, kinship, and role are fomalized by means of digraphs and matrices. All empirical content disappears and only bare relationships remain; all the original subjective familiarity is replaced by austere symbols. One can no longer recognize one's experience with relatives in the $C^{-1} W^{-1}$ and the FFZSS of formalized kinship.

Empirical interpretive concepts are the locus for the formalist's heuristics, his creativity, and even his playfulness. Consider, for example, Boulding's stock of dramatic characters (1962, pp. 27-32): the saint, the publican, the regenerate sinner, the yogi, and the devil, which turn out formally to be curves on a graph. Or notice McPhee's warning: "The technical reviewer will run into some awfully strong verbal interpretations; but since the last thing I find social scientists lack is the quarrelsome instinct, it is not surprising that in trial readings. . .the first thing they do is come back and bite the interpretation that led them into the formal argument in the first place. That is all it is there for" (1963, p. 2). The suggestiveness of interpretive concepts also has the serious function of helping the formalist find new formal ideas or modifications of old formal ideas in his empirical cases. For example, if international diplomacy is perceived as an empirical exemplification of a 'game,' one is thereby led to look for examples of the derivative formal concept—players, rules, strategies, payoffs, etc. One must mull over such familiar but vague things as diplomatic communiques, presidential speeches, reminiscences about cabinet meetings and private conversations, press conferences, an emperors' marginal notations on a telegram, in each case looking for a pure game concept hidden away in the empirical morass. In the course of this search one may find new formal concepts as well as old ones—suggestions for a new kind of player (universal player), a new role (integrative role), new kinds of strategy (stop fighting rather than eliminate an essential actor), new strategic dilemmas—and these concepts enrich the formal theory (M. Kaplan, 1957).

While the formalist has no theoretical use for the holist's concepts because of their vagueness, he can accept them as observation concepts, that is, as interpretations of some abstract system. For example, case studies of empirical kinship systems can be treated as interpretations of formal kinship models (White, 1963, ch. 3).

Thus the holist concepts, in which theory and observation are held in close unity, are always fragmented when they are borrowed by practitioners of other methods. When experimenters or survey researchers borrow them for theoretical purposes, the observational aspect is dropped and ignored as prescientific; when formalists borrow them for empirical purposes, the theoretical aspect is rejected as unformalized speculation.

These changes are not the product of perversity or prejudice; they are only what is necessary to adapt old concepts to new uses. The experimenter or survey researcher who takes a psychodynamic concept or proposition out of its clinical, observational context and treats it as a bit of theory is making the only use of it he can; he cannot use it to guide his precise, controlled observation. Similarly when a formalist ignores the theoretical aspect of a case study he does so because he cannot use such vague "theory" in his precise formal work.

On the other hand, it must be remembered that these borrowed and adapted concepts are not identical with the original concepts, and the propositions constructed out of them are no longer parts of a holistic theory. The survey researcher or experimenter who operationalizes psychoanalytic concepts cannot claim to be working directly with psychoanalytic theory, either by way of confirmation, disconfirmation, or modification. Psychoanalytic concepts are designed to guide direct observation of particular cases, not to yield predictions of questionnaire or laboratory responses.

The above account of concepts differs slightly from Bruyn's (1966, pp. 31-40), though I have used his terms where possible. Bruyn's primary interest in participant observation led him to simplify somewhat his account of other methods and to neglect some differences among them. Consequently he lists only four kinds of concepts, while I think one should distinguish at least six kinds, as follows:

	case-study methods	survey-research and experimental methods	formal methods
theoretical	anthropomorphic-sensitizing	speculative	formal
observational	concrete	operational	empirical-interpretive

Concrete concepts are prominent in case studies. They are derived direct-ly from the subject matter, from the speech and action of the people being studied. Concrete concepts are those used by these people to organize and interpret their experience, to construct their own world and give meaning to it. Consequently an account of these concepts enables one to enter into their life-world and vicariously share their experience. Each culture has its own concrete concepts embodied in its ordinary language and action, and each subculture has its own derivative technical concepts. The participant-observ-er or clinician must first learn these concepts as he is socialized into his sub-ject matter, and then try to describe them to his fellow scientists in his case study. So Polsky expounds the hustler's argot: speed, heart, short-con, dump-ing, lemoning, the fish (Polsky, 1967, ch. 2). Goffman develops the gambler's concepts of "hotness" (in Archibald, 1966, p. 154) and "action" (Goff-man, 1967, pp. 181-194) and the con man's concept of "cooling the mark" (Goffman, 1962). Hunter investigates such concepts as "real thinker" to clarify the ideology of the power elite (Hunter, 1959).

The concrete concepts of a subculture of the observer's own culture can be described by translating them into the familiar language from which they are derived, but those of a different culture are more difficult to translate. Redfield describes a typical frustration of the participant observer:

> I remember my feeling of achievement when I thought I had come to under-stand that a certain Maya word had a complex meaning of considerable subtle-ty, only to realize that no English words would do justice to the meaning of the term I had come to share with the native. I had, of course, encountered the inevitable problem of translation. I gave up, in this case, the translation as too difficult, and put the Maya word right into my English account (Redfield, 1960a, p. 92).

The best solution to the problem of translation is not to put the native word into the text, though that is frequently done, but to use a different kind of concept, an anthropomorphic or sensitizing concept. Sensitizing concepts are not directly derived from the culture of a single community, but are developed in the comparison of cases by finding similar or common elements among them all. They refer to the general rather than the unique and thus make cross-cultural understanding possible. Their meaningfulness in the observer's own culture being studied enables him to enter into it empathically. Thus they provide a bridge between two worlds. Every good case study should be built on a combination of sensitizing and concrete concepts, the one leading the reader into the case and the other making him at home in it.

Sensitizing concepts are also the basic component of holistic theories, as I have indicated, because they refer to what is general to many cases. The familiar sensitizing concepts of ritual, authority, kinship, role, identity, com-munity, anxiety, are each central to an important holist theory, and their meaning has developed along with the theory. Thus the interaction between concrete and sensitizing concepts is part of the continuous and close inter-action between observation and theory in case study methods, and this interaction is a solution to the attachment-detachment problem, the problem of entering into one's subject matter and becoming part of it while remaining detached enough to achieve some objectivity in one's description.

The problem of the experimenter and survey researcher is that of achieving enough precision in observation to make possible statistical control and manipulation of data, while retaining enough looseness of theory to avoid being tied down to one specific type of experiment or questionnaire or interview. This problem requires special kinds of concepts for its solution. Operational concepts provide the necessary precision and objectivity of observation; speculative concepts provide the necessary heuristic fertility. Speculative concepts are the source of new insights and hypotheses, which in turn suggest new questions, indices, and experimental designs.

Finally, the formalist desires theoretical precision and dependable deductive manipulations. His formal concepts are defined by the logical or mathematical relations into which they can enter and the deductive manipulations that are permitted with them. But this theoretical precision inevitably brings empirical vagueness with it, since his models have no exact analogues in the real world. Empirical exemplifications of a model are always approximate and always include empirical residues or deviations that do not appear in the model. However, these deviations can be heuristically useful as the source of new formal ideas, as modifications of a model or as the basis of an entirely different model. In addition, empirical examples are also sometimes used as "heuristic interpretations" to lead mathematically unsophisticated readers through a formal argument. So the formalist needs empirical or interpretive concepts to describe the loose and approximate exemplifications of his models.

Definitions

Holistic definitions are also explained by reference to the requirements of case studies. The holist uses neither operational nor relational definitions, because neither kind is suited to his purposes. Operational definitions serve to focus attention on specific responses to specific experimental or questionnaire operations. They are useful for the scientist who wishes to engage in careful control and measurement of some variable, but are not good for the holist because they isolate "variables" from their context and close off the wider observation he thinks is essential. Relational definitions serve to focus attention on the logical context of a term and indirectly point to the logical system in which the term is located. Such a focus is useful for the formalist, who wishes to construct and analyze logical systems, but is not good for the holist because it would take him away from direct observation and lure him into (what seems to him to be) abstract, idle speculation.

It may appear that the holist does not use definitions at all, because definitions are instruments of precision, and the holist, it may seem, is not interested in precision. Actually, he locates his precision elsewhere than practitioners of other methods, and thus merely seems imprecise according to their different standards of precision (and they by his standards). The holist is precise in his observation and description of *particulars*. Field workers will be precise and detailed in their diaries and field notes—note, for example, Herskovits' advice (1948, p. 89) to be sure to notice and record whether the basket weave is clockwise or counterclockwise, and Firth's warning that even little paint smudges on the wall may be important (Firth, 1951, pp. 24-26). Clinicians will be meticulously detailed in their probing of a dream (cf. Freud, 1925, pp. 78 ff, 114 ff) or of a patient's associations (p. 189 ff). (Cf. also Malinowski, 1922, p. 14; 1967, p. 290; Colvard, 1967, p. 349.) But these are not places where definitions are in order, since definitions are general.

Holist definitions are likely to be long, complex, and open-ended. The definitions of such concepts as institution, function, folk society, or role will take a chapter or a long article and will really be essays in theory. Such concepts may have a vague core meaning, but the core shades off rapidly into a series of variants, circumstances, aspects, standpoints, and relations or contrasts with other concepts. And no such "definition" will pretend to be complete; there is always more to be said and discovered. Each of the above holist concepts has a history of successive reformulations in which it takes on increased richness of detail and context and increased definiteness of boundary.

These definitions serve to organize observation by providing a large theoretical context for specific observations. The context serves to suggest interpretations and lines of observation that will clarify and expand the meaning of the initial observation. The openness of the definitions enables the observer to make his own modifications and additions to fit his own experiences. These uses are much the same as the uses of theory in general, and holist definitions are hardly to be distinguished from holist theories.

In my discussion of holist concepts and definitions I have stressed the appropriateness of these concepts for the holist's purposes. Perhaps it would be well to remind the reader that just as all tools have limits of usefulness, these concepts are not suitable for certain kinds of use. First, because of their vagueness, holist concepts are suitable only for theorizing that is continually controlled by reference to observation, to cases and examples. As soon as this sort of theory is separated from empirical contacts it becomes loose, uncontrolled speculation. Freud's speculations about monotheism and totemic religion come to mind as examples, and Parsons' theorizing in the last few years has similarly moved away from his many earlier empirical studies. The many vague nuances and hints packed into holist concepts lead idle thought in all directions, and their strong subjective and anthropomorphic elements give full play to unconscious motives. This, of course, is what they are supposed to do in the context of observation, but the result must be under continuous, precise control by direct observation. There ought to be a law forbidding any holist to engage in original theorizing until he has done at least one field or clinical study himself and read many others, and another law forbidding him from theorizing beyond the general area of his own empirical studies.

Second, the vagueness and generality of holist concepts make any definitive verification of hypotheses impossible. To do that, it is necessary to nail down hypotheses unambiguously, and this is not a characteristic holist tactic, for very good reasons. But in consequence the holist should remember that his theories are always tentative and subject to change. I refrain from raising the question whether the experimenter ever achieves definitive verification, but at least this is sometimes said to be his proper aim.

Logic

Holistic concepts are frequently, though not always, related dialectically. Two concepts are dialectically related when the elaboration of one draws attention to the other as an opposed concept that has been implicitly denied or excluded by the first; when one discovers that the opposite concept is required (presupposed) for the validity or applicability of the first; and when one finds that the real theoretical problem is that of the interrelation between the two concepts, and the real descriptive problem that of determining their interrelations in a particular case. This is known to dialecticians as the principle of interpenetration of opposites.

I shall give several examples of dialectically related concepts and then try to suggest why this characteristic often (though not always) appears in holist theories (cf. also L. Schneider's discussion of dialectic, 1964, pp. 375-386). The basic polarity is between culture and personality; the dialectical relation between this pair has long been recognized, and a whole body of theory has grown up around it. When one studies the dynamics of cultures, how they selectively incorporate and adapt elements from the cultures around them, maintain their identity amid changes, develop and differentiate, one is led to the realization that all these changes are the product of the human adaptive process and that variations in cultural dynamics are partly to be explained by variations in basic personality and its adaptive capacities. To cite just one example, in Bunzel's study of the historical development of decorative patterns on Pueblo pottery, she notes that in recent decades the patterns have become more uniform and stereotyped, esthetically less interesting. She attributes this cultural development to a decline in creativity, which in turn is part of the general rigidity and encapsulation that constitute the Pueblo response to Western domination (Bunzel, 1929). Conversely, when one studies the varied forms taken around the world by human desires and needs, aspirations, and habits of action, one comes to realize that these personality factors are shaped by culture acting through the institutions of family and occupation, and that personality is a reflection of culture. Thus the study of personality, which begins by implicitly excluding social and cultural factors, leads to the discovery of culture as that which makes personality determinate and real; apart from culture, personality is indeterminate, amorphous, potential.

The study of how these two factors interpenetrate, conflict, and develop reconciliations has been a primary concern for anthropologists and psychologists. For example, Turner (1964, p. 30 ff) observes that all the main ritual symbols of the Ndembu have two clearly distinguishable poles of meaning, an ideological pole composed of norms and values and a sensory pole composed of desires and feelings. Ndembu ritual unites and reconciles these conflicting principles.

The culture-personality polarity can perhaps be derived from the man-nature polarity that is implicit in anthropological work. Culture is the product of man in his struggle to survive in nature; it is the instrument for adapting to nature by which man makes himself human. Personality is the locus of the natural factors, physiological and biochemical, that condition and limit human development. Alternatively, Radcliffe-Brown suggests that the fundamental polarity is not between man and nature but between two conflicting conceptions of nature, the mechanistic and the social or spiritualistic, which are both present in every human society (Radcliffe-Brown, 1952, p. 130). Moving in an different direction, each of the original pair of concepts has been gradually polarized again in recent decades of theorizing to yield the fourfold division of system-types appearing in Parsons' work: organism, personality, social system, and cultural pattern.

A more abstract polarity is that between unity and diversity, consensus and conflict, in human systems of all kinds. Dialectical logicians can easily run through the formalities on this one, showing how unity makes sense only as an overcoming of diversity, how systematic conflict is possible only within a framework of agreed-on rules, values, or beliefs, how autonomy can persist only in and through consensus, and so on. These relationships have been known since Plato, who in the *Philebus* gave an amusing account of the student logician's discovery of the One and the Many. Anthropologists and sociologists, however, have rediscovered these relations empirically. Thus Turner finds that the same Ndembu rituals that symbolize the unity and closeness of certain social relations also dramatize separation and conflicts in those relations (1964, pp. 21-27). Murphy argues that in one case at least a contradiction between kinship terms and social relations is a necessary condition for social harmony (1967, p. 164).

Within cultures we have Redfield's distinction between peasant and urban culture, the "little" and the "great" tradition (1960b; 1953). Peasant culture is different from folk culture in that it is dependent on the city. The peasant sells his produce and labor in the city and gets back manufactured goods, government, and legal and military protection. His moral and religious culture is dependent on the priest, the school teacher, and the other learned and literate men who come from the city. The city in turn depends on the peasantry for food and population and for the folk elements that enrich art, music, religion, and literature. Yet the two cultures are opposites and can be mutually destructive. The city, with its superior power, exploits the peasantry and justifies the exploitation with its persuasive religion, learning, and law.

Redfield's distinction is an ancient one and can be found, for example, in the pages of Hegel's *Philosophy of Right* (par. 203-204, 247-248). On a larger scale, the distinction reappears as nationalism-internationalism, a conflict and interdependence between the small land-, tradition-, and folk-oriented areas and the great urban commercial and financial centers. The nationalist areas need the capital, technology, and ideas of the urban centers to modernize and even to survive as integrated entities, while the trading centers need the raw materials and manpower of the ethnic areas to survive. The urban exploitation of the peasantry that Redfield discusses reappears as imperialism in its various forms, political, military, financial, and cultural. Yet exploitation is not inevitable; The dialectical opposition can be overcome and transformed insofar as the dynamic of capital accumulation loses its autonomy by being brought under social control.

A pervasive social dialectic within families, groups, organizations, and societies is captured in Parsons' and Bales' instrumental-expressive distinction (Parsons, 1951, p. 49; Parsons, Bales, and Shils, 1953, p. 123 ff.; Parsons, et al., 1955, p. 47 and passim). Parsons expresses the distinction as contrasting functional prerequisites: any social system, to survive as a system, must solve the adaptive problems posed by its environment and must at the same time maintain its unity or integrity. Adapting to the environment includes such processes as producing goods that can be exchanged with surrounding social systems for needed resources, satisfying the physiological and psychological needs of members, developing techniques for controlling and exploiting the physical environment, and accommodating beliefs and values to the surrounding culture. Maintaining integrity includes such processes as developing and maintaining shared beliefs and values, resolving internal disputes and maintaining acceptable levels of tension and disagreement, socializing new members, and symbolizing the system to itself in ritual, ceremony, symbolic leaders and objects.

The two prerequisites are interdependent. Any systematic productive or adaptive activity requires organization of effort, an acceptable level of tension, and properly motivated members; the achievement of integrative tasks requires resources that must be obtained from the environment as well as temporary cushioning against environmental influences. But the achievement of each prerequisite tends to thwart and undo the other. Adaptive achievement, especially productive activity, requires impersonal attention to the task in hand, a sensitivity to cause-and-effect sequences and the technical imperatives of action, a belief in impersonal efficiency. Integrative achievement requires sensitivity to the feelings of people and to the symbolic meanings of persons, places, and things, ingenuity in devising acceptable compromises and redefinitions, and an ability to express and accept emotions.

The two sets of habits and attitudes are incompatible; the sober impersonality of task-orientation involves subordinating feelings and symbolic meanings to the objective requirements of getting something done on time, while the emotional sensitivity and expressiveness needed for dealing with interpersonal problems prevent one from attending to the objective schedules and rhythms of task achievement.

Human groups typically resolve the conflict by differentiating task-oriented and emotion-oriented phases in group activity. Bales found both these differentiations in small groups (Parsons, Bales, and Shils, 1953; Parsons et al., 1955), and Zelditch found a general cross-cultural tendency to differentiate family roles in the same fashion (Parsons, et al., 1955). Other writers have studied the same dialectical conflict (for example, Stogdill, 1959).

In studies of personality, the dialectical principle of ambivalence is very pervasive. Clinical psychologists find that love conceals hatred and hostility serves to repress affection, that submissiveness and rebelliousness go hand in hand, that stern emphasis on moral prohibitions derives its energy from repressed desires for the prohibited objects, that carefree enjoyment grows out of and conceals guilt feelings and fears, and in general, that any strong emotion or belief is locked in conflict with a concealed opposite that both nourishes and destroys it. Radcliffe-Brown similarly finds ambivalence at the root of joking relationships (1951a, pp. 20-22; 1952, pp. 109-110). A similar ambivalence has frequently been observed in certain kinds of colonial situations, where the cultural and moral pressure of the governing power tends to fragment the dependent group into submissive (progressive) and rebellious (conservative) factions. The former try to assimilate the superior culture and join it, while the "conservatives" reject the outsider and cling to the old way of life (Fallers, 1960, p. 84). Deeper study discloses the same ambivalence within the individual: the progressive's respect for the superior culture is accompanied by self-hatred and a deeper rejection of the culture (Kardiner and Ovesey, 1951, ch. 9), and the rejected progressive turns into the extreme nationalist rebel.

Dialectical thinking is also apparent in the conception of roles as reciprocal. It is observed that in any sustained interaction between two people, each role is largely shaped by the perceived or expressed expectations of the other. One's conception of self is thus a product of interaction with others, as G. H. Mead suggested, and one's presentation of self reflects the perceived expectations of the audience. This is perhaps a special case of the general principle of interpenetration of inner and outer worlds. Inner desires, fears, and inhibitions are projected into the perceived outer world, and external demands and examples are introjected as part of the self. Conflicts between self and other are also inner conflicts, and inner conflicts are projected out again to involve other people. Thus Leach (1965) argues that war is an outward expression of the inner self-other conflict.

The interpenetration of opposites is only one phase of dialectical logic, whose phases include among other things the generation of distinctions, the overcoming or transformation of opposites, and the transformation of subject matter. This is not the place for a thorough study of dialectic in science, so I limit myself to one additional snippet of dialectic, that is, the "principle" of the transformation of quantity into quality, (a principle often rendered meaningless by mechanistic interpretation) which is important in the work of the developmental functionalists such as Eisenstadt (1963), Apter (1965), Binder (1961), and Almond (Almond and Coleman, 1960, introduction). I shall illustrate the principle first and then explain it.

My illustration is from Eisenstadt's impressive study of centralized bureaucratic empires (1963). Eisenstadt locates this type of political system between feudalism and capitalism in his developmental typology (p. 10) and explains the characteristics of the type by its position in the typology (pp. 22-26). The bureaucratic empires differed from their immediate predecessors—feudal systems, patrimonial empires, and nomadic conquest empires—in that they had a partly autonomous political system. "Autonomous" here means, among other things, specific political goals determined by political circumstances, a set of specific political roles, a specific political community with territorial boundaries, and a specifically political decision-making process (pp. 19-24).

The survival of a bureaucratic empire depended on a number of political factors, such as maintaining a balance between two contradictory modes of legitimation and accountability. It especially depended on maintaining a moderate supply of free-floating resources, i.e., "resources—manpower, economic resources, political support, and cultural identifications—not embedded within or committed beforehand to any primary ascriptive-particularistic groups" (p. 27). The central administrations used these resources to maintain the partial autonomy of the political system, and Eisenstadt describes at great length their continuous attempts to maintain an adequate supply. In some cases, resources dwindled and disappeared: the merchants were overtaxed and went bankrupt, or they bought land and became local gentry, thus tying their resources down to a locality; the soldiers and officials became attached to a locality and lost their more general loyalty; and so on. In such cases the empire collapsed into feudalism. In other cases free-floating resources multiplied until they got out of hand: the merchants grew rich, the soldiers and officials became powerful and legitimate enough to take control of the bureaucracy and transform it into a modern capitalist state. In still other cases, the central administration managed to maintain a precarious balance for several centuries before succumbing in one direction or the other.

The "principle of transformation of quantity into quality" appears in the treatment of these free-floating resources. Fluctuations in resources continued, perhaps for centuries, until their quantitative value passed an upper or lower critical limit. At this point the whole political system underwent a qualitative transformation—a "process of total change" (p. 363)—into a different type of system, either feudalism at the lower limit or capitalism at the upper. Thus the "transformation of quantity into quality" is crucial for understanding the historical development of political systems in Eisenstadt's work. For another example of this principle, see Gluckman (1968, pp. 223-224, 233); cf. also Eisenstadt (1964) for a brief summary of his argument.

Dialectical thinking is by no means universal among holistic thinkers and theories. It is prominent in a few cases (for a recent example, see Turner, 1969), important though incomplete and unsystematic in many others, and absent in some. An example of the latter is Wittfogel's study of oriental despotism (1957), which contrasts nicely with Eisenstadt's dialectical treatment of the same subject matter.

In contrast with dialectical thinkers, Wittfogel distinguishes sharply between man and society. Human nature is treated as a fixed, unchanging set of strivings—for example, "Man pursues recognized advantage" (p. 16)—that work with the opportunities provided by nature. Society is never a cause, but only an effect of human strivings; it represents the cumulative deposit of the achievements of many men. Society affects man only negatively, by smothering his innate creativity to a greater or lesser extent. Relatively open societies, like feudalism (p. 419), do not smother men much and consequently allow great and rapid social development. Relatively closed societies, like oriental despotism or Soviet totalitarianism, smother men completely and so are completely stagnant.

To Wittfogel, history is an account of the relatively infrequent open periods when man has a genuine choice (pp. 9, 17) and of the long intervening centuries of stagnation. Neither man nor society undergoes any dynamic historical development; human nature does not change, and society is an artifact that changes only when men are able to change it. The resulting picture of oriental despotism reminds one of Mill's account in *On Liberty* (ch. 3): one reads of a static society that rigidly persists until an outside force (Western imperialism) breaks it up and releases the long-suppressed energies of individuals, who then go to work creating capitalism and democracy. (Cf. also Eisenstadt, 1958, for further criticism.)

Eisenstadt's picture of the same empires is dynamic and dramatic. They are characterized by basic internal contradictions that they may neither resolve nor intensify (Eisenstadt, 1963, pp. 149 ff, 268 ff, 317 ff); they depend on the steady maintenance of resources that continually tend to dwindle away or expand explosively. Key groups are continually shifting allegiance, values, or power, and reforms and renovations are continually working at cross purposes with other forces and trends. The central administrators maintain a precarious and harried foothold for a time, but finally fail and go under in the transformation of the system. Eisenstadt's account is supported by Binder's close-up view of a single case, modern Iran (Binder, 1961), where internal contradictions are sharp, continuous, and manifold.

Despite its deficiencies, Wittfogel's static snapshot or tableau is valuable as a supplement to Binder's and Eisenstadt's dialectical dramas. It reminds us that these empires did persist for a long time and that most of the dynamics went nowhere. Also Wittfogel's capitalist bias enables him to present vividly the point of view of the enterprising merchant or official who is fleeced or imprisoned or killed and who longs to be free to create capitalism and democracy. This picture supplements Eisenstadt's systemic or central administration point of view, from which the merchant is a valuable free-floating resource to be tended carefully and harvested periodically.

What accounts for the frequent occurrence of dialectical thinking among holists? The most obvious answer is that scientists are forced to think dialectically because the world is in some ways dialectical. While this may be correct, it cannot be a sufficient answer because practitioners of other methods do not think dialectically. The question then becomes, what is it about field and clinical methods that enables their users to think dialectically?

One possible answer is suggested by Redfield's treatment of dialectic (1960a, ch. 9). Redfield suggests that if one combines opposing one-sided descriptions of a human whole, the result is a more nearly adequate account of reality:

> It seems to me that with the recognition of the influence of personal choices on the resulting description we arrive at the possibility of combining two contrasting viewpoints into a combined viewpoint of the protean and unattainable absolute reality. I think we may well conceive of the process by which understanding of human wholes is advanced as a kind of dialectic of viewpoint, a dialogue of characterizations. 'This,' but on the other hand 'that,' is the orderly swing of the mind toward truth (1960a, p. 137).

Dialectic serves to counteract the human tendency to be biased, one-sided, abstract; it is a way of making thought and science more nearly concrete. One begins with some historically or empirically suggested viewpoint and develops it until its shortcomings are clear enough to suggest the outlines of an opposing, formerly excluded, viewpoint; then the latter is developed and related back to the first. In some cases the first viewpoint is a systematic theory that has been developed far enough to make its shortcomings obvious. Specifically, Parsons early was impressed with the shortcomings of neoclassical economic theory, which reappeared as the "instrumental" pole of his categories. Similarly, personality and culture theorists approached their synthesis through a recognition of the incompleteness of the viewpoints of both Freud and Durkheim taken separately. Redfield developed his peasant-urban dialectic through a recognition of the shortcomings of his folk society ideal type, and social psychologists came to emphasize the interconnectedness of self and other, of inner and outer, to counteract the obvious abstractness of individual psychology. In general, in this view holists adopt dialectical thinking to get closer to the particular, the concrete, and they adopt it whenever a line of thought has developed far enough to reveal its abstractness. Dialectic is the logic of the concrete.

However, this explanation may not fit all the cases, particularly the Freudian emphasis on the interconnection of opposite feelings, and it certainly is not a complete account of dialectic. Another possible partial explanation is the holist's abhorrence of dualism and of atomism. No human whole can be broken into two or more independent parts and still remain whole; the main subdivisions of a whole must be internally related, interpenetrating. One who has a bias toward seeing things whole will be suspicious of dualisms and atomisms and favorably disposed toward internal relations. Dialectic, as the logic of internal relations, would be used to overcome dualism and atomism.

The first of these two lines of thinking, that dialectic is a correction of one-sidedness, also serves perhaps to explain why many holistic works are not dialectical. Life is short, and it is not always necessary to insist on completing a total account of some subject matter. Most people must be satisfied with working out a partial account, even a purposely one-sided account, in order to be able to bring out and organize a sufficient amount of detail. Consider specifically the personality-culture polarity. Whole traditions of scientists have conciously and systematically limited themselves to one of these two levels of analysis without feeling in the least hemmed in. Many of them have recognized that the dynamics of culture work through personality and vice versa, but have left that problem to others. The culture and personality theorists who have explicitly focused on the dialectical relation could do so adequately only because they could build on the one-sided, perhaps distorted work of their predecessors and coworkers.

In any case, dialectical thinking is an important holist contribution to social science theories. There are abundant examples of theories that are erroneous due to one-sidedness, theories that badly need an injection of dialectic for their correction. Let us consider a few.

Whole political and economic theories have been built on the assumed principle of self-interest. Theorists have realized the limitations of this principle but have rationalized their own narrowness to themselves by suggesting that they would be just as happy with the opposite principle of altruism, which is equally one-sided; or they have suggested that in reality "self" means family or group, not individual; or they have put on an appearance of broad-mindedness by admitting that although most conduct is selfish there are also many altruistic actions, and although most people are rationally selfish there are also some who are insane; or they have even suggested entertaining an alternative principle that conduct is random. By these seeming concessions they have sought to convince themselves that they are broad-minded enough to recognize the empirical limitations of their theories. Actually all the alternative principles except the last are basically the same in that they all assume a ready-made self or group or family with all its interests agreed on and made consistent. Recently Mancur Olson (1965) has proved that if one assumes a ready-made self one cannot also have a ready-made group, but he did not question the assumption of the ready-made self. But the historical evidence (for example, that collected in Eisenstadt, 1963) shows that throughout history groups of

various kinds have often been better organized than individuals and therefore more capable of rational action. The rational self-interested individual
is unusual and needs explaining just as much as the ready-made rational
group. He is in fact, as Weber observed, nothing more than an idealization
of the capitalist man.

What is needed is a dialectic between a theory of the self or family or
group in the making and a theory of the actions of an already-made self.
The one theory deals with internal processes of conflict resolution, boundary maintenance, self-conceptualization and symbolization, socialization,
and so on, while the other deals with modes of action toward a securely
externalized environment. Both types of theory are already in existence
and the way toward combining them has been shown by Parsons' categories, but one-sided theorizing is still common.

A second dialectic is equally necessary for the correction of these same
theories. When one assumes a ready-made self or family or group, one
is faced with the problem of how these actors are to relate to each other.
The general assumption has been that interaction takes the form of exchange;
yet Hobbes argued long ago that in a society of rational self-interested men,
interaction takes the form of war, not exchange (cf. also Parsons, 1937,
pp. 89-94). The theory of interaction as exchange thus is seen to presuppose an opposite kind of theory that deals with the ways of holding a society together and thereby making exchange possible. Such a theory would
deal with how rules of exchange are established, maintained, and policed;
how desires, aspirations, and life styles are co-ordinated so as to make
exchange possible; how the units that exchange are recognized and certified;
and so on. We need such a theory in the small-group field as well, to supplement the current interest in interpreting small-group interaction as exchange.

Another similar example of a one-sided theory is that of the ready-made
national state. Both nations and states are assumed to be fixed entities with
definite boundaries and purely external relations with one another. But here
again systematic relations among externally related entities presuppose some
sort of noncontractual international order in which nations and states are
internally related. We need a theory of how international order is established and maintained, of how international unity and national diversity develop together and from each other. The basis of such a theory could well
be Redfield's principle of the interpenetration of the little and the great tradition, the interdependence of the little national groups and the great international financial, political, and religious centers. There is no adequate
theory of this kind; consequently, when international conflict occurs there is
no adequate set of principles available for resolving it. Instead, appeal
is frequently made to a principle of national self-determination, a fallacious
principle that is useful only for propaganda because it is based on the incorrect assumption that nations are purely external to one another (Diesing, 1967). Problems resulting from the objective interdependence and
interpenetration of nations and states must be resolved not by unstable

imperialisms or self-contradictory attempts at national self-determination, but by codetermination of some sort.

An opposite kind of one-sidedness occurred among some early functionalists, who developed a theory of the unity of cultures and societies that was so extreme as to exclude autonomy and diversity. We were sometimes given a static picture of a culture in which there was complete agreement on norms, in which each institution had a necessary function, and in which justice was automatically achieved by following the rules. Later functionalists corrected this picture by showing how norms develop and are accepted through disagreement and conflict (Llewellyn and Hoebel, 1941), how apparent agreement can mask actual disagreement and diversity (Bott, 1957; Leach, 1954), how conflicting norms can coexist in various ways, how the same institution can be functional for some groups or subsystems and dysfunctional for others (Kluckhohn, 1944; Merton, 1949, ch. 1), how unity is achieved through conflict (Coser, 1955, chs. 5, 7) and through autonomy (Goulder, 1959).

In the methodology of science, one-sidedness is exemplified by a theory that defines science entirely in terms of the achievement of rigor and precision. According to this theory, science is differentiated from pre-science by the precision of its definitions and measurements and the rigor of its deductions and experimental controls. The business of science is to verify hypotheses, and for this purpose hypotheses must be exactly stated, experimental controls must be thorough and rigorous, the measurement of results must be precise. Against this view I have argued that every scientific tradition I have examined contains a balance of precision and vagueness, rigor and suggestiveness, but that different traditions apportion the two elements in different fashions. The various kinds of balance serve the conflicting scientific needs of creativity and control: vagueness and suggestiveness facilitate creativity, and precision and rigor are means of control, either empirical or logical. If a tradition begins to overemphasize rigor and precision it moves toward theoretical stagnation and empirical preoccupation with detail, as experimental learning theory has at times done—and has been rescued each time by fresh outside ideas, first probability theory and later cybernetics and information theory. If a tradition overemphasizes vagueness, it moves toward diffuse and uncontrolled speculation, as psychoanalytic theory has done in the metapsychoanalytic speculations of Jung and the ethnohistorical speculations of Freud. A central problem of scientific methods is to keep a balance between precision and vagueness and to relate the two in such a way that they enrich rather than destroy each other.

Actually the one-sided philosophies do recognize both aspects of science, creativity and control, and the related needs for vagueness and precision. The deficiency of these philosophies is that they separate the two aspects sharply and thus make both of them abstract and static. The accounts of the logic of hypothesis testing, where precision dominates, forces one to realize that there is another side to science, the creative side, which is presupposed by the hypothesis-testing side. But this other side is then separated entirely from logic and becomes completely free and undisciplined, so that nothing systematic can be said about it. Conversely, the "logic" side becomes completely rigid and unchangeable because all creativity has been drained out of it and assigned to the nonlogical side. The result is that science is robbed of its dynamic, its historical development.

Structure

In Abraham Kaplan's terminology, the structure of holistic theories is concatenated rather than hierarchical (Kaplan, 1964, p. 298). That is, these theories are composed of several relatively independent, loosely linked parts, rather than of deductions from a few basic postulates. Each section of a concatenated theory is developed and tested independently of other sections, is based on its own body of evidence, has its own typology, and is not deduced from any other section. Each section in turn is likely to be composed of several relatively independent subsections. When a theory is applied to a case, each section illuminates a different aspect of the case, so that the whole theory together gives many-sided illumination and guidance to case studies and comparisons.

For example, psychoanalytic theory includes a section on topography (conscious-preconscious-unconscious, or primary and secondary processes), a section on drives or psychic energy, a section on personality structure (id-ego-superego, etc.), a section of the dynamics of personality functioning (conflict, defense, mastery, adaptation to reality), and a section on the stages of development and the etiology of neuroses (Hartmann, 1959, p. 13; Ross and Abrams, 1965, pp. 307-328).

Parsons' version of functionalism, which focuses on four basic functional prerequisites, includes the following sections: (1) the four prerequisites and the four specialized subsystems—economy or technical subsystem, polity, community, and pattern-maintenance subsystem—that develop to satisfy them; (2) the six interchange systems (Parsons, 1966b, p. 108 ff); (3) the seven levels of generality, as resources are transferred across subsystems (Parsons and Smelser, 1956, p. 139); (4) the four generalized media of interchange (Parsons, 1969, ch. 14-16); and (5) the phase movements—the phases of personality development and disorganization (Parsons et. al., 1955, ch. 2), the therapeutic cycle (Parsons, 1964), phase movement in task-oriented groups (Parsons, Bales, and Shils, 1953, ch. 5). The whole theory of functional prerequisites is itself only one section of functionalist theory, though a very important one. Another coordinate section is the theory of the pattern variables, which has a long and independent developmental history; the pattern variables are used to classify whole systems. (Parsons and Smelser, 1956, pp.33-38; Parsons, 1967, ch. 7). A third section is the theory of the evolution of social systems, which has come to the fore in the past few years. And finally there is the theory of structural prerequisites, of structural variations and their relations to function and process, which has been developed by other theorists. The various sections and subsections are closely linked together but cannot be deduced from a few basic postulates.

The theory of symbolic interaction has not to my knowledge undergone a similarly complex development. It may be that symbolic interactionists are less interested in abstract speculation and more interested in case studies and typologies; for instance, types of organizations, types of encounters, types of ritual. However, G. H. Mead's classic formulation of the theory has three distinct sections: (1) communication, symbolization, and meaning, (2) the self, including I, me, and the generalized other, (3) society, including the theory of the religious, economic, and scientific communities and the theory of social dynamics and development (G.H. Mead, 1934).

Finally, the theory of multilenear evolution has been somewhat delayed in its development, but we can get some idea of its intended shape from Steward's prospectus (1953) and from various specific contributions that have appeared. The theory, it appears, will be focused on an extended and growing typology of socioeconomic systems. The component types, such as patrilineal bands, irrigation systems, slash-and-burn agriculture, will be much more restricted than the broad, all-encompassing "savage-barbarian-civilized" types developed by the "unilinear" evolutionists, but will be more complex than, say, a "Bronze age" type that is defined by a single essential characteristic (Steward, 1953). Each type will be defined by a considerable number of specific characteristics that have regularly appeared together; this is what I have called an empiricist "real type." Each type will have a separate section of the general theory of evolution devoted to it. The theory will explain how and why various characteristics are combined in the type— a pattern explanation—and will state laws of development that apply to that type—presumably a deductive explanation.

Complex computer simulations are also concatenated; in this case the modules are the separate sections, and they are linked together in the flow chart. Mathematical models, in contrast, are all hierarchical.

Why are case study theories concatenated? I can imagine four possible reasons. For one thing, these theories grow out of typologies, and the typologies themselves are empirically derived. This means that each type is discovered separately through the examination of a series of cases and is tested and developed separately. Consequently one type cannot be deduced from another, and one typology cannot be deduced from another. One cannot deduce one defense mechanism from another, nor deduce a typology of defense mechanisms from a typology of developmental stages or of primary and secondary processes.

But this reason is not conclusive, since it is possible to arrange many empirically derived propositions and even typologies in a hierarchical order if one tries hard enough. One can possibly imagine some basic postulates that underlie all the far-flung domains of a holistic theory and find some formal term for which a whole list of types can serve as alternative empirical interpretations. However, as soon as one imagines such a process, one realizes that holists do not think in this way. Their thinking is not mathematical-deductive, but empirical in the sense that they always do their theorizing by reference to specific cases they keep close at hand. Indeed, they find deductive theorizing repugnant because it forces them to pin down their key concepts in a rigid, formal calculus, whereas they prefer continually to change and enrich the meaning of the terms as new case data come in.

This reason is not conclusive either, since it is always possible for a misguided mathematical thinker to pick up a holist theory and formalize it. In this case, the difficulty would consist in the fact that holist theories are usually unsuited to mathematical formalization (cf. ch. 8); their concepts are rich in empirical content and are often (though not always) dialectically related. An appropriate formalization would involve either the use of computers or entirely new formal languages; in either case, the result would still be a complex concatenated theory.

Finally, a simplifying mathematical formalization of a holist theory would largely destroy its usefulness as a guide to case studies. A concatenated theory, with its several independent sections and subsections, provides many-sided guidance to observation. Each section of the theory focuses attention on one aspect of the case and provides one way of organizing and interpreting data. The several sections supplement each other and provide a well-rounded interpretation.

A hierarchical theory, in contrast, is always one-sided. It takes one set of relations, one structure or process, one set of criteria, and abstracts it from the concrete case for logical study. For example, a deductively minded political scientist will abstract the exchange or the coalition or the bargaining or the voting or the symbolization aspect out of the total political process. A deductively minded economist will focus on processes of exchange or of resource allocation. A psychologist will focus on learning or on attitude formation. A deductively minded philosopher will abstract the logic of confirmation or of explanation from the whole scientific process, and so on.

Now I would be the last person to deprecate formal deductive theory, whose importance I have often expounded and defended against empiricist criticisms. But despite its great value in other respects, deductive theory is not very useful as a guide to case studies. Its inevitable one sidedness narrows and distorts observation, and the abstractness of its concepts draws attention away from the empirical case and toward the logical structure being developed. The case becomes a source of new formal concepts or an exemplification of old concepts rather than a center of interest in its own right. Consequently a hierarchical rearrangement of holist theories would reduce their unique value as a guide to case studies.

The following chapter deals in more detail with the use of holist theories.

16

The Use and Verification of General Theory

The discussion has now moved step by step from the specific to the general, from case study to controlled comparison to typology to general theory. I have argued that in current clinical and field practice, general theory does not develop directly out of specific observation, but rather out of a controlled comparison of cases. One selects a representative sample of cases, as determined by one's typology, and locates elements common to all the cases in constructing a general theory.

The reverse movement, from general theory to specific case, which we consider in this chapter, is also not direct. Theory is used to direct observation and suggest explanations; but general theory, which states what is characteristic of all cases, is too abstract to provide detailed guidance in a specific case. What is needed to direct specific observation is a less abstract theory, one that specifies the various ways in which universal elements manifest themselves in specific cases. Thus it is not enough to know that all human beings defend themselves against threats to their integrity; we need to know in addition the various types of defense mechanisms and the circumstances in which each is predominant. It is not enough to know that all societies must preserve some consensus on values as well as some dissensus and some deviance; we need to know the various types of value patterns, the circumstances in which each is predominant, and the kinds of dissent, deviance, and breakdown that accompany each. It is not enough to know that all scientific methods must somehow balance and combine precision and vagueness or activity and passivity; we need to know the various ways in which these are done and the circumstances in which each occurs and is effective.

In short, what is needed to direct observation is a typology that will classify a case and will state what can be expected in that class of cases. Typologies provide the less abstract, middle-range theory that controls observation. General theory, in turn, is used to organize and reorganize typologies, and only indirectly to control specific observation (cf. on this point, Bendix, 1963).

I suggest that general theory performs three functions for typologies. First, it explains individual types, that is, it explains how and why the various elements that have been continually found together in actual cases belong together. It explains by stating the connections—causal, logical, structural-functional, expressive-symptomatic, means-ends, theme and variations, etc.—that relate the elements to each other. Second, in specifying the connections it shows which elements or clusters of elements are most important in making the type what it is. This specification makes the type a more reliable guide to classification and observation, by focusing the observer's attention on essentials, on inferred depth factors rather than observable symptoms. It also leads to reorganization of the type and its subtypes and variants on the basis of essential rather than superficial characteristics. Third, it explains a typology by ordering it in some fashion. If the typology is diachronic it orders the types in a sequence of development and specifies the modes of transition from one stage to the next; if the typology is synchronic it specifies the essential principles that distinguish the types and shows that the resulting classification is complete.

For example, Fromm's revision of psychoanalytic theory (1947) centers on a typology of character consisting of two polar ideal types, the productive and the nonproductive orientations. Cross-cutting this typology is another typology of four ideal types, the receptive, the hoarding, the exploitative, and the marketing orientations. Each type is described by a long list of characteristics (1947, pp. 114-116) and an account of observable behavior (pp. 62-78). The theory explains and points to the essentials of each type, giving the basis of classification for both typologies.

Fromm argues, following Freud, that observable behavior is to be understood as the expression of character, an unobservable, largely unconscious organization of motives (1947, pp. 54-57). Character is what gives unity, coherence, and intelligibility to the wide diversity of a person's behavior. A person's character is his way of acting, of relating to the world. The variety of human character is endless, but each character can be understood as a unique combination of a few essential ways of relating to the world. The understanding of these essential ways is thus the key to the understanding of character and of behavior. Each of Fromm's ideal types is a description of one way of relating to the world, showing how that way appears in all the various spheres of action toward human and nonhuman objects. The whole typology is a classification of all possible ways of relating to the world, all possible character traits.

Note that Fromm's theory does not directly explain any particular bit of observable behavior. It explains directly only the ideal types, by showing in each case how all the many behavioral traits are a manifestation of a single mode of relatedness. The types in turn can be used to describe character, by showing how a particular character combines elements from each type. Finally, inferred character can be used to explain observable behavior.

The question of why a person has developed his particular character pattern is answered by a second part of Fromm's theory, his theory of social character (1948, 1949). Fromm argues that character arises out of an interplay between interpersonal relations in the family and the inner pressure of physiological maturation; family patterns in turn are related in some way to economic, political, and cultural determinants. The exact relations between family and society, personality and culture, have not been worked out beyond some rather impressionistic studies of two cases, capitalism and nazism (1955, 1941).

Both parts of Fromm's theory, the structural and the genetic, must be taken together to understand any particular person's behavior. Fromm's theory is a concatenated theory.

For a second example, consider Erikson's revision of the same theory (1950, ch. 7; 1959b; 1964, ch. 4; 1968). Where Fromm converts Freud's stages of psychosexual development into a synchronic typology of character, Erikson retains Freud's diachronic typology but revises the explanation of the types. In Erikson's theory each type represents one essential problem in human development, and the whole typology represents the whole sequence of developmental problems one faces through life. Each developmental problem is produced by a combination of social demands and physiological pressures and capacities resulting from maturation. These demands and pressures require for their satisfaction a level of personality organization that does not yet exist in the person; they break up the previously established personality integration and demand a new one. The conflict among new demands, new physiological pressures, and old personality produces a crisis that can be resolved only by personality change. A solution is made possible by the inner strength accumulated in the solution to previous crises and by help coming from other people. Erikson stresses that a solution to a developmental crisis always requires help from another person and that such help is always a two-way, mutual affair (1964, ch. 4 and p. 114). He calls this the "cycle of generations," since people at different stages of development can help each other with their respective problems and thus contribute to this continuous cycle of human development.

The solution to a developmental crisis produces, in the changed personality, a specific virtue or strength that is available for the next problem and for helping others. Conversely, each solution has an inadequate aspect and each virtue has its negative which necessarily accompanies it (1964, p. 139; note the dialectical thinking) to produce complications in some future developmental crisis. These complications appear clinically as regressions, that is, as the reappearance of an unsolved earlier problem during a later stage of development. In sum, each crisis contains within it some elements of the problems left over from previous crises as well as partial anticipatory solutions that were prepared in the solutions to previous crises.

Note how Erikson's theory explains the familiar Freudian developmental stages—oral, anal, genital, etc.—by showing how each centers on a developmental crisis and how each observed characteristic of the stage plays a part in the crisis. The theory also explains the whole typology by showing why each stage occurs when it does and how each stage prepares the way for the next stage and leads into it. Erikson's types are real types, in contrast with Fromm's polar ideal types, and so could be modified by evidence of new cases from previously unstudied types of cultures; they have in fact already been changed somewhat by Erikson. However, these types are so interlinked in the general theory that drastic change (such as the insertion of a ninth stage) is unlikely. This interlinking marks the difference between an empirically discovered and a theoretically explained typology.

A typology that has been explained by general theory is a better guide to observation than an unexplained set of real types. Explained typologies have been reorganized around supposedly basic or essential characteristics rather than superficial observables, and the observables have been related to the essentials as symptoms, expressions, superstructures, secondary institutions, and so on. Consequently, observation is directed immediately to those observables that will point to the basic characteristics of the case—the particular developmental problem being faced, or the particular mode of production, or the degree of autonomy achieved by certain subsystems, or the basic function that this type of subsystem performs and the structural characteristics it consequently must have, or the basic self-other relation. By directing attention to these essentials, theory prevents observation from getting lost in superficial details and facilitates a more rapid grasp of the basic structure of the case. To be sure, as I have already mentioned, theory can also overpower observation and prevent the discovery of novel factors in the case.

A theoretically explained type also improves one's control over comparisons. An empirical or "real" type controls comparison by ensuring that the two cases to be compared are likely to be similar in most respects, and that the meaning or systemic context of similar elements is also likely to be the same. A theoretically explained type does more than this: it provides a systematic list of essential characteristics for both cases, and comparison can then be an orderly point-for-point affair rather than a random search. An observed difference on some point is already half explained, because its connections to other characteristics are already specified.

We turn now to the question of how general theory is verified. When scientific method is treated as a heuristic or search process, verification is a check point in the process, a test. It consists in determining whether something—a variable, a factor, a hypothesis, a concept, a theory, etc.—is an improvement over what preceded it; or, looking forward instead of backward, it consists in estimating whether further search in the same direction is desirable. Falsification of the null hypothesis, for example, tells us there is evidence that something nonrandom worth investigating is present in a certain direction. The question of how high the required level of significance should be set is one of cost; the answer specifies how good the evidence has to be before we are willing to invest resources in further search. Significance levels are thus not arbitrary or should not be, but are justified in terms of the satisfactory allocation of scientific resources.

The criterion of improvement is determined by the use of the element being tested or verified. If the element is used to describe, the criterion would be some measure of descriptive adequacy; if the element is used to explain, the criterion would be explanatory power; and so on. Thus, scientists use different kinds of criteria for testing different kinds of scientific elements.

The argument of the preceding five chapters suggests that we should distinguish four levels of testing in case study methods: testing of a theme, of a configuration or case-descriptive model, of a type, and of a general theory. Bruyn suggests a fifth level prior to these four, verification of a meaning (Bruyn, 1956, pp. 237, 255 ff), but in the examples that occur to me I have difficulty distinguishing this level from verification of a theme or a configuration.

A theme is the lowest level of interpretive statement in a case study; it is like a pawn, easily gotten and easily discarded. It asserts simply that a certain uniformity exists in the data, that some sort of clustering or syndrome exists in the system being studied. Any such descriptive statement predicts that the uniformity will continue to appear in new data, and consequently it is tested by seeing whether further instances do appear. If only a few turn up it is inactivated, and if more than one or two negative instances appear it is discarded.

Arlow provides an example of clinical verification of a theme:

> During an initial interview I asked a patient how long he had been married. He answered, 'Sixteen months, three weeks.' The overly exact quality of this response aroused in me the suspicion that I was dealing with a person whose character structure was colored by obsessional thinking and compulsive traits. To confirm my suspicion I asked further, 'How long did you know your wife before you married her?' He answered, 'Two years, three months.' At this point, inwardly, I made a further set of predictions concerning this individual's mental traits. I guessed that he would be especially concerned with money, that he would have a passion for accumulating it, keeping meticulous records of his financial transactions, and that he would be most reluctant to spend it. A further set of predictions concerned his relationship to cleanliness . . . . Questioning confirmed each of these predictions in minute detail (Arlow, 1959, pp. 206-207).

More elaborate tests involve specifying how new instances will appear in new kinds of data, or specifying the exact nature or the exact location of the expected new instance. The requirement that the theme appear in new kinds of data provides a cross-check on the reliability of the data source—observation, informants, psychological tests, questionnaires, etc. Predictions about the nature and location of new instances serve to check the accuracy of one's interpretation. These tests can be used when the theme is already partially verified and one wishes to map its contour more exactly.

Note that verification occurs during, not after, the discovery of a theme, and is actually an integral part of the process of discovery. The first vague statement of a tentative theme is followed immediately by a search for further instances, which serve simultaneously to verify the existence of the theme and to specify its nature more exactly. After it is clear that the theme does exist in the data, its range of occurrence may next be investigated, and this search simultaneously serves as a test of its importance. The distinction between discovery and verification is analytical, made after the event.

A configuration or model is tested in a somewhat more elaborate fashion. Since a configuration is used to organize a set of themes into a systematic description of a case and in this sense to explain the themes, it is tested by its explanatory power. Testing involves three elements: first, how many themes are included in the configuration and how many are left out; second, how coherent or well-organized the themes are; and third, whether new themes fit into the model as well. Acceptance or rejection of a configuration, however, depends on the availability of a better alternative. The model that includes the most themes in the most coherent fashion is tentatively retained, and improvement in its inclusiveness and coherence is attempted. This contrasts with the treatment of a theme, which can be summarily rejected on the basis of two or three negative instances. The basis for the difference is that a theme is usually a simple, all-or-none affair, which either exists or does not exist, whereas a configuration can be modified and improved indefinitely; and unless a better prospect is available, a poor configuration is therefore improved rather than discarded. Some complex themes are also improvable in their formulation and can also be retained despite negative evidence. Conversely, a simple theme can be definitively verified by a small number of instances, while a configuration can be retested and improved indefinitely as new data come in.

Types and typologies are used to control comparisons and are tested by their fruitfulness in promoting understanding of the individual case and in developing theory. The instances of a type are supposed to be similar to each other in important respects other than those used to define the type. Consequently, when a researcher compares his case with others of the same type or with the mode for the type, he expects the other cases to suggest characteristics of his case that he might not otherwise have noticed. If the other cases are consistently or frequently misleading, he decides that his case is of a different type and that the initial similarities were superficial. Several experiences like this would constitute a disconfirmation of the type, in the sense that researchers would begin to distrust it and would look for a more reliable basis of classification. This is essentially what happened to the "savage" type that was inherited from the early social evolutionists; ethnologists (treating the type, perhaps mistakenly, as a real type) found too many differences among the cases classified as "savage," so that comparison within the type yielded many negative and few positive results.

More frequently, researchers find that a type is partly helpful and partly misleading; they react to this partial disconfirmation by trying to improve the type rather than discarding it outright. If the type is too broad and general, improvement will take the form of finding subtypes and variants; this is essentially what has been happening to Redfield's "peasant" type. If the components of the type appear in one's cases but do not seem to connect to each other in any intelligible way, one suspects that the type is mistakenly described. It may be defined too much in terms of surface characteristics rather than underlying dynamics, accidentals rather than essentials. In this case improvement takes the form of a search for the essentials, for the underlying dynamics of the type. This is essentially what has happened to the "schizophrenia" type in its various metamorphoses summarized earlier.

Both of these developments seem to have occurred in the social anthropological typology of residence rules. In the early decades of the century there was a standard typology: patrilocal, matrilocal, bilocal, neolocal, and miscellaneous. This was a complete set of real types: either a husband moved in with his wife, or she with him, or either with the other, or both moved out to a new location, or some confusing combination occurred. But as case studies accumulated, these types were seen to be too heterogeneous, and subtypes were distinguished according to where the husband was living when the wife moved in with him or vice versa (Murdock, 1949, pp. 16-17, 71). The Trobrianders were now classified as *avunculocal,* or *avunculvirilocal,* while for Malinowski they were simply patrilocal. New subtypes burgeoned, and the use of Latin dictionaries increased. The new subtypes were bewildering only to those who had not already been bewildered by the ever-increasing variety of residence rules discovered.

However, even with new subtypes, two observers might classify the same case differently (Goodenough, 1968), and so further changes were necessary. It became apparent that a census of geographical residence was not enough to determine unambiguously what residence rule was being followed. One had to determine *why* a couple lived where they did: how they defined the locality, what obligations they were fulfilling in moving there, or what characteristics permitted them to live there. These "depth" factors, such as kinship obligations and land ownership, rather than the superficial observable fact of geographical location, became more central in describing a type and in classifying a particular residence rule (Goodenough, 1968). This was the beginning of a shift from direct observation to theoretical explanation as the basis of the typology.

General theory is used primarily to organize (explain) and reorganize types and typologies, and thus is tested by its explanatory power. I have previously divided the explanatory function of general theory into three parts: (1) It states the connections between the elements that make up an empirical type, that is, it gives the dynamics of the type. (2) It specifies the elements or groups of elements that are most important in a typical dynamic, distinguishing depth factors from symptoms. (3) It organizes a typology into a developmental sequence or into a set of alternative solutions of a basic problem or in some other way. In each case the effect is to make the typology more useful and reliable as a guide to working with particular cases, both descriptively and practically. A well-explained typology facilitates the rapid and correct classification of a case, and a well-explained type suggests the essential etiology and dynamics of a case, rather than merely a list of things to look for.

Consequently the explanatory power of a general theory is tested by the usefulness of its associated types. When a theoretically explained type proves to be misleading or not very helpful in a number of cases, it shows that something is wrong with the associated general theory. It is then necessary to improve the theory by reinterpreting the underlying dynamics of the type and by changing the basis of classification of the typology. For example, every modification of Freud's various typologies by Rank, Horney, Hartmann, Fromm, Erikson, etc., was simultaneously a greater or lesser modificationof psychoanalytic theory.

The four levels of discovery-verification are closely related. One tests a general theory only indirectly, by testing the usefulness of its associated typology. The usefulness of a typology is measured by the adequacy of the case descriptions it makes possible, while the adequacy of a case description is determined by its success in organizing and explaining its constituent themes. Conversely, the discovery of a theme depends largely on theoretical suggestions brought to bear on the case by some typology, and the discovery or improvement of a type depends on the theoretical interpretation of an array of case materials. In general, discovery and improvement depend on ideas coming down from higher levels of theory, and these higher levels are tested in terms of the adequacy of lower-level statements. Only a theme, at the lowest level, is tested by direct empirical criteria, such as specific and immediate predictions, frequency counts, and statistical operations.

This account of the four (or five) levels of verification is perhaps a little too neat and orderly to be true; in fact, I strongly suspect that the reality is a good deal more complex and rambunctious than I have made it out to be. But of one point there can be no doubt: in case study methods, general theory is not tested in the same way that one tests a theme. Ignorance of this distinction has been one cause of the nonsense that philosophers of science have frequently produced on the subject of verification and falsification I select one especially obvious example to illustrate this point.

Sidney Hook claims that for forty years he has been asking psychoanalysts the question, "On what specific evidence would you decide that a child did not have an Oedipus complex?" (Hook, 1959, pp. 210, 214). He seems to have in mind a universally quantified empirical generalization of the following kind: for any x, if x is a human being, x has an Oedipus complex. He seems to suppose that this is one of the propositions of which psychoanalytic theory is composed. His question then is, what conceivable empirical evidence would falsify the proposition, or falsify psychoanalytic theory in general. He expects that there is none, that psycho-analytic theory is not empirically falsifiable, and that therefore it has no scientific, testable meaning.

Now this is nonsense. Holist theories are not composed of universal em-pirical generalizations and are not tested like empirical generalizations. The clinician does not approach each new case with the question, "Does this person have an Oedipus complex, yes or no?" What he tests is not a proposition but a type in a diachronic, development typology. The type he tests is a description of the oedipal stage of development: the essential prob-lem facing the personality at this stage and its main lines of variation; the origin of this problem in the solution of a previous problem and the way in which the earlier solution can affect the form of the new problem, and var-ious typical solutions, the symptoms by which one recognizes them, and the implications of each for later problems. He tests this type by using it to guide his observations of the oedipal aspect of a particular personality. Since the type is theoretically explained, it is supposed to guide him right to the essentials of his case. If it does not do so, if it misleads him into mis-interpretations and important omissions, this constitutes a partial discon-firmation of the type. In some such cases, all that is necessary is a minor change, some correction of a variant or a symptom list. However, a con-sistent disconfirmation would indicate that something is wrong with the theo-retical explanation of the type, and this would call for major recasting of psychoanalytic theory.

The theory of the oedipal stage has been tested in this way in thousands of case studies. These tests have provided partial confirmations and partial disconfirmations and have led to many changes in the theory, both major and minor. In one major change, that of Fromm (1947), the whole type has disappeared; in another, the name has disappeared (Erikson's stage three); in others, the name is retained but the dynamics have changed. The theorist's focus has shifted from biological factors to cultural factors (con-ceptions of authority and how it is supposed to be exercised) and social factors (family structures and functions). Along with this shift, the "neces-sity" of the stage has partly shifted from biological to functional; it is now seen as a stage that is necessary to the proper development of personality, in addition to being a necessary aspect of maturation.

The dialogue between Hook and Arlow (Hook, 1959, pp. 208-211, 216-219) is a good example of lack of communication. Hook is asking for a specification of evidence that would falsify psychoanalytic theory; Arlow re-plies with a characterization of a person who has skipped the oedipal stage. This answer indicates why the oedipal stage is necessary, that is, what es-sential phase of personality development occurs in it. If such a case history were to occur, it would provide confirmation, not falsification, of psychoana-lytic theory in that the theory suggests an explanation of the dynamics of the case: this person behaves as he does because he has skipped the oedipal stage. Hook thanks Arlow politely but does not understand his answer and is still not satisfied; at the close of his comments he is repeating his question as if nothing has happened (p. 219). Plainly his question is not a request for information; it is a hostile attack, and the proper reply is the defensive indignation that Hook says he has so often received.

Several more examples of the same error appear in Hook (1959); see also Nagel (1961, pp. 528-531) and Buck (1956). Buck's attack is on general systems theory, a formal method, but the same point holds: the basic concepts of systems analysis are tested not by specific predictions deduced from them but by their fruitfulness. The proper question is not "What characteristics are there which any object or group of objects could have, such that they would fail to form some kind of system?" (Buck, 1956, p. 226) but rather, "What can profitably be regarded as a system?" (Rapoport, 1966b, p. 129). The answer is, "Anything that suggests, by empirical exemplification, formal concepts that can be used in the construction or improvement of a mathematical model." In addition, since the general systems analyst is interested in constructing models of very wide applicability, he needs a wide range of diverse empirical examples, each suggesting the same formal concept. Unfortunately, Buck appears to have no understanding of the model-building method of the general systems analysts, and the message of his essay may be summed up in his oft-repeated phrase. "So what?"

17

Structural–Functional Theories

Functionalism, or structural-functionalism, has meant many things to many people. For some, the theory is summed up in Merton's 1949 chapter; for others, the term refers to Parsons' work from 1949 on. For some, it is a theory that flourished from about 1925 to 1940 and has since been replaced by symbolic interactionism except for a few stubborn survivals (according to Martindale, who later changed his mind); for others, "we are all functionalists now" since Radcliffe-Brown's ideas became generally accepted in England and similar ideas came to prevail in America (cf. K. Davis, 1967; Firth, 1955, pp. 237, 247). Some find two varieties of functionalism (a good and a bad, naturally); others find four or more uses of the term *function*; for still others the term *functionalism* has no definite meaning and there is no functionalist school (Radcliffe-Brown, 1952, p. 188).

My concern in this chapter is to suggest a particular interpretation of functionalism. I shall argue first that functionalism is not a timeless essence but a historically developing group of ideas. No one stage of development is definitive for the theory; it *becomes*, rather than *is*, something. Each functionalist statement or criticism should be understood in its historical context, as an attempted clarification or solution of problems present in earlier stages and as a locus of latent problems that lead to further development. Second, functionalism has developed in conjunction with participant-observer case studies. Consequently each functionalist statement should be understood in its methodological context as an attempt to solve problems presented by a particular subject matter and to make conclusions from that subject matter available for use in future case studies. I shall not insist on any particular terminology; since no one has yet registered *functionalism* or *structural-functionalism* as a trade mark, the reader is free to give any name or names he wishes to the ideas I shall discuss. Nor shall I argue whether or not Merton or Gouldner or Etzioni or Easton was a functionalist when he made his particular contribution to (functionalist?) theory. My concern is with ideas and methods, not labels, though I could suggest, for instance, that Gouldner used Mertonian functionalist ideas in his early participant-observation studies and largely dropped them about 1955 when he shifted to statistical surveys and factor analysis.

Most of the various interpretations and misinterpretations that appear in the polemics about functionalism result, I suggest, from taking a particular theoretical statement out of its historical and methodological context and thus losing its original meaning, that is, from treating it as a definitive account of what functionalism is rather than as one step in a disorderly process of becoming. Some critics who have located inadequacies in a functionalist statement have regarded them as permanent and ineradicable defects that provide sufficient reason for abandoning the theory rather than as one among the difficulties that have challenged the theory's adherents to further development. Philosophical critics in addition have tended to place too much reliance on functionalist statements *about* functionalism, treating them as faithful descriptions rather than as (in part) myths charting a hoped-for course of development and (in part) provisional attempts to clarify some continuing puzzle. Their criticisms have focused too much on specific definitions, treating them as complete accounts of what a concept means. This procedure is appropriate in studying formal theories, where a definition does embody the whole formal meaning of a term; it is also partly appropriate in survey research, where a definition embodies, if not the whole meaning of a concept, at least the whole meaning that will be operative in a particular study. But it is not appropriate in studying holistic theories, where the meaning of a term is located partly in its diffuse relations to other terms and cannot be adequately captured in a short definition; the term *function* is part of a cluster of terms including *structure, process, meaning,* and *functioning,* among others. Finally, the philosophical critics have at times applied standards that are not appropriate to functionalism, such as the deductive model of explanation and the hierarchical model of scientific theory.

I shall develop my interpretation of functionalism by making a brief survey of its history, which I arbitrarily divided into eight stages.

1. *Functionalism* is sometimes used in a very broad sense to include such theorists as Lowie, Boas, and Morgan. There is also a narrower sense in which it refers to those social scientists who were influenced by the work of Durkheim, Radcliffe-Brown, and Malinowski. I shall use the term in this second and narrower sense. The origins of this brand of functionalism are traditionally located in the 1907 and 1915-1917 participant-observer studies of Radcliffe-Brown and Malinowski (Radcliffe-Brown, 1922; Malinowski, 1922 and later works), and beyond them in Durkheim's theoretical work.

I suggest that two meanings of the term *function* can be distinguished in these studies, a general meaning and a special, more limited one. Probably Radcliffe-Brown and Malinowski did not distinguish the two, but when we are familiar with the later history of the concept, with its many distinct meanings, we can look back and find two of them in the early studies. The two meanings appear as senses two and three in Firth's discussion of "function" (1955, p. 244) In both cases one can define the function of an institution as "the part it plays in social life" Malinowski, quoted in Merton, 1949, p. 24; Radcliffe-Brown, 1922, pp. 229, 328; 1952, p. 180), but this vague phrase means different things in different contexts.

a. Primarily and generally, the function of an institution, the part it plays in social life, is its working interdependences with other specific institutions. Functionalism, in these early works, is an interest in finding and bring out the interdependences among the institutions of a particular society. Malinowski expresses his interest in "the manner in which two aspects of culture functionally depend on one another" and gives as an example the way in which Trobriand "economic enterprise and magical ritual form one inseparable whole, moulding and influencing one another" (1922, p. 515). He also shows the relation of kinship with production and distribution, the relation of both with political structure, and the relation of kinship and status with the ritual exchange of the Kula. Malinowski was also concerned with the relation between institutions and sentiments, or the "legal-intimate" polarity (1922, p. 19), suggesting that the survival of an institution might be defined as its degree of emotional vitality for the people participating in it (1922, p. 20). Radcliffe-Brown, in his later studies of kinship, committed himself to the hypothesis that "between the various features of a particular kinship system there is a complex relation of interdependence" (1952, p. 53). By this he meant such things as the interrelation of kinship terms and prescribed social relations (1952, p. 59) and the relation between kinship terms and preferred marriage customs (1952, p. 85). He also pointed out the frequent interdependence of exchange and social structure (1952, pp. 197-198).

What does "interdependence" or "functional dependence" mean? Its significance was at first primarily negative. Malinowski and Radcliffe-Brown were reacting simultaneously against the historical reconstructionists and the diffusionists. Both these schools attempted to explain particular items of a culture by relating them to presumed historical events, so that a whole culture was seen as the accidental combination of a number of independent historical sequences. This was the "shreds and patches" view of culture, a phrase of Lowie's that both men seized on to epitomize the view to which they were opposed (Malinowski, 1944, p. 38; Radcliffe-Brown, 1952, p. 186; cf. also Murdock, 1949, p. 322).

Against this view they asserted the basic holist assumption that a culture should be understood as an "integrated whole" or a "functional unity," by seeing how its parts were related with one another rather than with antecedent historical events. This assumption has continued to be fundamental in most functionalist theory and is, I believe, the basic theoretical accompaniment of the participant-observer method.

The positive meaning of "functional dependence" is more difficult to specify. For Malinowski it seemed to mean that each of two institutions was made determinate in some of its details by the prescriptions of the other, and was changed or preserved from change by those prescriptions. For instance, the kinship system determined who inherited one's trading partner or who got the best yams in one's garden; agricultural and magical techniques determined how many yams there were to deliver. Functional dependence also referred at times to a complex system of activities in which each activity prepared for and then set off one or more other activities (much as one actor's words function as a cue to other actors), and so on in a complex of cycles. Radcliffe-Brown (1952) used a variety of ambiguous phrases: "self-consistent" (p. 85), "faithful reflection" (p. 59), "different ways of applying or using" a structural principle (pp. 68, 81), a principle which itself is a hypothetical abstraction from the facts (p. 75). All these phrases are intended to exclude a causal relation between institutions (pp. 60, 68). Levi-Strauss, in discussing the interdependence between kinship terminology and social relations, rejects the above phrases and substitutes the equally momentous phrase, "dynamic integration" (1963, pp. 38-39). Evans-Pritchard, in discussing the interdependence of Azande beliefs, uses logical terms: "Witchcraft, oracles, and magic thus form a complex system of beliefs and rites which makes sense only when they are seen as interdependent parts of a whole. This system has a logical structure. Granted certain postulates, inferences and action based on them are sound" (1962a, p. 99). Radcliffe-Brown also referred to logical consistency as a special case of functional consistency (1935).

I suggest that this vagueness and ambiguity in the meaning of "functional dependence" or "functional unity" are due to the fact that several different kinds of interdependence exist in the cases studied, including perhaps some that were not fully understood. In all cases one could say that the "function" of an act, belief, story, institution, etc., consisted of the "part it played" or the "contribution it made" to social life as a whole. But its part or contribution might consist in justifying a practice, or setting up conditions for the next activity in a cycle, or specifying detailed obligations, or expressing a belief or principle, or reinforcing a sentiment, or providing evidence to support a belief. In each case a part of the system is "explained" (Radcliffe-Brown) or "made intelligible" (Evans-Pritchard) by specifying its relations to other parts, that is, by a pattern explanation; but different kinds of patterns occur in society, and descriptions of them in a case study will vary accordingly. Unless one has several of these patterns in mind as examples, the phrase "the part it plays" will necessarily seem vague.

b. One can also distinguish a special kind of contribution that certain institutions make to other institutions. I will illustrate this concept first and then define it. In *The Andaman Islanders,* Radcliffe-Brown discusses three things: social organization, ceremonies, and legends. He explains the latter two by showing how they preserve the former:

> I have tried to show that the ceremonial customs are the means by which the society acts upon its individual members and keeps alive in their minds a cer-

tain system of sentiments. Without the ceremonial those sentiments would not exist, and without them the social organization in its actual form could not exist. (1922, p. 324).

(Cf. also pp. 233-234; for legends, cf. p. 399; cf. also 1952, ch. 7). Similarly, both Malinowski and Radcliffe-Brown also studied primitive law, and they both treated it (with characteristically contrasting emphases) as an institution that served to ensure the performance of social obligations and to settle disputes (Radcliffe-Brown, 1952, pp. 198-199; Malinowski, 1926).

We find here a distinction between two kinds of institutions. On the one hand is the social structure or social organization, which includes kinship, production, and exchange; these institutions are in continuous operation. On the other hand are a set of secondary institutions that operate intermittently to repair, restore, maintain, or modify social structure; these include ritual, ceremony, legend, law, witchcraft, and politics. The secondary institutions can be said to have the function of maintaining the social structure in good working order. In this more limited sense, only secondary institutions have functions; social structure as a whole has none. Discussions of social structure take the form of showing the interdependence of its parts, which is the first sense of "function" discussed above.

2. A focus on social structure as the core of society continued in the later work of Radcliffe-Brown and his followers, British, American, and French. In this tradition, which continues to the present, one finds studies of kinship and marriage, of political systems, and also of "secondary" institutions such as ritual and witchcraft in their effect on social and political structure. The latter studies are modeled on Radcliffe-Brown's study of Andamanese ceremony and legend, continuing to test and modify his conclusions about them.

The studies of social and political structure were guided originally by Radcliffe-Brown's view that social anthropology is (or should become) a natural science whose aim is the discovery of laws or generalizations (1957). As tentative examples, he suggested, "One such law, or necessary condition of continued existence, is that of a certain degree of functional consistency amongst the constituent parts of the social system"; "a second [is that] any human social life requires the establishment of a social structure" (1952, p. 43; cf. pp. 43-47 for more examples). These laws he called, in an unguarded moment, the "cause" or "origin" of unilineal descent (1952, p. 46).

In order to discover laws one had to compare cases, and in order to control comparisons one needed typologies (Radcliffe-Brown, 1952, p. 195). Consequently the structuralists developed typologies of descent, of kinship terminology, of residence rules, and of political systems, and described these types as expressions or applications of basic structural principles. The search for "laws" has undergone various vicissitudes in the ensuing thirty years, including its complete abandonment (Evans-Pritchard, 1962a, pp. 20, 64; Siegel, 1963, p. 215), but the development and description of types and the search for limited generalizations about a type continue. Indeed, the typologies of kinship have become so numerous that the subject seems almost to be dissolving in chaos.

As time passed and case studies accumulated, the concept of function changed and became less central in structuralist studies, but did not disappear. Radcliffe-Brown provided an appropriate re-examination of the concept in 1952: " 'Function' is used to refer to the relations of process and structure . . . Process is dependent on structure and continuity of structure is dependent on process" (1952, p. 12). An illustration of what he means is provided by Evans-Pritchard's interpretation of Nuer feuding (1940, p. 150 ff). Nuer political structure expresses two contradictory principles of fission and fusion: the closer and more co-operative two political units are, the greater is their hostility (1940, p. 150; note the dialectical thinking). The feud is a process that sets this structure in motion; it activate's both principles and thus maintains the balance between them and preserves the continuity of the structure (p. 161). "The function of the feud . . . is, therefore, to maintain the structural equilibrium between opposed tribal segments which are, nevertheless, politically fused" (p. 159). A feud is similar to exercise, which, by activating the muscles of the body, keeps them in condition so they can be exercised some more.

The structuralist tradition has developed some similarities to formal theories that have made possible some mutual borrowing of concepts and techniques. The structuralists tried to abstract "principles" from which particular structures could be deduced and which provided a kind of deductive explanation of the structures (for example, Radcliffe-Brown, 1952, ch. 1). They constructed models, even semimathematical models, of structural types and tried to deduce intuitively some of the models' characteristics (for example, Banton, 1965, chs. 2-4). These models were originally real types but gradually became more idealized, more like formalist ideal types; in some cases, primary interest seems to have shifted away from empirical cases to abstract types and their component structures. The confusions and problems resulting from the appearance of formalist ideal types in an empiricist tradition have been cogently discussed by David Schneider (Banton, 1965, pp. 67-72 and passim). In general, this segment of the functionalist tradition seems to be moving toward some sort of crisis and reorganization.

3. After Malinowski had largely finished reporting his Trobriand field work, he turned to elaborating and teaching the theory of functionalism. The elaborated theory appears in his writings of the thirties and early forties; it does not appear in the Trobriand case studies, unless I have missed a passage somewhere.

Functionalism, in this later elaboration, is a theory of human needs and their satisfaction by culture. There are seven basic biological needs that are satisfied by culture: metabolism, reproduction, bodily comfort, safety, movement, growth, and health (Malinowski, 1944, p. 91). These needs are described as abstract summaries of a number of physiological drives or impulses like breathing and pain avoidance, rather than as real biological mechanisms (1944, p. 77). The cultural institutions that satisfy basic needs must themselves be maintained, and this imposes a new set of requirements on man. The derived needs are four in number: economic, educational, social control, and political (1944, p. 125)—obvious predecessors of Parsons' four functional prerequisites. Derived needs get their power from basic needs, and the ultimate function of an institution is its contribution to the satisfaction of a basic need, an organic impulse (1944, pp. 83, 159).

Malinowski claims that his theory is descriptive and empirical and that functional explanations are nothing more than elaborate descriptions (1944, p. 116-117). This statement has set off philosophical ruminations about the logical distinction between description and explanation, but from the context we see that Malinowski merely means to reject historical reconstructions and evolutionary speculations. This is also what he means by his rejection of "hypotheses" (1926, pp. 128-129; cf. also pp. 127-128, on the meaning of "explanation" for Malinowski). In positive terms, he means that his theory serves to focus attention on what is now observable in field work, rather than on what may have happened long ago. His theory serves as a guide to observation; it provides "recipes for the organization of perspective in field-work" (1944, p. 115). Specifically, it directs the field worker to locate the various functional problems in his case and see how they are being solved. The result would be a functional explanation of institutions showing how they contribute to specific solutions of problems *in this case*. The explanations would relate the institutions to what is happening at present rather than to what may have happened in the past, and in this sense would be "descriptions."

Unfortunately, the theory of basic needs cannot do what Malinowski wanted it to do, because basic needs are not observable, even indirectly, by a participant observer. The satisfaction of derived needs can be observed indirectly; one can, for instance, estimate the relative efficiency of a tribe in solving the "economic" problem by comparing labor inputs with product outputs over time (for example, Firth, 1939, pp. 133-142, appendix I); in a complex economy one can estimate gross national product or foreign exchange reserves and the like. If Parsons is correct (1969, chs. 14-16), one can deal with other functional problems analogously. Consequently, one can roughly determine the differential contribution of an institutional change or process to the solution of a particular functional problem. But one cannot do this with basic biological needs, because the biological element cannot be distinguished from the cultural element. Malinowski cites studies by Firth (1939) and Richards (1939) as examples of the use of his ideas in field work (Malinowski, 1944, p. 80); but Firth finds that he cannot distinguish biological and cultural determinants of dietary needs (1939, pp.

41-43, 32-37; cf. also Richards, 1939, pp. viii-x for the same comment; also Firth, 1951, p. 34).

The satisfaction of biological needs can perhaps be observed and measured in an experimental context by a physiologist. Malinowski refers to Hull and Pavlov in this connection, and seems to regard learning theory as the psychological basis for functionalism. He uses learning theory to argue for his claim that all parts of a culture must have some function. The argument is that according to learning theory unrewarded habits are extinguished; institutions are habits; and if any institution does not satisfy some basic or derived need it gets no reward and therefore must become extinct (1944, p. 142). The theorem that unrewarded habits are extinguished is indeed true, a priori, from the formal definition of the terms, but it cannot guide observation because specific habits, reinforcement schedules, and extinction rates cannot be isolated for study in the field. Consequently, the field worker cannot say of any specific practice whether it is being rewarded in some hidden way or whether it is in process of extinction or perhaps both. Because the concepts of learning theory are formal and experimental rather than holistic, they cannot be used to direct field observation as Malinowski intended; in effect, he imposed external and unobservable absolutes on the field situation.

Malinowski's theory of basic needs, as distinct from his theory of derived needs, has not to my knowledge been used by field workers after the initial attempts he cites, though it does have an occasional defender (for example, Piddington, in Firth, 1957). Its contribution was rather to set a problem for functionalists: how should one conceptualize the psychological concomitants of cultures? The solution to this problem has been attempted by the culture and personality theorists, to whom we turn next.

4. Culture and personality theory comes out of a variety of sources, including the later Boas and the later Sapir, Benedict, and Mead, as well as the work of Malinowski. Even Radcliffe-Brown stressed the importance of psychological investigations, though he did not carry them out himself: "The usages of a society work or 'function' only through their effects . . . in the thoughts, sentiments, and actions of individuals [and] an essential part of the task is the investigation of the individual." (1952, p. 185). When he defines functional unity as the absence of "persistent conflicts which can neither be resolved or regulated" (1952, p. 181) or argues that an inconsistency between kinship terms and attitudes produces a strain that leads to change (1935, p. 532), he is implicitly assuming psychological mechanisms.

The problem was to develop psychological concepts that would be useful in field work. This meant moving away from the unobservables of basic needs to the observables of personality and from the abstract universals of human nature to more limited and variable concepts that could be related to specific cultural phenomena. The solution was the concept of basic, or modal, or status personality, originally developed by Kardiner (1939). This was a real type, a concrete universal—human nature particularized and made determinate in a specific culture—which could be observed in the field and whose interrelations with its culture or subculture could be investigated. The various types in turn had to be explained by a general theory of personality, and the obvious holistic theory available for this purpose was psychoanalytic theory in its various versions.

The many field studies of modal personality led to many developments and clarifications of the concept. Among other things, it was found that generally only a minority of the inhabitants of a community would display the community's modal personality type, that two or more modal types could be found in the same community, and that the range of variation in two cultures could overlap greatly even though the modes of the two ranges were different (B. Kaplan, 1968, pp. 334-337). The chief theoretical issue was that of the relation between "culture" and "modal personality." Here were two different systems composed of the same elements, the same behavior. They were therefore in a sense identical, two aspects of the same thing; but they were also interdependent, antagonistic, and to some extent autonomous —a typical dialectical relationship.

The concept of function was doubled in this theoretical framework. It seemed that the Radcliffe-Brown functionalists had captured only half of the picture, the culture half; as Linton complained, "the picture of culture which emerges is that of a mass of gears all turning and grinding each other. There is no focal point for all this activity. . . . Each culture system appears mechanical and two-dimensional" (in Kardiner, 1939, p. viii; cf. also Nadel's reply, which goes back to Malinowski; Nadel, 1951, p. 367 ff.). With the addition of personality, the "two-dimensional" picture became three-dimensional, and the activity had a focal point. Cultural institutions were interdependent indirectly (unlike gears, which mesh directly), though the mediation of various personality factors and in various ways; and the integrity of personality was similarly maintained, supported, and challenged by culture factors. Consequently, function conceived as functional unity or interdependence now became a rather intricate affair, since there were two interdependent systems, each with a functional unity mediated by the other. And if function was conceived as the "contribution of an institution to the maintainance of . . . ," there were now two kinds of systems to be maintained.

Consider, for example, Mandelbaum's interpretation of the meaning of an institution—*meaning* being a term that is sometimes identified with function and sometimes distinguished from it: "What is the meaning of the Dry Funeral? What does performing it do for these folk? The 'meaning' of the Kota is its relation to other parts and periods of their lives, its effect on various of their systems of behavior." The implicit meanings are "those which help maintain the group's coherence and order, and which contribute to personal coherence and order" (Mandelbaum, 1954, pp. 89, 102). Similarly Kluckhohn proposes that "we must examine systematically the contributions which the witchcraft pattern assemblage makes to the maintenance of personal and social equilibrium" (1944, p. 79).

The "part it plays in social life" has now become two parts.

5. Probably the most important single development in functionalism has been its application to the study of complex modern societies. This shift led to major theoretical and methodological changes and set problems that have not yet been fully solved. It began in the twenties, when Malinowski's first students began studying African societies, and other field workers picked up his ideas and those of Radcliffe-Brown. Then in 1930 Warner and his associates, armed with ideas from Radcliffe-Brown and Durkheim, began to study Yankee City, and functionalism had come to the United States.

The basic shift of attention in these studies is from whole to part. The more complex a society is, the harder it is to study the whole society by participant observation; and in some areas like West Africa and India one cannot even locate a plausible "whole society." One necessarily focuses more on parts and their relation to other parts, on subparts, overlapping parts, and aspects of parts. Of course, even in the Andamans and the Trobriands it was necessary to study parts; but the whole was always present in experience, and one could eventually complete the study of the major parts and then construct a model of the entire society. With complex societies this is hardly possible.

For societies that are only moderately complex and moderately large, one might still reconstruct a model of the whole by skillful use of sampling and quantification. One could select three or four representative areas for intensive study (for example, Colson, 1954); one could use standard questionnaire forms to interview large numbers of people superficially, either within a sample area or scattered throughout the whole society; one could use census and tax data on even larger populations. These are the statistical techniques I discussed in chapter 12. In each case, census and survey data would have to be supplemented by direct observation, interviews, participation, and so on, so that each type of data could be checked for adequacy and interpreted in the light of other types of data.

However, for very complex and very large societies, these techniques are inadequate to reconstruct the whole system. In such cases, a typical response is to select a part that has important holistic qualities and treat it as a whole. One could study a village or small town, as Warner did, or a factory, a gang, a small group, a city neighborhood, a hospital, an organization, and in each case treat it as a whole society. It is also possible to expand one's powers of observation by taking a team into the field, as Warner did with his thirty or more observers and analysts, and by using various statistics and sampling designs. But these techniques only enable one to study a slightly larger part a little more adequately and to trace out a few more of its relations to other parts. In any case, the whole disappears from sight; what remains are numerous connections and leads that suggest the complex interdependence between the observed part and the other parts.

When researchers focused on the relation of parts to one another, several empirical findings soon emerged. First, it became clear that these complex societies were very loosely integrated. Major institutions like economy and kinship might be based on quite different organizing principles and be in active conflict with each other, in contrast with what Malinowski found in the Trobriands. Major groupings might be in continuing conflict, as in the frequent schisms found in some African kingdoms and in the Indian caste systems. Institutions like religion and ritual, which according to Radcliffe-Brown were supposed to integrate a society, were found to break it up or at least to express pre-existent conflicts (Bateson, 1936; Geertz, 1967). Different cultures and subcultures were found in the same locality, accommodating, conflicting, and changing.

Second, what integration did exist was a complex and devious affair, with overlapping and cross-cutting lines of influence. Control of deviant behavior, for example, might be accomplished simultaneously by internal personality factors, informal sanctions such as those Malinowski emphasized, and formal controls; motivation for economic activity might be similarly complex. Any one of these controls or sources of motivation might be in partial conflict with any other, or in internal conflict within itself (cf. Eisenstadt, 1961, on these two points).

Third, a different kind of integration occurred. For Radcliffe-Brown kinship was the basis of social structure and the essence of society. Warner found that class structure instead was the essential skeleton around which the institutions and groups of Yankee City were organized (1941, pp. 81-82), and a similar kind of integration was found in West Africa. Caste in India and politics in some African areas were perhaps other bases of integration (and simultaneously of conflict, of course).

Numerous theoretical implications were drawn from these findings, but we shall consider only what happened to the concept of "function." First, the concept of functional dependence or functional unity or interdependence became too vague to guide observation and was usually dropped (but cf. Warner, 1941, pp. 4-5, where "disfunctional" is treated as equivalent to "disorganized"; and Warner and Low, 1947, pp. 176-177, where Radcliffe-Brown's "functional consistency" appears. Warner's concepts remain close to those of Radcliffe-Brown.). Theorists wrote instead of *levels* and *types* of integration and disintegration. "Function" came to mean the contribution of one institution to the maintenance of some other institution, group, personality, or even of the whole society if there was such a thing. This meant that it was necessary to specify the unit being maintained, since an institution could contribute to the maintenance of one unit at the expense of some other unit. It also was necessary to specify what it was about the unit that was being maintained, or what "maintenance" meant in this case. And since any institution could have damaging "dysfunctional") as well as maintaining ("functional") effects, one could perhaps add up a sum or "balance" of functions and dysfunctions. This could be done either for the maintaining institution or for the one maintained. One could, for instance, estimate the dysfunctions of Navaho witchcraft for everything in sight, then estimate its functions, and then perhaps "add" or "balance" them. Or one could determine what institutions were tending to maintain personality structure (or anything else) and what institutions were tending to break it down, and then estimate the combined result of all these influences. Finally, one could specify duplications, or "functional alternatives," either actual or potential. A good summary of these various concepts appears in Merton, 1949, ch. 1 (cf. also Nadel, 1951, pp. 375-378).

As the concept of function became fragmented, functional analysis also diversified and developed in several directions. One important direction is represented by Merton's work, which has been influential in sociology. Here functionalism becomes the study of the effects, and especially the unanticipated effects, of something on something else—for example, the effects of theory on research or of research on theory (1949, pp. 11-12), the effects of goal-norm conflicts on personality and on political machines, the unintended effects of bureaucratic structure on personality and thereby on organizational efficiency, the consequences of diverse social structures for science (1949, p. 289), and so on. In Merton's theoretical statements he sometimes uses "consequences" and "functions-dysfunctions" interchangeably (1949, p. 68), and at other times seems to think of the latter as the subset of consequences relevant to "adaptation or adjustment." But this latter concept remains vague and does not seem to exclude much.

Merton's type of functional analysis is explicitly causal and not noticeably holistic. He can concern himself with the causal relations or interrelations between two abstract variables or with more complex causal interdependences in more specific situations. His theorizing is usually the rather loose and abstract speculation appropriate to the survey research method; it ranges over a mass of case materials and previous theoretical work and ends with a series of hypotheses to be tested or questions to be answered by statistical surveys. In some of his historical work (Merton, 1965) he is a diffusionist, plotting the incidence of some important concept in the history of ideas, tracing influences and borrowings, and even trying to locate the ultimate source of the diffused concept.

In short, I suggest that Merton's work represents the transfer of functionalist theory from a participant-observer framework to a survey research framework. This involves dropping the holistic and dialectical aspects of the theory and transforming it into a set of hypotheses about the effects of institutions, status personalities, etc., on one another. Other people, such as Karl Deutsch (Jacob and Toscano, 1964, ch. 4) have done the same thing. The transfer itself is part of the general borrowing between the two methods that has been occurring in sociology, producing mutual enrichment. From the standpoint of a borrower like Merton, I expect that participant observation and its related theories are seen not so much as a separate method but rather as an adjunct to the more recent, more refined techniques of social research. The case-study method is older and cruder, but may be regarded as still valuable as a preliminary source of insights and hypotheses.

Those philosophical and methodological discussions of "functionalism" that treat a functional relation as a causal relation backwards are based on Merton's variety of functional analysis. Such accounts may be correct for Merton and his followers, but not for other types of functionalists; for instance, Radcliffe-Brown explicitly excluded causal relations from his theorectical statements. For him, the notion of "cause" probably referred to historical cause, in which he was not interested.

6. A tendency to concentrate on the effects of parts of a society—institutions, modal personalities, value patterns—on one another is a natural and appropriate response to the problem of understanding complex societies. It is a way of isolating and specifying many detailed interrelations bit by bit and thus doing away with vague, global statements about the whole society. But the result is a fragmented picture in which basic, long-run system dynamics disappear from view. The many partial accounts do not combine in any clear way, and the various detailed dynamics do not seem to produce any over-all result.

An attempt to keep the dynamics of the whole society in view even while studying parts in detail has been central in the functionalism of Parsons and his many associates and students. Parsons began his functionalist theorizing in the late thirties with an examination of the central concept of "social system" (Parsons, 1949, p. viii). To him, a social system is a structure of social relations that tends to maintain itself. It is analogous to a biological organism in that both are self-maintaining systems; but self-maintenance for an organism consists of staying alive, while for a social system it consists of maintaining a boundary against environing social systems and maintaining a distinctive structure and a unified value pattern inside the boundary (Parsons and Shils, 1951, pp. 107-109; Parsons, 1951, p. 42). In his later theorizing, Parsons developed the concept of self-maintenance considerably.

Systems maintain themselves by coping with stresses and strains, by dealing with problems through more or less conscious purposive activity. The problems that social systems face may be classified into groups called functional problems or functional prerequisites (Parsons and Shils, 1951, pp. 120-123; Parsons, 1949, pp. 6-7, 48-51; 1951, pp. 26-36). The concept of a functional prerequisite was present in the early formulations of functionalist theory, appearing as Radcliffe-Brown's proposed "laws" and Malinowski's derived needs, but as these two formulations were discredited and abandoned, it became less important for a time. It is given only brief, programmatic treatment in Parsons' early functionalist work, but then Parsons' students began to focus on it (Aberle et al., 1950; Levy, 1952) and it received its first systematic treatment shortly thereafter (Parsons, Bales, and Shils, 1953). It has since become the central focus of Parsons' theory, so much so that the concepts of structure and later of process have been pushed ever farther into the background.

Parsons' theory of four functional prerequisites brings together and systematizes much earlier functionalist work. Radcliffe-Brown's requirement of functional unity or functional consistency appears as the integrative function, which is roughly the requirement that the parts of a system be coordinated so they support and carry out one another's activities. Parsons' early work on motivation as well as much culture and personality work deals with the pattern-maintenance function, which is roughly the requirement that the individuals participating in an action system be properly socialized and motivated to carry out their tasks, and that the tasks themselves be properly specified and re-interpreted in changing circumstances. The work of institutional economists such as Schumpeter and Myrdal relate the resource-mobilization function, performed by the economy, to the consequences resulting from performance of the integrative and pattern-maintenance functions. That is, performance of the integrative function in a society results in a specific class and occupational structure, and performance of the pattern-maintenance function results in individuals with certain motivations and values, among other things; and all these factors affect the economy and are affected by it in determinate ways. The work of political scientists on how politicians maintain electoral support, for example Easton, 1965, relates the class and occupational structure to the political structure (goal-achievement function) in determinate ways. Malinowski's list of basic needs reappears as the functional prerequisites of organisms, not social systems, and the culture-personality problem reappears as the problem of the fourfold articulation of organism, personality, social system, and culture. Finally, work on simpler societies is related to work on complex modern societies by the proposition that societies develop by differentiating subsystems that specialize on one functional prerequisite (Parsons and Smelser, 1956, ch. 5). The simpler societies are relatively undifferentiated; the complex are differentiated.

Parsons' theory is designed to be used in the study of parts of a complex, highly differentiated society—families, status systems, developing economies, organizations and bureaucracies, professions, political systems. For each part or subsystem the theory identifies a probable primary function and the resulting particular pattern of functional problems it faces, as well as its probable structure, values, and relations to other subsystems. But the study of a part never deals simply with its effects on other parts or the effects of other parts on it, as it did for the functionalists discussed in the previous section. Instead, the emphasis is always on the interplay of opposed but complementary functional requirements. In small groups, families, therapy, and personalities, these opposed requirements are met by a "phase movement" (Parsons, Bales, and Shils, 1953, ch. 5; Parsons et al., 1955, chs. 2-4) back and forth between opposed functional problems. In larger organizations, the opposed requirements are met by functional specialization at each level of the organizational hierarchy (Parsons, 1960, chs. 1-2), and the conflicts between requirements are reflected in intraorganization conflicts. In the primary subsystems of a society the opposed requirements are met by specialized subsubsystems (Parsons and Smelser, 1956, ch. 4) and by systematic interchanges with other subsystems, and the conflicts become subsystem conflicts, such as the conflict between capital and labor. Finally, in a whole society the conflicts among functional requirements become so important that they are handled by six specialized interchange subsystems using four media of exchange (Parsons, 1969, ch. 14-16; 1966b, pp. 107-112).

Thus the theory of the four functional requirements serves to keep the dynamics of a whole system in view in the study of parts, and relates the activities of parts to system dynamics. It also makes functionalism a voluntaristic theory of social problem solving (Parsons, 1937) in contrast to Merton's cause-and-effect functionalism. The conflicts among the functional requirements produce a semi-dialectical theory of social dynamics, in contrast to the way the adaptation-and-adjustment functionalists tried to add and subtract functional consequences to get their "net balances."

The concentration on social problem solving in Parsons' functionalism makes it necessary for him to develop explicit criteria of success in problem solving and self-maintenance. How can one tell that a system is successfully maintaining itself? Can one also distinguish degrees of success? The biological criterion of success is survival, but this makes little sense in dealing with social systems, because societies do not die and disappear except in extreme cases; they change. Earlier functionalists provided several alternative suggestions, from Malinowski's "emotional vitality" through Kardiner's frustration-satisfaction balance and Merton's net balance of functions-dysfunctions to more complex concepts of a balance between conflicts and the mechanisms for dealing with them. Etzioni in particular has observed that if a set of functional alternatives is available, one alternative may well be more effective than others in performing a given function, and he has attempted to estimate the relative effectiveness of different organizational structures in performing a pattern maintenance function (Etzioni, 1961, p. 78 ff).

All these criteria for success apply more readily to parts of a society—institutions, roles, substructures—than to a whole society. Parsons' systematization of the functional prerequisites makes it possible to develop a criterion that applies to a whole system. His criterion is whether there is an equilibrium among the functional interchanges. Since each solution to a functional problem affects the status of other functional problems, each solution indirectly feeds back on itself and determines how severe the problem will be the next time it comes up. Insofar as all these feedbacks are in a steady state, the system is maintaining itself. The steady state in turn can be measured by examining the inflation-deflation cycles of the four media of exchange (Parsons, 1967, pp. 341-345). If these fluctuate around a steady level, the system is maintaining itself. Self-maintenance need not involve structural persistence, value persistence, or indeed persistence of any particular characteristics of a system; but it does imply that these characteristics will change at an "equilibrium rate of change."

The concept of self-maintenance as a steady state of the functional interchanges immediately suggests its own extension. As Harold Kaplan observes, if a system of feedbacks can be in equilibrium, it can also be in an upward or a downward spiral (Kaplan, 1967, pp. 26-27). He calls the upward spiral "development," and defines it as an increase in the level of a system's performance (pp. 246-247). Kaplan provides a series of indicators for measuring adaptive and integrative development or decline (pp. 247-249). Parsons has the same concept, but calls it "growth" (1969, pp. 345-348). Growth is an increase in a system's capacity to solve functional problems, and is measured by the amount of power or other resource possessed by the system. Parsons cites Weimar Germany and the French Fourth Republic as examples of political systems that ran out of power and went politically bankrupt (1969, p. 493).

In his empirical interpretations of American society Parsons consistently expresses the belief that the American social system is solving all its functional problems pretty well, maintaining an adequate supply of social resources and perhaps growing a bit (Parsons and Smelser, 1956, pp. 147-149, 153, 158-161; Parsons, 1967, pp. 243-256; "The pressure of political cleavage...tends automatically to bring countervailing forces into play", p. 245; Parsons, 1969, pp. 162, 248, 279-280, 284). However, this optimistic ideological element has no necessary connection to his theory, which is neutral on the question of how well social systems are dealing with their functional problems these days. The charge of conservative bias can be made against Parsons personally but not against his theory.

7. If we avoid the assumption that social systems are normally successful in boundary maintenance, the existence of a system becomes a matter of degree. Systems in decline may shrink in resources or their boundaries become less distinct until they become part of an environing system; or internal cleavages may become more distinct until the system breaks up or reorganizes. Subcollectives or organizations may expand or develop more distinct boundaries and internal differentiation until they become relatively complete systems. The concept of "system," with its implications of secure boundaries, clear internal differentiation, and multiple functional interchange balances, becomes an ideal limit toward (or away from) which actual quasi-systems develop.

This version of functionalism requires several new concepts. First, we need a concept of "quasi systems," loosely organized structures whose governments are trying with indifferent success to solve one or another functional problem, or several problems simultaneously, in order to develop a secure boundary and a viable normative order. We think for example of the emerging and dissolving quasi nations of modern Africa, or the earlier shifting and overlapping African kingdoms, each achieving some partial measure of unity and resource mobilization and then loosening or coming apart temporarily again. We think of the St. Lawrence Island Eskimo, developing a somewhat effective polity and then becoming absorbed into the larger Alaskan polity (Hughes, 1966). The subsystems of these quasi systems need not have the same boundary; a religious community, a kingdom, and an economy, each with fairly definite boundaries and boundary-maintaining processes, may each overlap the other and provide passable functional inter-changes (for example, R. Cohen, 1964, p. 518). The terminology for quasi systems is not standardized; one finds the term *system* used loosely, as well as *society*, *group*, and *polity*.

Second, we need a concept of the environment in which these quasi systems come and go. Here there is a standard term, *field*. A field is a spatio-temporal continuum of interdependent processes that vary in tension, looseness, and harmony (Swartz et al., 1966, pp. 8, 26-31; Mitchell, 1966, pp. 56-60). A field may have a vague, fluctuating boundary or it may tighten up and assume some of the characteristics of a system. The term *arena* is some-times distinguished from and sometimes used interchangeably with *field* (Swartz, 1968, pp. 8-18). Note that history reappears in the "field" concept, and that it is not an abstract "structural time" history but a "real time" his-tory of real events. Evans-Pritchard's argument that functionalists should use historical data and concepts (1962a, chs. 1, 3; originally published, 1950) has finally been accepted though perhaps not as fully as he wished.

A third basic concept is "process," a standard functionalist concept that has for the first time become centrally important. With quasi systems form-ing and dissolving, functions performed poorly and erratically, and struc-tures fluctuating, processes are the most regular and dependable things left for study. Process is not, as with the structuralists, merely something that sets structures in motion and thereby keeps them fit; it is studied for its own sake. Compare, for instance, Evans-Pritchard's incidental treatment of Nuer feuding as something that activates political structure (1940) with the direct theorizing by Swartz et al., about the phases of a political conflict (1966, pp. 32-39, 50-51); or consider Gluckman's shift from considering Zulu re-bellions as a puzzling clue to Zulu political structure to his direct interest in rituals of rebellion in Africa (Fortes and Evans-Pritchard, 1940, ch. 2; Gluckman, 1963, pp. 20, 23, and ch. 3).

Because of its central interest in process in a field, this tradition may be called "process functionalism" We now have one branch of functionalism in which "structure" is the central concept, one in which "latent functions" are central, one in which "functional prerequisites" are central, and one in which "process" is central. The process functionalists are similar to the symbolic interactionists in their empirical concerns—both study micro-processes of interaction—and one may expect the two traditions to interact increasingly.

The process functionalists developed as offshoots or opponents of British structuralism and are still closely related to the structuralists. (Cf. R. Cohen, 1970; also Gluckman, 1968, p. 234: "We are all of us struc-turalists.") Max Gluckman, seeking to understand the puzzling data of Zulu political history, was one of the earliest to shift from a concern with static political and social structures to a concern with process in a field. He concludes, "I now abandon altogether the type of organic analogy for a social system with which Radcliffe-Brown worked....We have, as

Fortes and Firth have stressed, to think of a field of social action in which
we can delineate certain processes" (Gluckman, 1963, pp. 38-39; for Fortes'
use of the "field" concept, see Fortes, 1949, p. 286 ff). Gluckman's views
were further developed by Turner (1957) and others, and then spread
more or less rapidly (Swartz, Turner, and Tuden, 1966; Swartz, 1968).

However, the movement carries within itself as its internal other (in
Mead's sense) the "functional unity" ideas of Radcliffe-Brown and the "social system in equilibrium" ideas of Parsons. These concepts are now ideal
types to which existing quasi systems approximate in a fluctuating way.
Process case studies are concerned not merely with types and stages of process but also with how these processes are involved in the continuing stuggle
of quasi systems to solve functional problems.

8. The developmental functionalists take off in a different direction from the
work of Parsons and others (Levy, Almond). Instead of focusing on mi-
croprocesses within fluctuating semi systems, they examine the long-run development of whole political systems. By "development" is meant the complete transformation of a political system from one mode of organization
to an entirely different one—the transformation of small, independent city-states
to a large centralized empire, of autocratic empires and kingdoms to capitalist democracies, of tribal kingdoms and stateless societies to bureaucratic
one-party states. The impetus to this kind of study came from the availability of new subject matter, particularly the new states of Africa and Asia
that were striving to modernize their traditional societies and politics. Here
were societies that were changing rapidly, rushing pell mell from tribalism
to modernity, in which traditional and modern elements were still combined
in most incongruous mixtures.

The standpoint needed for studying these new states is just the opposite of
Parsons' standpoint. For the new states, "self-maintenance in a steady
state" or even a gradual "equilibrium rate of growth" means failure, not
success. A successful state is one in which the functional prerequisites of the
old order are not satisfied at all, in which internal contradictions are intensified and brought to a head rather than contained, in which old normative
orders are destroyed and rebuilt. Indeed, the standpoint of the developmental
functionalists is close to that of the Marxists, who are also concerned with
the radical transformation of whole societies and who are similar in other
important points of theory, logic, and method (cf. Lockwood, 1964, on this
point).

And yet it is just Parsons' systematic study of the functional prerequisites
of self-maintenance that has made developmental functionalism possible.
If one knows what is necessary for the self-maintenance of a society, one
also knows by negation what is necessary for its self-transcendence. For
example, Eisenstadt (1963) uses a Parsonian theory of functional prerequisites
to spell out in detail the conditions necessary for the self-maintenance of
the historical bureaucratic empires. He can then show how and why these
empires broke up and were transformed when the central bureaucracy failed

to satisfy the functional prerequisites—how one kind of failure produced a transformation into feudalism and an opposite kind of failure produced a transformation into capitalism. For a modernizing bureaucracy or revolutionary party, of course, the latter failure would constitute success, and success in self-maintenance would constitute failure.

Parsons represents the systematization and completion of several strands of earlier functionalism, but it is precisely this achievement that enables his followers, by building on his achievement, to take a new direction "brought to a head, it topples over." Parsons' Marxist critics, who accuse him of a static, consensus bias, are themselves taking a static view of science. They are correct mechanistically but not dialectically.

The central problem for the developmental functionalists is that of working out a typology of the stages of development of whole societies. To study the self-transformation of societies, one needs a theory that specifies from what and to what these societies are changing and that also describes the mechanisms by which the transformation from old to new takes place. Little more than a start has been made on this problem. The obvious typology to begin with is the "traditional-modern" one, but despite some theoretical clarification (Almond and Coleman, 1960, introduction; Apter, 1965; Gusfield, 1967), it remains an ill-defined continuum along which existing systems can only vaguely be located. The structure of the "modern" pole is not clear, the mechanisms of transformation are not clear, and it is not even clear in what sense the transformation is radical and in what sense gradual. Apter's mobilization-reconciliation typology (1965) makes good functionalist sense but does not seem to be developmental, unless one can describe development as a dialectical spiral between the two poles (the A-I poles, in Parsons' terminology). Probably the best typology is that offered by Eisenstadt (1963, p. 10), but it remains completely vague on the crucial type 7, "modern societies of various types." Until an adequate typology is developed, one cannot distinguish superficial change within a system from radical transformation of the system, nor can one distinguish progression to a later stage of development and retrogression to an earlier stage. Eisenstadt's typology enables one to make these distinctions, but not for "modern" systems. Recent Marxist writers have some contributions to make on this topic.

Note that history has not only reappeared but has moved to the center of functionalist attention. The kind of history studied is that of the development of societies through successive stages. Two kinds of time are distinguished in it: (1) normal time, in which there may be continuous cyclical or fluctuating change of the kind studied by Parsonians, by process functionalists, and by symbolic interactionists, but in which the basic structure of society, its basic personality, and its values remain much the same; and (2) revolutionary time, in which the functional contradictions of a society become extreme, and its structure, values, and personality are transformed. The concern of developmental functionalists is with revolutionary time, namely the present, but they have not yet clarified the mechanisms and termini of this time.

All of the six current varieties of functionalism I have distinguished are in various stages of development. The oldest variety, structuralism, seems to have completed its development some years ago and is now apparently in a critical period of change to something else, though many structuralists have already shifted to process functionalism while others are continuing with the structuralist program. Parsonian functionalism is still developing steadily, and especially accumulating empirical studies, but its main theoretical structure is reasonably clear by now. The two newest varieties—process and developmental functionalism—are just beginning to develop, and we can expect important advances in the near future when they get their typologies clarified. For example, it is instructive to read about the problems and prospects of revolution in Iran (Binder, 1961), but we need a similar study of the United States, which, like Iran, seems to be in a period of intensifying conflict and radical transformation. We need further processual studies of the kind summarized by Gluckman in his remark, "If we treat the mine and the tribe as parts of a single field, we see that within all the areas where it operates capitalist enterprise produces similar results" (1963, p. 223). Gluckman shows how the prosperity of the Rand gold mining corporations depends partly on the continued poverty of the native reserves, which provide cheap labor in prosperous times and a dumping ground for surplus labor in hard times; an obvious parallel is the way the prosperity of the California corporate farms depends on the continued poverty of Mexican laborers, who are imported when wages need to be kept down and exported again during economic recessions. On a larger scale, the false consciousness of the American worker is bought partly by profits and raw materials from American investments abroad, by profits from Venezuelan oil and iron ore, Bolivian tin, etc.; the show of democracy in America depends in part on the continuation of oligarchic government in Latin America, including C.I.A. "advisers" to various governments (*Manchester Guardian,* March 20, 1969, p. 5), anti-guerilla advisers in the armies, and American community development workers in the villages to keep the peasants happy (cf. Peattie, 1968, p. 63ff). Whether or not my particular examples are empirically sound, they represent the kind of interaction that stands out clearly when one studies processes in a field but is hidden when one treats the United States as a self-sufficient system in equilibrium.

Several lines of development can be seen in this history of functionalism. The main line is a continual differentiation of the originally vague concept of functional unity. It includes a differentiation of the functions that must be performed by an ongoing system, the kinds of structures needed to perform the functions, the processes and mechanisms involved, the interrelations among the functional requirements (including contradictions and facilitations), signs of failure in performing a function, and the consequences of various kinds of failure.

Another line of development is the expansion of subject matter from the original small "savage" societies to the full range of human systems—personalities, small groups, organizations, states, and empires.

Still another line is the reinclusion of originally excluded ideas as one pole of a pair. The early functionalists excluded history and change from their accounts, describing societies that maintained themselves against time because of their amazingly thorough internal unity. Historical changes were viewed as unknowable accidents, to be ignored along with the speculative reconstructions of diffusionists. But later this remarkable changelessness was seen to be characteristic only of a certain limited stage of historical development—or in some cases entirely an ethnographic fiction (Leach, 1957, p. 126). Attention shifted to the way stability and change alternate in the development of societies, and historical studies again became important. The early functionalists told us of self-maintaining societies, but logically a self-maintaining society is also implicity a self-transforming society. Change can be an adaptive success as well as a failure of self-maintenance, and persistence can be failure to develop as well as success in resisting disorganization. A village that has maintained its integrity can also "choose progress" without losing its integrity (Redfield, 1950), and new lives can be substituted for old (Mead, 1956).

The early functionalists tended to see conflict as a sign of disorganization and, under Durkheim's influence, studied the ways in which social cohesion and moral consensus were maintained. They recognized that there was plenty of conflict in the societies they studied, and that conflict was not only inevitable but also, as regulated conflict, essential to consensus (Malinowski, 1926; Radcliffe-Brown, 1952, p. 181 n). As increasing attention was paid to conflict and deviant behavior, it was recognized that even "unregulated" conflict was important in developing, maintaining, and changing consensus (Llewellyn and Hoebel, 1941; Coser, 1955). Conflict and consensus thus are a dialectical pair, each requiring, maintaining and destroying the other; and their interrelation in each specific case must be a focus of functionalist attention.

Similarly, the Durkheimian exclusion of personality factors from functionalist attention, though still practiced by some of Radcliffe-Brown's followers in England, is now justified as a deliberate narrowing of attention rather than as a necessity for all functionalist case studies. It is defended as a way of avoiding facile psychological explanations that would obscure important characteristics of social structure (Needham, 1962, p. 126), and also of avoiding dabbling in matters that are beyond the competence of sociologists (Gluckman and Devons, 1964, p. 17). But a more fundamental solution to the problem of competence is for the anthropologist to study personality theory or to team up with a psychologist, so that the detailed interrelations of personality and culture can be studied. However, there are still topics in which personality factors need not be directly considered.

Finally, the basic concept of "system," which gradually came into focus in the development of functionalist theory, is now seen by many as a limiting concept, with "field" as its polar opposite. The processes of self-maintenance and self-development are set on this continuum with neither extreme regarded as healthy. Changes in the permeability of boundaries around systems and subsystems are seen as part of the history of all system growth and decay.

These historical developments have been partly a response to problems internal to funtionalist theory, including problems pointed out by critics. But they have also been a response to problems encountered in understanding particular cases, as participant observers successively studied first small and primitive communities, then large and complex societies, then parts of modern societies, then developing economies, nations, and political systems.

In all these areas of study, functionalist theorizing has involved organizing and reorganizing types and typologies in order to make them more effective in controlling observation. The development of functionalist theory has largely consisted of this process. Malinowski inherited the "savage-barbarian-civilized" typology of the evolutionists (cf for example, Malinowski, 1922, p. xi), and his theoretical work essentially consisted in transforming this typology from historical to ahistorical, shifting it from diachronic to synchronic. He transformed the "savage society" type from a lowly predecessor of modern society to its equal, showing that both types of society faced and solved the same existential problems, though in quite different ways.

This transformation immediately suggested two new questions: what were the basic existential problems and what ways were there of solving them? This was apparently part of what Radcliffe-Brown had in mind when he called for the discovery of the "laws" of human society through the classification and comparison of cases. The response was a series of structural typologies, of kinship, political structure, economy, and the like. For example, Warner's class-caste-kinship-polity typology (1941 pp. 35, 81-82) suggested that every society had to have some essential structure around which all its institutions could be integrated, and that there were at least four types of essential structures.

The functionalist study of modern society produced a demand for a classification of institutions within a society, which led to the various functional typologies. Institutions were classified according to the predominant functions they performed, with the functional prerequisties providing a basis and explanation for the classification (for example, Parsons, 1960, pp. 44-47). As some researchers despaired of finding "the whole society" in the complex tangle of modern institutions and groupings and turned instead to the observable realities of process, they found they needed a typology of processes and of stages in processes. Finally, a renewal of interest in history led to a demand for a developmental typology, and the old "traditional-modern" pair was polished up and pressed into service pending the development of a better one.

We may now be in a position to consider once more the original question: what is functionalism? Granted that it has meant many things to many people, what does it really mean? I think it is clear from its history that if we are looking for some logical structure as the essence of functionalism, there is no such thing. Functional analysis is sometimes causal, sometimes noncausal; teleological and nonteleological; historical and ahistorical; holistic and nonholistic; sociological and psychological and political; focusing sometimes on consensus, sometimes on conflict or contradiction; and so on. Most versions of functionalism have been holistic and have had the logical characteristics discussed in chapter 15, but some do not. If we were to declare that those characteristics constituted the essence of functionalism, Merton and his followers and predecessors would be pushed out to the fringes of the tradition, which would be unfair and unwarranted. As for the various logics of functional analysis developed by philosophers, I hope I have shown that their relation to reality is very tenuous. They may still be good logic, but their chief use for the social sciences seems to be as a handy polemic weapon for antifunctionalists. They make sense only if interpreted as limited misinterpretations of one branch of functionalism at one point in its history.

If there is no logical essence of functionalism, might we find a genealogical essence? I have used a "genealogical" criterion above, including only descendants of Durkheim, Radcliffe-Brown, and Malinowski in my account. But as soon as we appeal to the kinship analogy, we are reminded of the structuralist discovery that every kinship system necessarily is built out of contradictory principles, such as consanguinity and affinity, because everyone has two parents a generation apart from him. Similarly, every scientist is influenced by more than one predecessor and is a member of a new generation, so that any specific influence chart is necessarily partial and misleading. The personality and culture people, the Mertonians, and the Parsonians all have learned from a variety of sources and have departed from, reacted against, or returned to a variety of earlier positions; so on a genealogical basis they must be called functionalists, nonfunctionalists, and antifunctionalists. The process functionalists, in particular, might just as appropriately be called process antifunctionalists, except that the name is awkward.

Should we use a subjective criterion, then, counting as functionalists only those people who think of themselves as functionalists? This would work well in some cases, but we would have to exclude Radcliffe-Brown in one of his anti-Malinowski moods (1949; 1952, p. 188). Similarly, a great many people might answer the question either "yes" or "no" or "yes and no" according to mood and circumstances.

Finally, if we use a criterion of communication and community we find that there is something of a boundary around some of the eight stages of functionalism I have distinguished, but I doubt whether any boundary of any kind could be found around all eight of them.

In short, I am inclined to agree with Kingsley Davis when he says that there is nothing special about functional analysis, that there are nearly as many varieties as there are varieties of sociological theory. On the other hand, one must admit that there are people, such as Martindale and Gouldner, who certainly are not functionalists (though one of my informants disagreed with even this statement about Gouldner). It would also be possible to construct a good "functionalism index" out of the indicators discussed above, but that would be a different approach to scientific method from the one in this book.

I conclude that functionalism *becomes* rather than *is* something, that it becomes something other than it is, and that, speaking superficially, this is how science develops. Speaking less superficially, functionalism has developed by negating and excluding alternative theoretical approaches and then returning and reincorporating them in modified form; by systematically developing central concepts like "functional unity," "system," and "self-maintenance" and then rejecting them and focusing on their opposites.

These remarks could also be made about other holistic theories, and especially about psychoanalytic theory, which has been frequently misinterpreted. Psychoanalytic theory is misunderstood whenever (a) it is taken out of its clinical context and treated as pure speculation, and (b) whenever one forgets history and tries to find out what Freud's theory "really was." (Marcuse, 1966, for example, commits both of these errors.). To understand Freud one should read his cases and put them and their theoretical accompaniments in a historical sequence (like that provided in Ross and Abrams, 1966.) In addition, one should not impose alien methodological requirements on psychoanalytic theory. One should not expect a clinical, holistic theory to be hierarchical-deductive, to contain rigid formal definitions, or to yield predictions and deductive explanations. Its task rather is to provide revealing classifications of cases and to sensitize one to what is happening in a case.

18

The Practical Use of Case Studies

The skeptical reader may by now be somewhat disillusioned by my account of case study methods. Case studies, it appears, are used to test and modify typologies, and typologies are used to control comparison and thereby to contribute to improved case studies. General theories are used to explain and improve typologies so they will be more useful in classifying cases and directing case studies, and the improved case studies provide ideas for modifying general theories. And so it goes round and round, with both theory and description changing in the process. Where, it may be asked, is the payoff in all this? When do we get to Science?

Actually the same question may be asked about the methods that produce general laws. Laws are used to suggest new experiments which in turn lead to modification of the laws, and we are again in a circle. The theoretical payoff in these methods is better laws, and the theoretical payoff of case study methods is holist theories. There is no valid reason to suppose that holist theories are a waystation on the road to some future set of general laws; I find no movement occurring in that direction. Nor, on a more descriptive level, is the classification of cases a procedure characteristic of infant sciences only, any more than the construction of mathematical models is a procedure limited to advanced sciences. Such views are simply fictions. Model-building and the classification of cases are alternative ways of bringing theory to bear on observation, and one need not lead to the other to be useful.

There is, however, one way of getting out of the circle, and that is in application to practical problems. The payoff of science is practice. The pay-off of case study methods is the particular kind of practice they make possible. Each of the major social science methods produces its own special kind of knowledge, and each kind of knowledge is especially adapted to a certain kind of practical use. The difference among these practical uses is one of the bases for distinguishing different methods—if one can prevent the distinctions I am about to make from collapsing and disappearing in a maze of intermediate cases, combinations, and transitions.

The experimental method, when used as an independent method and not as an exploratory adjunct to model-building, produces lawlike variables and correlations between them. Such correlations tell us that under specified conditions the introduction of an independent variable will produce a specified change in the value of a dependent variable. This kind of knowledge is suitable for producing changes that someone desires to produce. The desired change is the dependent variable; one produces it by setting up the required conditions and then introducing or manipulating the independent variable. The relation between science and its user is one of means and ends: the user specifies a desired end, and science, in the form of laws or correlations, specifies the means that will achieve it.

Consider, for example, the many experimental studies of small-group cohesion, morale, leadership, etc. These studies are relevant to the desired goal of increasing group productivity or efficiency. Insofar as a correlation can be experimentally demonstrated between productivity and empathic leadership (Golembiewski, 1962, p. 251 ff) or member compatibility (pp. 270-273) or motivation to produce (March and Simon, 1958, p. 47 ff.), and insofar as these variables in turn can be correlated with other variables under the control of management, it becomes possible to increase group productivity by manipulating the independent variable. Conversely, the many nonsignificant or negative correlations between productivity and job satisfaction, morale, group cohesion, etc., show that these are not the proper means to use in increasing group productivity.

Lewin's experimental work illustrates the same use of science as a means to a desired end. Lewin and his associates found, for example, that changes in eating habits were much more highly correlated with group decision than with lectures. Consequently, if one wanted housewives to drink fresh milk or eat whole wheat broad or organ meats, the proper technique was not to lecture them about these foods but to have the group discuss them and decide "on its own" to use them (Lewin, 1951, pp. 229-233, 184-185). His experiments in group atmospheres suggested to Lewin that if we want to make Germany more democratic we should train German democratic group leaders, who in turn would set up the proper atmospheres (Lewin, 1948, pp. 39-42, ch. 3).

Shock therapy, drug therapy, and prefrontal lobotomy also illustrate this use of science. In each case there is an empirical generalization which states that under certain circumstances the therapeutic agent produces a desirable change in behavior. Behavior therapy is a more complex variant of shock therapy in which pleasant shocks as well as painful ones in small doses are used to produce the desired changes. Teaching machines also illustrate this way of using science; here the desired end state is a subject who knows something.

From the holist standpoint, this use of scientific knowledge is a form of manipulation in which the subject (patient) is used as a means to an end. Even if the subject himself specifies the desired end state it is manipulative because he does not participate actively in the process of change. Instead, he is passive and controlled, and the change is produced by the independent variable in the hands of the controlling scientist. Such a procedure seems immoral to a holist because it shows a lack of respect for human freedom and dignity.

Survey research methods produce a variety of kinds of knowledge, including statistical generalizations, multivariate correlations, and factors or clusters of correlations. A more detailed study would probably lead one to distinguish several different survey research methods according to the kinds of knowledge produced, and would probably turn up more than one kind of practical application. But in general these methods are usually applied to large numbers of cases, to mass behavior, whole populations, all the societies of the world. Although the actual cases examined by the researcher may be small in number, they are treated as a sample from a larger universe, and the resulting generalizations are meant to apply to the aggregate of cases rather than to the sample alone.

This sort of knowledge, it seems to me, gives up the practical aim of controlling the individual case in favor of statistical control of large populations. If one knows, for example, that a certain vaccine or contraceptive or advertising campaign is effective 80 percent of the time, one can use this knowledge to achieve a desired mass effect without necessarily achieving it in any single instance. If one knows the statistical chances for success of various kinds of entering students, or therapy patients, or prospective married couples, or criminals up for parole, or home mortgage applicants, one can set up a selective admission or approval procedure that will maximize the proportion of successes to failures.

This sort of use is not as open to the charge of manipulation because it focuses on the aggregate rather than on the individual. The individual is not put under any experimental controls but is left in his natural state, and no particular result is expected of him or induced in him. To be sure, in admission or approval procedures he is either accepted or rejected, but this would presumably have to be done anyway because of scarce resources, and a selection criterion based on scientific knowledge is no more manipulative or degrading than an arbitrary criterion. It is manipulative only if a discriminatory criterion is used under the pretext of being scientific.

The reason the individual cannot be manipulated through the practical application of statistical correlations is that these correlations do not specify the mechanism by which a result is achieved in a single case; they merely describe and predict aggregate results. A marriage counselor or parole officer who predicts success or failure is not determining the future course of events or even any exact outcome; he is merely consulting his actuarial table and reporting past results for a class of persons. He is listing and adding up advantages and handicaps but not specifying how the individual will deal with them to produce his own result.

The distinction between experimental and statistical survey applications is not sharp and is probably diminishing rather than increasing as experimenters incorporate more and more statistical elements into their designs. But this raises doubt about whether the application of experimental knowledge really does result in manipulation. After all, the experimentally discovered correlations are statistical too; they indicate only a probability of achieving a desired result in an individual case and do not necessarily specify the mechanism by which the result is brought about. Consider, for example, the way March and Simon (1958) are able to organize the experimental literature on organizations around a decision-making model, thus suggesting that rational decision-making is the mechanism underlying these correlations. If one increases productivity by decreasing employee turnover, accomplishing this by making the job more interesting and important and by increasing the employee's autonomy (March and Simon, 1958, pp. 94-95), is that manipulation? Yes, it is; but there seems to be a great difference between achieving a desired end by such means and achieving it by operant conditioning. And yet if one tried to specify in particular experimental studies where rational decision-making ended and operant conditioning began, it would be extremely difficult. Does one end and the other begin when the experimenter offers not autonomy but positive inducements? Negative inducements? When he limits the resources available to the subject? When he controls information and structures the alternatives being discussed, as Lewin did in his group discussion experiments? When he deceives and distorts perception? When he mobilizes unconscious fears and drives to get his desired effect, as in some of the so-called sensitivity training exercises? When he smothers cognitive processes by sleep deprivation and drugs? All of these tactics and more occur in experimental work and in the practical application of experimental generalizations. Certainly the last two or three tactics are strongly manipulative, and some holists and formalists might argue that manipulation occurs in all of them. If so, there are several forms of manipulation, some considerably more humane than others. At this point the concept of manipulation itself begins to move into one's focus of attention. "Manipulation" is to some extent an ideological concept, used by the clinician to emphasize his distinction from, and superiority to, the experimenter.

I have already discussed the practical uses of formal models in chapter 7 and shall merely summarize them briefly here for contrast. One use is to find a course of action that will optimize some value relative to existing constraints and resources; the other is to predict the relative effects of various possible courses of action. One finds an optimum course of action by adding the constraint of optimization to the model and then solving its equations to see what initial value or set of values will satisfy this constraint. Optimization is possible with certain kinds of mathematical models, especially those using differential equations or matrix algebra. With differential equations one finds the optimum by setting some derivative equal to zero and solving the equations; with matrix algebra one maximizes some profit or value vector derived from the relevant matrices (Kemeny and Snell, 1962, ch. 9).

Computer models and some mathematical models such as those using digraphs (Kemeny and Snell, 1962, ch. 8) are not well suited to optimization, but approximate optimizations can be discovered by special search techniques.

One predicts the effects of various possible courses of action by representing the action as an input value, a parameter value, or a change in an equation or subroutine and then solving the model. Computer models are especially adapted to this use because of the enormous number of changes that can be made in a model and the ease and rapidity with which the effect of each change can be determined. Indeed, as the speed of computers increases it should soon be possible to run a whole series of changes through and get an almost immediate report of the effect of each.

Formal models are especially adapted to these two uses because they describe the logic or inner working structure of a system or process. The logic acts as a constraint on any possible input and any possible practical action. Sometimes the constraint takes the form of absorbing an input so that it has no effect on output (for example, a transition matrix with one absorbing state); sometimes it takes the form of channeling an input to a determinate output or range of outputs; and sometimes it specifies a certain combination of inputs as necessary to achieve a certain output. The practical use of a model consists in seeing how its constraints affect various proposed actions.

This kind of knowledge differs from empirical generalizations, both experimental and statistical, in that it deals with a logical system of relations rather than with individual empirical correlations or sets of correlations. It describes an inner mechanism that constrains any possible output, whereas empirical generalizations give actual input-output correlations.

The question of manipulation is not easy to answer for formal models because of the great variety of models in existence. Some models, such as learning models, can be used to manipulate because they specify the means needed to achieve a specific desired end. More frequently models can be used to give one party a differential advantage over other parties in a system; the party who specifies the values to be optimized in a model can optimize his values at the cost of other parties. For instance, an employer can use a queuing model to minimize his employees' time spent waiting for customers, at the cost of longer waits by customers; or he can use a communication model to optimize his control over communication at the cost of other links in the network. Still more frequently, however, the optimization or improvement is not at any specific person's expense but results from general increase in efficiency. A model can increase efficiency by optimizing inventory levels or eliminating redundant records and accounting procedures (see examples in Churchman, 1957) or apportioning tasks fairly by line-balancing (Hoggatt and Balderston, 1963, ch. 8) or minimizing cash shortages and surpluses in a banking system (Kemeny and Snell, 1962, ch. 6) or minimizing traffic accidents and bottlenecks. Some game models can be used to facilitate cooperation in a complex interdependent situation (Amnon Rapoport, 1967) such as cooperative disarmament and arms control (Saaty, 1968). Finally, some models such as the conflict and conformity model (B. P. Cohen, 1963) have no apparent practical use at all.

Case study methods also provide information about the internal mechanisms and dynamics of a system. However, these mechanisms and dynamics are not conceived as formal logic, as the necessary outcome of combining abstract mathematical relations in a structure. Instead they are conceived as psychological mechanisms of defense, integration, cognitive balance, perceptual structuring, symbolization, and the like; or as social mechanisms like communication, commitment, persuasion, coercion, and inducement. The constraints do not take the logical form of necessary or probable implication but the normative one of expectations, obligations, commands, self-concepts, and aspirations. Inputs do not take the form of initial or parameter values, but appear rather as stresses, strains, problems, and opportunities, as compatibilities and incompatibilities. To be sure, a formalist could reconceptualize most of these in mathematical terms, but that would eventually lead to a formalist kind of knowledge and practical application. Computer models partly bridge the gap between the two because they broaden the concept of "logical implication" so considerably.

The kind of knowledge of a living system that case study methods provide is essentially suited to enabling a person to work within the system, to become an active participant in its self-development. The participant observer and the clinician work their way into the system they are studying and try to become an active part of it in order to understand it from the inside. They conceptualize their knowledge in terms that the system members themselves use or could understand, though they also try to go beyond the understanding that system members have achieved. They test the objectivity of their knowledge in part by seeing whether it is intelligible and acceptable to system members, and in part by attempting to act on it and seeing whether their actions are understood and accepted in the system. Consequently, an adequate description of a system enables a person to act within it as a regular member. This is even more the case if a person uses knowledge he has himself gathered, because he can then rely also on the intuitive understandings that he cannot make explicit.

This kind of practical use is directly opposite to the use of empirical correlations. In the former the user works within the system in terms of its own needs and standards; in the latter the user manipulates the system from the outside to achieve externally imposed objectives. The use of formal models is midway between: with some models the values to be optimized can be set by a power external to the system or by one participant in it, while with other models the governing values are shared by system participants. The use of statistical generalizations to achieve aggregate results also falls somewhere between the two extremes.

"Working within the system" may take a great variety of forms. Essentially the worker brings his personal resources into the system and uses them there; and there can be great variation in the resources brought in, the roles in which they are used, and the problems on which they are used. The worker may take an ordinary role or a leadership role; he may provide emotional support or intellectual challenge; he may act like a politician, mediating conflicts and interpreting conflicting parties to each other, or he may take an agitator's role, championing and stirring up some oppressed or forgotten part of the system (cf. Dahl, 1963, pp. 88-90); he may work internally, interpreting the system to itself and bringing unrecognized parts to public attention; or he may work externally as an interpreter and a liaison between a system and its environing systems (cf. Beattie, 1965, p. 56).

To work effectively within a system in any of these ways, a worker needs knowledge: knowledge of the main problems of the system, its resources for dealing with these problems, and by inference, what additional resources would be helpful. As he begins to act, he also needs to know in a general way how his actions will affect the system. This is just the sort of knowledge that a good case study will provide.

The goal of working within a system may be described simply as helping the system work on the problems it is facing, or sometimes as stirring up latent problems that it could be facing. The result of such activity presumably will be an improvement in functioning, in mental health or integrity or development. Many writers have discussed this sort of goal, each with a slightly different emphasis; see for example, Rogers (1961, chs. 8, 9) focusing on the therapy patient, Sanford (1966, ch. 2) focusing on educational institutions, Brownell (1950) focusing on small communities, H. Kaplan (1967) focusing on political systems, and Etzioni (1968) focusing on "society."

However, in a more important sense the worker does not bring any operationally clear goals to his participation in the system; instead, he gets them from the system. The "fully functioning person" or the "active society" is not an operational goal but a regulative ideal whose content must be specified in each case. This is part of the meaning of "working within the system," as contrasted with external manipulation. The participating worker does indeed bring preferences and predispositions—value biases—to his participation, but as he is socialized into the system these are tested for their compatibility with what is already there and are either accepted or excluded. When the participating worker takes a mediating role between the system and its social environment, he transmits and interprets environmental demands, but these take the form of stresses to be managed rather than goals to be achieved. Indeed, he may on occasion help the system resist and reject environmental demands, as Tax did when the Federal Indian Service intensified its coercion of the community in which he was working (Gearing et al., 1960, p. 199 ff).

To amplify these general remarks somewhat, let us consider several areas in which holistic case study knowledge is put to practical use. The best known and best developed tradition of practical use is in psychotherapy, so we will begin there.

When we survey the types of therapeutic technique, we find a few general similarities and many variations of degree and emphasis. The variations are due partly to differences among the various psychodynamic theories, partly to differences in the personal resources each therapist brings to his work, and partly to differences in the needs, problems, and inner resources of each patient. Otto Rank stressed long ago that different patients require different kinds of help, that a strategy appropriate for a hysterical patient is the opposite of one appropriate for a compulsive patient (Rank, 1947). The similarities are due to the fact that each kind of therapy is in one way or another aimed at helping a person face and master his inner conflicts.

Given this aim, the first thing any therapist must do is temporarily insulate the patient from the demands and stresses of his social environment. Since every internal strain and conflict is partly a reflection of environmental stress (and vice versa), the reduction of stress immediately reduces the intensity of the patient's problems and makes it easier for him to face them. Stress reduction is limited by the facts that the patient projects internalized environmental demands onto the therapist, and that escape from the social environment can only be temporary.

The most complete insulation occurs in Bettelheim's milieu therapy, where the patient is placed in a complete therapeutic environment (Bettelheim, 1950, 1955). More usually, insulation consists of the therapist's emphatic refusal to make demands on the patient, to evaluate and criticize. This refusal is nicely symbolized in Baruch's play therapy by the empty room, the half-open closet door revealing various toys, and the therapist's statement, "You don't have to do anything you don't want to do here. You don't have to do anything" (Baruch, 1952, p. 12). Remember that this is a particularized refusal, adapted to a case in which stress took the form of a demand to perform.

The positive aspects of insulation from social pressures are the therapist's acceptance of the patient and his problems, his willingness to take the patient seriously and to work co-operatively with him. These two factors, insulation and acceptance, provide the setting for the therapeutic process. At the same time they provide the setting for clinical inquiry, since inquiry and therapy, getting knowledge and using it, occur together. The present account abstracts one side of this process.

The therapeutic process itself consists of the patient's becoming aware of himself, changing himself, and changing his conception of himself. "Becoming aware" has both an emotional and an intellectual component; the one involves the patient's experiencing himself, his feelings and wants, more vividly and directly, while the other involves his verbalizing and thereby achieving a measure of detachment and control. The relative importance of the two components varies in different psychodynamic theories and also in different patients, as Rank has emphasized (1947).

The therapist's role varies on an active-passive dimension in different theories and cases. In older Freudian therapy and in nondirective therapy today, the therapist is a passive, even invisible listener, whose only task is to interpret the patient to himself. More usually the therapist helps by asking questions and thus joining in the search. Still more active therapists take a role that the patient offers out of his unconscious, thereby dramatically revealing the patient's inner life to himself. The patient's conception of the role and his reaction to it are revealed simultaneously, and he has an opportunity to restructure his conception and to practice new reactions. Role-playing is important in group therapy and reaches an extreme in psychodrama, where the patient, the therapist, and assistants all play out the drama of the patient's unconscious life.

One role the therapist takes in all forms of therapy is that of interpreter, holding the mirror up to the patient so he can see himself. Interpretation has both a verbal and a dramatic, emotional aspect. In nondirective therapy, interpretation is ideally limited to those feelings that are just on the threshold of the patient's awareness, while in other types of therapy, interpretation may go somewhat deeper. In any case, the therapist limits himself to what the patient can manage. His task is to insure that the patient is not overwhelmed by difficulties and forced to retreat, but is able at all times to cope with the situation. Here knowledge of the patient's inner dynamics provides a crucial control; it enables the therapist to estimate the amount of tension that would be generated by any proposed interpretation. The more active the role a therapist takes, the more he needs to be guided by knowledge of the case. Insofar as his knowledge is adequate and he succeeds in keeping tension to manageable levels, the patient is placed in a position where he is able gradually to face himself, accept himself, and change himself.

Some readers may wonder why I have not taken seriously Eysenck's supposed evidence that psychoanalytic therapy has no effect at all (Eysenck, 1965, 1952). I believe the proper comment on Eysenck's work is that his blatant and consistent misuse of statistical techniques should not prejudice one against these techniques, which are valuable when used properly. By "misuse" I mean, for example, using unrotated factors when rotation is obviously called for (Rokeach and Hanley, 1956) and justifying this by saying the unrotated factors fit the theory he is trying to prove; using vague operational definitions and treating the results as final rather than as a preliminary step in locating improved definitions; ignoring margins of error and variants and thus achieving a spurious appearance of precision. Eysenck defines "cure" so vaguely that a psychoanalytic cure, a behavior therapy cure, a student counseling termination, and spontaneous remission of symptoms are all counted as cures in spite of their obvious differences. He adds and averages numbers from many different reports without evaluating the accuracy and comparability of the various estimates (cf. also Rosenzweig, 1954). Christie sums up his critique of an earlier Eysenck study as follows: "Errors of computation, uniquely biased samples . . . scales with built-in biases . . . and unjustifiable manipulations of the data" (Christie, 1956, p. 450). See also Stieper and Wiener (1965, pp. 13-15) for a more extended list of Eysenck's critics and for further critical comment.

In any event, a statistical evaluation of clinical therapy of the kind Eysenck proposes is inappropriate. It blots out the distinction between working within a system and working on a system externally. Eysenck's statistical evaluation treats therapy as an external variable that is uniformly applied to a mass population and achieves a desired, prespecified effect in a certain percentage of cases. But the clinician is not an external agent out to work his will on a passive patient; he is a participant with the patient in a co-operative endeavor (cf. for example, Erikson, 1964, pp. 52-55, 80), whose direction and objective are determined from day to day by the patient. Any change that occurs is accomplished by the patient and therapist jointly, and no "cure" is possible unless the patient wants it and finds it acceptable. From this standpoint, some "spontaneous remissions" may be similar to therapy in their outcome, though they are accomplished without the aid of a professional therapist. Others may result from changes in external stresses rather than personality change, and some may even signal an intensification of the person's problems.

Statistical evaluation of therapy may be appropriate if one is comparing alternative uses of public resources for a public policy goal such as urban renewal. In this case the desired goal is specified in advance; one is not interested in what the individuals involved may desire to do about themselves, but is concerned only with predictable aggregate results. But this is a matter of public policy, not therapy; cf. Sanford (1966, ch. 19), for a study of the contrast between the two.

A proper statistical evaluation of therapy would be one that treats the whole therapeutic situation as a change process whose goals are set within the situation. The most important and difficult phase of such an evaluation would be the search for situation variables that correlate significantly with therapeutic outcomes, and for criteria of change that are not externally imposed but derived from within the situation. Stieper and Wiener (1965) exemplify such a search for variables and criteria and also illustrate its difficulties. They consider such variables as the patient's "motivation," his desire to change, his willingness to assume responsibility for changing himself, the therapist's personality and its appropriateness to the patient's personality, and various modes of therapeutic interaction. Change criteria include rating procedures by therapists, patients, and outside observers. The authors point to the serious empirical and conceptual difficulties in all the variables and criteria they consider, thereby demonstrating that the search has a long way to go.

An earlier example of statistical evaluation is the Rogers and Dymond study (Rogers, 1961, ch. 11) which Eysenck mistakenly dismisses (1965, pp. 113-115). The design of this study is entirely appropriate, since it compares a patient with himself, before and after, to see what change has occurred during therapy. No other comparison is meaningful. Eysenck wants a statistical design that measures the effect of the therapist on the patient when all other factors are held constant or randomized; Rogers and

Dymond are interested in measuring the effect of the total therapy situation, including therapist and patient working together.

A more substantial objection to the present interpretation of therapy comes from studies that seem to show that therapists achieve their results by operant conditioning (for example, Bandura, 1961). These studies show that the therapist emits subtle verbal and postural cues that express his approval or disapproval of statements by the patient. The cues are picked up by the patient and act as rewards and punishments. In the early stage of therapy the patient is freed from external expectations and allowed to emit random responses; then the therapist begins to reward him selectively, first over a broad spectrum of behavior and then more and more precisely. Bit by bit, in the manner Skinner has demonstrated so well, the patient's verbal behavior is shaped in a direction acceptable to the therapist. The therapist, in turn, must by his previous conditioning emit a higher percentage of favorable responses as this happens, and the asymptote of this negatively accelerated positive-feedback system is a state in which the two sets of verbal behaviors reinforce each other strongly enough to prevent further change in either set. (Note the implicit mathematical model that looms up as soon as we start thinking this way.)

This objection illustrates nicely the contrast between a formal and a holist (functionalist or psychodynamic) theory. A formal theory is constructed of abstract concepts relationally defined, and interest is focused on the implications of patterns of relations among these concepts. Learning theory includes such formal concepts as response, reinforcement, extinction, desensitization, conditioning, and counterconditioning. Such a theory is applied by finding an empirical exemplification and studying the logical implications of the particular pattern found there. Note that the same empirical situation can exemplify a variety of formal models; thus a therapeutic interaction can be interpreted as a learning situation, or as a game, or as communication and information processing, or even as bilateral monopoly. The same behavior may be reinforcement in one model, a signal in a second, and a bid in a third. In each case primary interest is in the model, not in the whole situation; only those aspects of the situation that exemplify the model or can be put into an improved model are noticed, and the rest are ignored as empirical residues.

From a holist standpoint, formal models are always one-sided and abstract. (I make an exception here for computer models.) The formalist always focuses on one aspect of a situation and ignores the rest, while the holist tries to box in the whole situation. One way he does this, as I have indicated earlier, is by using polar or dialectically related concepts—need and press, self and other, I and it, projection and introjection, all the ambivalences and reaction formation. Such concepts, I suppose, are greeted with rage and despair by the formalist, who finds them too slippery either to comprehend or to test. The formalist's mind works mathematically, and dialectical logic is invisible to him; all he sees is equivocation and confusion (see for example Hook's futile attempt to understand dialectic, 1940, ch.

11). He would rather go on being one-sided and clear, even at the cost of incurring the holist's reproaches for his one-sidedness.

In the case of therapy, certainly conditioning occurs; so also do strategic interaction, communication and information processing, even pricing and exchange. Approval and disapproval is one of the means by which the therapist participates in the therapeutic situation. But it is only part of his participation. For instance, in Parsons' interpretation of therapy, "conditional reward" is one of four functionally necessary processes that occur. A complete holistic account of therapeutic processes must include some reference to approval and disapproval, among other things; but a formal model that selects out approval and disapproval in no way invalidates the more rounded account I have given above.

One can also reverse the foregoing proposition. If the formal concepts of learning theory yield a one-sided account of psychotherapy, they yield an equally one-sided account of behavior therapy. The behavior therapist is led by his theory to specify the behavior to be changed and to look for reinforcers that are maintaining it or that would change it; everything else is empirical residue of no interest to him. However, some of these residues may be of central interest to the psychodynamic therapist. In addition, the behavior therapist has no theoretical interest in the specific reinforcers used; they are all equally reinforcers, and their selection is a technical question rather than a theoretical one. His interest is focused on such problems as schedules of reinforcement and time span between behavior and reinforcement. Yet from a psychodynamic standpoint, the kind of reinforcement and its empirical setting may make all the difference in the outcome. At one extreme, behavior therapy may consist of strapping the patient to a hospital table, attaching electrodes, and shocking him at prescribed times. The therapist-technician, dressed in a lab coat, may sit at a control panel watching dials and pressing buttons, or he may impersonally note and record the patient's spasms and utterances. At the other extreme, the setting may be a playroom and the therapist a pretty, smiling, accepting and approving teacher, who gives candy, pats of approval, snacks, and movies, within a structured interpersonal relationship (cf. Hamblin et al., 1969). Both situations would be described in the same learning-theoretical terms, yet from a psychodynamic standpoint they are quite different.

The use of holistic knowledge in education is relatively less familiar to me, but its general characteristics are not difficult to make out. First, although (as in therapy) there is insulation from environmental stress to keep the student's problems at a manageable level, the insulation is much thinner. The teacher acts more as a mediator between the student and his cultural environment, introducing him selectively to successive portions of the environment that are judged to be within his range of mastery. Second, the primary focus of educational activity is on problems of development and growth rather than on the student's inner conflicts. The teacher's role is a more active one, challenging the student with new difficulties rather than waiting for him to dredge up his buried anxieties and conflicts and then working on them. Third, the teacher focuses more attention on the student's mature self, his conscious ego-processes, and less on his unconscious, repressed, infantile self. His interpretations focus more on the student's preconscious techniques of mastery than on his unconscious wants and images.

Consequently the teacher needs less knowledge about the student's unconscious personality and relatively more about his conscious and preconscious ego-processes. In fact, he needs considerable knowledge of the latter to maintain a proper intensity of challenge and to interpret environmental ideas and demands in ways that are intelligible to the student. The achievement of such knowledge requires close and extended personal contact involving both emotional and intellectual components. Where personal contact is not possible, the holist program fails. Education in a large-scale, impersonal, lecture-recitation situation is necessarily governed by statistical knowledge, with its prediction of probable aggregate result.

The main barrier to holistic education, to "the child-centered school," is not lack of knowledge but our bureaucratic educational structure. A hierarchical structure is suited to efficiency in production, to achieve goals set from above. The superintendent collects evidence of his productivity in the form of regular quantitative reports from principals and counselors and must therefore specify what is to be included in the reports as evidence of achievement. The principal in turn requires lesson plans and monthly reports from teachers, to show that he is in control and is getting results. Even the classroom materials emphasize the same point: a funny picture will have under it the caption, "Purpose—to help children appreciate humor." The conscientious teacher learns that to be a good teacher she must manipulate the children skillfully enough to achieve the goal in the allotted time.

Even these very general remarks must be qualified by reference to Rogers' proposal regarding education as nondirective group therapy. (Rogers, 1961, chs. 13-15). Rogers believes that the student can control his own development and actively seek out challenges, that the cultural environment is already available in books and the teacher need not mediate between it and the student unless called on to do so, and that the teacher's proper role is therefore that of accepting and clarifying the student's ideas as he pursues his self-education. Students give very mixed reports on the effectiveness of nondirective education, but it does come as a surprise to them.

When holistic knowledge is used to control participation in organizational and community problem-solving, the researcher's usual role is that of mediator. The participating worker tries to reduce excess strains, and then interprets the conflicting elements to each other and looks for mutually acceptable courses of action that will provide a place for all active tendencies in the situation (see for example, Lewin, 1948, ch. 8;

cf. also Gearing, 1960, pp. 182-197, 216-227, 294 ff; Kuriloff and Atkins, 1966). It is also possible to take the role of agitator, a calling the attention of the organization to a neglected subgroup or a buried conflict that could be re-examined and restructured. The basic difficulty with community problem-solving in complex societies is that most of the problems in small communities are part of the problems of the surrounding society. The same difficulty appeared in a theoretical context when functionalists tried to adapt case study techniques to complex societies.

The functionalist case studies by anthropologists have gone through two stages of practical use, colonial and postcolonial. In addition, of course, they are of indirect practical use as a comparative basis for understanding our own society and culture.

In the colonial period, the main problem of non-Western societies, most of them small and nonliterate, was their threatened disintegration under the powerful impact of Western culture. The participating anthropologist's attention was focused on this sometimes overwhelming stress (for example, Malinowski, 1922, pp. 464-468), and he sought to find ways to reduce it to bearable proportions. One way was outright resistance to Western values and a glorification of native values; another was to encourage the development of a mediating mechanism or group that would maintain contact with Western ways and selectively incorporate the least destructive of them. Both of these tactics were already in use before the anthropologists arrived; people were borrowing from the white man what they thought they could use—tools, weapons, foods, conveniences—and secretively protecting what they thought was endangered—ceremonies, legends, magical practices, native laws and moral obligations. Anthropologists participated in one or the other of these tactics according to their situation and their preferences. Some helped maintain the integrity of ceremonial and social life and encourage resistance to the white man's ways. They recorded and preserved legends, participated in ceremonies, provided equipment, and accepted and appreciated the old ways; they acted as spokesmen for their societies when a destructive colonial administrative move impended, and sometimes they even supported confrontation and resistance. Others, particularly those attached to colonial agencies as advisors or administrators, emphasized selective acceptance of what the white man had to offer. They concerned themselves with estimating the destructive effects of colonial policies and tried to suggest less destructive policies or less destructive ways of implementing policies. For example, when they realized the functional importance of bridewealth in certain African cultures, they succeeded in persuading colonial administrators to tolerate the practice instead of attempting to destroy it.

The kind of knowledge needed for this defensive mediation was, first, a knowledge of the sources of stability in societies and cultures. How did societies, especially preliterate ones, maintain their integrity against external threats? What functions were essential to self-maintenance, what alternative ways were there of doing this, and what practices (if any) could safely be given up without loss of stability? Second, they needed knowledge of the strong and weak points in the defenses of their particular colonial society. This knowledge would enable them to estimate the relative threat posed by a particular policy and to suggest less threatening alternatives. Third, they needed knowledge of their society's coping mechanisms, those by which it maintained its patterns against stresses and reintegrated its deviant, Westernizing members. Such knowledge would enable them to locate possible improvements in coping mechanisms adapted to the expected threats of Western influences.

The early functionalist case studies, including culture and personality studies, provided just this kind of knowledge. They brought out the interconnections of institutions in a functioning whole, showing how each contributed to the operation of others; they described the working of the repair and maintenance mechanisms; and they described the typical ways in which people coped with the problems of their own culture and the powerful new culture. Perhaps it would be going too far to say that this knowledge took the shape it did to enable anthropologists to help colonial peoples resist change. But it did take its shape from the dominant concern of the people being studied, which was to resist or come to terms with Western influence; and this concern was reflected in the case studies in the emphasis on self-maintenance and resistance to change.

To be sure, other concerns were present also, and in some societies a concern with Western influence was minor or nonexistent. The studies of such societies reflected *their* dominant concerns; for example, the intense Nuer concern with cattle and the pervasive Siriono food anxiety dominate the reports of Evans-Pritchard (1940) and Holmberg (1950). In these studies we read of ecological adaptation rather than of self-maintenance against disruptive culture stress.

The anthropologist who knew roughly how his society functioned was in a position to resist or adapt Western influence more effectively. He could see, as the natives often could not, the long-run destructive effect of sending young men to work in mines and plantations or of adopting European foods and religions. He could find other Western cultural elements that were less destructive or even helpful, and could watch for disruptive effects when they were being introduced. Note that anthropologists did not invent the goal of resisting Western influence, did not impose their own preferences on the societies they studied. They found these societies preoccupied with the problem of maintaining their integrity against Western influence, and they merely joined in working on the problems that were already present. Thus their activities in resisting colonializing changes did not involve, as Manners claims (1968, p. 164), an abandonment of cultural relativism.

Applied anthropology in the colonial period was bound to be a losing battle. The colonial cultures were doomed by the Indian Bureaus and Colonial Offices, by the missionaries, traders, and large corporations seeking profitable uses for their capital, and all the anthropologists could do was help make the process less painful and less destructive. Their task, as Malinowski put it, was to consider "how a minimum of natural wealth [could] be left to the Native" (1945, p. 131), or to see that there were "safeguards for Native interests and a compromise reached when these clash with European attempts at exploitation" (1945, p. 146). Gluckman put it more acidly in his critique: "Malinowski's compromise . . . appears to me as the anthropologist crawling on his knees to beg some white groups for a few more crumbs for the Africans, and then asking the missionary to preach a religion that will be an opiate" (1963, p. 219). Sometimes even this minimum program was not possible; as Manners (1968) and others have observed, the colonial administrator did not have to take the anthropologist's advice. In the period of transition to national independence, a Malinowskian program could even be reactionary, since attempts to preserve a traditional integrated culture would support the power and legitimacy of the tribal chiefs against the modernizing anticolonialist forces (Maquet, 1964; Wallerstein, 1966, pp. 1-3; Balandier, 1966, pp. 54-57). The attempt to preserve traditional cultures against the disorganizing effects of change served also to integrate the native culture into the colonial regime and so helped to preserve colonialism.

In the postcolonial period, which overlapped the colonial period in time, anthropologists found that progress and a desire for progress were important concerns in the societies they were studying. They found villages and societies that "chose progress" (Redfield, 1950) and were struggling with the problems of remaking themselves. The much-noted conservatism of primitive society disappeared with the colonial administrator and turned out to be a defensive reaction to the destructive pressure of capitalism and Christianity. When this pressure was reduced, societies acquired a forward-looking time sense, orienting themselves to a better future rather than to a nostalgic past. The concepts of "aspiration," "policy," and "mood" became important in studying such societies (Redfield, 1960a, pp. 106-107). This shift of emphasis represented a more fundamental solution to the problem posed by Western influence. Instead of resisting defensively by encapsulation and boundary maintenance, societies tried to gather strength to resist as an equal.

Political independence was the basic first step in the process of achieving equality. It represented a symbolic affirmation of the determination to be responsible for one's own development. Other symbolic acts followed, such as the expulsion of anthropologists from Indonesia as representatives of colonialism. These symbolic acts of themselves reduced the immediate psychological stress of Western influence to more manageable levels, thus enabling attention to be focused more on problems of development. Internal sources of weakness had to be eliminated and strength had to be created and mobilized, involving both the building up of economic strength by industrialization and the recovery of spiritual strength from the indigenous cultural heritage—for example, the revival of Hebrew in Israel and the move to ancient or entirely new inland capitals from the colonialist seaports in Asiatic countries (Murphey, 1957).

The newly independent governments soon worked out ambitious national plans and launched large development projects. Anthropologists and anthropological knowledge were called on to adapt these plans and projects to local conditions, fitting the new technology into existing cultural and social patterns as far as possible (cf. M. Mead, 1955; Spicer, 1952). Community development experts with anthropological knowledge were called on to help carry out plans and projects at the village level by anticipating and overcoming local resistance. Unfortunately, in many cases the community development expert is not too different from his colonialist counterpart (cf. Manners, 1968). Development is undertaken with American aid to provide profitable outlets for American capital, and the interests and aspirations of the natives are largely ignored or treated as resistances to be managed. The community development experts employed by development corporations are there solely to ensure that the local community remains peaceful and provides the necessary labor for the mines and plantations.

And so we find again the old "resistance" role of the participant observer, this time directed against the neocolonial development corporations. An example is provided by Peattie, who organized community resistance to a new sewer line running to the riverbank where the people of her barrio laundered and bathed (Peattie, 1968, ch. 7). Here again the participant observer's values, goals and interpretation of the situation were taken from the community being studied (cf. Peattie, 1965, pp. 366-369). The sewer line was a community development project planned by a Caracas corporation that wanted to facilitate the development of two American-owned iron mines; the local villagers figured in the planning only as cheap labor. Peattie contributed resources to the struggle—communication skills, status, and transportation—and her knowledge of the community enabled her to use the resources where they were most needed.

It is doubtful that this newer type of resistance will be any more effective than the earlier resistance to colonial policies. One notes that Peattie's employer was the same development corporation that was laying the sewer line, and that she left Venezuela soon after her role in organizing resistance came to the attention of the planners in Caracas, at a time when the controversy was still unsettled. The knowledge and resources appropriate to community problems are not appropriate for problems that involve national and international fields of interaction. What is needed in dealing with the problems of American neocolonialism is the kind of knowledge provided by process and developmental functionalism. The process functionalists can bring out the interconnection of processes in far-flung fields of conflict and locate the points at which resources can be applied most effectively. The developmental functionalists can study the dynamics of capitalist society and try to locate the transition mechanisms leading to the next stage of development. Such knowledge is not yet available in detail, but I hope that social scientists will endeavor to provide it.

The foregoing account of the practical uses of case studies is not complete; it merely picks out some prominent areas to illustrate varieties of emphasis as well as the essential characteristics common to all uses. Nor have I meant to imply that there are four sharply distinct ways in which social science knowledge may be used; these are simply benchmarks to help one keep his bearings as he studies the many forms of practical use. In particular, there are several combinations and continuities worth mentioning. First, the extensive incorporation of statistical techniques into experimental work leads to the experimental production of statistical generalizations that are more suitable for mass action on large populations than for the controlled manipulation of a single case. Many of the social-psychological experiments on small groups exemplify this. Second, the gradual shift in learning theory from an empirical to a formal method was accompanied in some cases by a retention of the experimentalist's manipulative ideal. Behavior therapy illustrates this combination. Third and most interesting, the continuing development of techniques of multiple correlation and the incorporation of holistic elements into statistical survey methods produce a kind of knowledge that is semiholistic in its use. The availability of multiple correlations enables the applied scientist to choose courses of action that are adapted both to his resources and to the problems of the population he is studying. The holistic elements enable him to appreciate the problems of his population more or less from the inside, to estimate the amount and kind of strain a policy would produce, and therefore to select actions that will limit strain to bearable levels. See, for example, Langner and Michael (1963, pp. 26-29); in this example, the goals of action are still specified by the scientist's employer rather than by the population studied; the authors still have basically a public health approach rather than a community self-development approach, but the distinction between the two has become considerably attenuated.

Nor do I mean to imply that one particular use of scientific knowledge is always morally superior to the others. Each use has its own appropriate conditions, and no one use is appropriate to all the problems of men. However, from a holist standpoint there is a hierarchy of desirability in these four uses. The holistic use exhibits the most respect for human dignity and freedom because it enables a person to work with, not on, his case, to treat him (or them) as fellow human beings rather than as things. Formal uses also work with, not on men, though in a great variety of unequally acceptable ways; and statistically controlled action with mass populations is also acceptable because it essentially avoids manipulations. But behavior therapy, shock therapy, is an abhorrent affront to human dignity. It is suitable for training pigeons, chickens, and flatworms, but can only degrade a free human being.

19

Weaknesses and Problems
of Case Study Methods

Scientists react to the weaknesses of a method (and all methods have weaknesses) in two different ways. If they are not using the method themselves, they cite its weaknesses as sufficient justification for ignoring the method and its results, for despising it as unscientific or inadequate, and for not allowing their students to learn it. If they are using the method, its weaknesses become problems, challenges that make work interesting and results an achievement. The following discussion takes the latter approach.

One continuous problem for the holist is that of drawing the best boundaries around his subject matter. How large a system should he include in his observations? He wants to study a whole system, not just a fragment, and this requires a continually expanding boundary as he finds his subject matter participating in larger systems. But he also wants a thorough, detailed study of all the important interrelations in his system, and this requires him not to dissipate his energies too widely. He cannot satisfy both of these contrary requirements fully; no matter which way he turns, his work will lack something—in comprehensiveness or in completeness of detail or in both.

The same problem occurs in the historical dimension. A complete study of the meanings and functions of an important event or artifact —a trial, a dream, a myth, a ritual, a set of needlecases—requires weeks and months of work in which leads are followed, interviews taken, connections traced. But if one takes the time necessary to make this detailed a study, there is not enough time to study adequately all the events and conditions that surround it. And if the historical background and wider contemporary context of the main event are studied only briefly or ignored, the particular event cannot be fully understood. Conversely, if one collects a comprehensive historical record over a period of months or years, one has no time to probe into any particular event fully enough to understand even its historical significance.

The early functionalists do not seem to have worried much about this problem. The proper boundaries of their subject matter were natural ones that already existed in reality. They were studying a whole tribe or culture, physically isolated on an island or in a valley or desert or, as with the plains and coast Indians, isolated from other tribes by warfare. The tribe was small enough so that in a year or two one could make a complete study of customs and behavior; or if this was not possible, one selected the most prominent village, the chief's village or the biggest one, for intensive study and assumed that the rest were similar. The assumption of homogeneity thus enabled one to study a sample and generalize. The historical problem was met by assuming that the tribe or culture had no recent history of importance other than that preserved in story and legend. Or, alternatively, a deliberate choice was made to see how far it was possible to explain a culture synchronically, without reference to history. Such antihistoricism represented a deliberate break with the earlier historical-diffusionist approach.

This plausible and effective solution broke down simultaneously in three directions. First, the development of personality and culture theorizing made anthropologists realize that an adequate understanding of their tribe required intensive study of individuals and families by means of projective tests, life histories, and detailed observation. Second, the shift of study from small, isolated tribes to communities in modern society or to complex African and Asiatic societies removed the convenient "natural" boundary and provided no plausible substitute. Third, the heterogeneity of the more complex and modern societies, as well as theoretical work on the importance of deviants for culture change and even for culture persistence, made it impossible to generalize from a small intensively observed sample. One had to study Fantan the interpreter and Gregorio the hand-trembler as well as Maliseni the financier and Left-handed the good family man.

As a result, any solution to the problem of boundaries can now be criticized as inadequate. If one proposes to follow the classic lead and study a small community of 500 to 3,000 people intensively for two or three years, the objection is that with such a large group one can get only a superficial, generalized picture, missing both the deviants and the deeper psychological processes. If one proposes to get at deeper processes by intensively studying and interviewing a few sample families, it is objected that interviews still provide only typical behavior, generalizations rather than actual process. One must therefore study a single family through a single day, spending months if necessary to unravel the complexities of interaction on that day; or if this is still too complex, one must concentrate on a few key events, perhaps a quarrel or a dream. But to understand the day or the quarrel fully, one must be familiar with the history that led up to it, a history going back to the beginning of the family, or the beginning of the individuals' lives, or their parents' lives. And if one is to study a single family fully, even on a single day, one finds family members participating in many formal and informal groups and institutions that must also be studied as they affect the family member. Moreover, to study these groups only from the perspective of the family member would be a distortion and would prevent even an understanding of the perspective, so the groups must be studied in the round. And since these groups and institutions are part of an economy, a polity, or a larger society, one must study that as well, including its relevant history. But obviously such a large picture must be quite general, and we are back where we started.

By now it is clear that the holist ideal of studying all the important aspects of a particular human whole is unattainable, and we must be satisfied with approximations. The various solutions that people have devised have moved in two opposite directions, or have combined parts of both. One direction is for the investigator deliberately to circumscribe a limited area of study, making his limits explicit and hoping that others will supplement his efforts in other areas. This is generally the line suggested by Gluckman and Devons in their study of the problem (1964); they add only that the investigator should keep an open mind about whether the closed system he has set up is an appropriate one. As his investigation progresses he should be ready to shift boundaries to include important new factors in his system. The other direction is to study a little of everything—normal and deviant personality profiles, individual life histories, families close-up and over generations, economic and ecological relations, class and occupational groupings, religious and ethnic subcultures—using a variety of statistical and qualitative techniques and a battery of specialists and generalists from all the social sciences. This direction is usually taken by the personality and culture theorists, since their theory ranges widely over many aspects of human systems. For example, Leighton's study of Stirling County lists an even 100 participants in the ten-year study, plus 123 clerical assistants and many consultants (1959, pp. 427-434). A wide-ranging study of this sort will necessarily have several foci that are studied in intensive detail either because they are typical or because they are of crucial importance, while other factors are studied less intensively.

Another very general problem is that of observer bias. This problem occurs throughout the social sciences but takes a special form in clinical and field methods. Every scientist must perceive and interpret his subject matter from some standpoint and thereby bias his conclusions. Also every scientist must be active with his subject matter in some fashion and must therefore change it as he studies it. Even the act of singling somebody out for attention has an effect on him, as we have long known. But the participant observer is more thoroughly and more continuously active than practitioners of other methods. He cannot take the detached, neutral pose of the experimenter and the survey researcher, but must actively involve himself in his subject matter emotionally, cognitively, and behaviorally. He must accept and work within the belief systems of the people he studies, take the roles that are offered him if possible, and form genuine, not feigned, attachments. But any such socialization process is transactional, with influences coming from socialized as well as socializer. Beliefs are selectively taken on and reinterpreted, roles are creatively modified, and attachments are necessarily selective if they are genuine. This is true even in the socialization of the smallest infant but is much more obvious with a fully developed adult. In addition, the participant observer continually changes his subject matter as he works with it in his newly learned roles, and the changes necessarily reflect in part the contributions he has made to his own socialization. Thus one could say that the participant observer not only perceives his subject matter from a bias, as all scientists do, but also that he remakes the subject matter in his own image as he studies it.

The experimenter tries to solve the problem of objectivity by detaching himself from his experiment and his subject matter as fully as possible, emotionally and physically. In this way he hopes that experimenter bias will have a minimal effect on the results. It might be argued that this is also the proper solution for the participant observer. Though he cannot, in the nature of the case, be as detached and objective as the experimenter, he should still try to imitate him by remaining detached and passive wherever possible.

However, this solution will not do because it takes the heart out of the method. Participant observation depends essentially on the creative use of bias to discover things that would otherwise not be observable, so the minimizing of bias and involvement would destroy the method. An observer who is not emotionally involved will be unable to empathize, to see things from the perspective of his subject, and therefore will miss much of the meaning of what he sees. Consequently he will not know how to ask the right questions (cf. the informant Bidaga's complaint: "I have been trying to explain these things to you for thirty years, but you never asked me the right questions." [Ladd, 1957, p. xiv]) and look in the right places. In addition, an emotionally detached person cannot as readily be accepted into intimate activities because his coldness will disturb the atmosphere. There are situations in which detachment is welcomed, such as quarrels, and there are public situations in which the observer's attitude is unimportant; but in personal, intimate activities, detachment is a barrier. Finally, an observer who does not actively probe and provoke will miss important aspects of his subject matter: its defenses against threat, its reactions to crises and problems, the limits of its tolerance.

How then can objectivity be achieved? We may divide the problem into two parts, the problem of observer bias in which observation reports are distorted and mistaken, and the problem of participant bias in which the participant changes the subject studied. Redfield has suggested a solution to the first problem (1960a, pp. 132-137, cf. also Mydal, 1944, appendix 2); he proposes that the same case be studied by two or more investigators with different biases, so that each can reveal and correct the exaggerations and omissions of the other. Objectivity is approached by combining the accounts and by rechecking where there is direct disagreement; the sign of falsehood is either direct contradiction or the incompatibility of different accounts.

This procedure is frequently followed in team research, where efforts are made to recruit observers with differing biases. It also frequently happens that several individual researchers will independently study the same case; thus the Hopi, the Navaho, and the Sioux have been studied often and from various perspectives. Or if there is only one study of a particular case, it may be possible to compare and combine treatments of a number of similar cases—for example, the many studies of Japanese villages and organizations, of American community political systems, of village India. Unfortunately it is not easy to combine two biased and partial accounts. The result of disagreement is more likely to be an acrimonious and inconclusive dispute than modest harmony, as in the dispute between Radcliffe-Brown and Murdock about Australian marriage rules (Lawrence and Murdock, 1949; Radcliffe-Brown, 1951b; Elkin, 1953; Leach, 1951, pp. 31-34) or the current dispute over who governs the American city. One notes also that Oscar Lewis did not take kindly to Redfield's characterization of their two accounts of Tepoztlan as equally biased and supplementary; Lewis agreed that Redfield was biased but demurred at applying the term to himself. Conversely, when two or more researchers happen to agree, this may indicate a coincidence of bias rather than pure objectivity; or the agreement of a team of researchers may indicate that the biases of the project director have dominated research rather than that the contributions of different perspectives have been harmonized.

The problem of participant bias is most acute in clinical work and action anthropology, where the subject is studied during therapeutic change and where participation is used both to evoke change and to produce information. Participants with different biases will produce different changes, and presumably there is no way of telling which of these changes, if any, are "objective" or "true." However, I suggest that if the participants have been properly socialized, all the changes are "objective." They all represent possible lines of development of the subject and therefore reveal a partial truth about the system being studied. It must be remembered that the clinician, if he is properly socialized, does not produce changes at will on a passive patient. Instead, he works within the patient's world, helping to release and develop changes that are already beginning, or helping to bring latent forces to the surface. Thus the changes are a selective development of the subject's immanent tendencies and reveal something about those tendencies, rather than being simply an expression of the clinician's biases. The same is true of the more incidental changes produced by the actions of participant observers; the responses to those actions represent existing mechanisms and potential lines of development within the subject.

The problems of observer bias and of participant bias are similar in one respect: in both cases, bias results in a partial or one-sided account of what the subject is like and also of what his potentialities for change are. But observer bias can be checked and corrected by another observer with a different bias, and this is hardly possible with participant bias. It is extremely unlikely that two or more clinicians will treat the same patient, and impossible in any case for them to treat him simultaneously. It might be possible to cross-check and combine their reports on similar patients, but the problem of determining which patients are similar enough in crucial respects would be difficult to solve.

When a bias cannot be checked against the output of a different bias or perspective, it can still be checked for its compatibility with the subject being studied (this is essentially Mannheim's solution; 1936, p. 95.) A bias is misleading or inappropriate insofar as it prevents the researcher from entering into the world of his subject and acting within that world. When the researcher's actions and responses are inappropriate from the standpoint of the subject, when they produce confusion and misunderstanding, the researcher is acting on premises that are different from those of the subject. This always happens during the period of the researcher's socialization, but if confusion and misunderstanding persist they show that a persistent bias of the researcher which is unacceptable to the subject is preventing him from understanding the subject. Consequently the researcher can check the appropriateness of his biases to his subject by noting persistent difficulties of communication and rapport. Such checking is, of course, easier to do if the reseacher is aware of his biases and can take a somewhat detached attitude toward them.

A clinician who is prevented from understanding his subject by inappropriate biases can still interact with him and produce changes, but he cannot explain or interpret the changes from the standpoint of the subject. Nor can he verify and correct his interpretations because of the difficulties of communication and rapport. Consequently, unless some other method of control and verification is used, his account of the changes cannot be reliable.

It must be admitted that this way of checking and controlling bias is not very satisfactory, because it requires the biased person to check on himself. The same biases that lead him to misperceive his subject can also lead him to misperceive difficulties of communication and rapport, and so his misunderstanding may continue indefinitely. Consequently the solution I have offered is a counsel of perfection rather than a solution.

Closely related to the theoretical problem of bias is the ethical problem of avoiding damage to one's subject. Since the participant observer necessarily changes his subject matter while studying it, he is responsible for those changes and should make sure they are not hurtful. This problem is familiar in experimental social psychology, where deception is frequently thought to be necessary during an experiment and where the experiment itself may be traumatic. The usual solution is to tell all after the experiment is over, in the hope that this will somehow cancel the changes and return the experimental subjects to their pre-experimental condition. At least one experimenter (Kelman, 1965) has had doubts about this solution and resolved to try to avoid deception, but found that it is not easy to conduct a controlled experiment with full disclosure to the subjects.

The participant observer does not have to use deception because he does not set up experimental controls; on the contrary, he lets the subject control him. Novice field workers sometimes are deceptive about themselves because they are not sure how they will be accepted if they tell the truth, but this is more an expression of their anxiety and ambivalence than an objective necessity of the method. In fact, deception is scientifically harmful in field and clinic because it sets up a barrier to communication and involvement. Deception by the researcher is felt and reciprocated (for example, Wax, 1960, p. 94), and the results are a mutually suspicious, distant relationship and unreliable data. This does not mean that the researcher must reveal everything about himself immediately; it means honesty in the relationship and an honest, intelligible statement of research aims when people express an interest in them. Here deception is a personal problem of integrity and self-confidence rather than a methodological problem, unlike experimental work, in which it is a true methodological problems.

The wider problem of responsibility for the changes one produces during participation is very real. The basic solution is to be as passive as possible in the initial stages of research and to become active only later, hoping that by the time a more active role is necessary one will have learned enough to estimate the consequences of one's actions and thus avoid damaging acts. The basic difficulty here is observer bias; one may easily misestimate the effects of his actions or substitute his own values for those of his subject. So observer bias is a dual problem, affecting both descriptive reports and normative judgments.

Note that I am rejecting the idea that one can be a "secret" participant observer who intentionally deceives his subjects by denying that he is observing them and pretending to be doing something else. Such a process is not participant observation because the continuing deception prevents any real involvement with the people being studied. For example, I regard the study by Festinger, Riecken, and Schachter (1956) as a field experiment rather than as participant observation. The authors came to their case out of an experimental tradition; they were interested in the case purely as a means of testing a hypothesis; and they used continuous deception as a way of maintaining control over incidental variables.

A closely related ethical problem is that of the researcher's indebtedness to his subjects for the knowledge he gets by studying them. The subjects take time to talk to the researcher, they befriend him, make a place in their lives for him, concern themselves with his work and seek out ways to be helpful. What can the researcher do for them in return? Gusfield expresses the researcher's feeling of indebtedness nicely: "The WCTU was my 'bread and butter' . . . They had been pretty helpful to me in many ways, and I was using them. This kind of situation is bound to fill the field worker with ethical misgivings, and I had a sincere feeling that they deserved some kind of repayment" (1960, p. 106).

Indebtedness is not a problem in experimental work, because experimental subjects are paid by the hour for their participation, and this is thought to be a sufficient discharge of the experimenter's obligations. One would expect it to be a problem for survey researchers, who ask their subjects to take up to several hours to fill out questionnaires, take tests, or give interviews; however, I have never come across any expressed recognition of this problem, either oral or written. Field workers, in contrast, frequently express awareness of the problem. Perhaps the difference is due to the participant observer's more personal involvement with his subject, which contrasts sharply with the tester's or questionnaire writer's impersonality. Or perhaps the greater contributions of the field workers' subjects produce a greater actual indebtedness.

Several solutions have been devised for this problem. Probably the most important form of repayment is the continual small courtesies of the field worker; he should be a good listener, express genuine respect or deference in attitude, perform small favors, participate seriously in ceremonies if asked (Wax, 1960). In a few cases native informants may charge by the hour, enabling repayment at least for specific interviews. Sometimes it is possible to make a gift to the whole community being studied; for example, the Leighton group provided a free psychiatric clinic for Stirling county (Leighton, 1959, pp. 7-8), and Redfield gave two large gas lamps to Chan Kom so the village could engage in night festivities (Redfield and Villa Rojas, 1934, p. 279). Or one may find other ways of being helpful to the community during one's stay; for example, when I was studying the Fox project I eagerly accepted the task of organizing and cataloging a pile of interviews, field notes, diary entries, and carbon copies. In clinical work and action anthropology, repayment takes the form of using one's knowledge to work out a program of assistance to the people studied.

But no matter what form of repayment is found, there is always a residual indebtedness that is inherent in the diffuse relationship the field worker develops with his subject. In a specific, quasi-contractual relationship, indebtedness is also specific and can be completely discharged by a specific payment, but in a diffuse interpersonal relationship, indebtedness is diffuse on both sides and can never be definitively eliminated. The result is a lingering sense of debt and guilt on the part of the field worker. This may express itself in overidentification with his subject, a reinforcement of the identification and involvement that normally results from participant observation (Gans, 1967, p. 444; S.M. Miller, 1952, pp. 97-99). The researcher may become a spokesman for the people he has studied, defending them

This becomes a scientific against attack and stressing their good qualities. problem when his research report also takes on a defensive tone, eulogizing virtues and playing down weaknesses. Here, then, is another source of observer bias of which both the researcher and his readers should be aware.

20

The Implicit Ontology
of Case Study Methods

One consideration that induces the holist to persevere in using his method despite its weaknesses and despite the slanders heaped on it is his feeling that it gets at something real that other methods miss. This sense of what is real and what is less real or unreal is what I have called an "implicit ontology." Perhaps *ontology* is too formidable a word for what is more a matter of vivid, immediate experience; yet I suspect that the great ontologies of the past were rationalized out of just some such experience. But words are not important, and the dissatisfied reader can substitute "existential concern," "personal knowledge," "precategorical experience," "secondary reinforcement," "substitute object-cathexis," or any other phrase that suits him.

The experience of which I speak may be described as a sense of communion with something vivid and fulfilling, of being at home with something that reacts and responds to one's actions. A formalist feels most at home with his clear, orderly models; there is nothing murky or opaque, nothing alien to his mind in them. He knows how to work with them and get an intelligible response, and their regular but unexpected transformations in his hands are a source of delight. Experimentalists and survey researchers are similarly rewarded in their encounters with statistical regularities. There is nothing more exciting and fulfilling for a survey researcher than to feed a meaningless mass of data representing a year's work into a computer, turn on the "varimax rotate" routine, and watch the regularities come tumbling out. It is like the experience of a miner who hauls up a bucket of mud and sloshes it around and around until only a few bright bits of clean gold are left on the bottom.

A holist finds his experience of reality in the human community. Koestler has described the experience inarticulately and well:

The lesson taught by this type of experience, when put into words, always appears under the dowdy guise of perennial commonplaces: that man is a reality, mankind an abstraction; that men cannot be treated as units in opera-

286

tions of political arithmetic because they behave like the symbols for zero and the infinite, which dislocate all mathematical operations (in Crossman, 1950, p. 68).

This formulation is more suitable for a clinician; a participant observer might rather say that human communities are real, while the forms of thought invented to manage them are abstractions. Families, groups, friendships are living entities that will always transcend any attempt to capture them with static intellectual categories.

When this experience is formulated more soberly it becomes a statement about causation, a standard ontological topic. Men are the only real causal agents in society; numbers, laws, logics, are causal only as they enter into human acts. Social causation is not a matter of being pushed or of regular sequences as on a movie screen, but rather a matter of perception, interpretation, and decision. The world that affects human beings is a perceived world, and external factors must be perceived and interpreted to have an effect. (This presumably does not apply to the laws of natural and biological science, since these apply to man as a natural object rather than as a social being.) For example, experimental controls, instructions, and rewards must be perceived and interpreted and then enter into a decision before they affect the subject's behavior. In order to understand how the controls act, one must find out how they are perceived and interpreted by each individual subject. Similarly, a logically possible strategy or a logically necessary conclusion must be recognized and attended to before it can be effective in action.

As a result, the output of most social science methods has a good deal of unreality, reporting surface manifestations rather than the realities of behavior. Statistical generalizations tell us that certain regularities occur a certain part of the time, but say anything about the actual inner or interpersonal transactions that bring them about. To see why a regularity appears in one case and not another, one must enter into the two cases and see how the particular perceptual and cognitive processes produced the two results. Similarly, logical models state what must necessarily be the case at asymptote or equilibrium; but these are abstract states and abstract necessities that human beings can take their time in reaching.

A proper knowledge of man should get at these realities by focusing on the worlds that human communities construct for themselves. Such knowledge will still be an abstraction, but it will be less abstract than the laws and models coming out of other methods. A proper logic, if one is needed, should reflect the continuous change and growth of real life rather than impose an unreal rigidity and exactness on life. These prejudices may be expressed more abstractly by saying that to be socially real is to be a self-maintaining system, where "self-maintaining" logically implies self-developing and self-transcending. A self-maintaining system establishes a boundary between itself and its environment and maintains control over interchanges through its boundary. It takes a hand in all influences impinging on it and shapes them as far as possible to fit its own requirements. In this way it endeavors to maintain its own integrity, that is, its own characteristic pattern of activity.

The fact that systems have boundaries does not mean that they exist independently of one another, like Aristotelian substances. A system depends for its continued existence on interaction through a boundary; but all such interactions tend to stabilize and grow and to develop boundaries of their own, thus becoming systems in turn. Conversely, internal interactions also at times stabilize and segregate themselves within boundaries or semi-boundaries, thereby becoming subsystems. Human society, therefore, consists of systems within systems, each with boundaries that are continually changing their permeability. Nor is there one fundamental type of system, say, the individual, that is more real than other types of system. Individuals become and develop within larger systems of activity and depend on the continuation of these larger systems in some form for their own continued existence and integrity. Cut off from human culture, the individual dies immediately; cut off from society he also dies, though more slowly. And in any case, radical changes in environing systems of activity produce changes in the personality of individuals, so they are not the same persons any more.

A more important criterion for locating a real system is the degree to which it maintains a characteristic pattern of action within a boundary. Patterns of action and interaction are continually fluctuating in society, and in this sense systems gradually take shape and gradually disappear, merging into other systems. This is true both for large and for small systems. In the large, it happens that a number of systems may interact in a rather haphazard and fluctuating way, so that the environing system is more a field of action than a determinate system. Sometimes these interactions become more regular and self-stabilizing, so that a larger system comes into being; at other times the larger system may decay into its component parts or be divided among neighboring systems. In the small, a tightly organized system may be all of a piece with no regular subsystems; then sometimes two or more subsystems gradually define themselves and succeed in maintaining themselves even at the expense of the environing system. Alternatively, subsystems, systems, and supersystems may all succeed in maintaining their integrity in a complex pattern of joint activity.

Existence is thus relatively precarious for systems at all levels of complexity. Boundary maintenance is never absolutely successful, and repair goes on continually. To say, therefore, that systems maintain control over boundary interchanges and take a hand in all influences impinging on them is to state an ideal that is only partially achieved. Systems can be broken down and overcome by overwhelming inputs, and they can decay through inadequate inputs and outputs. The maintenance and improvement of system integrity becomes an ideal, a practical task toward which participant-observer and clinical methods can contribute useful knowledge and in which they find their ultimate justification.

III

Methods in the Philosophy of Science

... eine besondere Philosophie «ewiger Wahrheiten»,
die über den Einzelwissenschaften stehe, sei überhaupt
nicht mehr notwendig.

Robert Havemann

21

The Participant–Observer Method

In Part III, I consider several methods that philosophers of science have used to study scientific method. My purpose is to bring out some contrasts and similarities between the method of the present study and methods used by other philosophers; I also wish to apply some conclusions from previous chapters to the topic of philosophic method itself. These are matters in which I am more personally involved and have studied less carefully than the topics of the previous chapters, so I do not have as much confidence in my conclusions.

The method used in the present work was described at some length in chapters 1, 11, and 13, and I wish here only to emphasize two characteristics that distinguish it from other methods used to study the same subject.

The participant observer approaches scientific method from the inside; he attempts to take the point of view of the scientists who are using a particular method. He does this by becoming, as far as possible, a member of a scientific community, sharing its activities and discussions, familiarizing himself with the literature, problems, and personalities that are discussed, helping with the daily work in whatever way he can. Taking an inside point of view consists of taking one's concepts, distinctions, problems, logic, values, from the scientific community rather than imposing externally derived concepts and distinctions on it. One learns concepts and distinctions not just by asking people or reading an article but by participating in innumerable activities. In this way one is able gradually to note the distinctions that are made habitually, almost unconsciously, the procedures that are carried out routinely, the goals, assumptions, and modes of inference that are taken for granted in activity as well as in speech. In the terminology of communication theorists, one learns by communicating rather than by metacommunicating.

The participant observer tests the adequacy of his account by seeing whether its various parts are acceptable and intelligible to the people he is working with, though not necessarily identical to their own verbal formulations. He does this not by asking their approval of an article—which tests mainly friendship and politeness—but in informal discussion continued over a period of time. Or, expressed somewhat differently, he tests the adequacy of his understanding by acting on it and seeing where his actions are unintelligible or puzzling to others.

Very few philosophers of science, to my knowledge, try to take an inside point of view in the social sciences. Everyone agrees that one should try hard to understand a scientist before criticizing him; but the usual method of achieving understanding is to take a sentence or paragraph or word out of an article and ask, "What might this mean?" Various possible meanings are suggested, and each one in turn is tested to see whether it makes sense. But this procedure throws the philosopher of science back into his own culture and closes off the culture of the scientist he thinks he is studying. The suggested meanings and distinctions are possibilities that exist in the culture of the philosopher, and the tests of making sense are taken from his own logic, standards, and concepts. Most philosophers simply do not realize the extent to which they are members of a distinct philosophical subculture, and how different it is from some of the scientific subcultures. When they say, "is ordinarily understood to mean. . ." or "In the ordinary method of science . . .," they are referring to concepts in their own subculture rather than in the scientific subcultures. The few exceptions, such as Churchman and Kaplan, stand out and compel my respect by their uniqueness.

Consequently most philosophical critiques of a scientist or method that I have seen are nothing more than ethnocentric expressions of culture shock.

Like most ethnocentrism, the ethnocentrism of philosophers tends to be accompanied by a sense of superiority; their attitude is that philosophers are experts at clarity and clarification whose mission is to clarify the thinking of the less fortunate. When they study a scientific work or tradition and have difficulty with it, they take this as a sign of the scientist's confusion rather than of their own failure of understanding. When they succeed in making distinctions that are not present and not needed in a work they are examining, they regard it as a sign of their superior clarity and the scientist's confusion, rather than a sign that they have failed to understand the scientist. When I suggested to one philosopher that he might try a little harder to understand a particular group of scientists, he replied, "You talk as if I, a philosopher, have to stick to the vague, ambiguous, and philosophically naive things an anthropologist says" (personal communication).

The participant observer takes the inside approach not only to understand scientific work but also to evaluate it. When he points out weaknesses in a line of research activity and suggests improvements, he tries to use standards and goals drawn from the method or tradition to which the research belongs. Each scientific method or tradition has its own standards and goals that have been developed and modified in practice, and the participant observer uses these standards rather than alien ones drawn from philosophy or physics or elsewhere. He discovers them not by asking people or reading their methodological pronouncements, since these may reflect inoperative ideals or language they picked up from some philosopher to look respectable. He locates them, rather, by observing and participating in actual practice and by comparing practice with written or verbal statements about method. Operational standards are not normally formulated in an explicit, consistent, and comprehensive fashion, particularly if they are still being worked out in practice; or if an explicit and comprehensive statement has been worked out, practice may have moved beyond it. Consequently it may be necessary to reformulate standards before applying them, but the reformulation should reflect actual practice.

If a method is developing rapidly, as nearly all methods seem to be doing these days, reformulation can be a complex and difficult process. A method may develop by repudiating familiar techniques and borrowing new ones from any or all of the social sciences; or old techniques may be modified in response to criticisms and examples coming from neighboring methods or to problems set by changing subject matter. Interdisciplinary co-operation may induce a merging of diverse experiences and skills or may combine weaknesses rather than strengths. Side by side with all these changes, the old techniques may continue in use and be defended with all the old arguments. Consequently even the preliminary question of what a method "is" at a given time may be unanswerable in any clear and coherent fashion. In addition, the modification in standards and perhaps in goals required by new techniques cannot be apparent until they have been used for a while. For example, when experimental gaming was first tried about fifteen years ago, no one knew the requirements for a good gaming experiment. It took some years of experience and a great variety of experimental designs to bring out some of the peculiar problems involved in using this sort of formal model in an experiment, and even now we cannot claim to have a definitive set of standards for gaming experiments.

The question of what are the indigenous operational standards and goals of a method is therefore difficult and may have more than one plausible answer. However, it is clear that the sensible question is not which standards are "native" and which are borrowed and adapted from other methods. All social science methods have borrowed extensively from one another, and the borrowed elements of a method may have become an essential part of it. The question should be, rather, which standards are now an intrinsic, necessary, operational part of a method and which remain alien, unusable formulas. An example of an alien standard is the statement that all scientific theory, and therefore also functionalist theory, should be hierarchical-deductive in form. Easton makes this statement (1965, p. 9) but recognizes immediately that the standard cannot be applied to his version of functionalist theory at the present time. He therefore calls it an ideal and quite properly ignores it in the rest of his work.

Here again, most philosophers of science today, as far as I can tell, insist on imposing standards and goals on the social sciences. They claim to know a priori what science must be and what scientists must do, and do not hesitate to criticize social scientists for deviating from these externally imposed standards. In particular, they hold that there is a logic that is valid for any scientist whether he likes it or not. For some philosophers, this logic is formal logic and for others it is informal logic, and the two groups of absolutists engage in continuous and interminable argument. From this absolutely valid logic is drawn a set of requirements that are presumed to be binding on any scientist and are used to evaluate and criticize particular scientific work.

For example, Helmer and Rescher make the following statement: "But once a new fact or a new idea has been conjectured . . . it must be capable of objective test and confirmation by anyone. And it is this crucial standard of scientific objectivity . . . to which the social scientist must conform" (1959, p. 27). I do not say that Helmer and Rescher are absolutely wrong; I am merely pointing out that they did not discover this standard in the work of social scientists but laid it down as an a priori obligation. Even this would not be objectionable if they had only bothered to express the obligation in a form relevant to the work of social scientists. Everyone wants to be objective; but what does "capable of objective test and confirmation by any one" mean for an action anthropologist or a computer simulation of a particular engineer's designing procedures? The phrase makes sense to an experimentalist—it means replicability to him—but what it means in some other methods would be very difficult to determine. These difficulties, I believe, are due to the one-sidedness of the standard. If Helmer and Rescher had investigated what "objectivity" might mean in, say, a case-descriptive simulation, they might have come to see the abstract one-sidedness of their principle and reformulated it to make it relevant. They might have discovered that in some social science methods objectivity presupposes and includes subjectivity; that since human behavior is telic, one is objective or faithful to one's subject matter only by helping it change itself. A simulation of an engineer's designing procedures is accurate, objective, only insofar as its clarification of his aims and standards enables him to improve his procedures (cf. Mitroff, 1967, 1969). Once one discovers what objectivity means in the social sciences, the origin of the principle of objectivity in its unmodified form is no longer important; what is important, as with all culture borrowing, is its relevance or usability in the new culture.

Let us consider the "inside" approach to scientific method in more detail. The participant observer begins by familiarizing himself with a particular scientific community, learning its techniques and technical concepts, its ceremonies and legends, its history and its theories, in the manner I have described in chapter 11. That is, he moves into a community. However, "inside" is not a static location where one can settle down comfortably; it is more like a seat on a roller coaster. Almost immediately one becomes aware of variations in technique and disagreements over method. One finds scientists clustered in small, close-knit groups or schools, each group a little different from the others, and one is faced with the problem of deciding which of these groups are insiders, which are outsiders, and which are borderline. Also, each of these groups will be in intercommunication with a wide variety of other groups that must be classified in turn. The insiders, of course, must be studied, but the outsiders must be studied somewhat too, to make sure they really are different. Thus one is led imperceptibly on to studying wider and wider circles of scientists using different methods.

Classification involves comparison, and one is thus almost immediately involved in comparing different groups of scientists. As I indicated in chapter 13, it is hardly possible to do a case study without comparing it with other cases. Comparison serves, among other things, to clarify a method by contrast. The differences that show up have to be explained: why does this kind of experiment run on for so many trials, hundreds of them? Why does this kind run only one trial per day, but for so many days? Why do these experimenters get so personally involved in their experiments, conducting interviews and personality tests, observing in various ways, even participating as subjects, while those other experimenters try to design experiments that can be run by machine? Why do these experimenters spend ten years on one topic, while those pick a new topic for each experiment? Why does this group of theorists fail or refuse to learn mathematics, while that group limits itself to calculus and analytic geometry, another group to statistics and probability theory, still another group mainly to game theory, while still another group is composed of all-round mathematical virtuosos? Some of these questions can be disposed of with trivial answers, some point to minor variations in a method, and some lead directly to basic characteristics.

Comparison can also reveal what a method is failing to do or not doing well and thus point to potentialities for its further development. Similarly, criticisms of a method by users of other methods may, if properly restated, reveal weaknesses and problems, although they may also reveal mere misunderstandings. In addition, parallels between different methods may sometimes point to general problems or tasks that both are facing; this enables one to describe one's method in a deeper and more theoretical way, as a solution to certain problems that other methods also face. In short, the comparative process that takes one outside a method is necessary for full understanding. The "outside" is an essential part of the "inside" point of view.

As more cases—more methods and variants of methods—accumulate, it is possible to move toward broader generalizations. If one could collect a representative sample of all methods and study each intensively, one could even develop a theory of scientific method in general by seeing what all methods have in common. Such a theory, which does not yet exist anywhere, would be very useful for understanding a specific method: it would point to the essential problems that the method is solving in its own unique way, and thereby enable one to explain why the method is what it is. It would also enable one to distinguish essential characteristics from surface characteristics, and to classify variants on an essential rather than a superficial basis.

The present work has hardly any such generalizations about scientific method in it. I have not been able to collect enough case studies to provide a representative sample and have preferred to minimize generalization rather than present a distorted account. Some generalization is unavoidable if one wishes to control comparisons—one cannot study the particular case without using some general principles—but I have tried to limit myself to this minimum.

If I had to generalize at this premature stage, I would be inclined to point to the problem of the One and the Many as the essential problem of scientific method. Any scientific account of human society must somehow deal not only with the uniqueness of which human history and individual life histories consist, but also with the regularities of various sorts that appear in history. If the primary focus is on regularities, the unique inevitably shows up, first as something to be controlled, then as a source of ideas about new regularities, and finally as something to be intuitively reconstituted in the practical application of regularities. If the primary focus is on the particular history, regularities inevitably show up as concepts for describing particularities, as bases for controlling comparisons, and as generalizations to be achieved inductively. If I were to work out this problem in detail to determine how adequately various methods deal with it, case study methods would come out on top. They include both the particular and the universal within science instead of consigning the particular to intuition, practical application, or history; they exhibit the universal within the particular instead of segregating the two in one way or another; and they move from particular to universal and back by gradual steps rather than in one grand jump. But the fact that my own method comes out best in this account is itself conclusive evidence that the account is biased, or unmediated as a dialectician would say, and therefore inadequate.

Several other generalizations have suggested themselves in my studies as suitable for further testing and reformulation. For one thing, all methods I have studied combine theory and observation, using theory to control and guide observation and observation to correct and improve theory. This mutual control leads to observations that the casual observer could not make and ideas that the nonscientific thinker could not conceive. This does not mean that each scientist must observe and theorize in equal proportions —there can be a division of labor—but that both elements must be distributed and related somehow in each method. All or nearly all methods seem to involve some combination of activity and passivity in the scientist's interaction with his subject matter. His activity consists not merely of thinking but also of acting on or with his subject matter, and his passivity consists in being acted on without his interference. This does not mean that each scientist must be both active and passive—again there can be a division of labor—but that both elements must be distributed and related somehow in each method. All methods seem to involve some combination of vagueness and precision, vagueness related mainly to search or discovery and precision usually related to testing operations, but sometimes also to search. Vagueness and precision are not correlated with observation and theory; in some cases theorizing is precise and observation vague, in some cases observation is precise and theorizing is vague, and sometimes both are mixed. Nor is it necessary for each scientist to be sometimes vague and sometimes precise, as long as the two qualities are distributed and related somehow. Finally, all methods are fully self-corrective. There is nothing in science that is immune to change, no hypothesis so completely verified that it is beyond question, no completely perfected technique, no a priori truth about the world or about method, no one ultimate model. The continual influx of new young scientists eager to prove their worth by knocking cherished truths guarantees this point.

In chapter 1, I used the anthropologist's term "cultural relativism" as an alternative name for the inside-outside or comparative point of view. The relativist holds that a culture or community should be understood and evaluated by means of its own concepts and standards. This does not mean that one should limit himself to concepts and standards that are explicitly in the consciousness of scientists; as I have indicated, one appeals in addition to practice, to concepts implicit in a line of development, and even to usable examples set by practitioners of other methods. Nor does one assume that each community has quite different standards and categories; if this were the case, communication between communities would be impossible rather than merely difficult. The fact of extensive communication and collaboration throughout the social sciences indicates that there are underlying continuities and similarities even among methods that seem quite different. There may even be universal standards of scientific validity, and if so, more extensive participant observation should reveal and clarify these standards.

The reader may object that the position I am describing is not relativism as he understands the term. It would be inconsistent for a relativist to insist absolutely on any particular terminology, so for such readers I offer the substitute term "absolutism," which I borrow from Barrington Moore (1958, p. 94 ff). According to Moore, an absolutist is a person who believes that scientific knowledge can improve our understanding of valid human values and who therefore uses scientific techniques to develop standards for appraising human behavior. With regard to scientific method, an absolutist would be one who thinks we can improve our understanding of correct scientific method by the systematic study of scientific practice, and this is exactly what the present work claims to do. Perhaps the term "absolutism" in turn has offensive connotations for some readers, and I offer them "pluralism" as a vaguer substitute. Or one might say the method is relativistic in its treatment of individual cases and becomes gradually absolutistic as it moves toward broader generalizations.

A second characteristic of the participant-observer method as I have used it is its historicism. There are several varieties of historicism, so this term too may cause some misunderstanding. I mean here the view that science develops over time. Its goals develop, its methods develop, its logics, its concepts, its theories, its practical uses all develop. The chief output of the social sciences is their own self-transformation; they produce not laws but better ways of knowing. This means that if one wishes to understand a scientific work or method or concept one must place it in its historical context. The work usually turns out to be an attempted solution to problems that plagued its predecessors or, in some cases, a reaction against one-sidedness in its predecessors. In turn, it contains implicit characteristics and latent problems that become clearer in its successors. Its contemporaries are also relevant, because it usually expresses a choice from several perceived alternatives and an understanding of which alternatives will clarify the nature of the choice.

Historicism also means that the standards for evaluating scientific work develop over time. As a new method develops, the standards and goals implicit in it are gradually worked out into clarity, and leftover standards from previous methods are gradually discarded. A standard or principle may be very important for a time, then gradually become a hindrance to new work, and finally be replaced by a new one.

This book covers too short a time-span—two or three decades, in the main —to suggest any clear generalizations about how scientific methods develop. One sees various kinds of change occurring over the decades, but no consistent pattern is apparent. One line of development is the dead end line, exemplified by Hullian learning theory, British structuralism, and perhaps in earlier times by German and American diffusionism. Here a community of researchers turns inward on itself, perfecting its techniques, developing ever greater precision and concern for technical details, producing distinctions and disputes of ever greater complexity and subtlety, until the whole effort suddenly collapses and takes a radical new direction. Another line of development is open, exemplified by survey research methods and culture-personality theory, in which techniques and ideas are borrowed from all over and there is steady though apparently haphazard growth. Apart from providing occasional hints about how science develops, two or three decades are only sufficient to provide a historical context for specific groups of works—where they came from, what the perceived alternatives are, and where they are heading—and that is the extent of historicism in the present work.

Historicism is rather rare among contemporary philosophers of social science, as far as I know. The logical positivist program in particular aims to lay down ultimate criteria that are valid for all science for all time. These philosophers give one a picture of a science that essentially has no history. There was a period of pre-science or pseudo-science characterized by abject submission to Aristotelian dogma; then science was invented by Galileo and Newton, and ever since has been steadily moving on to the next decimal place or the next higher generalization or the next floor (cf. Walker, 1963, p. vi). Newton—a mythologized Newton—is still held up as the model for all scientific work to imitate, and classical mechanics is still the model that all science will someday imitate perfectly. More recently there have been important historicist treatments of the physical sciences by Kuhn, Feyerabend, and Toulmin, and my work can be regarded as parallel in spirit to theirs. It should be clear by now that I disagree with Popper's comments on historicism (1957), as well as with his views on scientific method, dialectic, Freud, Plato, Hegel, social change, etc. Even his otherwise sound criticism of the principle of national self-determination is superficial because it is non-dialectical (cf. Diesing, 1967). The whole of this book is, in passing, a defense of Mannheim against Popper's criticisms, so further general comment is perhaps unnecessary.

I conclude with an example to show how historicism and the inside point of view work out in practice. This is not an example of which I am proud, because it shows up both the weaknesses of the participant-observer method and my own shortcomings in using the method. But it does deal with a topic that several other philosophers have discussed, and so it affords an opportunity to illustrate the contrast between an inside, historical point of view and an ethnocentric point of view.

Milton Friedman's much-discussed methodological argument (1953, ch. 1) has been examined in detail by Nagel (1963), by Massey (1965), by Cyert and Grunberg (1963), and by Melitz (1965), among others. Nagel begins his article by summarizing deftly and clearly what Friedman seems on the surface to be saying. He then notes that a controversy has developed over Friedman's contention that the postulates of a scientific theory do not need to be realistic as long as the theory is accurate in its predictions. Nagel proposes to clarify this controversy and does so by distinguishing three senses of "realistic," which he illustrates with examples from physics. Now he has his Procrustean bed, and he next proceeds to force Friedman onto it. He observes that Friedman's use of "realistic" is ambiguous, vacillating between sense 1 and sense 3; but that is not all, because if Friedman picks sense 1, his argument becomes trivial, and if he picks sense 3, much of what he says loses its point or is mistaken. There is just no way Friedman can come away from that bed in one piece.

Grunberg follows the same procedure. He first lays down "the meaning of these terms in methodology" (Cyert and Grunberg, 1963, p. 299), namely in Hempel's theory of explanation, and then proceeds to belabor Friedman because his argument becomes ambiguous when expressed in Hempel's terminology. Massey (1965) picks up from Friedman the problem of whether the assumptions of a scientific theory need to be realistic; then he proceeds to consider some characteristics of a fully axiomatized science, in order to clarify the problem and solve it. For an example of a fully axiomatized science, Massey cites an axiomatization of geometry by a philosopher. Then he returns to Friedman's argument and shows that it does not hold for a fully axiomatized geometry. Whether it holds in economic theory, or whether this really was Friedman's problem, he does not bother to consider.

Melitz' article (1965) illustrates well the ethnocentrism of which I spoke previously. He says such things as: "If Friedman's thesis is to be meaning-ful, he must be maintaining, in effect. . ." (p. 46); "On the basis of current philosophical usage. . . " (p. 57); "the adjective 'definitional' is usually understood. . . " (p. 57); "The general trend in philosophy . . . " (p. 58); "according to general understanding in logic. . ." (p. 59). Melitz means, "My friends and I talk this way, but Friedman talks differently, so he is con-fused and misleading." As for who is confused, we find Melitz asking rhe-torically, "What are some examples of unwanted implications of postu-lates?" (p. 47), when Friedman provides two in the text, namely the tree and the billiard player. Massey expresses the same ethnocentrism when he contrasts Friedman's "idiosyncratic use" of a term with "the customary logical one" (1965, p. 1158).

I do not mean to say that the substantive views of these philosophers are incorrect; in particular, Nagel's substantive statements are clear and con-vincing, as are also Hempel's comments (1965, pp. 31-32). My point is that none of them try to take Friedman's point of view to understand his meaning; they all interpret him with the concepts of their own subculture. Nor do any of them look for the historical context of the argument and for the substantive developments in economic theory underlying it; they all treat it as a timeless statement about Science. But Friedman was not writing about science in general, nor was he writing for philosophers; he was writing about economics for economists, both friends and enemies, whom he knew personally. As Baker Brownell one observed in an unduly neglected work,

> I can address only people whom I know and whose response, by the time-less magic of projection, affects me before it is given. My statements cannot find their destinations in the anonymous abstraction called "people in gen-eral." When deprived of concrete, human context they lose way and their meanings have no particular reference. Under these conditions directive language breaks down. Circuits cannot be completed with all persons at once, nor can statements have a universal direction, for there is no universal direction. Universals of this sort are wingless things that clutter up the directive course of language (1950, p. 215).

In order to understand a social scientist, one must locate the personal and cultural context in which he is working and the historical context of the problem he is working on, and the philosophers have not done this.

I decided to investigate Friedman's article because the controversy about it among economists puzzled me. I could not fit the various ideological positions, especially Friedman's, into the picture I was trying to work out of the model-building method or methods. When Nagel's smooth, skillful hatchet job came out it convinced me that Friedman was just wrong and could be ignored; but I couldn't manage to keep him ignored. Too many other people were discussing him, and the controversy did not make sense. In other words, this was a negative instance for my developing picture, and negative instances are important to a participant observer as foci of re-structuring. Friedman's article was one of many such foci that I used to restructure again and again my picture of the model-building method.

I began by recalling my original intuitive reaction to the chapter in 1954: I didn't like it. This is a significant datum because I know some of my biases and can interpret my reaction in the light of that knowledge. Next I placed the chapter in a historical context. I noted Friedman's reference to a 1950 Alchian article as presenting another version of his position, and this reminded me of a 1962 Gary Becker article which also develops Alchian's ideas, and Becker was associated with Friedman at Chicago at one time. So Becker's article brings out more fully one line of development in Fried-man's thought. Next, a footnote led back to a Machlup-Lester controversy in the 1940's. I now had a context. Friedman's opponent is the institutional-ist Lester, his ally is the marginalist Machlup, and his own view is further developed in Becker. The differences between Machlup and Samuelson, and between Samuelson and Friedman, which loom large in the journals, are secondary to Friedman's own interest. By "realism" Friedman means the *institutionalist's* "realism," which is different from any of Nagel's three senses, but approximately combines senses 1 and 3. Thus Nagel also falls into place; and my own initial dislike fits in, since I don't like the marginalists. In addition, Friedman's examples of the tree and of the billiard player fit this new scheme nicely. These examples have puzzled and annoyed some commentators (cf. Cyert and Grunberg, 1963, pp. 303-309), but they seem well-chosen to me.

Next I checked this hypothesis against a new type of datum: I found an informant, Claude Hillinger, a student of Friedman. First I asked him to give his account of the position, listening carefully for his structuring of the issues. Sure enough, the institutionalists showed up as the alternative posi-tion. Then I asked him to interpret certain paragraphs, to compare with my own interpretations, and then I tried my interpretations on him. I didn't expect our views to be identical, and they weren't, but I wished to check the acceptability of my interpretation. It was necessary that my interpretation be acceptable *and* that the differences of detail between us be related to the dif-ferences in our location (in ideological space) vis-à-vis Friedman. Both events occurred; he accepted my interpretation, I accepted his, and the dif-ferences of emphasis were intelligible. Finally, I reread Friedman's article in the light of my informant's comments and found no new points.

My interpretation of Friedman's views then was as follows: Considerable empirical evidence had turned up in the thirties and forties to show that most people most of the time do not act in an economically rational man-ner. They do not maximize. The institutionalists gleefully picked up this evidence and declared that their old enemies, the marginalists, had been disproved and discredited. The proper task of economists now was to join with sociologists in empirical studies of consumer behavior, which would duly be published in the *American Journal of Economics and Sociology.* Such a proposal would, of course, make a marginalist scream in anguish, so Friedman and Machlup moved to the defense. Friedman's defense consisted simply in shifting the locus of rationality from the individual to society, arguing that rationality is really a selective social mechanism that rewards those businessmen who for whatever reasons act "as if" they were rational and punishes the rest. In other words, he suggested a new empirical interpretation of the old formal models. He did not argue substantively that the models had been conclusively verified, but he did argue methodologically that evidence from consumer behavior did not count as disconfirmation. Friedman's argument could now be brandished by marginalists like a crucifix to ward off methodological criticisms, while they went about their business of constructing and elaborating models as before (cf. for example Downs, 1957, p. 21).

Computer modeling represents, in my opinion, a more fundamental solution to this controversy. The computer people took seriously the evidence that people are not maximizing-rational and decided to find out by empirical study how decisions actually are made. Thus they became, in a way, heirs of the institutionalist program—though the institutionalists would surely disinherit them if they could. One of the things they inherited was the institutionalists' enemy, Friedman, so a sorcerer (Hempel) was invoked to nullify Friedman's defensive methodological witchcraft. Unlike the institutionalists, the computer people did not leave their material at the level of empirical generalization; their apparatus enabled them to construct formal models of decision-making that were much more complex than those of the marginalists and much more adequate empirically. Their models do not replace the marginalist models but supplement them, since the two point in different directions. The computer models deal with the actual logic of business decisions; the marginalist models deal with long-run logical necessities in society, not with behavior in individual cases.

There are still several difficulties in this interpretation that cast doubt on it. One is Samuelson's views, which still puzzle me. I gather, on the basis of Samuelson's discussion of consumer behavior (1966, part 1), that he would prefer the alternative formalist route of changing one's postulates rather than changing one's empirical interpretations when a model needs correction, but I am not sure. It may also be that, as Lerner suggests (1965), Samuelson's methodological views and his substantive work are dissimilar. But a full investigation of Samuelson's views would take at least as long as the investigation of Friedman's views, so I regretfully postpone it—regretfully, because a thorough study of Samuelson's work might clarify my interpretation of Friedman. On the other hand, Machlup's more recent work fits nicely into my interpretation; cf. Machlup, 1967 (p. 2), where he qualifies and reinterprets the much misinterpreted phrase "unrealistic assumptions." I also agree with Krupp (1963).

A second source of doubt is the fact that I had only one informant and talked to him for two hours only, and so may have misinterpreted him. In particular, we may have exaggerated the amount of agreement between us. Nor did I take notes immediately after the interview, as a good participant observer should; I depended on memory. My excuse is that at the time I had no idea what method I was using and in any case had no idea that the interview would be important; it was just another of the many discussions I had been having. This, incidentally, is a good illustration of why new field workers are urged to take precise, detailed notes of everything; they can never tell what may be important to them years later.

A third source of doubt is the fact that my explanation fits too well one of my biases, that of moving from initial disagreement to final agreement. Therefore it may be that I have misinterpreted Friedman to make him more agreeable to me personally. On the whole, I would not be too surprised if Friedman were to rise up and declare that I had twisted his views.

These loose ends illustrate another characteristic of the participant observer's work: it is never finished.

22

The Method
of Rational Reconstruction

I take the title of this chapter from Hempel (1965, pp. 10, 44 and passim) to refer to what is probably the dominant method used by philosophers of science today. This method was developed by the school of philosophers who called themselves "logical positivists" or "logical empiricists." The school developed its ideas in the twenties and thirties in work by the Vienna Circle—Wittgenstein's *Tractatus,* Carnap's *Aufbau,* work by Schlick and Feigl among others—and by Reichenbach in Germany and A. J. Ayer in England. The concern of these philosophers originally was to put science on a sound foundation by cleansing it of metaphysics and ideology, which they felt were claiming a spurious prestige by pretending to be scientific. Metaphysics and ideology, they felt, were composed of vague, emotion-laden ideas that were immune to rational evidence and rational argument and that expressed themselves in irrational and barbarous behavior like that of the Nazis. One could not prevent people from thinking this way, but one could at least exclude such ideas from science, by imposing a strict criterion of rational verifiability on it. Since metaphysical ideas were immune to correction by facts, such a criterion would expose and discredit them as nonscientific.

Over the years the original positivist program has been modified a great deal, and in the work of recent exponents such as Hempel, Topitsch, and Brodbeck has absorbed ideas and aims from other sources. However, there is still a prominent interest in verifiability and in rules for verification or confirmation. Science is still conceived to be a set of laws, or hypotheses, or propositions, which are to be tested and confirmed by empirical evidence according to strict, impersonal rules and criteria. Those laws that have been adequately confirmed describe the world (in some sense of "describe") and predict the way it will continue to be. Physics is the most advanced science, measured in quantity of confirmed laws, and the other sciences must strive to imitate physics as they increase their stock of confirmed laws.

This view of science, without the original aims of the twenties and thirties, is widely accepted by social scientists and even assumed as self-evident by many. It is even accepted by some philosophical opponents of the logical empiricists, who are thus reduced to defining their task as one of opposing science.

I am by no means an expert on the ideas of the rational reconstructionists, and the following account is an outsider's view, even a view from afar, which insiders may feel contains misinterpretations and distortions.

A common tactic for understanding something unfamiliar is to locate something familiar that is similar and compare the two. Accordingly, in attempting to understand the rational reconstructionists I ask, "Which of the methods of the social sciences does the method of rational reconstruction most resemble?" To answer this question, I must examine the way in which the method distributes its vagueness and its precision. Clearly it is vague and imaginative in its treatment of empirical cases and precise in its reasoning. Examples are described briefly and carelessly; if one is studying explanation, for instance, a sample explanation a few sentences long is picked up for examination, its context ignored, and its meaning assumed to be clear. A logical point or characteristic is located in the example and the shift to abstract reasoning is made as rapidly as possible. There the pace slows down drastically. Extreme caution is exercised in examining a logical characteristic; each implication drawn from it is studied at great length, cooperatively by many philosophers, and the crucial results are derived and stated in symbolic logic.

This distribution of vagueness and precision suggests that rational reconstruction is a formal method. Further examination turns up other characteristics that support this classification.

1. A sharp distinction is made between fact and logic, between fact and law, between fact and norm. Consequently the distinction between scientists, the guardians of fact, and philosophers, the guardians of logic, is sharp and clear. So also is the distinction between science and ethics. This is similar to the formalist's sharp distinction between logic and fact, between a model and its empirical exemplifications, or between a model and its practical applications.

2. In the development of theory, the rational reconstructionist begins with the logically simplest and most abstract case and gradually adds complications to make his account more adequate empirically. Thus Hempel begins his work in explanation with a deductive-nomological model and later moves to inductive-statistical and deductive-statistical models. In his study of deductive explanation he begins with the most abstract case of complete, true, certain knowledge and gradually incorporates incompleteness, possible truth, and probability. Similarly the various studies of confirmation begin with simple, formalized languages. This characteristic movement from logically simple and empirically abstract to logically complex is similar to mathematical modeling rather than to computer simulation.

3. The type of logic used is formal and symbolic. Even when reasoning is verbal it is guided by the requirements of formal logic, and when the argument approaches a crucial point it becomes more clearly formal and sometimes shifts completely into symbols.

4. There is even an apparatus of axioms or postulates (Hempel, 1965, pp. 30-35, 102, 247-248, 367-368) which must be included in a satisfactory theory.

5. Like all formal theories, those of rational reconstructionists are one-sided. The holistic participant observer tries to give a complete account of how all aspects of his case fit together, but the formalist selects only one aspect for formalization and leaves the rest as unknowable empirical residues. Specifically, the rational reconstructionist works only with the context of justification, not the context of discovery, and so his account of science is purposely one-sided. His reason is that justification can be given a strict logical reconstruction but discovery cannot. Discovery is a form of creativity; it does not embody any logic and therefore is unknowable, unpredictable. (This is, incidentally, false; discovery can be formalized in computer models.) Science is thus broken into two completely different parts, discovery and justification, and neither can contribute anything to the task of the other. In order to put the two parts together again and give a complete account of a scientific method, it would be necessary to shift from formal to dialectical logic, but this would be impossible for a rational reconstructionist. Even the thought of turning dialectical would be abhorrent to him.

I conclude that the rational reconstructionist is a formalist, a model-builder similar to the mathematical model-builder but using symbolic logic as his formal language. His models are similar to mathematical models of rational behavior; that is, they describe what the ideally rational scientist would do and serve as ideals or norms for ordinary scientists.

In constructing a model, say, of explanation or confirmation or concept formation, the rational reconstructionist first sets up his axioms and postulates. These are general conditions that any model must satisfy to be adequate. The axioms seem to follow from the nature of logic, for example, Hempel's consequence condition (1965, p. 31): "If an observation report confirms every one of a class K of sentences, then it also confirms any sentence which is a logical consequence of K." Some postulates seem to be part of or to follow from a very general conception of the essential nature of science. For example, the postulate that any adequate observation report must in principle be replicable by any qualified observer seems to be part of a conception of science as essentially general and impersonal. This conception of science was developed earlier in the history of the method and, as I have indicated in chapter 21, is one-sided, emphasizing the universal at the expense of the particular and the narrowly objective at the expense of the subjective and participative.

Having got his postulates clear, the rational reconstructionist next takes an example of the process he is modeling, usually an example from physics. He picks physics because this is the most advanced science and therefore the one in which activity approaches closest to the ideal limit of rationality. He lets his imagination play over the example, trying to locate the logic implicit in it. Having located and written down the supposed logic, he tests it against other examples to see whether the same logic is also present there. Then begins a long process of testing and correction of the model. It is tested against the relevant axioms and postulates; its parts are checked for internal consistency; its consequences are deduced and similarly checked; and the whole model is tested against many other examples. Testing and correction is a co-operative process involving many philosophers and lasting many years. During the course of testing, the axioms and postulates are also subject to revision; new postulates may be required to account for regularities in the examples, and old postulates may be restated in more general or more precise form.

The final model must be adequate both formally and materially: formally it must satisfy all relevant postulates and axioms, and materially it has to provide a close approximation to the logic implicit in the examples studied (cf. Hempel, 1965, p. 34). An adequate model is regarded as a rational reconstruction, or explication, of what physicists do.

The next step is to locate the limits of relevance of the model. Does it also explicate the activities of other scientists besides physicists? Examples from chemistry, physiology, astronomy, are examined one by one. Here is where the social sciences come in; they are approached with the question of whether a model developed in physics applies to them as well. The expectation is that it will apply but not as well, because the social sciences are not as advanced as physics. It is also to be expected that as one moves into these new areas the basic model will have to be modified slightly to be relevant to the special characteristics of each field. Thus a set of variants of the basic model is gradually accumulated; for example, there are causal explanations, genetic explanations, dispositional explanations, explanations by reasons and by models, and functional explanations.

Other variants of the basic model are constructed by relaxing one or more of its assumptions. Thus Hempel complicates his model of explanation by constructing various forms of incomplete explanation (1965, pp. 415-424), just as a neoclassical economist expands his competition model by constructing various forms of imperfect competition. Confirmation theory is a variant of the model of verification, achieved by relaxing the requirement of 100 percent certain verification (Hempel, 1965, p. 4). Statistical explanations are a variant of nomological explanations, constructed by substituting statistical for deterministic laws; they have two subvariants, according to whether a single event or a class of events is to be explained.

So far the method of rational reconstruction looks just like the mathematical model-building method, and like the model-building method I regard it as extremely useful both in promise and in achievements. Its various models of scientifically rational procedure serve as norms that scientists can follow to make their behavior more rational, like other mathematical models of rational behavior. They can also be used as a baseline for exploration; to the extent that some body of scientific practice diverges in a regular way from the model, we know something else is going on that requires a different model. For example, Hempel's study of one version of functional analysis shows that these functionalists were not producing deductive explanations. From this finding Hempel correctly inferred that they were doing something different, namely investigating the self-regulating characteristics of various systems according to a heuristic program (1965, 3 pp. 329-330). Unfortunately Hempel did not go on to model the explanations that were resulting from this program.

This brings me to my one criticism of the way the method of rational reconstruction is currently practiced. Its practitioners have always clung very closely to a few basic models. For a time the inductive-statistical model of explanation seemed like a bold new departure, but it now looks very similar to the more orthodox deductive-statistical model; in the one case the probability number states the empirical probability, in the other it states the logical probability or degree of confirmation. This caution contrasts sharply with the practice of mathematical model-builders, who have constructed a large variety of models for every occasion.

The advantages of having several models are twofold: first, each brings out a different aspect of empirical reality, and second, each has an empirical area of greatest relevance where other models do not work as well. Some types of behavior are best explained by learning theory, some by game theory, some by a model of competition, some by a conflict-and-conformity model, some by a cognitive balance model, some by a cognitive reverberation model, and so on; there is no one master model that applies equally well to all human behavior. In Coleman's terminology, mathematical models are "sometimes-true theories" (1964, p. 516 ff; cf. also Hempel, 1965, p. 446, for the same point).

The rational reconstructionists have essentially one basic model of each scientific task. There is one model of explanation, one of confirmation, one of concept formation, one of the structure of scientific theory, and so on. This severely and unnecessarily limits the usefulness of their work. Their models are useful in some areas of science where they are directly relevant but are confusing and even quite misleading in other areas.

In particular, their models are of uneven usefulness in the social sciences. This is after all to be expected, since the basic models were presumably derived from a study of examples taken from physics. Specifically, I find that the models apply quite well to experimental work and with some modification also to statistical survey methods. Some models, including those of explanation and of the structure of scientific theory, apply nicely to mathematical modeling, but others, such as confirmation and definition, are misleading and apply only with considerable reinterpretation of terms. With computer models, especially case-descriptive models, the situation is still worse. Finally, all the models are seriously misleading when applied to clinical, participant-observer, and some historical methods. In general, the reconstructionist models apply most readily when the objective of the scientist is the discovery of general laws; less readily when his objective is the discovery of relatively specific logical structures; and least readily when his objective is the understanding of particular empirical systems.

As a result, the application of the reconstructionist models to the social sciences has caused a great deal of difficulty, and it is hard to say, on balance, whether they have contributed more confusion or more clarification to the methodology of the social sciences. The confusion has taken two basic forms. First, when a reconstructionist applies some model, say, one of explanation or concept formation, to an area of the social sciences and finds that it does not fit, he reacts by condemning the social scientists rather than by adjusting his model or devising a new and more appropriate one. The social scientists affected may react with defensive polemics, thus wasting their time, or they may try to "correct" their ways and get themselves tangled up in inappropriate procedures. Their opponents within their own group gleefully seize on the condemnation as a weapon; thus I have heard a social scientist praising Hempel's discussion of functionalism (1965, ch. 11), saying in effect, "Hempel really showed up those lousy functionalists that time!" Also in Martindale, (1960, p. 465), one can read that Hempel has disposed of functionalism once and for all time. In both cases nothing constructive is accomplished.

Second, when a reconstructionist finds that a model does not fit well, he may engage in complex logical maneuvers to show that it does fit after all. After a good deal of hocus-pocus he may conclude, triumphantly, that properly interpreted it can be made to fit; but the resulting mass of interpretations may make the model so complex that it is no longer of any use to any social scientist. This has happened especially in discussions of historical methods; a not-so-hypothetical extreme example will illustrate. Suppose there is a historian who is interested in reconstructing the particular interrelations between ideological, economic, political, and social dynamics in a limited historical period. A rational reconstructionist could argue that Hempel's covering law model fits this case. The historical period is logically a member of a (nonexistent) class of periods exactly like it; each particular observed interrelation (implicitly) depends on an (unknown) law stating that this interrelation occurs with a certain (unknown) probability in a certain (unknown) set of conditions; consequently each interrelation is logically a member of a (nonexistent) class of interrelations; and so on. Now this is quite ridiculous; yet something of the sort, I gather, has occurred in discussions of historical methods and occasionally elsewhere. It is ridiculous because it serves only a defensive function and is in no way useful. The historian could not improve his method by applying the doctored-up covering law model because everything it points to—laws, classes, and conditions—is nonexistent. At most, he might succeed in eventually replacing his fairly adequate method by another that was no better.

I am not sure why the rational reconstructionists cling so defensively to their one basic set of models. It is a very good set, but that is not sufficient reason. The explanation is probably historical, having to do with some not-yet-discarded aspect of the original logical empiricist program. In any case, I hope that alternative models will soon begin to be explored.

Here Kaplan's work (1964) is especially important because he has put his finger on the alternative models: the pattern model of explanation and the concatenated model of the structure of scientific theory. The proper task of the reconstructionists, in addition to refining their existing models, should be to begin working out the logical characteristics of these two new models. They are well equipped for such a task, whereas the philosophical participant observer with his dialectical way of thinking is not likely to be very good at the required formalization.

23

The Typological Method

Some examples of the typological method of studying the social sciences are Briefs, 1960; Schwab, 1960; and Sacksteder, 1963a, 1963b. It has also been applied to the study of philosophical method by Pepper (1942), McKeon (1951, 1952), Stallknecht and Brumbaugh (1954), Sacksteder (1964), and Crimmel (ms.). A more detailed and systematic account will be provided by McKeon's forthcoming Carus lectures.

The investigator begins with a tentative typology of possible methods, which he inherits from previous work. Then he selects a social scientist for study and reads one or more of his major works. During the reading he runs through his typological check list of choice points for any method and tries to see which choices were made at each point in the work he is reading; he can then classify the work as an example of a specific type of method. Choice points include such decisions as what constitutes a unit of evidence (isolatable data or whole contexts), what constitutes a unit of meaning that explains or summarizes the evidence (a law, a model, or a case history), and what sort of relation exists between evidence and meaning (Sacksteder, 1963b, pp. 415-416). A scientist might choose one of four possible logics for manipulating his concepts: dialectical logic, an Aristotelian logic of essence and accident, formal logic, and informal logic (Crimmel, manuscript). In theory construction, the scientist might choose either to locate the least parts of his subject matter, for example, a conditioned reflex, and to built more complex explanations out of these units; or he might work out a series of partial approximations of an indescribably complex reality; or he might concentrate on solving specific middle-range problems (McKeon, Carus lectures).

Once the investigator knows the scientist's choices among these alternatives, he is in a position to interpret the scientist's work properly. The methodological choices determine in a general way the selection and perception of problems, the techniques available for solving them, and the range of acceptable solutions. The details of the work develop in accordance with these basic constraints; they represent the working out of the choices on a given subject matter.

Over the years, the basic typology is altered as the investigator and his colleagues examine more and more cases. The purpose of the typology is to distinguish methods that are different and to group methods that are the same in spite of superficial differences, so as the number of cases increases, the typology becomes more complex. Originally, I am told, McKeon's typology consisted of two types, Platonists and Aristotelians; later this was expanded to three, then to 3 × 2 and 3 × 3, then eventually to 4 × 4, and in the Carus lectures I believe there are 4 × 4 × 4, or 64 methods now available. Schwab (1960) locates five choice points with 5, 4, 2, 2, and 3 alternatives, for a total of 240 possible methods. Sacksteder (1963b, p. 418) recklessly speculates that there may be 2^9, or 512 possible methods, which in practice reduce to four main methods. Each of these classifications has some logical basis that makes it an exhaustive classification of all possible methods.

The purpose of the typology, and of the whole typological method, is first to facilitate an understanding of a scientist or philosopher by enabling one to read him from his own point of view. Second, one can pick a particular method and use it consistently, thereby avoiding the methodological confusion that would result from mixing methods or from being misled by people who use different methods. In short, the typology should enable a scientist to see more clearly what he is doing, to do it more efficiently, and to understand other scientists better.

The typological method is plainly quite similar to the participant-observer method. Classification and comparison are an essential part of participant observation, while in the typological method the detailed study of particular cases is essential to the improvement of the basic classification. Also both methods take the inside point of view in one way or another. The difference is that participant observers use real types, empirically derived, while typologists use formalist ideal types.

Real types are an attempt to describe in simplified form the classifications that social scientists themselves make in their interactions with one another. Close and continuous cooperation indicates that a method is being shared somehow; inconclusive polemics and disdainful avoidance point to differences. A more detailed study of interaction patterns and of attitudes produces complications of the basic picture, as one finds subcommunities, liaison groups, travelers, and all sorts of borrowing across boundaries. These patterns point to variants and changes of method that must somehow be included in the basic typology and that may lead to extensive changes in the original classification scheme.

Formalist ideal types are discovered by a formalist type of induction, in which empirical cases remind one of logical distinctions that one already knew about. These distinctions are then collected and organized into a typology, which can be illustrated by typical empirical cases. The purpose of the preliminary empirical investigation, the induction, is to guarantee the relevance of the typology one is constructing, but the basic process of construction is logical. That is, one takes the distinctions that have appeared in the cases and combines them into a set of idealized methods, each consistent, complete, and adequate. None of these ideal methods may be perfectly exemplified empirically, but one may find approximations to them. This kind of typology is always clear and regular, while the empirically constructed real types tend to be uneven and incomplete, with variations and exceptions pinned to them in unexpected places and with patches and seams from corrections of earlier versions still visible. Formalist induction is rather similar to the process I have discussed in chapter 4, describing experimental work with mathematical models.

One can also apparently skip the induction, as Sacksteder (1963a, 1963b) seems to do, and construct the typology by enumerating the a priori possibilities.

Another difference between the typological and the participant-observer method is that the former is nonhistorical. Typologists believe that the several methods were never invented; they have always existed as logical possibilities and were as fully available in Plato's and Aristotle's day as in our own. The history of science and of philosophy is cyclical, an endless sequence of the same methods, though not necessarily following in the same order in each era. There may be fashions in methods, with some lying unused for many years, or there may be rapid sequences and coexistences of many different methods.

Nor have I come across any allowance for individual development in the various typological accounts. One gets a picture of the great thinker, an Aristotle or a Keynes, beginning his lifework with his method clearly worked out and ending it without having made a single change. What the typologist would do with Franz Boas, Herbert Simon, Alvin Gouldner, or George Homans I do not know; but if he would deny the historical development of method in the work of these people he would be missing something important.

The typologist's response to the differences I have pointed out is to produce a typology of approaches to method in which both he and I are assigned their respective positions. He can always smother a disagreement by producing a classification which distinguishes the two positions. Thus I understand that in McKeon's Carus lectures there is a metatypology of possible approaches to method, and one of the possibilities listed there is historicism. My method occupies one cell in the metatypology, and McKeon's method occupies the neighboring cell. We are fellow-monks in the same monastery. No marriage is permitted in this monastery; that is, no process of conflict and cooperation between opposed methods is permitted, since that would lead to the development of method and thereby to history.

Other differences are that the typological method is applied to individuals rather than to a community, and it is applied only to written texts rather than to the total culture of a community of scientists. All these differences may be due to the fact that the typological method was originally invented with a view to understanding the great philosophers of the past, and it may well be modified as it comes to be applied to contemporary social scientists. The work of the great philosophers is completed and so has a spurious appearance of timelessness, like a polished statue, as Plato would say; the work of the social scientists is alive and growing, so no static set of types can capture it. And indeed when I consider Briefs' work (1960), which of all the examples cited has been the most useful to me, I find that all the modifications I would wish to see have already occurred. Briefs considers schools of economists rather than individuals: the institutionalists, the marginalists, the econometricians, and the "mathematical" economists. Nor does he limit his evidence to published work; he participated in discussions, watched work in progress, and consulted informants. There is even some recognition that methods develop over time, as Briefs suggests that the mathematical economists are gradually separating themselves from the econometricians as their own method develops. The irregularity and patchwork characteristic of a set of real types are also present; the title of Briefs' book promises three methods, but the body of the work presents nearly four. I find very little firm difference between Briefs' conclusions and mine, and if his work represents a future line of development for the typological method it may well become indistinguishable from participant observation.

There is, however, one important substantive difference between Briefs' conclusions and mine. I have, in Part I, of the present work, treated his "method of isolation" as a variant of his "mathematical" method rather than as a separate method. This variant is characterized first by the use of partial or *ceteris paribus* rather than total models; second, by an application of a model to a relatively specific empirical or logical problem without considering other possible applications; and third, by a relative preference for simple mathematics or even English in written exposition. A somewhat similar variant exists within the experimental method. I classify the "method of isolation" as a variant because both "method of isolation" and "mathematical" economists use the same models, borrowing freely from one another; both use the same concepts and the same logic or mode of thinking, and both use similar procedures in developing and improving a model; because a preference for English over mathematical exposition is more a question of rhetoric than of the economist's own thinking; and because there has been a continuous shift toward the "mathematical" in recent decades.

For example, Boulding's *Conflict and Defense* (1962) would count as a "method of isolation" case by all of Briefs' criteria. Yet Boulding uses game models and other models developed by "mathematical" thinkers, and his own mathematical thinking shows through the verbal exposition and appears clearly in the footnotes. He does distinguish economic problems from other types, but applies the same models to economic and noneconomic problems. Finally, "mathematical" thinkers have had no difficulty understanding and discussing this work, just as Boulding has had no difficulty understanding and using their work.

Briefs' reply would probably be as follows (cf. Briefs, 1960, p. 92): It is true that "mathematical" and "method of isolation" economists use one another's models freely; but as you yourself have recognized, such borrowing across methods occurs all over the social sciences. Each borrowing from a different method produces its characteristic distortions, and this particular kind is no exception. For example, Boulding does borrow various mathematical models, but when a model is inadequate for the empirical problem he is discussing he discards the model and uses some other tactic.

Actually, Briefs' account of the method of isolation serves to point to a blind spot in my own work. I have taken two standpoints in the foregoing pages, the formal, or "mathematical" in Briefs' classification, and the holistic, since two standpoints are the minimum necessary for even a partial understanding of anything complex. But this particular binocular approach has the defect of making the method of isolation invisible, supposing that there is such a thing. From a formal standpoint, the isolation people are simply implicit formal theorists, inadequately mathematical and therefore insufficiently rigorous theoretically. From a holist standpoint, the isolation people are not empirical enough; their seemingly empirical statements conceal an abstract mathematical model that narrows and rigidifies their thinking and prevents them from actually seeing the case they are studying. I even find to my chagrin that my rejection of certain marginalists as propagandists for capitalist imperialism is a standard holist attitude: Briefs says, " 'Method of Isolation' hypotheses seem narrow, abstract, unempirical, and in general, appear to confuse a particular political ideology with scientific economics" (1960, p. 88). Briefs' ability to take the "method of isolation" standpoint thus reveals a possible deficiency in my account of scientific methods. His description of the method makes it possible to investigate empirically whether it is an independent method or just a variant, a question about which I am still skeptical. And of course it could be an independent method in his formal classification and a variant in my empirical classification.

24

The Method
of Conceptual Analysis

The method of conceptual analysis is an outgrowth of Wittgenstein's study of how language conditions thought and how philosophers make mistakes when they used words in contexts for which they were not originally designed. Examples include Winch (1958), Peters (1960), Taylor (1964), and Anderson (1964).

The method may be described most directly as a way of doing the social scientists' conceptual work for them..Winch in particular has asserted that the social sciences are really a branch of philosophy and that philosophers are the true social scientists (1958, pp. 42-43). As the method is gradually applied throughout the social sciences, one subject matter after another is marked off and specialized in by various philosophers. Philosophical psychology is the main area investigated so far, but one also hears of philosophical anthropology and of course philosophical linguistics, and presumably philosophical sociology and economics will follow shortly. In the discussion below I shall confine myself to philosophical psychology, since that is the most developed field at present.

The method is basically very simple. The investigator picks a psychological concept, such as intention, motive, action, pleasure, dreaming and waking, and analyzes it by seeing how it is used in ordinary conversation. This includes seeing what other concepts it combines with in a sentence, what sorts of questions one can ask about it, what sorts of answers would be appropriate, and conversely what sorts of sentences, questions, and answers would be odd, pointless, puzzling, or senseless. This procedure is called "discovering the logic of the concept." To distinguish this sense of the word *logic* from that used by the rational reconstructionists, it is called *informal logic*.

The analysis of any particular concept is an endless process, since any interesting concept can be used (and misused) in an infinite number of sentences, so there are always new sentences remaining to be examined. It is

316

always possible that one of them will disclose an unsuspected wrinkle in the concept, a new kind of use. Nevertheless, one can be reasonably sure of the logic of a concept after several years of intensive study by many philosophers. Some concepts, including "good" and "intention," are pretty well cleared up now, and others, such as "motive" and "reason," should follow shortly.

The logic of a concept consists of the various kinds of uses to which it can properly be put in ordinary conversation, plus its misuses. A concept such as "good," for instance, turns out to have a bewildering variety of uses and misuses, each of which must be sorted out and classified. Two concepts can be compared by comparing their respective logical profiles; for example, philosophers nowadays are busily comparing the profiles of "cause," "motive," and "reason." Such a study clarifies the extent to which reason-type and motive-type words can be used in cause-type sentences, or in other words, the senses in which reasons and motives can act as causes.

Presumably the ultimate use of philosophical psychology would be to straighten out the concepts of scientific psychologists and help them avoid conceptual confusion. For example, scientific psychologists may mistakenly think of behavior as movement in space, although it actually consists of following a rule, or they may think of action as caused when it is really motivated, or they may suppose that computers can think, when actually they are only machines.

I believe that this method as it is currently practiced has no relevance for the social sciences at all. It is a perfect example of the ethnocentrism I discussed earlier. Its practitioners make the basic mistake of supposing that scientific language is the same as ordinary language, and that the culture of social scientists is the same as the culture of those philosophers whose stock in trade is ordinary language. Hempel has written an appropriate epitaph for the method (1965, pp. 485-486); Plato has also commented on it, in the *Protagoras*.

But all sorts of things happen in this world, and it is possible that some of these modern descendants of Prodicus may learn something about the social sciences and make themselves useful. One possibility is that conceptual analysis can be a source of hypotheses for use in constructing models and designing experiments. This has in fact already happened; see Sayre, 1965. Sayre argues that the computer models of pattern recognition have all along been based on an erroneous conception of what recognition is, and this error has been responsible for the failure of the models in recognizing handwriting. The models have treated recognition as a process of matching an input with a set of master patterns stored in memory until a match (to a criterion) is found. Sayre does a conceptual analysis and argues that the process should be reversed; in recognition we actively generate a series of patterns and try to match these to the activity producing the input. Sayre's ideas parallel those of Halle and Stevens, 1962, where this type of recognition is called "analysis by synthesis." Sayre's hypothesis can now be tested in revised recognition models. Another possibility is that a conceptual analyst could actually study the social sciences after he has made his distinctions and clarifications, to see whether they are relevant. For example, after Brown (1963) found nine uses of the term "explain" in ordinary language, he tried to see which of these uses were also current in the social sciences, and found seven. The danger of this approach is that the philosopher may confine his efforts to looking for illustrations of his a priori categories and distinctions, instead of trying to see whether the distinctions are appropriate and relevant to actual problems. I have no objection to the clarification of concepts, but most of the "conceptual clarification" these people have provided, such as their discussion of whether computers can think, has no relevance to the problems of social scientists. Here again there are exceptions, such as the work of Sayre (1965) and Mischel (1964, 1966).

It may be objected that conceptual analysts have made an important contribution by bringing out the importance of subjective elements in understanding behavior. They have shown that people follow rules, carry out intentions, and give reasons for their actions. However, these things have been known by social scientists for many years, certainly since the development of marginal utility theory a century ago. Nearly all the important pioneers —Durkheim, Freud, Weber, G.H. Mead, Thomas, Veblen, etc.—have made subjective elements central in their theoretical and empirical work, and their successors have come to take the importance of subjective elements for granted. That issue was settled long ago. The rediscovery of rules by people like Winch is good news but hardly represents an advance in social science methodology. What is needed is further investigation of the various ways currently used to study subjective elements and to relate them to more objective determinants of behavior. We need to study the strengths, weaknesses, and prospects for improvement of methods currently in use, and the cooperation of conceptual analysts in this enterprise would be welcome, if unexpected.

Wittgenstein's influence is also cited as one source of still another method, the hermeneutic (Habermas, 1967) or hermeneutic-dialectic (Radnitzky, 1969) method. From what little I have read about this method, the present work is thoroughly hermeneutic in intent. This indicates that my account of the method of conceptual analysis, which also derives from Wittgenstein and must be somehow implicitly or potentially hermeneutic, is erroneous and needs revision.

25

Science, Philosophy, and Astrology

Is Astrology Scientific?

The philosophers of science with whom I have occasionally discussed my ideas have usually disagreed with these ideas. In particular, my suggestion that one could find standards for scientific method implicit in the actual practices of scientists has been unacceptable to listeners. They have insisted that one must know in advance what is to count as good science, lest one be led astray unwittingly by some pseudo-science and gradually lose all bearings. People do all sorts of things nowadays; how is one to know which of these things are science unless one already has some criterion or definition of scientific method? My absorption in current practices and willingness to accept and study what was actually happening has been a source of surprise, shock, and dismay to such listeners. More than once as I talked I have noticed a look of amazement and apprehension spreading over a listener's face; then as he found to his horror that I could even accept psychoanalytic theory as scientific he would say to himself, "This man has no standards *at all*. He will accept *anything.*" Then he would ask me, "What about astrology? Astrologers also claim to have a scientific method of their own. Could you study this method, look for its implicit norms, and come up with standards for good scientific astrology?"

To this question I have always replied that I do not know anything about astrology and so have no opinion on whether or not it is scientific. This answer is partly facetious, and it is possible to give a more thorough answer. I do have a working definition of science which I have used all along to determine what is to count as science. The definition, however, is an empirical one. A method is scientific if it is used by members of the scientific community. The criterion of membership is the empirical one of regular, effective collaboration with other members. Community boundaries are marked by non-

319

interaction, misunderstanding, and polemics. In cases where interaction between two groups is partly friendly and partly hostile I have marked off subcommunity boundaries and have looked for subcultural differences to explain the partial hostilities. The partial cooperation, in turn, has indicated the existence of cultural continuities which make joint activity possible.

By the criterion of interaction and collaboration the whole of the social sciences eventually form a single community. The community is by no means homogeneous, but rather consists of a somewhat rambling, irregular network of the sort Bott (1957) finds in large cities. Within this network there are clusters of intensive interaction linked by looser and weaker interactions, but no sharp and absolute divisions. The collaboration boundary around the social science is somewhat sharper, perhaps sharp enough to justify treating the social sciences as a single community. However, even here one finds it impossible to draw a sharp collaboration boundary between social and natural sciences. Social and natural scientists collaborate actively in the areas of physiological psychology, ecology, epidemiology, ethology, urban geography, and electrical engineering. In each case collaboration is made possible because both social and natural scientists share the same method. Thus ethologists use participant observation to study ape societies, ecologists use mathematical models, and physiologists use laboratory experimentation and computer modeling. Collaboration is defined as a two-way process, excluding one-way borrowing. The practitioners of dianetics, for example, who borrow various psychological ideas but give nothing in return, are not counted as scientists according to the collaboration criterion.

Are astrologers part of the social scientific community? So far as I know, they are not. I have never come across any collaboration of any sort with astrologers, through the journals, personal communication, or colloquia, though I may have missed a reference somewhere. Whether they are natural scientists I do not know.

The criterion of interaction and collaboration is supplemented in practice by more theoretical secondary criteria. The community of social scientists has developed and continues to develop a set of standards and goals which define what is to count as science for them, and the natural scientists presumably have done the same. One would expect to find sharp divergences between the standards developed by natural scientists and those developed by astrologers, and the divergences would explain lack of collaboration. For instance, if astrologers use inadequate controls and haphazard procedures or fail to search for negative instances, by current natural or social science standards, this would explain the lack of collaboration.

In Praise of Science

Astrologers may object that I have misinterpreted their claim. They do not claim to be social or natural scientists as I have defined the terms; their claim is rather to posses a different way of knowing that is the equal of the scientific way. There are a variety of ways by which man achieves knowledge; science is one way, but there is also art, philosophy, theology, mystical experience and finally astrology.

Some philosophers have urged the same objection on me. Their strongest disagreement has been with the way I have seemed to assimilate philosophic and scientific method and thereby turned philosophers into scientists. They have thought it ridiculous of me to describe my method as a variant form of participant observation, and regarded it as an insult to describe Hempel, Nagel, and Carnap as model-builders. (I regard it as high praise.) Philosophy, they say, has its own unique method of knowing, namely conceptual analysis, which has nothing to do with science but is just as good as the methods of science if not better.

To this objection I reply that the social sciences are a rather remarkable human achievement, and philosophers and astrologers would be fortunate if they could do even remotely as well. I do not wish to belittle our centuries-old philosophic heritage of great ideas, and I agree that these have been essential to the development of science and are still valuable. But if one wishes to speak of truth, the goal of science, that is a different matter. Over the last century or so we have come to realize that truth is a much more difficult thing to achieve than was earlier supposed, and our critical standards have risen accordingly. The difficulties that have been discovered may be summed up under three heads, associated with the names Freud, Marx, and Durkheim. They are the difficulties of unconscious personality bias, class bias, and cultural bias. The remarkable thing about the social sciences is that they are able in some measure to overcome all these difficulties, while philosophers, I am afraid, rarely even recognize them.

It is not at all easy to discuss these three forms of bias, because one's biases appear even in the manner of discussing them. If one's biases lead him to deny the existences of one or another bias in himself, if would be inconsistent of me to try to use rational argument to show that neither I nor my audience was rational. Accordingly, I shall limit myself to a few tentative, and certainly biased, suggestions, which are intended to appeal only to those who already agree with them.

The social sciences deal with the problem of individual bias in three ways. First, science is a cooperative enterprise, not an individual achievement. The variety of methods and of tasks within each method provides a place for all kinds of personalities. Thus each person's unconscious drives provide energy for his particular scientific task, and the great variety of drives more or less, sooner or later, supplement and check one another. Second, all science is ultimately empirical; it does not entirely depend on analysis and speculation, even cooperative speculation. It uses observation which is controlled in some way for observer bias and sharpened by a great variety of specialized techniques and instruments. Controlled observation does not completely eliminate bias, but provides some objective checks on the subconscious determinants of perception and thought. Third, reasoning is partly assisted by the use of mathematics and computers, so the endless mistakes of human reasoning can in part be overcome. I do not claim that these measures provide a complete solution to the problem of unconscious bias or that they work at all rapidly; but they do provide a partial solution that would be difficult to improve on or even approximate by any nonscientific method. They make truth a possession of the scientific community with its continually developing instruments of observation and reasoning, rather than of individuals with their unconscious biases.

The problem of class bias is more difficult to deal with. Mannheim's suggestion is that insofar as social scientists are drawn from different classes and insofar as they can achieve a partial autonomy from their class background and a tolerant appreciation of other viewpoints, the various class-bound viewpoints can supplement and counteract one another somewhat. Mannheim's ideas were developed in the more optimistic period of the twenties, and one may question whether they can be taken seriously today. The question is not one of the class origin of social scientists but of their occupational experience and the financial and institutional control of their activities; and one could argue that American social science has by now been thoroughly corrupted and interwoven into the institutional structure of capitalism, imperialism, and militarism. Social scientists, it may be argued, are increasingly becoming businessmen whose stock in trade is ideas and techniques; they get their stock by appropriating ideas and techniques from the scientific community that has produced them, turning public into private property; and they sell themselves to the highest bidder, which is usually government or industry. Their occupational experience is hierarchical and authoritarian, and their reference group includes political, business, and military leaders. Consequently the products of social science serve to consolidate and justify military-industrial domination at home and abroad. Idealized pictures of American society are produced and disseminated, showing how our progressive democracy can solve its few remaining problems by liberal reforms—civil rights laws, anti-trust laws, poverty programs, financial aid to cities or farmers, industrial development programs. Techniques are developed for more efficient use and control of manpower and resources at home and abroad, and for soothing and retraining dissatisfied groups. And, worst of all, justifications are provided for the aggressive foreign policy that culminated in the war crimes in Indochina.

But it seems to me that this argument exaggerates. One can find strong capitalist-militarist elements of various sorts in American social science, but there are also anti-capitalist and anti-militarist tendencies as well as neutral elements. Moreover, these various elements can still cooperate on common scientific problems despite ideological differences. For example the anti-militarist Rapoport may be correct in asserting that a dialogue between him and exponents of the "strategic" mode of thought is impossible (Rapoport, 1964b, ch. 16); yet he can still cooperate with strategic thinkers in developing mathematical models of conflict and cooperation. This is more or less what Mannheim meant by the partial autonomy of science. Whether this condition can be maintained as capitalist military-industrial domination becomes more complete and more repressive I cannot predict. It may be that a rotten society gradually produces a rotten social science; or it may yet be possible to retain some autonomy and integrity.

The present work has intentionally avoided dealing with the various influences of society on science, not in the belief that there are no such influences, but in the hope that one can still treat the social sciences as partially autonomous without too much distortion. A more balanced picture must, however, include a description of the social influences.

The problem of cultural bias is also a difficult one. To some extent the social sciences have transcended the ethnocentric predicament by their extensive traditions of cross-cultural research, though cross-cultural sensitivity is still inadequately diffused. In addition one can see the beginnings of a partly autonomous culture of science, drawing its members from all over the world and thus incorporating elements from a variety of cultures. When Japanese, Malayan, Indian, and American scientists can cooperate in a comparative study of some effects of industrialization, or when political scientists from a variety of different countries can cooperate in setting up international data banks, the problem of cultural bias is beginning to come under control. Some of this cross-cultural cooperation appears on closer examination to be a form of American cultural imperialism tied into American Cold War strategy, but again I do not think this is the whole story.

The above suggestions will not impress those philosophers who deny the existence of uncontrollable bias in themselves. They may admit that some people are irrational, but their recommended solution is likely to be that of Russell: Be more rational, like me. For these philosophers the foregoing remarks serve only as a partial rationalization for my choice of the method used in this book. I have hoped, by joining the cooperative, empirically controlled enterprise of science, to subject my own biases to some measure of eventual control.

References

Abelson, Robert, and M. Rosenberg. 1958. "Symbolic psycho-logic," *Behavioral Science,* 3:1-13.

———. 1963. "Computer simulation of 'hot' cognition," in Tomkins and Messick, eds., *Computer Simulation of Personality.* New York: Wiley.

Aberle, David. 1961. "Matrilineal descent in cross-cultural perspective," in D. Schneider and K. Gough, eds., *Matrilineal Kinship.* Berkeley: University of California Press.

Aberle, David, et al. 1950. "The functional prerequisites of a society," *Ethics,* 60:100-111.

Adams, Ernest. 1960. "Survey of Bernoullian utility theory," in H. Solomon, ed., *Mathematical Thinking in the Measurement of Behavior.* Glencoe: Free Press.

Adorno, T. W., et al. 1950. *The Authoritarian Personality.* New York: Harper.

Ake, Claude. 1967. *A Theory of Political Integration.* Homewood: Dorsey.

Alker, Hayward. 1965. *Mathematics and Politics.* New York: Macmillan.

Allen, R.G.D. 1938. *Mathematical Analysis For Economists.* New York: Macmillan.

Almond, Gabriel, and J. S. Coleman, eds. 1960. *The Politics of Developing Areas.* Princeton: Princeton University Press.

Almond, Gabriel, and S. Verba. 1963. *The Civic Culture.* Princeton: Princeton University Press.

Anderson, Alan, ed. 1964. *Minds and Machines.* Englewood Cliffs: Prentice-Hall.

Apter, D. 1965. *The Politics of Modernization.* Chicago: University of Chicago Press.

Archibald, K., ed. 1966. *Strategic Interaction and Conflict.* Berkeley, Calif.: Institute of International Studies.

Arlow, Jacob. 1959. "Psychoanalysis as scientific method," in S. Hook, ed., *Psychoanalysis, Scientific Method, and Philosophy.* New York: N. Y. U. Press.

Arrow, Kenneth. 1951. *Social Choice and Individual Values.* New York: Wiley.

Ashby, W. Ross. 1956. *Introduction to Cybernetics.* New York: Wiley.

Balandier, G. 1966. "The colonial situation," in E. Wallerstein, ed., *The Colonial Situation.* New York: Wiley.

Balderston, F.E., and Austin C. Hoggatt. 1963. "Simulation models: analytic variety and the problem of model reduction," in Hoggatt and Balderston, eds.,

Symposium on Simulation Models. Cincinnati: Southwestern Publishing Co.

Bales, R.F. 1950. *Interaction Process Analysis.* Cambridge: Addison Wesley.

————— . 1953. "The equilibrium problem in small groups," in Parsons, Bales, and Shils, *Working Papers in the Theory of Action.* New York: Free Press.

Bales, R.F., A. Couch, and P. Stone. 1962. "The interaction simulator," in *Proceedings of a Harvard Symposium on Digital Computers and Their Applications,* Cambridge: Harvard University Press.

Bandura, Albert. 1961. "Psychotherapy as a learning process," *Psychological Bulletin,* 58:143-159.

Banfield, Edward. 1961. *Political Influence.* New York: Free Press.

Banks, Arthur S., and Robert Textor. 1963. *A Cross-Polity Survey.* Cambridge: M. I. T. Press.

Banton, Michael, ed. 1965. *The Relevance of Models for Social Anthropology.* New York: Praeger.

Baruch, Dorothy W. 1952. *One Little Boy.* New York: Julian Press.

Bateson, Gregory. 1936. *Naven.* Stanford: Stanford University Press.

Beattie, John. 1965. *Understanding an African Kingdom: Bunyoro.* New York: Holt, Rinehart, and Winston.

————— . 1968 (1959). "Understanding and explanation in social anthropology," in R. Manners and D. Kaplan, eds., *Theory in Anthropology.* Chicago: Aldine Publishing Co.

Becker, Howard S., and Blanche Geer. 1960. "Participant observation," in Richard Adams and J. Preiss, eds., *Human Organization Research.* Homewood, Illinois: Dorsey.

Becker, Howard S., et al. 1961. *Boys in White.* Chicago: University of Chicago Press.

Bendix, Reinhard. 1963. "Concepts and generalizations in comparative sociological studies," *American Sociological Review,* 28:532-539.

Benedict, Ruth. 1934. *Patterns of Culture.* Boston: Houghton, Mifflin.

Bernard, Jessie. 1945. "Observation and generalization in cultural anthropology," *American Journal of Sociology,* 50:284-291. Reprinted in R. Manners and D. Kaplan, eds., *Theory in Anthropology.* Chicago: Aldine.

Bettelheim, Bruno. 1950. *Love is Not Enough.* Glencoe: Free Press.

————— . 1955. *Truants From Life.* Glencoe: Free Press.

Binder, Leonard. 1961. *Iran.* Berkeley: University of California.

Black, Max, ed. 1961. *The Social Theories of Talcott Parsons.* Englewood Cliffs: Prentice-Hall.

Blau, Peter. 1964. "The research process in the study of the dynamics of bureaucracy," in Phillip Hammond, ed., *Sociologists at Work.* New York: Basic Books.

Blumer, Herbert. 1956. "Sociological analysis and the 'variable'," *American Sociological Review,* 21:683-690.

Borch, Karl. 1968. *The Economics of Uncertainty.* Princeton: Princeton University Press.

Bott, Elizabeth. 1957. *Family and Social Network.* London: Tavistock.

Boulding, Kenneth. 1953. *The Organizational Revolution.* New York: Harper.

————— . 1962. *Conflict and Defense.* New York: Harper Torchbooks.

Briefs, Henry. 1960. *Three Views of Method in Economics.* Washington, D. C.: Georgetown University Press.

Brodbeck, May. 1959. "Models, meaning, and theories," in L. Gross, ed., *Symposium on Sociological Theory.* Evanston: Row, Peterson.

Brody, Richard. 1963. "Some systemic effects of the spread of nuclear weapons technology: a study through simulation," *Journal of Conflict Resolution,* 7:665-753.

Bronson, Gordon. 1965. "The hierarchical organization of the central nervous system: implications for learning processes," *Behavioral Science,* 10:7-25.

Brown, Robert. 1963. *Explanation in Social Science*. Chicago: Aldine.

Brownell, Baker. 1950. *The Human Community*. New York: Harper.

Bruyn, Severyn. 1966. *The Human Perspective in Sociology*. Englewood Cliffs: Prentice-Hall.

Buck, R. C. 1956. "On the logic of general behavior systems theory," in H. Feigl and M. Scriven, eds., *Foundations of Science and the Concepts of Psychology and Psychoanalysis*. Minneapolis: University of Minnesota Press.

Bunzel, Ruth. 1929. *The Pueblo Potter*. Columbia University Contributions to Anthropology. VIII. New York: Columbia University Press.

Bush, Robert R., and F. Mosteller. 1955. *Stochastic Models for Learning*. New York: Wiley.

————. 1960. "Survey of mathematical learning theory," in R. D. Luce, ed., *Developments in Mathematical Psychology*. Glencoe: Free Press.

Byers, N.F. 1959. "Economic, logical, and mathematical systems," *Social Research*, 26:379-402.

Caplow, T. 1956. "A theory of coalitions in the triad," *American Sociological Review*, 21:489-493.

————. 1959. "Further development of a theory of coalitions in the triad," *American Journal of Sociology*, 64:488-493.

Catton, William. 1965. "The concept of 'mass' in the sociological version of gravitation," in Fred Massarik and P. Ratoosh, eds., *Mathematical Explorations in Behavioral Science*. Homewood: Irwin-Dorsey.

Christie, Richard. 1956. "Eysenck's treatment of the personality of Communists," reply by Eysenck and rejoinder by Christie, *Psychological Bulletin*, 53:411-451.

Churchman, C. W. 1957. *Introduction to Operations Research*. New York: Wiley.

————. 1963. "An analysis of the concept of simulation," in Hoggatt and Balderston, eds., *Symposium on Simulation Models*. Cincinnati: Southwestern Publishing Co.

Clark, Kenneth. 1965. *Dark Ghetto*. New York: Harper.

Cohen, Bernard P. 1963. *Conflict and Conformity*. Cambridge: M.I.T. Press.

Cohen, Kalman. 1960. *Computer Models of the Shoe, Leather, and Hide Sequence*. Englewood Cliffs: Prentice-Hall.

Cohen, Kalman, and Richard Cyert. 1961. "Computer models in dynamic economics," *Quarterly Journal of Economics*, 75:112-127.

————. 1965. *Theory of the Firm*. Englewood Cliffs: Prentice-Hall.

Cohen, Ronald. 1964. "Conflict and change in a Northern Nigerian Emirate," in George Zollschan and Walter Hirsch, eds., *Explorations in Social Change*. Boston: Houghton Mifflin.

————. 1970. Review of Swartz, *Local-Level Politics*. *American Anthropologist*, 72:112-115.

Coleman, James S. 1960. "The mathematical study of small groups," in H. Solomon, ed., *Mathematical Thinking in the Measurement of Behavior*. Glencoe: Free Press.

————. 1964. *Introduction to Mathematical Sociology*. New York: Free Press.

Colson, Elizabeth. 1954. "The intensive study of small sample communities," in Robert Spencer, ed., *Method and Perspective in Anthropology*. Minneapolis: University of Minnesota Press. Reprinted in Epstein, 1967.

Colvard, Richard. 1967. "Interaction and identification in reporting field research," in G. Sjoberg, ed., *Ethics, Politics, and Social Research*. Cambridge: Schenkman.

Coser, Louis. 1955. *The Functions of Social Conflict*. Glencoe: Free Press.

Crimmel, W. Manuscript. *An Introduction to Logics*.

Cronbach, Lee, and Paul Meehl. 1955. "Construct validity in psychological tests," *Psychological Bulletin*, 52:281-302.

Cross, John. 1965. "A theory of the bargaining process," *American Economic Review,* 55:67-94.

Crossman, Richard, ed. 1950. *The God That Failed.* New York: Harper (Bantam paperback edition).

Cyert, Richard, and E. Grunberg. 1963. "Assumption, Prediction, and Explanation in Economics," in Cyert and March, eds., *A Behavioral Theory of the Firm.* Englewood Cliffs: Prentice-Hall.

Cyert, Richard, and J. March. 1963. *A Behavioral Theory of the Firm.* Englewood Cliffs: Prentice-Hall.

Dahl, Robert. 1963. *Modern Political Analysis.* Englewood Cliffs: Prentice-Hall.

Dalton, Melville. 1959. *Men Who Manage.* New York: Wiley.

————. 1964. "Preconceptions and methods in *Men Who Manage,*" in Phillip Hammond, ed., *Sociologists at Work.* New York: Basic Books.

Davis, Kingsley. 1967 (1959). "The myth of functional analysis," reprinted in N. J. Demerath and W. A. Peterson, eds., *System, Change, and Conflict.* New York: Free Press.

Davis, Otto, 1969. Notes on strategy and methodology for a scientific political science. in Joseph Bernd, ed., *Mathematical Applications in Political Science, IV.* Charlottesville, U. P. of Virginia.

Deutsch, Morton. 1949. "A theory of cooperation and competition," *Human Relations,* 2:129-151.

————. 1962. "Cooperation and trust: some theoretical notes," in *Nebraska Symposium on Motivation,* pp. 275-319. Lincoln: University of Nebraska.

————. 1965. "Some psychological aspects of social interaction," in B. Wolman, ed., *Scientific Psychology.* New York: Basic Books.

————. 1966. "Rejoinder to Kelley's comments," in K. Archibald, ed., *Strategic Interaction and Conflict,* pp. 44-48. Berkeley: Institute of International Studies.

Deutsch, Morton, and R. Krauss. 1962. "Studies of interpersonal bargaining," *Conflict Resolution,* 6:52-76.

Diesing, Paul. 1967. "National self-determination and U. S. foreign policy," *Ethics,* 77:85-94.

Downs, Anthony. 1957. *An Economic Theory of Democracy.* New York: Harper & Row.

Dozier, Edward. 1954. *The Hopi-Tewa of Arizona.* Berkeley: University of California Press.

Easton, David. 1965. *A Systems Analysis of Political Life.* New York: Wiley.

Edwards, Ward. 1961. "Probability learning in 1000 trials," *Journal of Experimental Psychology,* 62:385-394.

Eggan, Fred, ed. 1937. *Social Anthropology of North American Tribes.* Chicago: University of Chicago Press.

————. 1954. "Social anthropology and the method of controlled comparison," *American Anthropologist,* 56:743-763.

Eisenstadt, S. N. 1958. "The study of Oriental despotisms as systems of total power," *Journal of Asian Studies,* 17:435-446.

————. 1961. "Anthropological studies of complex societies," *Current Anthropology,* 2:201-210.

————. 1963. *The Political Systems of Empires.* New York: Free Press.

————. 1964. "Processes of change and institutionalization of the political systems of centralized empires," in George Zollschan and Walter Hirsh, eds., *Explorations in Social Change.* Boston: Houghton Mifflin.

Elkin, A. P. 1953. "Murngin kinship re-examined," *American Anthropologist,* 55:412-419.

Epstein, A. L., ed. 1967. *The Craft of Social Anthropology.* New York: Barnes and Noble.

Erikson, Erik. 1950. *Childhood and Society*. New York: Norton.

————. 1959a. "The nature of clinical evidence," in Dan Lerner, ed., *Evidence and Inference*. Glencoe: Free Press. Revised in Erikson, 1964, ch. 2.

————. 1959b. "Identity and the life cycle," (selected papers), in George S. Klein, ed., *Psychological Issues*. New York: International Universities Press.

————. 1964. *Insight and Responsibility*. New York: Norton.

————. 1966. "The concept of identity in race relations," *Daedalus*, 95 no. 1:145-171.

————. 1968. *Identity, Youth and Crisis*. New York: Norton.

Estes, W. K., and J. H. Straughan. 1954. "Analysis of a verbal conditioning situation in terms of statistical learning theory," *Journal of Experimental Psychology*, 47:225-234.

————. 1959. "The statistical approach to learning theory," in Sigmund Koch, ed., *Psychology*, vol. 2, pp. 380-491. New York: McGraw-Hill.

Etzioni, Amitai. 1961. *A Comparative Analysis of Complex Organizations*. New York: Free Press.

————. 1968. *The Active Society*. New York: Free Press.

Evans-Pritchard, E. E. 1940. *The Nuer*. Oxford: Oxford University Press.

————. 1962a. *Essays in Social Anthropology*. London: Faber.

————. 1962b. *Social Anthropology and Other Essays*. New York: Free Press.

Eysenck, H. J. 1952. "The effects of psychotherapy: an evaluation," *Journal of Consulting Psychology*, 16:319-324.

————. 1965. "The effects of psychotherapy," *International Journal of Psychiatry*, 1:97-178.

Fallding, Harold. 1967. "The family and the idea of a cardinal role," in G. Handel, ed., *The Psychosocial Interior of the Family*. Chicago: Aldine.

Fallers, Lloyd. 1960. "The role of factionalism in Fox acculturation," in F. Gearing, et al., eds., *Documentary History of the Fox Project*. Chicago: University of Chicago.

Feibleman, James K. 1956. *The Institutions of Society*. London: Allen and Unwin.

Feigenbaum, Edward, and J. Feldman. 1963. *Computers and Thought*. New York: McGraw-Hill.

Feldman, Julian. 1962. "Computer simulation of cognitive processes," in H. Borko, ed., *Computer Applications in the Behavioral Sciences*. Englewood Cliffs: Prentice-Hall.

Feldman, Julian, Fred Tonge, and Herschel Kantor. 1963. "Empirical explorations of a hypothesis-testing model of binary choice behavior," in Hoggatt and Balderston, eds., *Symposium on Simulation Models*. Cincinnati: Southwestern Publishing Co.

Festinger, Leon, H. Riecken, and S. Schachter. 1956. *When Prophecy Fails*. Minneapolis: University of Minnesota Press.

Firth, Raymond. 1939. *Primitive Polynesian Economy*. London: Routledge.

————. 1951. *Elements of Social Organization*. London: Watts.

————. 1955. "Function," in W. Thomas, ed., *Yearbook of Anthropology*. New York: Wenner-Gren Foundation.

————. ed. 1957. *Man and Culture*. London: Routledge and Kegan Paul.

Fisher, Ronald. 1935. *The Design of Experiments*. London: Oliver and Boyd.

Forrester, Jay. 1961. *Industrial Dynamics*. Cambridge: M.I.T. Press.

Fortes, Meyer. 1949. *The Web of Kinship Among the Tallensi*. London: Oxford University Press.

Fortes, Meyer, and E. E. Evans-Pritchard, eds. 1940. *African Political Systems*. London: Oxford University Press.

Fouraker, Lawrence E., and Sidney Siegel. 1963. *Bargaining Behavior*. New York: McGraw-Hill.

Freud, Sigmund. 1925. *Collected Papers,* vol. 3. London: Hogarth.

Friedman, Milton. 1953. *Essays in Positive Economics.* Chicago: University of Chicago Press.

Fromm, Erich, 1941. *Escape From Freedom.* New York: Holt, Rinehart, and Winston.

————. 1947. *Man For Himself.* New York: Holt, Rinehart & Winston.

————. 1948. "Individual and social origins of neurosis," in Clyde Kluckhohn and H. A. Murray, eds., *Personality in Nature, Society, and Culture.* New York: Knopf.

————. 1949. "Psychoanalytic characterology and its application to the understanding of culture," in S. S. Sargent and M. W. Smith, eds., *Culture and Personality.* New York: Viking Fund.

————. 1955. *The Sane Society.* New York: Holt, Rinehart and Winston.

Gamson, W. A. 1964. "Experimental studies of coalition formation," in L. Berkowitz, ed., *Advances in Experimental Social Psychology,* 1:82-110. New York: Academic Press.

Gans, Herbert. 1967. *The Levittowners.* New York: Pantheon.

Gearing, Fred, et al., eds. 1960. *Documentary History of the Fox Project.* Chicago: Department of Anthropology, University of Chicago.

Geer, Blanche. 1964. "First days in the field," in Phillip Hammond, ed., *Sociologists at Work.* New York: Basic Books.

Geertz, C. 1967. "Ritual and social change: a Javanese example," in N. J. Demerath and W. A. Peterson, eds., *System, Change, and Conflict.* New York: Free Press.

Gladwin, Thomas, and Seymour Sarason. 1953. *Truk: Man in Paradise.* New York: Wenner-Gren Foundation.

Glaser, B., and A. Strauss. 1965. "Discovery of substantive theory: a basic strategy underlying qualitative research," *American Behavioral Scientist.* 8:5-12.

————. 1967. *The Discovery of Grounded Theory.* Chicago: Aldine.

Gluckman, Max. 1963. *Order and Rebellion in Tribal Africa,* Collected Essays. New York: Free Press.

————. 1968. "The utility of the equilibrium model in the study of social change," *American Anthropologist,* 70:219-237.

Gluckman, Max and E. Devons, eds. 1964. *Closed Systems and Open Minds.* Chicago: Aldine.

Goffman, Erving. 1962. "On cooling the mark," in A. Rose, ed., *Human Behavior and Social Processes.* Boston: Houghton Mifflin.

————. 1967. *Interaction Ritual.* Chicago: Aldine.

Goldberger, Arthur. 1959. *Impact Multipliers and Dynamic Properties of the Klein-Goldberger Model.* Amsterdam: North Holland.

Golembiewski, Robert. 1962. *The Small Group.* Chicago: University of Chicago Press.

Goodenough, Ward. 1968 (1956). "Residence rules," in R. Manners and P. Kaplan, eds., *Theory in Anthropology.* Chicago: Aldine.

Goodman, Leo. 1964. "Mathematical methods for the study of systems of groups," *American Journal of Sociology.* 70:170-192.

Gouldner, A. W. 1950. *Patterns of Industrial Bureaucracy.* Glencoe: Free Press.

————. 1954. *Wildcat Strike.* Yellow Springs, Ohio: Antioch.

————. 1959. "Reciprocity and autonomy in functional theory," in L. Gross, ed., *Symposium on Sociological Theory.* Evanston: Row, Peterson.

Grant, D. A. 1962. "Testing the null hypothesis and the strategy and tactics of investigating theoretical models," *Psychological Review,* 64:54-61.

Gray, D. J. 1962. "Sociology as a science," *American Journal of Economics and Sociology,* 21:337-346.

Greenberger, Martin. 1965. "A new methodology for computer simulation," in James

Beshers, ed., *Computer Methods in the Analysis of Large-Scale Systems*. Cambridge: M.I.T. and Harvard.

Guetzkow, Harold. 1962. "A use of simulation in the study of inter-nation relations," in Guetzkow, ed., *Simulation in Social Science*. Englewood Cliffs: Prentice-Hall.

————. 1963. *Simulation in International Relations*. Englewood Cliffs: Prentice-Hall.

Gullahorn, J. and J. 1963. "A computer model of elementary social behavior," in Feigenbaum and Feldman, eds., *Computers and Thought*. New York: McGraw-Hill.

Gusfield, Joseph. 1960. "Field work reciprocities in studying a social movement," in Richard Adams and Jack Preiss, eds., *Human Organization Research*. Homewood: Dorsey.

————. 1963. *Symbolic Crusade*. Urbana: University of Illinois Press.

————. 1967. "Tradition and modernity: misplaced polarities in the study of social change," *American Journal of Sociology*, 72:351-362.

Habermas, Jürgen. 1967. *Zur Logik der Sozialwissenschaften*. Tübingen: Mohr. Reprinted by Verlag Zerschlagt das Bürgerliche Copyright.

Haldi, J., and H. Wagner. 1963. *Simulated Economic Models*. Homewood: Irwin.

Halle, M., and K. Stevens. 1962. "Speech recognition," *IRE Transactions on Information Theory*, pp. 155-159.

Hallowell, A. I. 1955. *Culture and Experience*. Philadelphia: University of Pennsylvania Press.

Hamblin, Robert, et al. 1969. "Changing the game from 'Get the Teacher' to 'Learn'," *Trans-action*, 6:20-31.

Handel, Gerald, ed. 1967. *The Psychosocial Interior of the Family*. Chicago: Aldine.

Hanson, Norwood. 1958. *Patterns of Discovery*. Cambridge: Cambridge University Press.

————. 1963. *The Concept of the Positron*. Cambridge: Cambridge University Press.

Harris, Marvin. 1968. *The Rise of Anthropological Theory*. New York: Crowell.

Harsanyi, John. 1961. "On the rationality postulates underlying the theory of co-operative games," *Journal of Conflict Resolution*, 5:179-196.

Hartmann, Heinz. 1959. "Psychoanalysis as a scientific theory," in S. Hook, ed., *Psychoanalysis, Scientific Method, and Philosophy*. New York: N.Y.U. Press.

Hebb, D. O. 1949. *The Organization of Behavior*. New York: Wiley.

————. 1955. "Drives and the C.N.S.," *Psychological Review*, 62:243-254.

Hegel, G. 1945, originally 1821. *Philosophy of Right*, trans. by Knox. London: Oxford.

Helmer, Olaf, and Rescher, N. 1959. "On the epistemology of the inexact sciences," *Management Science*, 6:25-52.

Hempel, C. G. 1965. *Aspects of Scientific Explanation*. New York: Free Press.

Herskovits, Melville. 1948. *Man and His Works*. New York: Knopf.

Hiller, L., and R. Baker. 1962. "Computer music," in H. Borko, ed., *Computer Applications in the Behavioral Sciences*. Englewood Cliffs: Prentice-Hall.

Hirt, Michael, ed. 1962. *Rorschach Science*. New York: Free Press.

Hoggatt, A. C., and F. E. Balderston, eds. 1963. *Symposium on Simulation Models*. Cincinnati: Southwestern Publishing Co.

Holland, Edward. 1963. *Experiments on a Simulated Underdeveloped Economy*. Cambridge: M.I.T. Press.

Holmberg, Allan. 1950. *Nomads of the Long Bow*. Washington, D.C.: Smithsonian Institute of Social Anthropology.

Homans, George C. 1950. *The Human Group*. New York: Harcourt, Brace.

————. 1961. *Social Behavior:* Its Elementary Forms. New York: Harcourt Brace.

———— . 1962. *Sentiments and Activities.* New York: Free Press.

Homans, George C., and D. Schneider. 1954. *Marriage, Authority, and Final Causes.* Glencoe: Free Press.

Hook, Sidney. 1940. *Reason, Social Myths, and Democracy.* New York: Day.

———— , ed. 1959. *Psychoanalysis, Scientific Method, and Philosophy.* New York: N.Y.U. Press.

Hopkins, T., and I. Wallerstein. 1967. "The comparative study of national societies," *Social Science Information, 6/5:25-58.*

Horton, D. 1943. "The functions of alcohol in primitive societies," *Quarterly Journal of Studies in Alcohol.* Reprinted in C. S. Ford, ed., 1967. *Cross-cultural Approaches.* New Haven: HRAF Press.

Horvath, William J. 1965. "A mathematical model of participation in small group discussions," *Behavioral Science,* 10:164-166.

Huff, David. 1965. "The use of gravity models in social research," in F. Massarik and P. Ratoosh, ed., *Mathematical Explorations in Behavioral Science.* Homewood: Irwin-Dorsey.

Hughes, Charles C. 1966. "Social control among the St. Lawrence Island Eskimos," in Schwartz, Turner, and Tuden, eds., *Political Anthropology.* Chicago: Aldine.

Hull, Clark, et al. 1940. *Mathematico-deductive Theory of Rote Learning.* New Haven: Yale University Press.

———— . 1943. *Principles of Behavior.* New York: Appleton-Century.

———— . 1952. *A Behavior System.* New Haven: Yale University Press.

Hunter, Floyd. 1959. *Top Leadership USA.* Chapel Hill: University of North Carolina Press.

Hurwicz, Leonid. 1963. "Mathematics in Economics: language and instrument," in James Charlesworth, ed., *Mathematics and the Social Sciences.* Philadelphia: American Academy of Political and Social Science.

Jacob, Philip, and J. V. Toscano, eds. 1964. *The Integration of Political Communities.* Philadelphia: Lippincott.

Janowitz, Morris, and D. Segal. 1967. "Social cleavage and party affiliation," *American Journal of Sociology,* 72:601-618.

Jaques, E. 1952. *The Changing Culture of a Factory.* New York: Dryden.

Jarvie, I. C. 1964. *The Revolution in Anthropology.* London: Routledge and Kegan Paul.

Kaplan, Abraham. 1964. *The Conduct of Inquiry.* San Francisco: Chandler.

Kaplan, Bert. 1968 (1957). "Personality and social structure," in Robert Manners and D. Kaplan, eds., *Theory in Anthropology.* Chicago: Aldine.

Kaplan, Harold. 1967. *Urban Political Systems: A Functional Analysis of Metro Toronto.* New York: Columbia University Press.

Kaplan, Morton. 1957. "Balance of power, bipolarity, and other models of international systems," *American Political Science Review,* 51:684-695.

Kapp, K. W. 1961. *Toward a Science of Man in Society.* The Hague: Nijhoff.

Kardiner, Abram. 1939. *The Individual and His Society.* New York: Columbia University Press.

Kardiner, Abram, and L. Ovesey. 1951. *The Mark of Oppression.* New York: Norton.

Karsh, Bernard. 1958. *Diary of a Strike.* Urbana: University of Illinois Press.

Kelley, H. H. 1965. "Experimental studies of threats in interpersonal negotiations," *Conflict Resolution,* 9:79-105.

————. 1966. "A classroom study of the dilemmas in interpersonal negotiations," in K. Archibald, ed., *Strategic Interaction and Conflict.* Berkeley: Institute of International Studies.

Kelley, H. H., and Arrowood, A. J. 1960. "Coalitions in the triad: critique and experiments," *Sociometry,* 23:231-244.

Kelly, George A. 1955. *The Psychology of Personal Constructs.* New York: Norton.

Kelman, Herbert C. 1965. "Manipulation of human behavior: an ethical dilemma for the social scientist," *Journal of Social Issues,* XXI, 2:31-46.

Kemeny, John, J. L. Snell, and G. Thompson. 1957. *Introduction to Finite Mathematics.* Englewood Cliffs: Prentice-Hall.

Kemeny, John, and J. L. Snell. 1962. *Mathematical Models in the Social Sciences.* Boston: Ginn.

Kendall, P., and P. Lazarsfeld. 1950. "Problems of survey analysis," in R. Merton and P. Lazarsfeld, eds., *Continuities in Social Research.* Glencoe: Free Press.

Kerr, C., J. Dunlop, F. Harbison, and C. Myers. 1960. *Industrialism and Industrial Man.* Cambridge: Harvard University Press.

Keynes, John M. 1936. *General Theory of Employment, Interest, and Money.* New York: Harcourt, Brace.

Kluckhohn, Clyde. 1944. *Navaho Witchcraft.* Cambridge: Harvard University Press (Beacon Press reprint).

_____. 1949. "The Philosophy of the Navaho Indians," in F. Northrop, ed., *Ideological Differences and World Order.* New Haven: Yale University Press.

_____. 1967 (1939). "On certain recent applications of association coefficients to ethnological data," *American Anthropologist,* 41:345-377. Reprinted in Clellan S. Ford, ed., *Cross-Cultural Approaches.* New Haven: HRAF Press.

Kluckhohn, Clyde, and D. Leighton. 1946. *The Navaho.* Cambridge: Harvard.

Knopf, Irwin. 1956. "Rorschach summary scores in differential diagnosis," *Journal of Consulting Psychology* 20:99-104. Reprinted in M. Hirt, ed., *Rorschach Science.*

Köbben, Andre. 1961. "New ways of presenting an old idea: the statistical method in social anthropology," in Frank Moore, ed., *Readings in Cross-cultural Methodology.* New Haven: HRAF Press.

Kosok, Michael. 1966. "The formalization of Hegel's dialectical logic," *International Philosophical Quarterly,* 6:596-631.

Kroeber, Alfred. 1948. *Anthropology.* New York: Harcourt, Brace.

Krasnow, H. S., and R. A. Merikallio. 1964. "The Past, Present, and Future of General Simulation Languages," *Management Science,* XI, 2:236-267.

Krupp, Sherman. 1963. "Theoretical explanation and the nature of the firm," *Western Economic Journal,* 1:191-204.

Kuriloff, Arthur, and S. Atkins. 1966. "T group for a work team," *Journal of Applied Behavioral Science,* 2:63-94.

Ladd, John. 1957. *The Structure of a Moral Code.* Cambridge: Harvard University Press.

Langner, Thomas, and S. T. Michael. 1963. *Life Stress and Mental Health.* Midtown Manhattan Study, vol. 2. New York: Free Press.

Lave, Lester. 1965. "Factors affecting co-operation in the Prisoner's Dilemma," *Behavioral Science,* X, 1:26-38.

Lawrence, W. E., and G. P. Murdock. 1949. "Murngin social organization," *American Anthropologist,* 51:58-65.

Lazarsfeld, Paul. 1959. "Problems in methodology," in R. Merton et al., eds., *Sociology Today.* New York: Basic Books.

Leach, E. R. 1951. "The structural implications of matrilateral cross-cousin marriage," *Journal of the Royal Anthropological Institute,* 81:23-56.

_____. 1954. *Political Systems of Highland Burma.* Boston: Beacon Press.

_____. 1957. "The epistemological background of Malinowski's empiricism," in R. Firth, ed., *Man and Culture.* London: Routledge and Kegan Paul.

————. 1965. "The nature of war," *Disarmament and Arms Control,* 3:165-183.

Leighton, Alexander. 1959. *My Name is Legion.* New York: Basic Books.

Leighton, Alexander, et al. 1960. *People of Cove and Woodlot.* New York: Basic Books.

————, et al. 1963. *The Character of Danger.* New York: Basic Books.

Lerner, Abba. 1965. "Professor Samuelson on theory and realism: a comment," *American Economic Review.* 55:1153-1155.

Lesser, Alexander. 1933. *The Pawnee Ghost Dance Hand Game.* Columbia University Contributions to Anthropology, New York: Columbia University Press.

Levinson, D. J., et al. 1966. "Intraception: evolution of a concept," in G. Direnzo, ed., *Concepts, Theory, and Explanation in the Behavioral Sciences.* New York: Random House.

Levy, Marion. 1952. *The Structure of Society.* Princeton: Princeton University Press.

Levi-Strauss, C. 1963. *Structural Anthropology.* New York: Basic Books.

Lewin, Kurt. 1936. *Dynamic Theory of Personality.* New York: McGraw-Hill.

————. 1948. *Resolving Social Conflicts.* New York: Harper.

————. 1951. *Field Theory in Social Science.* New York: Harper.

Lieberman, Bernhardt. 1962. "Experimental studies of conflict in some two-person and three-person games," in Joan Criswell et al., eds., *Mathematical Methods in Small-group Processes.* Stanford: Stanford University Press.

————. 1964. "i-trust: a notion of trust in three-person games and international affairs," *Conflict Resolution,* 8:271-280.

Lindesmith, Alfred. 1968. *Addiction and Opiates.* Chicago: Aldine.

Lindzey, Gardner. 1961. *Projective Techniques and Cross-Cultural Research.* New York: Appleton-Century-Crofts.

Linton, Ralph, ed. 1940. *Acculturation in Seven Indian Tribes.* New York: Appleton-Century-Crofts.

Llewellyn, Karl, and E. A. Hoebel. 1941. *The Cheyenne Way.* Norman: University of Oklahoma Press.

Lockwood, David. 1964. "Social integration and system integration," in George Zollschan and Walter Hirsch, eds., *Explorations in Social Change.* Boston: Houghton Mifflin.

Lord, Edith. 1950. "Experimentally induced variations in Rorschach performance," *Psychological Monographs,* 64, no. 316. Reprinted in Hirt, 1962.

Luce, R. D. 1959. *Individual Choice Behavior.* New York: Wiley.

Luce, R. D., and Howard Raiffa. 1957. *Games and Decisions.* New York: Wiley.

Lumsden, Malvern. 1966. "Perception and information in strategic thinking," *Journal of Peace Research,* 257-274.

Macesich, G. 1961. "Current inflation theory: considerations on methodology," *Social Research,* 28:321-330.

Machlup, F. 1964. "Professor Samuelson on theory and realism," *American Economic Review,* 54:733-736.

————. 1967. "Theories of the firm: marginalist, behavioral, managerial," *American Economic Review,* 57:1-33.

Malinowski, B. 1922. *Argonauts of the Western Pacific.* London: Routledge.

————. 1926. *Crime and Custom in Savage Society.* New York: Humanities Press.

————. 1927. *Sex and Repression in Savage Society.* London: Routledge.

————. 1944. *A Scientific Theory of Culture and Other Essays.* Chapel Hill: University of North Carolina Press.

————. 1945. *The Dynamics of Culture Change.* New Haven: Yale University Press.

————. 1954 (1948). *Magic, Science, and Religion.* Garden City: Doubleday

Anchor Books (reprint).

Mandelbaum, David. 1954. "Form, variation, and meaning of a ceremony," in R. Spencer, ed., *Method and Perspective in Anthropology*. Minneapolis: Minnesota University Press.

Manners, Robert. 1968 (1956). "Functionalism, realpolitik, and anthropology in underdeveloped areas," in R. Manners and D. Kaplan, eds., *Theory in Anthropology*. Chicago: Aldine.

Mannheim, Karl. 1936. *Ideology and Utopia*. New York: Harcourt, Brace reprint HB3.

Maquet, Jacques. 1964. "Objectivity in Anthropology," *Current Anthropology*, 5:47-55.

March, J., and H. Simon. 1958. *Organizations*. New York: Wiley.

Marcuse, Herbert. 1966. *Eros and Civilization; a Philosophical Inquiry into Freud*. Boston: Beacon Press.

Marsh, Robert M. 1965. "Comparative sociology, 1950-1963," *Current Sociology*, vol. 14, no. 2.

Martindale, Don. 1959. "Sociological theory and the ideal type," in L. Gross, ed., *Symposium on Sociological Theory*. Evanston: Row, Peterson.

————. 1960. *The Nature and Types of Sociological Theory*. Boston: Houghton Mifflin.

Masling, Joseph. 1960. "The influence of situational and interpersonal variables in projective testing," *Psychological Bulletin*, 57:65-85.

Massey, Gerald. 1965. "Professor Samuelson on theory and realism: a comment," *American Economic Review*, 55:1155-1163.

McKeon, Richard. 1951. "Philosophy and method," *Journal of Philosophy*, 48:653-682.

————. 1952. *Freedom and History*. New York: Noonday.

McPhee, William. 1963. *Formal Theories of Mass Behavior*. New York: Free Press.

Mead, George H. 1934. *Mind, Self, and Society*. Chicago, University of Chicago Press.

Mead, Margaret, ed. 1955. *Cultural Patterns and Technical Change*. New York: New American Library.

————. 1956. *New Lives For Old*. New York: Morrow.

Meehl, Paul. 1950. "On the circularity of the law of effect," *Psychological Bulletin*, 47:52-75.

————. 1954. *Clinical vs. Statistical Prediction*. Minneapolis: University of Minnesota Press.

Melitz, J. 1965. "Friedman and Machlup on the significance of testing economic assumptions," *Journal of Political Economy*. 73:37-60.

Merton, Robert. 1949. *Social Theory and Social Structure*. Glencoe: Free Press.

————. 1965. *On the Shoulders of Giants*. New York: Free Press.

Messick, David. 1967. "Interdependent decision strategies in zero-sum games: a computer-controlled study," *Behavioral Science*, 12:33-48.

Miller, George A. 1964. *Mathematics and Psychology*. New York: Wiley.

Miller, Neal. 1959. "Liberalization of basic S-R concepts," in Sigmund Koch, ed., *Psychology*, vol. 2, pp. 196-292. New York: McGraw-Hill.

Miller, S. M. 1952. "The participant-observer and 'over-rapport'," *American Sociological Review*, 17:97-99.

Mills, C. Wright. 1951. *White Collar*. New York: Oxford University Press.

Milner, P. M. 1957. "The cell assembly, Mark 2," *Psychological Review*, 64:242-252.

————. 1961. "A neural mechanism for immediate recall of sequences," *Kybernetik*, I:76-81.

Mischel, T. 1964. "Personal constructs, rules, and the logic of clinical activity,"

Psychological Review, 71:180-192.

————. 1966. "Pragmatic aspects of explanation," *Philosophy of Science,* 33: 40-60.

Mitchell, J. C. 1966. "Theoretical orientations in African urban studies," in M. Banton, ed., *The Social Anthropology of Complex Societies,* ASA Monograph, #4. London: Tavistock.

Mitchell, William. 1962. *The American Polity.* Glencoe: Free Press.

Mitroff, Ian. 1967. "A study of simulation-aided engineering design." Working Paper No. 66, Space Sciences Laboratory, University of California, Berkeley, California.

————. 1969. "Fundamental issues in the simulation of human behavior," *Management Science,* 15:B-635-649.

Mooney, James. 1896. *The Ghost Dance Religion and the Sioux Outbreak of 1890.* Bureau of Ethnology, report 14, part 2, 1892-3. Washington: Government Printing Office.

Moore, Barrington. 1958. *Political Power and Social Theory.* New York: Harper Torchbooks.

Moore, Frank W., ed. 1961. *Readings in Cross-cultural Methodology.* New Haven: HRAF Press.

Murdock, George. 1949. *Social Structure.* New York: Macmillan.

Murphey, Rhoads. 1957. "New capitals of Asia," *Economic Development and Cultural Change,* 5:216-243.

Murphy, Robert. 1967. "Tuareg kinship," *American Anthropologist,* 69:163-170.

Murray, Henry A. 1938. *Explorations in Personality.* New York: Oxford.

Myrdal, Gunnar. 1944. *An American Dilemma.* New York: Harper.

Nadel, S. F. 1935. "Nupe witchcraft and anti-witchcraft," *Africa,* 8:423-447.

————. 1942. *Black Byzantium.* London: Oxford University Press.

————. 1951. *The Foundations of Social Anthropology.* Glencoe: Free Press.

————. 1952. "Witchcraft in Four African Societies," *American Anthropologist,* 54:18-29. Reprinted in C. S. Ford, ed., *Cross-cultural Approaches,* New Haven: HRAF Press, 1967.

Nagel, Ernest. 1961. *The Structure of Science.* New York: Harcourt, Brace and World.

————. 1963. "Assumptions in economic theory," *American Economic Review,* 53:211-220.

Naroll, Raoul. 1962. *Data Quality Control.* New York: Free Press.

————. 1968. "Some thoughts on comparative method in cultural anthropology," in Hubert M. and Ann B. Blalock, eds., *Methodology in Social Research,* ch. 7. New York: McGraw-Hill.

Nash, Manning. 1955. *Machine Age Maya.* American Anthropological Association Memoir no. 87. Menasha: American Anthropological Association.

Needham, Rodney. 1954. "Siriono and Penan: a test of some hypotheses," *Southwestern Journal of Anthropology,* 10:228-232.

————. 1962. *Structure and Sentiment.* Chicago: University of Chicago Press.

Newell, Alan. 1962. "Some problems of basic organization in problem-solving programs," in M. Yovits et al., eds., *Self-Organizing Systems,* pp. 393-423. Washington: Spartan Press.

Newell, Alan, and H. Simon. 1963. "GPS, a program that simulates human thought," in E. Feigenbaum and J. Feldman, eds., *Computers and Thought.* New York: McGraw-Hill.

Olson, Mancur. 1965. *The Logic of Collective Action.* Cambridge: Harvard University Press.

Orcutt, Guy, et al. 1961. *Microanalysis of Economic Systems.* New York: Harper.

————. 1963. "Views on simulation and models of social systems," in Hoggatt and Balderston, eds., *Symposium on Simulation Models*, pp. 221-236. Cincinnati: Southwestern Publishing Co.

Osgood, C. 1953. *Method and Theory in Experimental Psychology*. New York: Oxford.

————. 1958. "Behavior theory," in Roland Young, ed., *Approaches to the Study of Politics*. Evanston: Northwestern University Press.

Oskamp, S., and D. Perlman. 1965. "Factors affecting co-operation in a Prisoner's Dilemma game," *Conflict Resolution*, 9:359-374.

Parsons, Talcott. 1937. *The Structure of Social Action*. New York: McGraw-Hill.

————. 1949. *Essays in Sociological Theory*. Glencoe: Free Press.

————. 1951. *The Social System*. Glencoe: Free Press.

————, et al. 1955. *Family, Socialization and Interaction Process*. Glencoe: Free Press.

————. 1960. *Structure and Process in Modern Societies*. Glencoe: Free Press.

————. 1964. *Social Structure and Personality*. New York: Free Press.

————. 1966a. *Societies: Evolutionary and Comparative Perspectives*. Englewood Cliffs: Prentice-Hall.

————. 1966b. "The political aspect of social structure and process," in D. Easton, ed., *Varieties of Political Theory*. Englewood Cliffs: Prentice-Hall.

————. 1967. *Sociological Theory and Modern Society*. New York: Free Press.

————. 1969. *Politics and Social Structure*. New York: Free Press.

Parsons, Talcott, R. F. Bales, and E. Shils. 1953. *Working Papers in the Theory of Action*. Glencoe: Free Press.

Parsons, Talcott, and Edward Shils, eds. 1951. *Toward a General Theory of Action*. Cambridge: Harvard University Press.

Parsons, Talcott, and N. Smelser. 1956. *Economy and Society*. New York: Free Press.

Peattie, Lisa. 1965. "Anthropology and the search for values," *Journal of Applied Behavior Science*, 1:361-372.

————. 1968. *The View from the Barrio*. Ann Arbor: University of Michigan Press.

Pepper, Stephen. 1942. *World Hypotheses*. Berkeley. University of California Press.

Peters, R. S. 1960. *The Concept of Motivation*. London: Routledge.

Polanyi, Karl, ed. 1957. *Trade and Market in the Early Empires*. Glencoe: Free Press.

Pollis, A., and B. Koslin. 1962. "On the scientific foundations of marginalism," *American Journal of Economics and Sociology*, 21:113-129.

Polsky, Ned. 1967. *Hustlers, Beats, and Others*. Chicago: Aldine.

Popper, Karl. 1957. *The Poverty of Historicism*. Boston: Beacon Press.

Pruitt, Dean. 1967. "Reaction systems and instability in interpersonal and international affairs," ONR Technical Report No. 2.

Radcliffe-Brown, A. R. 1922. *The Andaman Islanders*. Glencoe: Free Press. Reprinted 1948.

————. 1935. "Kinship terminology in California," *American Anthropologist*, 37:530-535.

————. 1949. "Functionalism: a protest," *American Anthropologist*, 51:320-323.

————. 1951a. "The comparative method in social anthropology," *Journal of The Royal Anthropological Institute*, 81:15-22.

————. 1951b. "Murngin social organization," *American Anthropologist*, 53: 37-55.

————. 1952. *Structure and Function in Primitive Society*. Glencoe: Free Press.

————. 1957. *A Natural Science of Society*. Glencoe: Free Press.

Radlow, R. 1965. "An experimental study of 'cooperation' in the Prisoner's

Dilemma game," *Conflict Resolution,* 9:221-227.

Radnitzky, G. 1969. "Ways of looking at science," *Scientia,* 104:49-57.

Rank, Otto. 1947. *Will Therapy.* New York: Knopf.

Rapoport, Amnon. 1967. "Optimal policies for the Prisoner's Dilemma," *Psychological Review,* 74:136-148.

Rapoport, Anatol. 1957. "Lewis Richardson's mathematical theory of war," *Journal of Conflict Resolution,* 1:249-299.

————. 1963. "Mathematical models of social interaction," in R. D. Luce, ed., *Handbook of Mathematical Psychology,* vol. 2, pp. 493-580. New York: Wiley.

————. 1964a. "Review of *Computers and Thought,*" *Management Science,* 11: 203-210.

————. 1964b. *Strategy and Conscience.* New York: Harper.

————. 1966a. "Strategic and non-strategic approaches to problems of security and peace," in K. Archibald, ed., *Strategic Interaction and Conflict.* Berkeley: Institute of International Studies.

————. 1966b. "Some system approaches to political theory," in D. Easton, ed., *Varieties of Political Theory.* Englewood Cliffs: Prentice-Hall.

————. 1967. "Exploiter, leader, hero, and martyr: the four archetypes of the 2 × 2 game," *Behavioral Science,* 12:81-84.

————. 1968. Editorial comment. *Journal of Conflict Resolution,* 12:222-223.

Rapoport, Anatol, and A. H. Chammah. 1965. *Prisoner's Dilemma.* Ann Arbor: University of Michigan Press.

Rapoport, Anatol, and M. Guyer, 1966. "A taxonomy of 2 × 2 games," in L.V. Bertalanffy and A. Rapoport, eds., *General Systems,* vol. 11.

Rashevsky, Nicholas. 1951. *Mathematical Biology of Social Behavior.* Chicago: University of Chicago Press.

Redfield, Robert, 1941. *The Folk Culture of Yucatan.* Chicago: University of Chicago Press.

————.1947. "The folk society," in *American Journal of Sociology,* 52:293-308.

————. 1950. *A Village that Chose Progress.* Chicago: University of Chicago Press.

————. 1953. *The Primitive World and Its Transformations.* Ithaca: Cornell University Press.

————. 1960a (1955). *The Little Community.* Chicago: University of Chicago Press.

————. 1960b (1956). *Peasant Society and Culture.* Chicago: University of Chicago Press.

————. 1962. *Human Nature and the Study of Society.* Collected papers, vol.·1, M. P. Redfield, ed. Chicago: University of Chicago Press.

Redfield, Robert, and A. Villa Rojas. 1934. *Chan Kom.* Chicago: University of Chicago Press.

Reid, Russell. 1967. "Marriage systems and algebraic group theory," *American Anthropologist,* 69:171-178.

Reik, Theodor. 1949. *Listening with the Third Ear.* New York: Farrar, Straus.

Richards, Audrey. 1939. *Land, Labor, and Diet in Northern Rhodesia.* Oxford: Oxford University Press.

Riesman, David, and J. Watson. 1964. "The sociability project," in Phillip Hammond, ed., *Sociologists at Work.* New York: Basic Books.

Riker, William. 1962. *The Theory of Political Coalitions.* New Haven: Yale University Press.

————. 1967. "Experimental verification of two theories about n-person games," in Joseph Bernd, ed., *Mathematical Applications in Political Science III.* Charlottesville: University Press of Virginia.

Rochester, N., et al. 1956. "Tests on a cell assembly theory of the action of the brain," in *I.R.E. Transactions on Information Theory,* vol. IT-2, 3:80-93.

Rogers, Carl. 1961. *On Becoming a Person.* New York: Houghton Mifflin.

Rokeach, Milton, and C. Hanley. 1956. "Eysenck's tender-mindedness dimension: a critique," reply by Eysenck and rejoinder by Hanley and Rokeach, *Psychological Bulletin,* 53:169-186.

Rome, Sydney and Beatrice. 1962. "Computer simulation toward a theory of large organizations," in H. Borko, ed., *Computer Applications in the Behavioral Sciences.* Englewood Cliffs: Prentice-Hall.

Rosenzweig, Saul. 1949. *Psychodiagnosis.* New York: Grune and Stratton.

————. 1954. "A transvaluation of psychotherapy—a reply to Hans Eysenck," *Journal of Abnormal and Social Psychology,* 49:298-304.

Ross, Nathaniel, and S. Abrams. 1965. "Fundamentals of psychoanalytic theory," in B. Wolman, ed., *Handbook of Clinical Psychology,* ch. 14. New York: McGraw-Hill.

Rotter, Julian. 1954. *Social Learning and Clinical Psychology.* New York: Prentice-Hall.

Rotwein, E. 1959. "On 'The Methodology of Positive Economics'," *Quarterly Journal of Economics,* 73:554-575.

Saaty, Thomas. 1968. *Mathematical Models of Arms Control and Disarmament.* New York: Wiley.

Sacksteder, William. 1963a. "Diversity in the behavioral sciences," *Philosophy of Science,* 30:375-395.

————. 1963b. "Structural variation in science," *Synthese,* 15:412-423.

————. 1964. "Inference and philosophic typologies," *The Monist,* 48:567-601.

Sampson, E., and M. Kardush. 1965. "Age, sex, class, and race differences in response to a two-person nonzerosum game," *Conflict Resolution,* 9:212-220.

Samuels, Ina. 1959. "Reticular mechanisms and behavior," *Psychological Bulletin,* 56:1-25.

Samuelson, Paul A. 1963. Discussion, *American Economic Review,* 53:231-236.

————. 1964. "Theory and realism: a reply," *American Economic Review,* 54:736-739.

————. 1966. *Collected Scientific Papers.* Cambridge: M.I.T. Press.

Sanford, Nevitt. 1966. *Self and Society.* New York: Atherton.

Sayre, Kenneth. 1965. *Recognition.* Indiana: University of Notre Dame Press.

Schachtel, Ernst. 1966. *Experiential Foundations of Rorschach's Test.* New York: Basic Books.

Schafer, Roy. 1954. *Psychoanalytic Interpretation in Rorschach Testing.* New York: Grune and Stratton.

Schapera, Isaac. 1953. "Some comments on comparative method in social anthropology," *American Anthropologist,* 55:353-362. Reprinted in C. S. Ford, ed., *Cross-cultural Approaches.* New Haven: HRAF Press, 1967.

Schneider, Louis. 1964. "Toward assessment of Sorokin's view of change," in George Zollschan and Walter Hirsch, eds., *Explorations in Social Change.* Boston: Houghton Mifflin.

Schubert, Glendon. 1959. *Quantitative Analysis of Judicial Behavior.* Glencoe: Free Press.

Schwab, Joseph. 1960. "What do scientists do?" *Behavioral Science,* 5:1-27

Schwab, William B. 1960. "An experiment in methodology in a West African urban community," in Richard Adams and J. Preiss, eds., *Human Organization Research.* Homewood: Dorsey.

Schwartz, Jacob. 1961. *Lectures on the Mathematical Method in Analytical Economics.* New York: Gordon and Breach.

Sears, R. R. 1943. *Survey of Objective Studies of Psychoanalytic Concepts.* New York: Social Science Research Council.

Shneidman, Edwin. 1965. "Projective techniques," in B. Wolman, ed., *Handbook of Clinical Psychology*. New York: McGraw-Hill.

Shubik, Martin. 1959. *Strategy and Market Structure*. New York: Wiley.

———. 1963. "Some reflections on the design of game theoretic models for the study of negotiation and threats," *Journal of Conflict Resolution*, 7:1-12.

———. 1964. *Game Theory and Related Approaches to Behavior*. New York: Wiley.

———. 1968. "On the study of disarmament and escalation," *Journal of Conflict Resolution*, 12:83-101.

Siegel, B., ed. 1963. *Biennial Review of Anthropology*. Stanford: Stanford University Press.

Siegel, Sidney, and L. E. Fouraker. 1960. *Bargaining and Group Decision-making*. New York: McGraw-Hill.

Simon, Herbert. 1954. "The construction of social science models," in Paul Lazarsfeld, ed. *Mathematical Thinking in the Social Sciences*. Glencoe: Free Press.

———. 1957. *Models of Man*. New York: Wiley.

———. 1963. Discussion, *American Economic Review*, 53:229-231.

Simon, Herbert, and A. Newell. 1956. "Models, their uses and limitations," in L. D. White, ed., *The State of the Social Sciences*. Chicago: University of Chicago Press.

Skinner, B. F. 1938. *The Behavior of Organisms*. New York: Appleton-Century.

———. 1959a. *Cumulative Record*. New York: Appleton-Century.

———. 1959b. "A case study in scientific method," in Sigmund Koch, ed., *Psychology*, vol. 2, New York: McGraw-Hill.

———. 1966. "Contingencies of reinforcement in the design of a culture," *Behavioral Science*, 11:159-166.

Smelser, Neil. 1963. *Sociology of Economic Life*. Englewood Cliffs: Prentice-Hall.

Spence, Donald P. 1968. "The processing of meaning in psychotherapy," *Behavioral Science*, 13:349-361.

Spicer, Edward H. 1940. *Pascua, a Yaqui Village in Arizona*. Chicago: University of Chicago Press.

———. 1954. *Potam, a Yaqui Village in Sonora*. American Anthropological Association memoir no. 77. Menasha: Banta.

———, ed. 1952. *Human Problems in Technological Change*. New York: Russell Sage.

Stallknecht, Newton, and R. Brumbaugh. 1954. *The Compass of Philosophy*. New York: Longmans, Green.

Stephan, F., and E. G. Mishler. 1952. "The distribution of participation in small groups," *American Sociological Review*, 17:598-608.

Stephens, William N. 1968. *Hypotheses and Evidence*. New York: Crowell.

Steward, Julian. 1953. "Evolution and process," in A. Kroeber, ed., *Anthropology Today*. Chicago: University of Chicago Press.

Stieper, Donald, and D. Wiener. 1965. *Dimensions of Psychotherapy: An Experimental and Clinical Approach*. Chicago: Aldine.

Stogdill, Ralph. 1959. *Individual Behavior and Group Achievement*. New York: Oxford.

Suppes, Patrick, and R. C. Atkinson. 1960. *Markov Learning Models for Multiperson Interactions*. Stanford: Stanford University Press.

Swartz, Marc, ed. 1968. *Local-Level Politics*. Chicago: Aldine.

Swartz, Marc, et al., eds. 1966. *Political Anthropology*. Chicago: Aldine.

Taylor, Charles. 1964. *The Explanation of Behavior*. New York: Humanities.

Thibaut, J., and H. H. Kelley. 1959. *The Social Psychology of Groups*. New York: Wiley.

Thomas, W. I., and F. Znaniecki. 1958 (1920). *The Polish Peasant in Europe and*

America. New York: Dover.

Tolman, E. C. 1951. "A psychological model," in Talcott Parsons and E. Shils, eds., *Toward a General Theory of Action.* Cambridge: Harvard University Press.

Tomkins, Silvan, and S. Messick, eds. 1963. *Computer Simulation of Personality.* New York: Wiley.

Toulmin, Stephen. 1961. *Foresight and Understanding.* Bloomington: Indiana University Press.

Tullock, Gordon. 1967. *Toward a Mathematics of Politics.* Ann Arbor: University of Michigan Press.

Turner, V. W. 1957. *Schism and Continuity in an African Society.* Manchester: Manchester University Press.

————. 1964. "Symbols in Ndembu Ritual," in Max Gluckman, ed., *Closed Societies and Open Minds.* Chicago: Aldine.

————. 1969. *The Ritual Process: Structure and Anti-Structure.* Chicago: Aldine.

Tustin, A. 1953. *The Mechanism of Economic Systems.* Cambridge: Harvard University Press.

Udy, Stanley. 1959. *Organization of Work.* New Haven: HRAF Press.

Uesugi, T. K., and W. E. Vinacke. 1963. "Strategy in a feminine game," *Sociometry,* 26:75-88.

Vidich, Arthur, and Joseph Bensman. 1958. *Small Town in Mass Society.* Garden City: Doubleday.

————. 1960. "The validity of field data," in Richard Adams and Jack Preiss, eds., *Human Organization Research.* Homewood: Dorsey.

Vinacke, W. E. 1959. "Sex roles in the three-person game," *Sociometry,* 22: 343-360.

————, et al. 1966. "The effect of information about strategy on a three-person game," *Behavioral Science,* 11:180-189.

Vinacke, W. E., and A. Arkoff. 1957. "An experimental study of coalitions in the triad," *American Sociological Review,* 22:406-414.

Vogt, Evon, and E. Albert, eds. 1966. *People of Rimrock: A Study of Values in Five Cultures.* Cambridge: Harvard University Press.

Von Mises, L. 1960. *Epistemological Problems of Economics.* Princeton: Van Nostrand.

Walker, Marshall. 1963. *The Nature of Scientific Thought.* Englewood Cliffs: Prentice-Hall.

Wallerstein, Immanuel. 1966. *Social Change: The Colonial Situation.* New York. Wiley.

Warner, W. L. 1941. *The Social Life of a Modern Community.* New Haven: Yale University Press.

Warner, W. L., and Paul Lunt. 1942. *Status System of a Modern Community.* New Haven: Yale University Press.

Warner, W. L., and Leo Srole. 1945. *Social Systems of American Ethnic Groups.* New Haven: Yale University Press.

Warner, W. L., and J. O. Low. 1947. *Social System of the Modern Factory.* New Haven: Yale University Press.

Washburne, Chandler. 1961. *Primitive Drinking.* New York: College and University Press.

Wax, Rosalie. 1960. "Reciprocity in field work," in Richard Adams and Jack Preiss, eds., *Human Organization Research.* Homewood: Dorsey.

Webb, Eugene, et al. 1966. *Unobtrusive Measures: Nonreactive Research in the Social Sciences.* Chicago: Rand, McNally.

Weil, R. L. 1966. "The N-person Prisoner's Dilemma: some theory and a computer-oriented approach," *Behavioral Science,* 11:227-233.

Weiss, Robert. 1956. *Processes of Organization.* Ann Arbor: Survey Research

Center, University of Michigan.

White, Harrison. 1963a. *An Anatomy of Kinship.* Engelwood Cliffs: Prentice-Hall.

————. 1963b. "Review of *Mathematical Methods in Small Group Processes,*" *American Journal of Sociology,* 64:304-306.

Whitehead, A. N. 1941. "Mathematics and the Good," in P. Schilpp, ed., *The Philosophy of Alfred North Whitehead.* Evanston: Northwestern University Press.

Whiting, John, and I. Child. 1953. *Child Training and Personality.* New Haven: Yale University.

Whyte, W. F. 1943. *Street Corner Society.* Chicago: University of Chicago Press.

Winch, Peter. 1958. *The Idea of a Social Science.* London: Routledge.

Wittenborn, J. R. 1949. "Statistical tests of certain Rorschach assumptions: Analyses of discrete responses," *Journal of Consulting Psychology,* 13:257-267. Reprinted in M. Hirt, 1962.

————. 1950a. "Statistical tests of certain Rorschach assumptions: the internal consistency of scoring categories," *Journal of Consulting Psychology,* 14:10-19. Reprinted in M. Hirt, 1962.

————. 1950b. "A factor analysis of Rorschach scoring categories," *Journal of Consulting Psychology,* 14:261-267.

Wittenborn, J. R., and F. A. Mettler. 1951. "A lack of perceptual control score for the Rorschach test," *Journal of Clinical Psychology,* 7:331-334.

Wittfogel, Karl. 1957. *Oriental Despotism.* New Haven: Yale University Press.

Wolman, Benjamin. 1965. "Schizophrenia and related disorders," in B. Wolman, ed., *Handbook of Clinical Psychology.* New York: McGraw-Hill.

Yamane, Taro. 1962. *Mathematics For Economists.* Englewood Cliffs: Prentice-Hall.

Zelditch, Morris. 1955. "Role differentiation in the nuclear family: a comparative study," in Parsons, et al., *Family, Socialization and Interaction Process.* Glencoe: Free Press.

Zinnes, Dina. 1968. "An introduction to the behavioral approach: a review," *Journal of Conflict Resolution,* 12:258-267.

Name Index

343

Subject Index

349